OUR STRENGTH IS IN OUR FIELDS

AFRICAN FAMILIES IN CHANGE

RAIJA WARKENTIN
University College of the Cariboo

KENDALL/HUNT PUBLISHING COMPANY
4050 Westmark Drive   Dubuque, Iowa 52002

To Henry, Tom, Tania and Jill

TABLE OF CONTENTS

PREFACE

University students often complain that ethnographies are so dry and academic that they do not give any sense of what it is to live in the culture concerned. The author sincerely hopes that this ethnography fulfills her primary goal of introducing sound anthropological knowledge in a more interesting and less formal way.

SUBJECT MATTER

This ethnography is a narrative about the everyday lives of rural and urban African families, as seen through the eyes of the author during twelve years of anthropological fieldwork among the Fofu of Zaire. Frustrated by the confined and dull existence of a bush pilot's wife, the author becomes curious about Zairean life. She starts to visit African families and then to study anthropology. In following the lives of her key informants over twelve years the author forms deep and trusting friendships. Her description of a myriad of incidents and conversations hopefully brings the Fofu society to life and gives the reader an insight into the way the Fofu think. A wide range of subjects is illuminated, including family and gender relationships, marriage negotiations, childrearing, economic pursuits, clan incest, witchcraft, burial rites and the anthropological fieldwork process itself. The book also casts light on the cultural confusion caused by urbanization and social changes made by both the white colonial rule and an insensitive Zairean dictatorship. This book, therefore, also has relevance to the present day political turmoil in Zaire.

INTENDED READERSHIP

Academic This book provides multidisciplinary case-study material for under-graduates. It is suitable for courses of cultural anthropology, sociology, human geography and women's studies. It has already been used in several university courses and students' comments have been very positive. Apart from finding the material enjoyable to read they have claimed that it brought the subject to life and gave them an idea what fieldwork is really like.

General The informal style of this book makes it accessible to the general reader. People interested in Africa or the Third World generally or, indeed, anybody who takes an intelligent interest in life in general will find this book useful.

Structure The book is divided into two sections dealing with rural and urban areas respectively. The Introduction describes the author's unconventional route to anthropology and her extraordinary study programme. Chapter 2 explains how the author became acquainted with the rural Fofu and describes both the area studied and how the fieldwork was organized. Chapter 5 covers the same topics with regard to the urban area. Chapters 1, 3, and 4 describe and discuss the lives of three families of the rural area and Chapters 6, 7 and 8 do the same in respect of three urban families. Drawing from the information in the narrative, Chapter 9 analyses and compares the rural and urban lifestyles. Finally, questions and topics for discussion are provided for the benefit of the students. Their potential uses are explained below.

How to Use the Book

It can be read solely for enjoyment or it can be used for exercises in courses on anthropology, sociology, women's studies and human geography.

Anthropology "Questions and Topics for Discussion" tells students how best to read the book when using it for an exercise in anthropological analysis. It also suggests topics for such an analysis and questions the students should keep in mind while reading. The topics can be used in connection with exercises on the rural and urban areas either separately or jointly. If both areas are dealt with together a comparative study results. To assist the student further an example of a comparative analysis is offered in Chapter 9. It is not, of course, exhaustive: an attentive reader will find more examples in the text and there are many other possible subjects to compare.

The author has used these analyzing exercises with encouraging results in her classes. For many students it was their first opportunity to apply textbook learning.

Sociology, Women's Studies and Human Geography Although "Questions and Topics for Discussion" is specifically designed for anthropological analysis, they can also be adapted for discussion or written assignments in these subjects.

General Readers Those reading this book for pleasure may also find that their enjoyment is enhanced if they consider some of the suggestions in "Questions and Topics for Discussion."

Female Perspective

Despite the recent increase in books by women who put the woman's point of view on various issues, there is still a need for this perspective to be presented on African issues. Virtually all the lives described in this book are those of women. The author shared the female experience of her African friends as she, like them, was also a wife and mother. She bore both her children and raised them to school age in Africa. This common ground doubtless nurtured a feeling of affinity which encouraged the Fofu women to express themselves openly.

Anthropological Issues

Observation Time Because of Western academic schedules, most anthropological books are based on one or two years of fieldwork. Occasionally authors have been able to go back to the field repeatedly over a long period of time, but their visits have usually been for relatively short periods ranging from a few months to about a year. This book is unique in that the author lived continuously in Africa for ten years and then returned to the same people twice for periods of two months and a year.

Sole Interpreters Anthropologists are beginning to question the authority of those ethnographers who act as sole interpreters of exotic cultures (Handler 1985, Clifford 1983, Tedlock 1979). In classic monographs the ethnographers do all the explaining and the natives rarely say anything. This tends to be the pattern in recent monographs about African women and children, although monographs about other geographical areas are increasingly expressing differing points of view. Life histories have been the traditional forum for natives to express their point of view, but as D. Tedlock (1979) has pointed out, even these are really monologues as they only allow a single native voice to be heard. In this book, Zaireans are allowed to speak for themselves and argue with the author. Often entire discussions with the author are reported, sometimes verbatim.

Dialogical Narrative Another problem of life histories is that the anthropologists who have done the interviewing have cut out their questions and given us their edited version of the native informant's monologue. A reader cannot tell how the interviewer's questions may have influenced the reply. In the proposed book, whole conversations and arguments are reported. This presents viewpoints less subjectively and also gives the reader a clearer idea of the fieldwork process. A reader gets a double analysis: of the ethnographer's culture and of the exotic culture (Sapir 1921, Handler 1985). This new style of writing has been called *self-reflexive* in sociology or *dialogical* in anthropology (Tedlock 1979), as well as *experiential, interpretive* and *polyphonic* (Clifford 1983).

Town and Country Very rarely, if at all, has there been a detailed study of an ethnic group living in rural and urban areas of a single geographical zone. Some anthropologists have suggested that such a comparison provides the best understanding of cultural change.

AUTHOR'S PLEA

It is easy to look at the Fofu through Western eyes and condemn them for their customs, such as the way women are treated and children are punished. However, the author urges the readers to withhold judgment and approach the Fofu customs from the point of view of the Fofu themselves in their cultural context. This approach is called *cultural relativism* and it is a good path to tolerance and appreciation of other cultures.

Acknowledgements

Over the years my research has been supported by the Academy of Finland as a member of a multidisciplinary project, "Personality, Mental Problems and Forms of Treatment in Changing Cultures" (directed by Dr. Anja Forssén) and by the Social Sciences and Humanities Research Council of Canada. I have never counted the flights I received free of charge from the companies whom my husband worked for and I am forever grateful for this concession. Thanks go to Henry, Tom and Tania who sometimes joined me on my visits to the villages and helped me make friends with the Zaireans. Their moral support for my anthropological endeavour was very important to me. Furthermore, Tom and his friend Khalid Yaqub gave me invaluable help with the computer conversion of files and Tom designed the kinship diagrams of each family. I would also like to thank Dr. Regna Darnell and Dr. Harold Barclay for their helpful comments on the manuscript, Lennart Smith for his practical advice, and Kaarina Alvarez, Genelda Cornfield, Homa Hoodfar and Kirsi Viisainen for their encouragement as the work progressed.

Because English is my second language I needed help in copy editing the manuscript. The initial chapter was edited by Bryan Alan. The most arduous work, however, was done by Gillian Smith who spent hundreds of hours editing and polishing my English. When we were pen friends in our schooldays she used to help me learn English by correcting my letters. Who would have believed that she would do a similar job, albeit much more ambitious, some thirty years later dealing with tales from Africa! I am very thankful not only for this hard work but also for her imaginative contribution towards other aspects of this book and her encouragement and steadfast belief that it would be a great success.

Finally I owe much to the families whose stories I have related. Words cannot express my gratitude for letting me share their lives with them and learn to understand and value cultures other than my own. I am also thankful to the communities where these families lived, for graciously letting me be there and explore the unknown. To preserve the privacy of the people whose lives I unashamedly describe, all the personal names (except those of my family) and most names of communities and ethnic groups have been changed. Thus if one looks for the term "Fofu" in the ethnic maps or lists of Africa, one will not find them. Let them stay anonymous.

INTRODUCTION

BREAKING WITH CONVENTION

INTRODUCTION:
BREAKING WITH CONVENTION

I became an anthropologist in an unconventional way, by accident rather than design. I did not plan to be one when I was at university in Finland. I was a loyal Finn: I gained my Master of Arts degree in Finnish Language and Literature, taught those subjects in a school and a university in Finland, and was expecting eventually to receive a pension from that work.

One Christmas holiday, however, I fell not only in the alpine snow of Switzerland but also in love with a handsome Canadian. He was on his way to Zaire (then the Belgian Congo) to be a bush pilot and was in Switzerland to learn French. The following summer I went to Africa to visit him and to see if I would like to live there as well. By then I was looking through rose-tinted spectacles: everything appeared exotic and romantic. Sarcastic remarks of some colleagues about "sunstroke," protests by my parents, and head shaking by my students did not deter me. I was going to leave everything, get married, and move to Africa.

I have since tried to analyze my motives. Falling in love was an obvious one and another one was a wish for adventure instead of steady work to build up a good pension. In addition, there was a desire to do something worthwhile, to help the poor of the world. Surely they would appreciate our work much more than the spoiled Finnish students appreciated my teaching! Raised as a devout Lutheran, I thought that my future husband's work as a pilot for the Protestant missions represented the ultimate sacrifice a person could make. I had not read anything about anthropology or development of the Third World countries and was to find out the hard way how unrealistic my thoughts were.

"Your life is so interesting!" was the usual comment on my letters back home. Of course, I was telling exciting stories about the "wild" land and people. As the wife of a pilot, I had the opportunity to travel around the country with my husband, and I took full advantage of it. I got to know all the main cities of the country and the many bush villages which had landing strips. I visited other African countries as well. But what I did not tell in the letters, except to a few trusted friends, was of my difficulty adjusting to different cultures, of which the American was the hardest for me. Most of our friends were Americans who thought that their culture was the best in the world and that everyone, including the Africans and I, should follow it. I felt lonely being the only Finn there and having nobody else to beat the drum for my own culture. Nobody understood me, not even my husband.

Boredom was the other difficulty I concealed in my letters. I only managed to travel a few days a month — the rest of the days were spent indoors, literally within four walls. It was the job of the wife of the mission pilot to flight follow her husband all day long with a single side band radio. Henry radioed his position every half hour as well as on take-off and landing. When the radio was on, its static filled the house. Those unaccustomed to the radio heard only the static and were unable to distinguish the human voice. Every weekday, all day, I was tied to the little noisy box. I felt that life was passing me by. I was living in the area without knowing anything about the surrounding people. Only on Henry's days off or on those days when he was doing maintenance on the plane, did I have the chance to look around.

We were moved around the country three times in two years. During the second year, we were living in Buva next to a Zairean family. I was fascinated by the life I saw when I looked over the fence into their yard: there were lots of people, noises, smells, movement, and colors. How I yearned to know something about that life instead of sitting inside tied to the radio.

I vaguely remembered that such a subject as anthropology existed and decided to start studying it. An anthropologist doing his doctoral fieldwork gave me some books and ideas. I took a three-month course in Swahili, studied my books, got somebody to take over the radio, and set off for a month's stay in a village to do my first field study. I could have started with my neighbors, but I had the idea that genuine tribal life existed only in the villages and that is what I wanted to observe first. I took my one-year old son Tom along with me. He, wearing only a loincloth, was happy exploring the surroundings with a Zairean nanny while I went to the fields with the village women, helped them pound and winnow rice or simply sat and chatted with them.

Soon after my first anthropological field trip, we spent a year in Canada on Henry's first furlough and I used the opportunity to study anthropology in a university. When we returned to Africa, I enrolled in a correspondence course with the University of Helsinki and continued my studies. I received hardly any credits for my year's work in Canada, so I had to start from the beginning. Also, I had to take my exams in the Finnish embassy in Kenya, since Finland was not diplomatically represented in Zaire. The trips to the embassy were not hard to arrange because, again, as the wife of a pilot, I could fly at no cost.

Did I say "not hard to arrange?" The first exam I took in 1975 was almost a fiasco. I arrived at the embassy at the set time and was greeted by a Kenyan receptionist who had no knowledge of my exam. The Finnish officer had apparently gone to the airport to meet a Finnish governmental dignitary. She phoned from the airport saying that she was sorry she had not been able to keep our appointment. I understood that a government official was more important than an insignificant student. But she went on to explain that the plane was late and she had to wait for him. Did I mind waiting at the embassy for an indefinite time? Now that was not so simple. I was scheduled to feed my baby Tania in a few hours. She was only two months old and was being looked after by my parents who had just arrived from Finland for their first visit to Africa. I asked whether she could tell me where the exam papers were so that I could sit the exam there and then. Absolutely no! The papers were in the safe and the exam had to be administered according to the rules provided by the university, i.e., under her personal supervision and in a specially prepared room. We set another time in the late afternoon for me to sit the exam.

I went back to our guest rooms but was unable to eat anything for the rest of the day — and probably produced nothing for my baby, either. In the afternoon I went back to the embassy and sat the exam under the meticulous supervision of the official in a room that had been cleared of dictionaries and other books that might help me in my writing. A month later I learned that I had received the grade "excellent" for the exam. It encouraged me to study further and there were no more complications with the exams later on when the embassy expanded and had more personnel.

Did I say "no more complications?" Yes there were. Sometimes my exam application was lost in my supervising professor's pile of correspondence. When this happened I had to keep on writing to him in Helsinki until I received confirmation that the exam had been sent by diplomatic mail. Then I had to wait until the embassy confirmed that they had received it. Once a shipment of textbooks took almost a year to reach me. Although I was not trying to break any records, it was frustrating to wait. I used my time doing fieldwork and reading the books I had. Some of the books I needed were only available in the departmental library in Helsinki University. On one of my annual trips to Finland I asked if I could borrow such a book — a Swedish ethnography — and send it back from Africa. The librarian was horrified but after second thoughts told me that she had the same book in Danish and she would not worry about taking the risk of losing that one as only the Swedish edition was heavily used.

"But I have never studied Danish!" I said.

"You might be surprised how easy it is once you get the hang of it." All Finns must study Swedish at school, so reading Swedish ethnographies was not too bad, but Danish — no way! As this happened just before the revolution in photocopying I had no choice but to take the Danish version with me.

Back in Africa, reading the book was slow and painful. I only had a Swedish-Finnish dictionary so I had to guess what an unknown Danish word might be in Swedish then look it up in that. I recorded all the words that I could not understand. Luckily, one day two Norwegians happened to come to the hospital for a medical check up and I used the opportunity to ask for their help with my Danish studies. We went through my word list in no time. In my next exam, I had a question about this ethnography and was able to answer it.

I am sure I worked much harder than the Finnish anthropology students. The fieldwork assignment is a good example. On my visit to Finland I learned that the Finnish students generally went to the open air market at the harbor in Helsinki and observed the activity while sipping coffee and eating delicacies. They finished their exercise in a few weeks and wrote up their report. In contrast to them, I visited my research village for two years before I wrote my report. Well, it did not matter. I was studying for my own interest more than for the grades and the university offered me structure and direction, for which I was grateful.

At this time, from 1974 to 1977, we were living on a Protestant mission station, called Nyanya. There was a large hospital with several American doctors, so Henry's flying was largely geared to the needs of the hospital. He flew a six-seater single engine plane and transported cargoes of imported medicines both to the hospital and to many other dispensaries over a large area. He also flew the doctors who visited the dispensaries and performed operations in the bush. The plane was, in fact, named after the doctor who used it the most. Henry often brought seriously ill patients from the bush to the mission hospital, sometimes saving lives, sometimes losing them in the plane. Although such losses were hard on him, he generally received great satisfaction from his work and was appreciated by others. Most of the time, the weather around the equator was ideal for flying. Usually he could go around the thundershowers or wait for a while for them to pass. Very seldom were there days when the clouds would cover the whole sky all day long.

Tom was two years old when we moved to Nyanya in 1974. When Henry finished his flights in the afternoon, Tom and I would walk through the African section near the hospital and beyond the mission station to the commercial section of the village. I was fascinated by the life I saw. My own life seemed sterile and dull compared with the busy and colorful life which went on here. Sometimes Tom got tired of walking and begged me to carry him. He was getting too heavy for me, so I merely reduced my speed and told him to keep on walking. The Zaireans passing by would chastise me,

"Your child is crying, you must carry him, carry him."

I showed them my arms and said, "Look I have no strength, I can't."

They did not agree, "You should try anyway, madam, try, try. The child is crying, crying!"

To please them, I picked him up and carried him for a few yards, before putting him down and letting him follow me whining and complaining. Suzana and Jacques were the first couple I became acquainted with through these walks. Theirs is the story "The Dissolution Of A Marriage" in Chapter 1.

Then in November 1974, I found the village of Yenyabo which became the focus of my main research over twelve years. From 1974 until 1977 I visited Yenyabo by car from our home at Nyanya. My visits were not on a regular basis but usually amounted to three separate days each week. Sometimes, however, I would stay in the village for a few days at a time. By then Henry and I had come to an arrangement which allowed me to leave the radio. We used a tape recorder which was sound activated. This was handy because Henry's calls were recorded but during the long intervals between, the tape was not running.

Figure 1.1 The author visiting a Fofu family with her children.

"Just make sure to listen to the tape at night when you come home. I don't want to sit with the crocodiles for many days," Henry commented dryly. This is what I did if he did not get home before me and it worked out fine. There were only minor hitches. Once, for example, I could not make out his final report, so I was anxious to find out whether he had arrived at his destination. However, judging from the tone of voice he was all right. Next day I talked to him on the radio and verified his condition. Later we taught Zaireans how to flight follow on the radio and let them do it. They were glad of any paid work.

In 1977, we went for a summer vacation overseas. We returned to Africa but did not work for the missions any more. We had become acquainted with a Zairean businessman who was planning to start a charter company in the beautiful city of Bululu. He had asked Henry to join him in the business venture and Henry had accepted the challenge. We therefore moved to the city, about 300 miles from Nyanya. It was not totally strange to us for we had visited it several times before. We were to live in Bululu for four years until we left Africa in 1981.

During those four years I studied the urban Fofu. How I got to know them and stories about their lives are contained in the section "Who Can Survive In This City?." I also continued to keep in touch with Nyanya and Yenyabo by flying back for visits. The new company gave me the same concessions as the mission had, so I could fly for nothing. Now I would stay in the village a week at a time once every two months. As I could only take a seat on the plane if no paying customer wanted it, I could seldom warn the villagers of my impending visit. But as one of them had always dreamt I would come, the villagers were never surprised to see me. As soon as I arrived, everyone seemed to know I was there. I presumed this was by word of mouth but I discovered there were other means as well. Once, for example, I was sitting by a house in the far outskirts of the village when a young fellow walked into the yard.

"Where is 'Madame Pilote' (Mrs. Pilot)?" he inquired.

"How did you know I was here?" I marvelled.

"I saw your footprints near the stream, your footprints," he replied loftily.

"How did you know they were my footprints?" I continued naively.

"No one else wears that kind of shoe here, that kind of shoe," he explained patiently. Only then did I pay attention to my shoes. Most people walked barefoot. Some wore shoes or sandals, but none of them American sneakers.

During the four years I lived in Bululu I worked on my Master's thesis, comparing childrearing in the village and in the city. I had been asked to join a personality study project sponsored by the Academy of Finland and so I also conducted several psychological tests, some of which involved drawing and clay modelling, on the Fofu children. I finished my Master's degree in 1980 and spent a further year of fieldwork on the personality studies and my own observations on the various families.

When we left Africa in 1981 we did not know whether we would return. I was hoping to continue university studies but had no firm plans. In fact, we did not know if we would settle in Canada or Finland. Our tickets were to Canada via Finland, but while in Finland, the love of my home country took over and I said enthusiastically,

"Let's live here!" Henry's attachment to Canada was not strong, having been absent from there over fifteen years and he agreed. We tried to settle down in Finland and I continued to work with the personality study project and to write up the results of my field research. However, Henry could not find work because the country was then quite closed to foreigners who were not fluent in Finnish.

After about a year we decided to move to Canada which proved to be better for our family as a whole. Henry soon obtained work with an airline as a mechanic and I enrolled in a university as a doctoral student. There was again the problem of credits. I had to do an extra year because of the different systems in North American and European universities. I felt like Sisyphus trying to roll a stone up a mountain and always meeting with setbacks. But tenacity and perseverance are Finnish traits so I kept on rolling the stone. I was preparing to go back to the Fofu to do my doctoral fieldwork.

In 1984, a year before the commencement of the fieldwork, I had a stroke of luck. Henry's former mission organization phoned and asked if he would consider going back to Nyanya to help out with the flying program over the summer. This would enable me to visit the villages and investigate the topic of my dissertation and so prepare a better proposal for the fall. Our children flew to their Finnish grandparents for the two months which we spent in Africa after three years of absence.

Naturally, it was great to see old friends again and hear their news. During the two months, I visited many villages, not only Yenyabo. Sometimes I was able to use a car but not often. And so I discovered a new mode of transportation for me: walking. A Fofu friend commented on it,

"Madam, when you were a young woman, you did not have strength to walk, to walk, but now as an older person you walk with ease, walk with ease." I was delighted with my new skill, myself.

I found walking had several advantages. In the first place, it was very good for talking: I would get into deep discussions on many issues with my informants during the long treks. Another advantage was that when alone on the road I could think better. I also saw things which I would not have seen if I had been going by car. Walking was physically exhausting, though, and I could not walk as fast as my African companions. My eyes were opened to see a "walking culture." One views the world differently according to the means of transportation: ten miles is nothing for a person travelling by car but it is a long distance by foot — and even longer if you carry thirty pounds of manioc on top of your head, which I did not.

One day I caught up with a woman who moaned rhythmically with every step. It sounded different from the wake mourning, which was more energetic and aggressive. I asked if she were sick. She told me that she was tired because she had walked from Lemura, a city thirty miles away. I had not known that people made that journey on foot but afterwards I realised that many people could not afford the bus fare and walked instead.

My final trip to the Fofu was from July 1985 to July 1986, when I conducted my doctoral field research. This time Henry worked for the commercial company he had started in 1977. To his dismay, it was not in good shape and there was not much he could do to improve the situation. He was stationed in Bululu and later in Buva, another city. This time our children came to Africa as well and attended an American boarding school some 500 miles from Bululu. We came together for one month at Christmas and another one at Easter. We also spent a long weekend together once every three months. We missed each other a lot during the intervals.

For the doctoral research, I worked among the Fofu in six locations: in three villages, at a Catholic mission station in Lemura, at a Protestant mission station at Nyanya, and in the city of Bululu. I was studying the influence of Christian missions, both Catholic and Protestant, on childrearing among the Fofu. Both missions provided me with accommodation when I was working at the stations. In the case of the Catholic mission, this was actually in the convent with the Zairean sisters. The Protestant mission gave me a house to stay in. When in the villages, I stayed with a Zairean family. In Bululu, I stayed in our own house, provided by Henry's company. I could not have chosen such a large variety of locations had I not laid the foundations years before. Wherever I went I knew people.

The custom of women marrying men from villages other than their own proved to be beneficial to me. In every place, there was a woman whom I had met at Yenyabo or Nyanya and who had since married into another village. As these women were now living in new and unfamiliar places they greeted me as a close relative who would alleviate their home sickness. To be so welcomed helped me to win the confidence of those I did not already know.

Since 1986, I have written my dissertation, received my doctoral degree, and been teaching anthropology in the Universities of Alberta, McGill and the Cariboo. At present I am working on several academic papers on various aspects of the Fofu. In these formal studies the information is, of course, handled in an analytical way. In this book, however, I have presented information about the Fofu in a less formal manner: about their work, their relationships, their joys and sorrows. I wanted, in short, to bring them to life and to convey a sense of what it is like to be a member of a different culture.

With this book, I hope to convey to the reader that one's culture permeates the minutiae of everyday life and one's way of thinking and that it is very difficult to get to know and understand a different culture. It took me years to learn to behave correctly and understand the people. Therefore, the second purpose of this narrative is to describe the path of a foreigner from ignorance to deeper understanding of the Fofu culture.

I am attracted to this self-reflexive style because it allows me to inquire into my own cultural background while I am trying to learn about the Fofu way of thinking. I was a lone Finn in Africa and felt that I had to defend my Finnishness to the Americans with whom I lived. Although I perhaps had more in common with the Americans I felt an affinity for the Fofu, because both our cultures were being threatened by the Americans, who behaved as if their way of life were the only "Christian," "civilised," and "good" way. Anthropologists have often been marginal people in their own societies and I certainly was one in the white community where I lived.

Although I felt this natural sympathy with the Fofu, it was still difficult to understand their ways. Their extreme politeness was one reason for this. They sometimes tended, at least initially to hide the truth from me and to tell me what they thought I would be pleased to hear. Over the years that I knew them I did, however, move from a position of ignorance about the Fofu to a deeper understanding of them. It is this long, challenging and immensely rewarding path that I want to describe.

PART I

OUR STRENGTH
IS IN OUR FIELDS

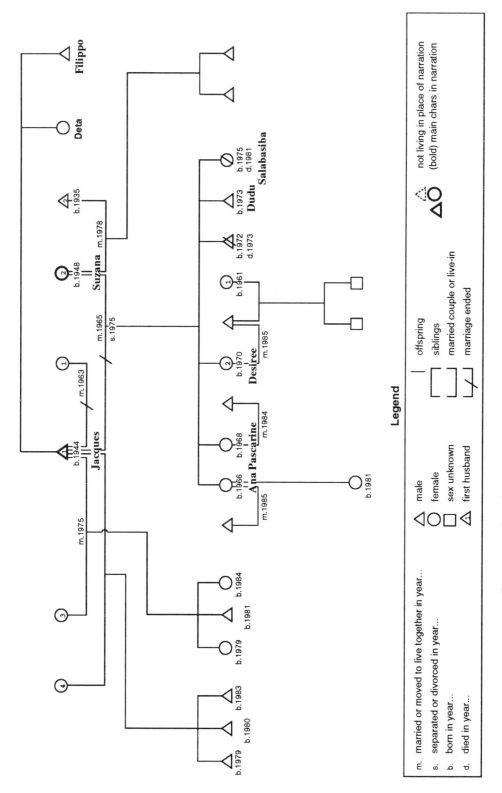

Figure 1.1 Family Diagram for "The Dissolution of a Marriage."

1 THE DISSOLUTION OF A MARRIAGE

A BOX OF MATCHES

I enjoyed going to the centre of Nyanya which was close to the mission station. It consisted of shops, private homes, beer houses, and brothels. Through it all ran the dirt road which was busy with pedestrians, cyclists, trucks, cars and buses, all in various stages of repair or disrepair. In the rainy season the road was muddy and very slippery. I remember walking on it as if I were walking on ice: inching my way up the hill with Tom trailing behind me holding onto my skirt to keep his balance. In the dry season, however, it was dusty and passing vehicles left a thick cloud behind them which made pedestrians cough. In no season was the road level, as it was never touched by a road grader. But despite its inadequacies, crowds of people were happy to use the road daily: caregivers of patients in the mission hospital shopped along it, for others it was the means of access to the near-by market which attracted people from far away to sell their garden and dairy produce or brooms or stools; and, of course, thousands of women from Nyanya itself and the near-by villages passed along it in the course of their everyday business.

The shops were made of various materials: mud; boards blackened with used motor oil; bricks; or cement blocks. They were always single storey buildings, a few yards in each direction, twenty by fifteen being the largest of all. They all sold similar items — a little bit of everything: salt, sugar, rice, margarine, milk powder, flour, soap, batteries, exercise books, children's clothing and material. Some carried more variety than others.

One September afternoon in 1974, soon after moving to the village, Henry, Tom, and I went to look around the shops. I bought a piece of material to make myself an outfit in the local style: a wrap around skirt and a top. I also bought half a kilo of salt and gave the sales clerk a plastic bag to put the salt into. He weighed it with old fashioned scales. Henry bought some nails. We went to another store and were welcomed by a man with a broad smile. He was out-going and it seemed natural for him to chat with us while I bought some matches. The man was a tailor who sewed in his shop. A tape measure hung around his neck and he treadled his Singer sewing machine steadily (there was no electricity in the village). I asked what he charged for making garments. In addition to his prices, I also discovered that he did not use any patterns but did his work by estimation.

While we chatted, his wife came to get some salt. She also smiled at us. That encouraged me to ask if I could go into her yard at the back of the house to greet her family. She was a bit surprised but agreed. The man stayed in his shop sewing and selling while we went outside and greeted the people sitting around in her yard. Tom started chasing some chicks which he had spotted and the woman promised to give him one when they grew bigger. We had met Jacques and Suzana.

Before I had found "my" village Yenyabo, I often used to go to their place and learn about their activities. I also became acquainted with their relatives who lived in their clan villages. Later I used to stop by their house on my way to Yenyabo in order to greet them and keep up with their news. Eventually their marriage dissolved, and as I did not get to know Jacques' new wife as well as I had known Suzana, I lost contact with the family. During the last two years of my stay in Africa, however, I found both Suzana and Jacques and renewed my acquaintance with them. I wanted to write this story to commemorate the first African family I knew well. In the beginning, I was green in anthropology and ignorant about Fofu customs. On top of this, Suzana's family were not confident enough to reveal themselves at first but tried to present themselves as they thought I wanted them to be. Little by little I began to see behind the masks and learn about Fofu culture through observing their lives.

A week after our first visit, Tom and I dropped by Suzana's and Jacques' again. But instead of finding Jacques at the sewing machine, I found a strange woman there. Apparently customers could pay to use the machine. I went around to greet Suzana and her children, and she presented us with two oranges which she had just picked from her tree. Jacques hurried after us to give us two bottles of soft drink. Tom gulped one of them immediately, glad to have a treat after the walk down the hill. A teen-age girl was taking care of the children. I later learned that she was Marata, Suzana's relative from her home village.

During this visit, I asked Suzana how she and Jacques had got married. I used the French word *mariage* but Suzana corrected me: they had never done *mariage* because Jacques had been married before. She meant that they had never gone through the church wedding ceremony because the Catholic church did not acknowledge Jacques' divorce. After this I learned not to use the French word, because it was invariably connected with a church ceremony rather than a traditional marriage. So from then on I used a Swahili word. This was not so simple either, because the Swahili word *kuoa* ('to marry' used for men) or *kuolewa* ('to be married' used for women) implied payment of bridewealth. In some cases, couples lived together although no bridewealth had been paid and were still regarded as married. To them I had to talk in terms of their coming to live together.

Suzana was sweeping the yard when Tom and I went to greet the family again five days later. She hastily fetched chairs for us and, since it was drizzling, set them under the overhang of the roof. Jacques' father was visiting from his home village, some six miles from Nyanya. I wanted to write down the names of Suzana's children and their meanings. Jacques' father helped Suzana explain the meanings of the names to me with great seriousness. Suzana had borne five children, one of whom had died a couple of years before. The first three of the surviving children were girls, the last a boy. The meanings of the girls' names expressed the frustration of having a female baby (boys were more desirable because the lineage was traced through males). The boy's name, Dudu, literally meant 'ground' but it pointed to the possibility of the child dying and being buried in the ground since death had already visited the family. Thus my innocent examination of names gave me an insight into the Fofu world. Later, however, I noticed that the family preferred to use European names for the girls, such as Ana, Pascarine and Desiree although they were officially forbidden in the country.

During a subsequent visit, I told Suzana that I would like to go and see her home village.

"But it is a little bit far away, far away," Jacques mused.

Suzana thought for a while. "I need to get some vines to plant sweet potatoes, sweet potatoes, maybe we should go," she then remarked.

I was ready immediately: "Let's go now!"

Suzana hesitated with a sour face. "What's the matter?" I inquired.

She sulked and Jacques explained, "If you take her now, how will she get back later in the afternoon?" I gathered that they did not expect me to stay all day with Suzana in the village but wanted me to go back for her.

"I'll go back to get her then," I promised. Suzana looked relieved and hurriedly prepared her two-year-old son and herself for the trip. Jacques ordered a man with a huge goitre to go with us and buy soap for his store in a town called Sezabo on our way.

The road ended at Sezabo but we continued to drive on a path as far as we could with bush branches scratching the car on both sides. We passed several villages and I was intrigued to see women grinding corn with rocks, instead of using a pestle and mortar which was more common. Finally we could drive no more and parked the car in someone's yard. Suzana knew the people, since they belonged to her clan and asked them to watch the car for us. We walked the rest of the way, each of us carrying our children. In the end, Suzana, seeing me struggle under Tom's weight, reached for him and carried both children. She was more accustomed to carrying heavy loads than I. We passed through a string of villages and Suzana repeatedly greeted people to the left and right. The villagers stared at us and I assumed that it was not very common for a European to walk there.

We arrived at Suzana's village and found her mother, father, and sisters-in-law busy with their various household activities. Marata was hoeing in a near-by field and came to greet us. I was thankful for a chair that one of the in-laws brought me. Suzana hurried into the hut and returned to present me with two eggs. Her mother and father seemed to be in good shape; they were about to go to the fields to hoe. Her grandmother, whom they estimated to be over 90 years of age, sat on a mat near the house and refused to talk to us. Old people were often unsociable, I had heard. Only later did I discover that she had lost her voice a decade ago and was not able to speak. Suzana's father told me that she was still capable of weeding the fields and worked a little every day.

Suzana's family was uneasy in my presence, since they were not used to foreigners visiting them. I soon left Suzana there to collect her vines and went back home. In the afternoon, when I returned to fetch her, everybody was busy. One of Suzana's brothers was pounding corn in a mortar as were two village girls. This pounding was in preparation for distilling liquor for the wedding of one of Suzana's brothers, although I did not know it then. Suzana's grandmother was studiously peeling manioc roots without even occasionally looking up and her father was building a rack for drying manioc. Suzana and her mother were tying two huge bundles of sweet potato vines for Suzana. The back of my station wagon was easily filled by them. Suzana was pleased with her day's work.

Little did I know then that her villagers and all those living in the villages we had driven through were envious of Suzana having a white woman do her a special favor. Suzana only told me this ten years later when we were looking at some photographs of the early days of our acquaintance. At the time I could not grasp the spirit of community which was the corner stone of the Fofu culture. I tended to treat my informants as individuals.

The next day Suzana came to visit me with her infant son and a young man, Filippo, who was Jacques' younger brother and was staying with them for the school holidays. He brought me fifty eggs from Jacques' home village. In the course of chatting with him I found out that he was attending a Catholic college in Lemura, some 30 miles from Nyanya. Jacques paid for his school fees and in return Filippo helped him in his store during the school holidays.

As we were drinking tea and eating banana bread, Suzana's son who was sitting on her lap waved his arms so vigorously that she could not eat her bread. I offered her Tom's high chair so she could be free of him. She was flabbergasted and when I obviously failed to understand why, my househelper, who had been observing what was going on with great interest, explained to me as if I were a complete simpleton, that a Fofu child would be afraid in the chair. Suzana showed her agreement by nodding her head.

I received the same reaction when I offered the chair to other Fofu and I finally got the message. It was neither the height nor the appearance of the chair that was frightening: mothers refused it because of the loneliness and sense of isolation they presumed a child would feel without physical human contact. Later I measured the length of time infants were carried or held in bodily contact during the daylight hours in a village and found out that it was almost 80% of the total observation time. This marked a substantial difference between African and Western child rearing.

When I next went to see Suzana I found her in front of the store standing in a deep ditch of brown water washing laundry. She was about finished and her three daughters carried a pail, a few basins, and the laundry home and started hanging it out on a string between the house and a fruit tree. Suzana and I followed the daughters into the yard. There Suzana proceeded to give her son a bath with warm water she had heated for the purpose. I noticed a black string with some colorful beads around his waist and wondered what significance it might have. Later I was to find out that most children wore them and they were for magical protection against diseases. Sometimes mothers bought special bundles of powdered medicine or shells which they tied to the string.

The girls, having finished hanging out the laundry, were trying to knock fruit off an orange and a pawpaw tree with a long stick. Some passers-by were helping themselves to fruit but nobody paid any attention to it. Soon the children were happily sitting on the ground eating their breakfast and throwing the peel all over the yard. I was offered some fruit and when I asked what I should do with the peel, they all stared at me not understanding why such a question could be asked and laughingly told me to toss it anywhere. Even so I felt guilty doing it. Suzana would eventually sweep all the peel and other garbage off the yard.

Suzana had hired a teen-age girl to help her with chores now that Marata had returned to her home village. This girl was now braiding a neighbor's hair. It was a long process — about two hours — but then the hairdo could last several weeks. Suzana had bathed her son to take him to the "kilo" at the hospital. This was what the Zaireans called the monthly well-baby clinic. Going to the "kilo" was an important occasion for both mothers and infants. The mothers invariably dressed themselves and their infants up in their best clothes, and armed with their carefully preserved attendance cards and, looking important, made their way to the clinic. That day I gave Suzana a ride since it was on the way to my home.

Suzana and I frequently visited her home village. I noticed that the preparations for the wedding of her younger brother were proceeding well. A new house had been built for the young couple about one hundred yards from Suzana's father's place and the father had erected a shelter for the guests. Relatives were busily preparing beer and liquor for the feast. Suzana's brothers were drinking beer while working and seemed a bit intoxicated. I told them that I would like to attend the wedding, too. There was no answer, no invitation but not a flat refusal either. I did not know then that it was not a Fofu habit to refuse flatly, refusal had to be expressed indirectly.

I was given another lesson in this some time later when I dropped into Jacques' store and asked if I could see Suzana.

"She has gone to the river to wash the laundry," replied Jacques casually.

"Then I'll just go and greet the children in the yard," I said.

"They'll be afraid of you," warned Jacques. That should have been enough to tell me that I was not wanted there but, totally oblivious to the signs, I walked around the store to the yard. There I met a huge drinking party, the members of which were all unknown to me. I had interrupted their pleasure and I was clearly not popular.

I hastened back into the store where Jacques offered me a chair. Suzana's brother, whose wedding was in preparation, was also there and we chatted about his marital plans. He told me that three goats and two cows had been paid as bridewealth and that this was not a problem to the family as his father owned many cows. He kept on pestering Jacques for batteries which he had set his heart on. Jacques ignored his begging at first but in the end he was worn down and snapped,

"All right, all right, take them."

No sooner had he said this than Filippo handed them over to the groom-to-be. I wondered how much Jacques had to give away to relatives and if his business was profitable despite these handouts.

Filippo and a son of a Protestant church elder then decided to open their hearts about Americans. They told me that they thought Americans were very proud people and they did not like them. I was intrigued because most of the Protestant missionaries were American. It must have been hard for the son of a Protestant church elder to live on the mission station under "American rule," if he disliked them. I also wondered if his father felt the same way. If he did, how could he handle being in a responsible position in the church and cooperating with the American missionaries? Did the Zaireans have two faces — one which smiled at the foreigners and the other which disliked them? Why did they not show their dislike openly? These were the questions I was to tackle in the years to come.

The young men went on to ask me to find them American girls as correspondents. Given that they had just finished telling me about their dislike of Americans that was very surprising. They had heard that American parents did not demand any bridewealth for marriage. That would suit them fine! They also thought that the parents of American girls might give young couples presents instead of the young couples having to wait on and do chores for the older couple as was the case with the Fofu. Such an arrangement would please them a lot! Perhaps the missionaries were originally accepted by the Fofu only on account of the money and other goodies they brought with them and distributed to the Zaireans.

When I left the store, a Protestant church elder who had been following the events from a distance, caught up with me and told me that I should not have friends like Suzana and Jacques. These people were Catholic and drank a lot. Today when I had arrived, Suzana had hidden herself from me so I would not know that she had arranged the party and Jacques had lied to me about her having gone to wash laundry. Catholic people were heavy drinkers and I should have nothing to do with them. Instead, I should choose my friends from the Protestants who did not have that habit. I tried to explain to him that I just wanted to learn how people lived, regardless of whether they drank or not, or whether they were Catholic or Protestant, or neither for that matter, but he did not understand me at all.

Another time when I went to greet Jacques and Suzana, Marata, who had returned to help her clan sister, told me that Jacques was somewhere in the neighborhood drinking and would be too embarrassed to come and greet me. I noticed that when drinking was under way my presence seemed to cause uneasiness. This feeling was confirmed later when Jacques came to see Henry who was sick with malaria. I told Jacques that I had decided not to attend the wedding of Suzana's younger brother after all. Jacques was very relieved and said,

"Good, because everyone would be drunk there!"

Protestant missions were very much against drinking alcoholic beverages but Catholic missions allowed it even though they did not approve of inebriation. Among the Zaireans being a "Poro," as the Protestants were called, meant that they drank coke, which was considered sugar water — at least in public — while the other, "normal" people, drank the real stuff. This difference tended to fade away in privacy, and I often met Protestants who had consumed stronger drinks than coke. Nevertheless, rural people were uneasy about their drinking habits in my presence because they knew that I was a Protestant.

The wedding was held without my presence and apparently everyone enjoyed it a lot. Soon afterwards, Suzana started talking about a great feast she was going to put on to honor the death of her son who had died over two years ago. It was a long time before the feast actually took place but it was preceded by much talk. Suzana was going to forget the sorrow and bitterness which she had felt after the death of her son. At the feast she would cut the black string tied around her neck as a symbol of mourning. She would also bathe and change from her dark clothes into brightly colored ones. She had to work hard to be able to purchase a new set of clothes and the beer and food for the feast.

About a week after the wedding Marata came to say that Suzana's father was very sick and Suzana would like to go and see him right away. I thought that it was a matter of life and death and got Tom and myself ready very quickly. When I arrived at Suzana's, however, she was not ready herself: she still had to bathe and change her clothes. While I waited I watched the children play with dolls which they made themselves out of corn cobs and mud. Jacques was treadling his machine, sewing someone's jacket. The children kept on going to the pile of scraps of cloth near him and choosing pieces as blankets for their sleeping "babies." When Suzana was finally ready we went, leaving the children, even the youngest this time, behind in Marata's care.

When we reached Suzana's home nothing seemed to be wrong with her father. When I inquired after his health, he merely murmured that he might have arthritis because his legs had been hurting at night. Apparently, the main trouble was that he was exhausted from the wedding celebrations which had lasted several days. He announced that he would rest very well before he even thought of arranging his youngest son's wedding.

The young bride was called to greet us. She was a young girl, barely fifteen, who cast her eyes shyly down and knelt on the ground to greet us. I felt ill at ease when she did this but Suzana seemed to take it for granted. Everyone gave commands to the young bride to run errands for them and she obeyed. Suzana's mother explained to me that the young girl whom she called *ngoli* (daughter-in-law), was now supposed to serve her and her husband for a couple of months until she, the mother-in-law, allowed the newlyweds to establish their own household.

"She works very well, very well, I must say," Suzana's father joined in the conversation. Apparently this was a big compliment. Then the *ngoli* was sent to the manioc field to cut manioc leaves for Suzana to take home. The mother and her older daughter-in-law went to the same field to dig up some manioc roots. They not only dug them out but also washed them and tied them into a bundle for Suzana who only sat and chatted with others.

I realised that the purpose of this trip was to get manioc leaves and roots for Suzana and her father's sickness was only an excuse for coming. I laughed to myself and did not tell Suzana that I had seen through the ploy. Her mother and one of the sisters-in-law carried all the bundles and a guinea pig to the car and we were off.

THE RUNAWAY GOAT

Jacques did not mind me visiting Suzana's village but he must have felt that my attention was too much on the female side of his family. He kept saying that one day he would take me to his home village, Gangu, to meet his parents. Finally he named the day. The route was a long narrow road, or rather, two ruts worn deep in the dirt. He and some other men, who came along with us, laughed at me when I stared at planks which were meant to be a bridge across a river.

"What if I miss the plank" I asked. I don't know why they laughed or what else I could have done other than try or turn back. I sent one of the men across the "bridge" to tell me if the wheels were in line with the planks and slowly drove across.

Jacques's father did not like the "noise" of the village so he lived near his fields, away from the main village. However, he was in the process of selling his house and fields to somebody from Lemura. In this area it had been customary to transfer the ownership of fields which belonged to the clan people without charge. But the mission station and the increasing commercial activity around it were bringing outsiders to the area thus causing land shortage and with it the commercial selling of land. Although this village was about six miles from Nyanya, its influence was felt here.

While going the last few hundred yards on foot, Jacques told me that his father had worked at gold mines further north during the Belgian colonial rule before the country's independence in 1960 but had then returned to his home village. It meant that Jacques had grown up in an area "foreign" to his clan village.

Jacques' parents came to meet us on the path. They were old and wrinkled and a bit stooped. I asked them in the local fashion,

"*Habari gani?*" (What is the news?)

The mother replied by fending it off, "Wapi!" which could be translated "Don't bother to ask."

Her husband answered, "Only illness."

Neither of the answers was polite but I was to learn that old people often took the liberty of snapping at younger ones in this way. The old woman was carrying a young child on her hip. I inquired,

"Is he your child?"

She replied "Oo-i," in Fofu agreement, but Jacques corrected her by explaining that the child was his older brother's and lived in the village.

I made the mistake of complimenting the old man on his house. This only made him belittle it. It was bad to elevate someone above others because the others would be envious and try to harm him with witchcraft in order to bring him down to their level. A social scientist (Foster 1965) has called this idea behind the peasant world view the image of "limited good": there is a limited amount of good in this world; if someone has more of it, it follows that the others have less of it. However, I did not know about this theory then.

If I had thought that my welcome was a bit cool I changed my mind when Jacques' father presented me with a shiny black goat. I thanked him profusely. He explained that it would be very bad of him not to give me something when I came to visit his homestead. Jacques' older brother gave me two eggs.

As we walked back to the car, one of the children led the goat by a vine rope. Jacques pointed at the trees growing near the path, they marked the graves of chiefs. His father's brother who had been a village chief a long time ago was buried near one of the trees.

This presented me with an opening to ask Jacques if the villagers took gifts to the graves of the deceased.

"No more," he explained. "We used to, but now civilization, has arrived and we no longer follow old customs, those old customs." Over the years I was to learn that the missionaries had fought vehemently against "ancestor worship" which they regarded as competition to the worship of the Christian God. They had destroyed shrines of the ancestors in private homes, in the fields and at the graves. In former times, the first fruit of the fields was always offered to the ancestors before anyone dared to touch the harvest. If something went wrong in the family, the head of the lineage offered libation and meat to the ancestors and prayed for better times. Ancestors were thought of as punishing recalcitrant lineage members, so the fear kept people in line. I gradually came to see that in their conversion from belief in ancestors to belief in the Christian God, nothing had replaced the fear which had had such a controlling influence on them. People could now break both the traditional and modern rules without feeling guilty.

I inquired about the face tattooing which Suzana and older women had. They had a vertical line between the eyes going down onto the nose and one round mark on each cheek under the eyes. Jacques explained that girls were decorated this way before "civilization" came to the country. Furthermore, their front teeth used to be filed to sharp points but this custom had also been abandoned. He went on to describe what their clothing was like before Western material became available: about the time when his father married his mother, people wore animal skins as loin cloths. Later I saw an old Belgian book which had pictures of Fofu in their native costumes: they had loin cloths — not of skins — but of grass.

Another custom I read about but Jacques did not mention, was that women used to wear round wooden plates in their lower lips. Old books debated whether this custom was for decoration or for protection from the Arabs: these enemies were not interested in women wearing ugly plates.

As we passed the school yard I noticed a car there and I wondered who else had ventured here. Jacques said it was the Catholic priest's who had arrived to hear confessions.

"Do you go to confession, too?" I queried.

"Not any more because I divorced, no more," he said in a matter-of-fact way. I noticed that the rules of the church were generally referred to unemotionally. As we walked he told me that he had attended a Catholic school intending to become a priest but had then abandoned the idea and married. But his wife was no good.

"Why was she no good?" I demanded.

"She never obeyed, never obeyed me or my father and she kept on running off to her home village. In the end I sent her away, away." I tried to find out where she was living. Jacques said that she had married someone in a city south of the area in another tribe's territory but he had also left her. I remembered that Suzana had told me that Jacques' first wife had no children and wondered what the real reason for the divorce had been.

"How are you doing with Suzana?" I dared to ask personal questions while driving back because the other men did not return with us.

"Fine" he said, "She is a good wife, a good wife."

"What makes a woman a good wife?" I inquired ignorantly.

"She obeys me, obeys me."

"Nothing else?" I persisted.

"I have a quick temper but she soothes and calms me down, calms me down. That is a good wife."

I referred to his first wife again and asked how his father liked him changing his wives.

"Oh, he was very glad, very glad. He did not like the first wife at all because she did not obey him either, him either." Jacques talked easily as if the matter had been simple. But I thought that it could not have been so at the time.

When we arrived back at his store, Suzana and Marata came to greet me. Jacques gave me two bottles of Coke to take to Tom and then he went to his sewing machine and continued his work immediately. His time was valuable and he had already been away from his work several hours. I went home to tie the goat up.

The goat gave us many headaches. We tied it carefully in the woods near our house where it could feed on the grass and bushes. But one day both goat and rope disappeared. I became anxious because the loss would be bad for my relationship with Jacques and his family and I walked around hopelessly searching for it. Later that day I went down to have my lesson in Kifofu near the airstrip. My teacher had caught the goat and was keeping it for me. Apparently, someone had seen the black goat wandering down the hill and asked around whose it was. My Fofu teacher knew about the gift and was kind enough to help me. He told me that to lose a gift was a serious matter and advised me to tie it more securely. I accordingly took the goat home and tied it up with many knots.

A few days later, however, I saw it wandering loose again. This time I gave orders to butcher it right away. I was very relieved when the meat was in our freezer, even though we would have got more meat if we had fattened it up first. Only when the goat could no longer escape did I dare to tell Jacques about its adventures. He listened to me seriously without his usual smile. When I had finished, he looked relieved and smiled again.

"If it had disappeared for good, we would no longer be friends, no longer be friends," he emphasized.

Did I ever let out a sigh of relief!

❑ ❑ ❑

Marata came to visit our home a few times with her friends. She liked to sit on the porch swing and look around. Once I asked her to help me with the trouble we were having with our fruit tree, namely that children came to pick lemons without asking. We were annoyed because it was *our* tree. Henry had confiscated a girl's basin and told her that she should return with her mother to get her basin back. She never did. Marata did not seem to understand what the problem was and reached for the lemons herself. That annoyed us even more. Then I remembered that Suzana let anyone pick fruit from her trees — passers-by simply helped themselves. Could it be that fruit trees were common property? Later years showed that it was. But the attitude to trees was changing. Ten years later I was walking in a village and met a man angrily shouting at children who had picked his mangos. My informant told me then that people were realizing the market value of fruit and were claiming ownership rights over trees but these were hard to enforce because many people were "stubborn."

Another time Marata was sitting on our swing when a young American couple came to our house straight from the mission swimming pool. They had their arms around each other and he was happily swinging a towel in the air. I introduced them to Marata and her friends. The girls were staring at the couple with wide eyes. I told the girls that the couple was engaged to be married in a few weeks. The girls were very surprised.

"With us, if the groom comes to visit the bride's village she will run away, run away," Marata claimed. After consultation with her friends she inquired,

"Are they sleeping in the same bed?"

"I don't think so," I replied, and the girls sighed with relief, "That's good anyhow."

This was my first acquaintance with Fofu sexual morality which focused on premarital chastity even more strongly than did the morality of the missionaries. Indeed, the girls were not happy for an engaged couple to walk together, let alone have their arms around each other. It was unheard of among the Fofu! Married couples did not walk together for that matter either; it was just not proper.

I also learned that a good bride had to look sad at her wedding to show her innocence. She was expected to resist going to the groom's place and cry when leaving home. Some time after Marata's teaching of Fofu chastity, an American wedding was held in the mission church, for a different couple from those Marata had seen. The church was packed full, about a thousand people. The American bride followed the American custom of showing her happiness by a radiant smile. The African audience stirred each time the smile flashed because it interpreted the smile differently from the Americans. The American missionaries did not appreciate this cultural difference.

Soon after this, Suzana and Marata quarrelled and Marata ran away from Suzana's. Actually Suzana told me only that Marata ran away. She didn't mention the quarrel, which I heard about from outsiders. Jacques claimed that he and Suzana decided to send her away because she was disobedient and therefore a bad example to the smaller children. A fourth story told by Suzana's sister-in-law was that Marata had become upset when Suzana sent her to the field to get some food. Be that as it may, Marata never came back to live with Suzana's family and for a long time the two females did their best to avoid each other completely. Marata appeared at our door a few times after leaving Suzana. She told me that she was in good standing with Suzana but had gone to live with another relative further away. Eventually we heard that she had married and moved to live with her husband.

As my visits to Suzana's home village grew more frequent I came to know her relatives better. Suddenly it dawned on me that her sister should not be living there with her husband. Why had they not followed the patrilocal residence rule (i.e. the residence of the young couple with the husband's kin)? Suzana's mother told me that they had not gotten along with his father and had moved. Later I noticed that each village had a few odd couples following the uxorilocal residence rule (i.e. the residence of the young couple with the wife's kin). The ideal pattern of all male lineage members (i.e. a set of kin who trace descent from a common ancestor through known links) living near each other in harmony was broken in these cases. I came to know that the attainment of this ideal was often hampered by accusations of witchcraft if sickness or calamity fell upon someone. Under the veneer of a united lineage, there were competition and ill feelings, as in all human relationships. A woman's side of the family had fewer claims on a person than the man's side, so living with a woman's relatives was more comfortable. Not all of Suzana's father's brothers lived there either. Some had moved further away in fear of the consequences of bad relationships, i.e., witchcraft.

In the following year, one of Suzana's uncles who had lived in a uxorilocation moved to live near Suzana's father. I met him when he was building a house for himself near Suzana's father's place. He explained his relationship in the Fofu fashion,

"Suzana's father is from the same father and the same mother, he left our mother's milk for me." This explanation was necessary because what we call "cousins" the Fofu call "brothers" and "sisters." Suzana's uncle wanted to make it clear that he was from the same nuclear family as her father. The uncle's wife had died recently but he had brought his son and his daughter-in-law with him. She was a young girl and she was treated as a *ngoli* by all of Suzana's relatives. By now the wife of Suzana's brother had served her in-laws long enough and was running her own household. She was now enjoying having a new *ngoli* to run errands for her!

SECOND WIVES SHOULD NOT BE SECRET

For some reason, Jacques' store closed down and the space was used for living quarters. It took some time before I found out what had happened. I gathered that Jacques' work as a tailor did not bring him enough money and he tried other business ventures. He never explained to me what he was doing, I simply caught glimpses of his activities and tried to piece them together.

One day Jacques was leaving for Kisangani some 200 miles away to sell cows and pigs. The truck, on which he was going to travel together with other passengers and their animals, was standing in the centre of Nyanya loaded with noisy and smelly animals. I looked at the truck and could not determine where the passengers would find any room. Jacques was not worried, however,

"We'll travel on the boards above the animals, above the animals." What a place to travel! To stand or sit on hard boards on a long and bumpy journey! Still more passengers were gathering around the truck to pay their fares. When I drove towards Suzana's home village later that day I met her three brothers who were hoping to travel with Jacques but by that time the truck had been declared full. In my estimation, it was full long before.

Jacques was away on his trip for two weeks. He was satisfied with his business deal. This time all the animals had arrived alive which was not always the case. On one occasion they had all died en route.

Jacques was often away on trips when I went to greet the family. Suzana did not know where he was but thought that he was trying to get a new licence to reopen his store. She did not show any anxiety to me but when we visited her parents, they often talked about it and said,

"Very bad, very bad indeed." Suzana was pregnant and an absent husband when the time for delivery was approaching was not a good thing.

In April 1975 Suzana came to visit me with a female clan sister. We drank coffee and chatted several hours. We talked about the future delivery of Suzana's baby later that month. We sat on the grass outside part of the time and Suzana commented on how slow the mission workers were at cutting grass. She appeared normal and I suspected nothing. In the afternoon, however, one of Suzana's children came to tell me that her mother had delivered a baby girl only one hour after she had left. I was amazed and felt cheated. But it turned out to be a good lesson in Fofu thought. Later that afternoon I ran to the market place to buy something. There I met Suzana's clan sister and discovered that Suzana had not told her about being in labor at my place, either.

"But I saw her grimace and guessed that she was in labor, she was in labor."

How could she behave as if nothing was happening? Why did the Fofu do it? The two women had left my place together and gone home. Only then did Suzana, accompanied by one of her daughters, go to the hospital to deliver.

In the evening, Tom and I went to the maternity ward of the hospital. Every one of some fifty beds in the huge ward was full. Mothers were feeding or cuddling their babies. Suzana was beaming now that everything was over. She confessed that the labor pains had been severe at my house but she had been able to hide them.

"Why did you not tell us?" I asked.

"You never talk about such matters to anyone, to anyone," she emphasized.

I realised how poorly I had behaved by Fofu standards. I too was pregnant at that time but I let everyone know about it. No wonder some Fofu men had laughed nervously: I had mentioned a taboo subject! When I later interviewed women about pregnancy they told me about the so-called "evil eye." This is the concept that people can cause others harm by wishing it upon them. If, for example, something went wrong with a pregnancy it was supposed that an ill-wisher had caused it. As one could never identify ill-wishers because everyone naturally appeared congenial and friendly to one's face, the women tried to reduce the risk of anyone harming their babies by never discussing their pregnancies. The fear of the "evil eye" did not diminish when the child was born. Once I innocently held a new born baby in a village. The next day when I passed by, the mother of the baby was angry at me,

"What did you do to my baby yesterday? After you left he did not stop crying. He cried all night!"

Suzana's child was another girl, the fourth one. I teased her about it and asked how she felt about having so many girls.

"Well, what can I do? This is how God brings them," she answered. She complained that she was in pain and I left her to rest.

A week later I passed by her house. She was healthy and busy doing her housework. She was now living in the new house that Jacques had been slowly building next to the old one. The new one was also a mud house with a thatched roof. Jacques was on another trip. Some of Suzana's friends dropped in and held the baby for a while before leaving. Suzana breast-fed the baby and laid her on the bed in the same room. The second youngest child who had been sleeping on the same bed, woke up and cried. Suzana commented that he was sick and cried all the time. She held him on her lap the rest of my visit. I noticed that the physical contact with the mother continued even after a new baby was born, at least, if the second youngest was sick.

A few days later, Suzana's mother, sister, and two sisters-in-law arrived to see the baby and the mother gave a name to the baby, Salabasika, which means "nothing but girls." Afterwards I wondered why Suzana waited so long to have her daughter named because I understood the Fofu custom was for a mother to stay in seclusion only for three days before bringing a daughter out for naming and four days if it was a boy. I never asked Suzana why she delayed the naming but when I talked to other Fofu women about it they said that having babies in the hospital frustrated their customs because they were not secluded at all while in the hospital. They therefore tended to discount that time.

By this time I was busy studying "my village" Yenyabo and did not spend as much time with Suzana as before. However, I often stopped by her house on my way to Yenyabo to hear the news. Sometimes I gave rides to the children if Suzana sent them on errands in the same direction as I was going. Once I dropped Suzana and her baby off near a river where she and a friend went to do the washing. When I had my second child, Tania, in the same maternity ward as Suzana had had hers, I went to show her to Suzana and her family. Not only Suzana but also the neighbors came to stare at the white baby.

"She is a big baby, a big baby," they commented. It shocked them to hear that she was eating porridge at two months.

"A baby of that age should not eat anything else but the mother's milk, the mother's milk," they said shaking their heads seriously. They were still saying it when Tania was six months old. One of Tania's admirers was Jacques' elder sister Deta. She had recently arrived to stay at Jacques', having left her marital home. Later I got to know her quite well.

Jacques' brother Filippo was home from his school which was at that time in Central African Republic. He begged me to get him into a Canadian university to study to be a chemist or agronomist. He did not like his school because there was a shortage of meat there. He was compelled to eat dog meat because there was no other meat available. Jacques was going to try to send him dried meat. I doubted whether any shipments would arrive with so many opportunities for thieves on the way. I could not help the brother get into a Canadian university because I did not have any contacts with Canadian agencies for scholarships: in fact, I had spent only one year in Canada. But we chatted about what it would be like to be a student abroad. He was enthusiastic, he would stay in Canada all his life! I reminded him that scholarships were often conditional upon the recipient going back to his home country for a couple of years. He smiled broadly,

"One can always get around such regulations, around. Who wants to live in this country, in this country?" I did not say anything but I was surprised that he did not consider his country worth living in with all his family around. I had thought that Zaireans valued their families above all. I was also disappointed that he did not seem to have any sense of responsibility for the improvement of his country. But maybe I judged him too harshly.

For some time I had been puzzled about the relationships in a family which both Suzana and I were friendly with. The mother of the family, Elisabeti, sold vegetables to me and I had become friends with her and often visited her home a few miles from Nyanya. I knew that she had a husband and seven children. A woman lived near her house with a child but no husband. I asked her how it was that she lived alone, because it was not common. She told me that her husband had beaten her so badly that she left him and came to live with her father's brother. I did not ask Suzana about the family but one day she volunteered the information.

"You know Elisabeti has a co-wife, a co-wife, but she is afraid to tell you so, tell you so." That was a surprise to me and I had mixed feelings. I was glad to know who the other woman was but upset that people felt unable to tell me.

"Why on earth did they not tell me?" I remonstrated.

"They were afraid to tell you because Elisabeti's husband used to be a Protestant preacher; they were ashamed, ashamed." I had heard that he had been active in the church but had never sought more details about it. According to Suzana, he had had to leave his position when he took the second wife. After Suzana's ground work it was easier for me to talk to Elisabeti and I soon let her know that I understood the situation and did not think anything of it. Our relationship improved after that.

Then Elisabeti gave me similar information about Suzana.

"Have you heard that Jacques has taken another wife, another wife?" What? Where? When? I was full of questions. Apparently he kept her in the city of Lemura and alternated between his wives.

Eventually, Suzana started talking about it spontaneously. Jacques had taken another wife without telling her. She found out from other people. Now that was not the proper way to take another wife! As I learned from Yenyabo, in villages the husband should approach the first wife, tell her about his intentions and ask for her permission. Only when this was granted could he go ahead with his plan.

Both Suzana and her family were very much in favour of polygyny — so much so that they once tried to convince me that even the Catholic church encouraged it, which I knew to be untrue. And Suzana did seem to take having a co-wife well at first. She joked about Jacques avoiding the subject and talked about it lightheartedly.

I learned later, however, that it bothered her very much. In fact, it was to cause a long and bitter fight between them.

At the end of one visit, soon after Jacques took his second wife, Suzana told me that she was tired of living there and that she would go and stay with her parents for a while. First, as she had said many times before, she would arrange a big feast for her dead child to be held at her parents' place. She would go to town and buy some new material for herself and corn flour to make beer. She would rejoice at her parents'.

And rejoice she did, according to Jacques who had sent children to spy on Suzana. Her family had laid on a big feast with lots of beer and dancing. Afterwards, Suzana wanted to stay on and relax for a while. Jacques' sister, Deta, kept me informed about Suzana's children who remained at Nyanya. She took charge of them while their mother was away. We made plans to visit Suzana in her village.

There was no trip, however. Jacques forbade it. Deta told me all about it on the morning of the planned visit. He was fuming about his terrible wife. The day before he had gone to Sezabo three miles away on business and had by chance met Suzana and her brother at a "buvette" drinking liquor. She had the baby with her. Jacques was annoyed and told her to leave immediately and return to her home village. Suzana's brother got up and told him that Suzana's whereabouts were none of his business now that she was at her father's place. Jacques had returned home furious and ordered us not to go to see his "bad" wife. He had been planning to let her stay with her parents and calm down about his second marriage. In time he would go and fetch her home with a gift to her parents. Now he dropped the second part of the plan.

This provided Deta with an opportunity to tell me that she had run away from her husband for the same reason: he had taken a second wife. She would not have minded if the second wife had been a young girl but she was a woman with four children whom she abandoned when she came to live with Deta's husband. Deta went on to explain the real problem between her and her husband: she had only two children, of whom the first one had died and the second one was already five years old. She had not been able to conceive again although she had wished to. Now that she was staying with her brother she could go to the hospital to ask for help to overcome her infertility.

That day we did not go to see Suzana as it would have irritated Jacques, although I was eager to see her and hear her side of the story. Instead, Deta suggested that we go to greet Jacques' father which pleased Jacques a lot. But this was not very successful. Jacques' family was not happy that we appeared without warning and his father was not even at home.

Two months passed before I saw Suzana again. She came to my house on her way to get medicine for her child who had been very sick but was improving. She looked fabulous: she was wearing a bright new wrap-around skirt with a matching top, a necklace, shiny dangling earrings, and her hair was braided in tiny neat braids which must have taken hours to do.

Figure 1.2 Dressed-up Zairean women.

She raged about Jacques. It was his duty to come and get her from her home village and return her to her marital home but that rascal of a man had not done it. Her brother's third wife had heard that Jacques was scouting for a third wife for himself. He had crowds of women! He used not to be as crazy and evil as now. The second wife was also mad at Jacques because of his running around with women. Suzana's children were staying with Jacques and the second wife and they were crying for their own mother. Suzana was ready to return to her marital home but she could not because Jacques was bad-tempered. His mother and sister were there, too, and she could not stand them. If she were to return she would kick them out immediately.

Suzana felt she would like to go somewhere far away to forget her sorrow. I asked her if she could not marry someone else.

"No way, Jacques would kill me, truly kill me!" she exclaimed. She waved her arms in the air wildly while speaking. Her former composed, gentle and balanced personality was gone. She spoke with a harsh voice vibrating with an anger which she did not even try to hide.

The situation in her home village was not bright either. A teacher had "stolen" the proposed bride of her youngest brother, although the goats had been paid for her bridewealth. Now he was living with another woman at Sezabo without any marriage payments. Her father was angry and threatened never to give even one cow for his marital payments.

Her brother with three wives was having difficulties keeping harmony in his household. The wives continually quarrelled and her brother yelled at them, threatening to beat each of them if the bickering did not end. One of the wives was living in Suzana's father's house to keep some distance from the others. Suzana forecast that one of the wives was bound to leave sooner or later because the situation was unbearable.

As her return to Jacques seemed uncertain Suzana had started her own fields in her home village. She had no knowledge of the state of her marital fields at Nyanya and she was not interested in them either. I noticed that to have recourse to a clan village and clan lands was a security for women. In some other African societies women did not have this economic and moral back-up.

A few days after Suzana's visit, Jacques' second wife and his sister Deta came to greet me. The second wife was a shy young girl who did not speak much but let Deta keep the conversation going. Deta boasted that she had worked hard in Suzana's marital fields now that Suzana was gone and explained what she had sown.

"When will Suzana return?" I asked innocently.

"I don't know. Jacques has not gone to fetch her yet, not yet," Deta replied.

"May she not return on her own?" I inquired.

"Oh, no! The husband will get angry if she does. It really shows that he loves her if he goes to get her," she explained.

Jacques' second wife was one of twelve children of a Catholic catechist from Sezabo. Deta praised how well she cared for Suzana's children and the house. She claimed that the second wife and the children were living in Jacques' city house. I did not know if it was true because Suzana mentioned having seen her children in Nyanya.

As for Deta herself, her husband had made two trips to fetch her back to her marital home.

"My spirit stays behind because in a few weeks he would beat me again and the same trouble would start, would start," she lamented and did not go with him.

I went to Finland with my children for the month of May in 1976. When I came back, Jacques dropped by. He accused Suzana of having been a disobedient wife. She had treated his parents poorly and lacked respect for him, which had caused him to look for another wife.

"Let Suzana stay with her parents, let her stay, I am angry with her!" he declared. I asked him about his work, if he continued to tailor. He explained that he had left tailoring temporarily and was now dealing in ivory. He bought from far away and sold to the truck drivers going to Uganda. He made good money and would soon have enough for an electric sewing machine which he would buy from me. It was news to me that I was to sell him a sewing machine but I did not worry about it then.

Two months passed and I heard nothing about Suzana. Then I decided to go and see her. I was driving towards her home village to find out what was going on when I spotted her father at Sezabo walking towards his village. I stopped the car and asked about Suzana.

"She is here in the chief's jail, in jail," the father said to my astonishment. "Jacques sent policemen for her three days ago."

"Is it possible for me to see her?" I inquired.

"Yes, but she went to get some medicine for her child, some medicine. Wait and I'll get her," the father went off to find her. Soon Suzana came with her baby and seemed happy to see me. She talked loudly,

"Jacques has forsaken me, forsaken me, and I thought you had forsaken me, too."

Apparently the jail was not too strict about her presence because she got into the car and said,

"Let's go home, home!"

As we drove slowly towards her village it started raining and the road became slippery and muddy. We had to sit in the car and wait for it to stop raining. This gave Suzana's father an opportunity to blame Jacques.

"Jacques is a bad man, a bad man," he scorned. "I have no idea why he sent the police to tie Suzana up." He elaborated on these themes until it cleared up.

At home Suzana's mother continued to blame Jacques. "He spreads the word around that we are bad, bad, and accuses Suzana of having another husband."

I asked whether she had one.

"No, she is here with us," the mother replied sternly. "He is a bad man. Suzana goes and cooks food for her children and he accuses her of poisoning them!"

Their complaining about Jacques colored my visit and I thought that it must have made Suzana feel good that her family supported her unconditionally in her marital dispute. It must have been nice to be able to fall back on your immediate family and lineage no matter what happened to you, even if you had been thrown into jail.

I noticed that Suzana's grandmother was still about but she did not pay attention to what was going on around her. A wife of Suzana's brother was carrying a new born baby and came proudly to show him to me.

It had been raining again and when we went to leave the car was stuck in the mud. Suzana's father called for help. He was wobbly after drinking liquor non-stop during the visit. About a dozen men pushed the car shouting and laughing, and later screaming when the tires of the car spurted mud over them. I was horrified to see the state they were in and asked Suzana whether I should give them some money to compensate them — a typical Western thought that money can replace everything.

Suzana shrugged her shoulders, "Don't do that. It should teach them, teach them to do better *salongo* (communal work), better *salongo* and keep their roads in better repair!"

At the chief's place Suzana got out of the car to inform the authorities that she was going to see me off. We drove to visit Elisabeti a mile away and then she walked back to the jail.

During the following week I heard various reports of her. Apparently she was out of jail. Someone had seen her waiting for transportation to the regional court some 10 miles away. Another told me that their house had died, which meant that they had divorced. Rumors were circulating that Suzana was pregnant by a clansman and that Jacques was so indignant that he was suing her for damages and the court case was dragging on. In going to court Jacques was a modern man. Ordinarily marital disputes were settled by the families.

A few weeks later I went to visit her in her home village with an English friend who was spending her holiday with us in Africa. Suzana was working in the fields but her mother sent for her. As she approached, we could see her big belly. She was obviously pregnant. Her youngest daughter who was now seventeen months old was crying on her hip. She looked tiny and sickly. Suzana let her suck her breasts which surprised me because Fofu mothers weaned their infants once they found out that they were pregnant again: a pregnant mother's milk was believed to be poisonous.

I asked her when she would deliver her new baby.

She looked at me straight in the eye and said, "I am not pregnant."

Confused, I turned my face to her mother who met my gaze and said slowly and firmly, "Suzana is not pregnant."

I finally got the underlying message not to bother them with the affair. Again, I had been too straightforward which was not regarded as good manners among the Fofu.

Suzana told me that her child had been very sick. She certainly looked unhealthy: her skin was covered with sores, her hair was falling out, and tears and mucus had dried on her cheeks. Although she was older than Tania, she did not walk yet as Tania did. Suzana lamented that once the daughter was weaned she would have to give her back to Jacques. It was the Fofu custom that the children belonged to the father in divorce if all the bridewealth payments had been made. She missed her children but was not allowed to see them because her husband had denied access. I wondered whether Suzana was wilfully neglecting her youngest child to avenge her husband or whether her emotional state was spontaneously and unconsciously reflected in the childcare.

I tried to ask how the court case had gone and who had to pay damages but she did not want to talk about it. That was an indication that she had had to pay. Once more she and her family members pronounced Jacques to be a bad man.

I inquired whether she would eventually remarry.

"Yes, I will, but I am not going to marry anyone from Nyanya or from Gangu (Jacques' home village), none of them, that's for sure!" Nor did she. But she did marry another tailor.

I went to see her after a couple of months. Her mother told me that Suzana had gone to fetch firewood from across the river and would not be back for a long time. I thought that she might be hiding in the house not wanting to see me. It would be about time for her to deliver the baby and she clearly wanted to keep me in ignorance of it. I had learned from others that becoming pregnant by a man of one's own clan was taboo necessitating negotiations between the lineages concerned. The children born of such unions suffered ridicule all their lives.

Suzana's youngest child was at home, however, and I noticed that she still looked miserable and coughed all the time. Suzana's mother blamed Jacques for leaving the child there instead of caring for it at Nyanya where medicine was available. Now that it was weaned he should have taken his child as was the proper custom.

The brother with three wives had built an extra house for one of the wives to keep peace in the family. The Fofu usually built a house slowly by carrying a couple of poles at a time on the shoulder when returning from fields near the woods. It took from several months to a year to build a new house. But this man had built it in a month. Suzana's family joked that one could build speedily if there was an urgent need!

I did not go to Suzana's home village for a year. I sensed that her family wanted to keep me out of the affair which put them under much stress. I was still a stranger to whom they tried to show a beautiful facade. I continued my trips to Yenyabo and each time I passed Jacques' store and house I turned to see if the family was home. I sometimes chatted with the second wife and with Jacques while Suzana's children ran around us. They seemed clean, healthy and happy, and on the surface, at least, everything was fine. Jacques had the broad grin on his face again, especially when his second wife bore a baby son. I gave her a gift when I went to see the baby.

I moved to Bululu the following year. Before moving, I went to Suzana's village once more to bid farewell but she was not at home. When I flew back to Nyanya from Bululu to visit "my village" Yenyabo, I never took the time to go and greet Suzana's family. Years went by and I heard that Suzana had married a man from another tribe and was living in the city of Lemura, 30 miles away. Jacques and Suzana's youngest brother bumped into each other at the market. They had gone for a drink together and decided to let bygones be bygones.

"I'LL COME TOMORROW"

Seven years passed until Henry and I came back to Nyanya for two months. I made a point of seeing how Jacques was. I found him just as he had been years before, sitting in his house sewing. He grinned broadly when he saw me.

"It's a long time, long time, madam!"

The children had grown and I had to keep the old family chart in front of me to help me guess who each one was. Suzana's only son Dudu was now twelve years old, a tall fellow. The second oldest daughter, Pascarine, was married and living elsewhere. Jacques made a point of mentioning that three goats had been paid for her bridewealth and three cows remained to be paid. The oldest daughter Ana was living with Suzana's parents after a scandal of which I heard later. I was not surprised to hear that the youngest child whom I had seen sick at Suzana's parents had died of *kwashiorkor* (malnutrition). After my departure, Jacques had sent Ana to fetch her and Ana had become her caretaker but she was unable to restore her health.

Jacques' second wife was now the first wife and had three children. She had gained weight and lost her girlish appearance along with her shyness. Jacques had taken another second wife who also had three children. There were children all over the place and I could not keep track of who belonged to whom.

Jacques did not own an electric sewing machine yet but still desired one and became very excited when he talked about the different stitches that the electric machines were said to have. The mission had laid an electric power line from Lemura, making electricity available to people outside the mission station.

When I asked about Suzana, Jacques told me that she had stopped by the house recently because she was staying at her home village. Years back he had told me that he divorced Suzana because of her disobedience but now he gave a different explanation: Suzana had destroyed his shop by taking his money to drink and to give away as gifts to her family. That is why he had told her to leave and stay in her own village.

Although I recalled Suzana leaving him of her own accord after he had taken another wife, I did not say anything because I realised that there are often many motives behind our actions. Which one we express at any given time depends on many circumstances. He did not, however, seem to have any anger left and he talked about her calmly. When I told him that I wanted to go and see her, he even volunteered to send his son Dudu with me to show the way, in case I had forgotten.

I caught up with the news in detail later when Jacques came to visit me in our house. His round face beamed like the sun.

"I thought we would meet only in heaven, in heaven, but here you are!" he exclaimed. He went over the major events of the past years in detail, starting with the sad news.

His father had died about the same time as his youngest daughter, just a few days apart. Fifteen-year-old Ana, who had been taking care of the child, was living with her grandfather at the time and had slept with the child a long time at night before realising that she was dead. This was about four years ago. A third troublesome matter arose soon after this: Ana became pregnant. Jacques had forced Ana to name her lover, who turned out to be Jacques' sales clerk although he vehemently denied his paternity. Jacques was persistent and dragged him to the hospital for a blood test which proved his paternity. Jacques then sued him but the lover's older brother settled the matter out of court. He agreed to pay the maternity bill, materials for the baby care and one cow — the last was still outstanding.

Jacques moved on to the better news. He had great plans of building a new family house and a brick school building for tailors on one of his three lots at Nyanya. I did not know he was so wealthy. He had heard that he might get funding for the building and sewing machines for the students through the Catholic mission and he would not mind me recommending him to the mission in this regard.

"Why should I keep my tailoring skills for myself, for myself only? I want to teach others." His altruistic tone sounded hollow. His youngest brother Filippo now lived in a city some two hundred miles away, owned a garage and ran two cars. He had promised to send Jacques a bus to make money at Nyanya. One of his elder brothers was planning to drive it.

"I am glad I paid his schooling, his schooling. Now I can reap the benefits, the benefits," he boasted. He went on to describe the glorious career Filippo had made for himself. It had been very profitable for him to study in the Central African Republic, rather than in Zaire, and to get to travel to seven other African countries. The Zairean embassy had arranged these trips for him and met him with an embassy car at the airports. He had also smuggled gold to Uganda and once he had been jailed for allegedly spying. Again, the Zairean embassy helped him and succeeded in negotiating his release. Filippo was not discouraged by those setbacks but continued "like a white man," always trying new things. Jacques patted his pocket,

"I have a hundred dollar check in my pocket, in my pocket, at this moment." Filippo was preparing to go to live in the capital and then make trips to France. Jacques himself might go to see him before he left on another trip.

Jacques' and Suzana's son Dudu was polite and quiet as children should be with adults. As he shyly showed the way to his mother's home village I realized that everything seemed different. The bushes had grown in eight years and we could not drive as far as before. Suzana's parents were in the yard when we arrived. They hardly looked older than when I had last seen them. Suzana's grandmother had passed away some years ago. The house was also different and in a different place from the previous one. A woman came to greet me from a house near-by and I recognized her as "the young bride" who had got married when I first knew the family ten years ago. Then she had been a subservient daughter-in-law kneeling down before other members of the family but now she was an outgoing, self assured woman with five children. The youngest one was now sucking her breast. Suzana's sister and her husband were still living in the village and so was the brother with the three wives and the two other brothers who now had two wives each.

Suzana had gone across the big river to get firewood for distilling liquor but was expected back any time. Her youngest child, a five-year-old boy, was sitting near Suzana's mother. He looked at me suspiciously. Suzana's oldest daughter Ana was now living here permanently. I wondered why and received a unanimous explanation from all present. Ana's relationship at home with Jacques was strained because of her illegitimate child and the fact that he and his brothers had not received any bridewealth for her. Ana had therefore decided to go to her mother's relatives. The mother's side of the family having no expectations or entitlement to bridewealth, felt less disappointment and could love her for herself.

When I inquired if Suzana got along with her present husband, her mother answered briefly that she had two children by him. That was explanation enough for her but I reminded her that Suzana had six children by Jacques and yet they divorced. The mother put the blame on him again,

"Suzana was willing to return to Jacques but he kept her away, he kept her away."

While I was showing pictures of my family and explaining what we had done over the eight years, Suzana walked in with a huge bundle of long pieces of wood. Although she had spotted me from far away she continued to walk at a steady pace, holding her head firm to balance her heavy load. She did not say anything at first but threw it down near the door. Then she wiped the sweat which was streaming from her forehead with clothes hanging on a string and smiled. Her smile changed into laughter and she came to hug me.

"Madam, I thought I will never see you again!" she shouted. She had visibly aged and her voice was cracking. Perhaps the heavy loads affected her neck muscles and vocal cords.

She remembered that I had come to look for her before moving to Bululu in 1977 but had not found her. She recited item by item what I had left for her as a gift (soap, baby powder, baby clothes), which I had forgotten. She claimed that she treasured those gifts and did not let anyone touch them.

She confirmed that she was married to the same man whom she married after divorcing Jacques, and had two sons by him. She was staying in her village to get some money by distilling liquor in order to buy some pieces of material. It was tough to live in the city, there were no fields to live off as there were here in the village and her husband's wages did not go far. However, Suzana seemed proud to mention that he was a tailor (like Jacques, I thought) and made the robes for the Greek Orthodox priest and suits for white men. One child had stayed with his father in the city; his sister had arrived to take care of him.

"I think I have finished child bearing, finished," she told me.

As we went to greet her relatives in the village I took pictures of her walking along the path, carrying her load, and sitting with her parents. A year later she remembered exactly what pictures I had taken and demanded all of them for herself.

"You did not bring the picture where I turned back to face you on the path in that field," she concluded. I was stunned because there were several similar pictures and I had only brought a selection. What a memory she had!

As Henry and I were going to the city on the following day to do some shopping I arranged to take Suzana with us so that she could show me her family and home in the city and then return to her parents' village with us. Next morning she was waiting for us on the roadside together with her sister's half-grown daughter who carried a bundle of food for Suzana's family. On the way Suzana told me that her youngest son was suffering from epilepsy. The family had tried all kinds of medication, native and Western, to no avail.

We had to park near the main street of Lemura and walk on a sandy path about half a mile. One could see all kinds of houses on the way: mostly made of mud, but a few were made of wood, cement blocks and bricks. The houses did not seem to be in rows and I wondered if there had been any official plan for this area. However, after I lived in a bigger city I realised that there was more space between the houses here than there was there. Also, some trees and bushes brought green to the sandy area.

Suzana's husband, a man in his fifties, stood in the yard smoking a cigarette. Suzana's older son sat near a fire while a woman cooked on it. The boy saw his mother first and ran to meet her. Suzana took him into her arms and walked into the house without a word to any adults. I knew that Fofu did not consider it proper for a couple to show any intimate feelings in public. It was usual for a returning spouse to greet everyone except his or her partner. The little boy was now leaning his head against his mother. Suzana's niece also entered the house to leave her bundle there. I had stopped at one end of the yard and stood watching until Suzana offered me a chair which the niece brought out for me. Then I greeted everyone and chatted a while before I left to do my business in town.

In town later I happened to meet Suzana's husband in the street. He looked gloomy as he talked to me.

"When is she moving back to us, moving back? How long is she going to stay there?" he asked twisting his head in the direction where he assumed Suzana's village would be. There was aggression and anger in his voice.

"I don't know. She told me that she is trying to make money to buy material," I tried to be neutral.

"How many pieces of material does she want? In five months she must have made lots of money, lots of money!" I had no idea that she had been away that long and I wondered if earning money was an excuse for something else. I even wondered if the woman in the yard was his sister, perhaps he had taken another wife. I did not ask any questions.

"The boy misses his mother, misses his mother," he murmured. I thought I had a solution,

"Suzana told me she was willing to take him along to the village." The man stiffened and announced,

"She is not allowed to do it, not allowed!" He continued to walk on slowly, looking annoyed.

In the afternoon I went to pick Suzana up. The husband stood like a statue of stone in the yard watching her prepare to leave. His sister was doing household chores. She turned to the boy and asked,

"Are you going along with your mother, along?" The boy declared in a clear voice,

"Not today but she will come to fetch me tomorrow!" Suzana's sister-in-law and the boy came to the car to see us off. Suzana was already sitting in the car when she stretched her arm towards her son and demanded,

"Dad, shake my hand!" I did not know why she called him dad. The boy's face twisted and he burst into tears. Suzana shouted laughingly,

"I'll come tomorrow to get you."

Her sister-in-law carried him away and we left. I asked if she was going to come back tomorrow.

"Of course not, but it is good to comfort a child, very good."

Brought up in a different culture which emphasized the importance of the "truth" I thought in my heart that Suzana was unethical. I was wise not to say it aloud and later realized that her promise was well-meant. Other women with whom I discussed this habit of mothers lying to children told me that a good mother did it out of kindness to show how much she loved the child. An anxious child was soothed when hearing the mother's affirmation of returning soon. He was happy again and would sleep well in the anticipation of the new day which would bring the mother home.

"Won't he feel cheated when the mother does not come as promised?" I insisted.

"Oh no, in his heart he knows that the mother wants to come but who knows what has happened, so she cannot come."

I suppose children might as well get used to this way of relating to others because it was prevalent among adults as well. A Fofu man told me that he would never show his dislike of a person. One day an aggressive man asked him for a bed for the night. He did not want to give it so he explained very regretfully that his house was full but that his relative would be glad to have him. Then he gave directions to the relative's house but these were totally wrong. The man would not find any houses in the place he directed him to. I was horrified,

"Won't he come back furious and kill you for the wrong instructions?"

"Oh no, he will leave my house happy in anticipation of a warm bed and in memory of my kindness. By the time he cannot find the house, he is too tired to come back." Another Fofu man told me that his uncle used to put up a show when

3guests came to his house. He would send one of the children to buy beer in the village. Some time later the child would return to report that the beer was finished. The uncle would then lament the situation and the guests would be happy about his kind thought. But the children never went to buy the beer, the uncle had instructed them only to pretend to do so. Sociability was highly valued among the Fofu.

I told Suzana about my encounter with her husband in town. She had talked with him as well. He did not want to let her go back but she told him that she had to go and get the other son from her parents but then she would return soon. She chuckled,

"What a good thing I left him there!" She had calculated everything carefully.

SHY AND ASHAMED

Shortly after arriving back to Nyanya after a year's absence, I was walking to the market to get some food supplies when someone behind me shouted,

"Madam Pilot!" I turned around automatically, although there were three other "Madam Pilots" at Nyanya then. A woman was running after me excitedly. I recognised her as Jacques' sister Deta whom I had not seen for nine years.

"Can it be you? I saw you walking by, walking by, and I thought it was you but then I thought you cannot be here. Yet no other white woman walks to the market but you."

She was exhilarated and hugged me many times, then she dragged me to her room which she rented in a long wooden house not far from Jacques' home. She had been in Nyanya for a few months to help with his children. Jacques had left for a distant city (where he had wanted to go already ten years ago) and was expected back soon. Deta had hardly changed in nine years; she was as slim and beautiful as before. She earned money by prostitution as many other women did. She had returned to her husband for a while but left him again.

Deta stayed in Nyanya for a few months and often came to my house to chat, usually bringing with her something from Jacques' garden for me. She insisted on accompanying me to places and introducing me to family members.

As soon as I could, I went to Jacques' house. Suzana's son was at home alone swinging a charcoal iron in the air to get fire going in the coals. A pair of wrinkled shorts was on a chair waiting to be ironed. When I arrived, he interrupted his work and went to fetch his stepmother. I gave her a little gift of guest soap and we chatted while the young boy ironed his shorts. Jacques had left for the distant city eight months ago to receive a car from his younger brother but something was wrong with it and it needed repairs.

"Do you get letters from him?" I asked. She answered in the affirmative.

"How many times has he written?" I inquired.

"One can't count, the letters come like water, at least one or two a week. He says he is coming soon, coming soon."

It was not a Zairean custom to write often, so I did not know whether to believe her or not. In the light of local gossip, I would say that she told me lies so as not to appear as neglected by Jacques as she really was.

Deta then appeared in the doorway. She looked a bit drunk having emerged from a beer party. As she saw me out, she told me that Suzana's son was treated poorly by his stepmothers. Indeed, he had no bed to sleep in, only the dirt floor. They did not feed him properly either but Deta gave him food. The marriages of the two older daughters, Ana and Pascarine, were not formally arranged even yet. Their situation was no better than last year: Pascarine's husband had not brought cows for her bridewealth and Ana's former lover had not paid the outstanding cow and she was now living with someone who had not paid anything either. The third daughter Desiree had eloped only last week to the annoyance of the family. Jacques was away and therefore the family had no man to take care of these matters. It was time that Jacques returned. She insisted that I go with her to see Suzana in her home village the following day. I was surprised that Suzana was still — or again — there and pleased that someone would go with me.

Although I was ready at Deta's before seven o'clock in the morning I was still scolded for being late. Deta had been waiting for me nervously a long time. Later I learned to get up at four to start such trips in order to avoid the hot sun. I had no car this year but I ventured on foot. Although we walked at least eleven miles that day, I did not notice it because of the interesting conversation and the people we met on the way.

Deta wanted to call at Desiree's which was at Sezabo, about half-way on the way to Suzana's village to get back her wrap around skirt which she had lent her to elope in! I could not quite reconcile the claim that she and the family were against Desiree's elopement with the fact that Deta had lent her skirt to Desiree. The boy friend was a married man with two children and it did not please Deta that Desiree was to be a second wife. He had frequented Jacques' tailor shop and made eyes at the young girl. When the girl had told her aunt about her plan to marry him and she had opposed it, Desiree had blamed her for being old-fashioned. Perhaps this induced Deta to collaborate with her. The first wife left when Desiree arrived, taking the youngest child with her and leaving the older one for Desiree to care for.

"I will be very uncomfortable with her fiance. I should not really see him but I want you to meet him." I was not asking her to take me to the place and could not understand why she broke her own avoidance rules just because of me. Nevertheless, I truly enjoyed observing avoidance behavior, of which I had read in anthropological text books. I knew that avoidance rules between certain in-laws were commonly followed in Africa and that an avoidance relationship typically existed between a woman and her son-in-law but now I learned that the rule also applied to a wider category of relatives. The avoidance relationships contrasted strongly with the joking relationships which existed between other relatives. On this trip, I saw both kinds of relationships and Deta kept me informed about how she felt about them. She had internalized the rules to her very being.

Deta first introduced me to the fiance's brother and his wife who lived on the opposite side of the road to the eloped couple. She stood at some distance from them with her back to them, explaining to me that she felt "ashamed" to face them. The situation was so tense that I found no words to chat with and I think that the brother-in-law was glad to see us leave. When we approached the fiance 's house Deta explained that both she and the fiance would be very ashamed.

"Which one has more shame?" I inquired.

"I, of course, as the bride's father's sister, especially when no goats have been paid. When he pays them, I need no longer be as ashamed as now, just a little bit ashamed."

The house looked attractive, it was built of mud and painted in two tones. The fiance was born here but had been brought up in a big city some 200 miles away. His living room gave the impression of a city home with carpentered furniture, table cloths and pictures on the wall. Deta sent me in first and only came in after I had greeted the fiance . We had never met and I explained to him that I had come to see his wife whom I knew as a little girl. He called for her and she came and greeted me by offering her shoulder for me to touch. It was a Hiha custom for a younger person to offer a shoulder to an older person as a sign of respect. When I first came to the area, only Hiha pastoralists were following this custom but now it was spreading among the Fofu. As I introduced myself Desiree was kneeling down on the floor in the fashion of a *ngoli*, a young daughter-in-law, a custom which I had first encountered at Suzana's home village. She looked down shyly, then sat down in the corner of the room holding her co-wife's sick child on her lap. The child was breathing heavily and was feverish. Desiree had quite a responsibility in her hands at the age of fifteen.

Deta avoided looking at Desiree's fiance , but he kept on glancing at her. Desiree brought her aunt the skirt she had borrowed, we sat a little while but the conversation was difficult with Deta's obvious anxiety. After she whispered to me "This is horrible" we got up and left. When we had walked a little distance away from the house Deta let out a sigh of relief,

"That was hard! But now we will go to my *semeki* (brothers-in-law), and I don't need to be ashamed. I may talk, laugh, joke, and walk freely, walk freely from house to house."

She felt this way about the village of her brother's ex-wife. Her thoughts returned to her niece's case.

"We are going to fetch the goats soon. It is important to get them very soon."

I wondered why the hurry when Desiree's two older sisters had not brought in their bridewealth payments either. Deta explained that Desiree's case was the most urgent because she had never been married before. I remembered that Ana had borne a child before this cohabitation but I did not know the details of the marriage of the second oldest daughter, Pascarine, except that the goats had been paid.

While walking I asked what the relationship was now between Suzana and Jacques after many years of separation. Deta replied that if, for example, they met on the road they would not greet each other or talk. There was still love between them, and because of this love, Jacques could still tear her clothes in rage. If there had been none, they could have greeted each other like human beings. This attitude was not typical of divorced couples. I knew some who remained on good terms.

Deta was happy to arrive at Suzana's home village. She talked all the time. What a contrast to her behavior at Desiree's place! Suzana, her mother, one brother and some children were at home. The two other brothers had gone to dig gold for the day. We sat outside, and when it became hotter, moved into the house where it was cooler. Part of the time Deta talked in Kifofu and Suzana's brother translated for me. Something had happened to his voice. He talked in a whisper.

"Illness," explained his mother.

"Drinking" said someone else. But I knew that everyone in the village drank, yet only he had lost his voice. I also remembered that Suzana's grandmother had lost her voice during the latter part of her life, perhaps it was genetic disorder.

Everyone was listening to Deta. She told the family that she had seen Jacques' very first wife in the city further south when she had gone back to her husband. The ex-wife was going bald now. Suzana and her mother clicked their tongues with amazement. Then Deta told them about a woman whose childhood home was in this village. Her husband was mistreating her. She would be coming home soon, for nobody could take such abuse. Her children had told her to leave, they would stay with their father. The fact that they were from a different tribe explained to Deta why they were "mean" people.

She also had a juicy piece of news: Jacques' present younger wife had gone to the city for an abortion. She had become pregnant after Jacques had left and feared that he would find out.

"Will he find out?" I asked. Everyone nodded.

"He will, he will. His family will gather to discuss the matter but usually we don't do anything about it. If he had stayed, the pregnancy would have been his, not another man's. It would have been his," Deta explained to the nods of the others. From other similar cases I had learned that the Fofu considered all adults to have the right to sexual relations. Those spouses who were away too long were depriving their partners of their rights and, therefore, it was understandable for the remaining partners to take lovers. Jacques was not expected to live in chastity either. I inquired how common abortion was and they all agreed that it was very common.

"Unfortunately," they added.

I don't know what prompted Deta to speak about the past but she then stood up and recounted a story, acting it out in the most dramatic places. Her grandmother had told it to her father and it was a true story. Everyone listened to her spellbound.

Her grandmother had borne only daughters, no sons. Once again she bore an infant and informed her husband that it was a girl. He went out, although it was dark, calmly dug a grave in the ground, put a banana leaf into it, took the child, set her in the grave and covered her with dirt, levelling it with his foot. The daughter cried three days in her grave. The man (I noticed that Deta did not use the word "grandfather") came out with a pestle and beat the grave with it. Here everyone was silent as Deta dramatically pounded the ground. The crying ended and the man told his wife not to mention it to anyone.

Then Deta linked the story with the present with such conviction that nobody could dispute it. Because of this sin, Jacques' family had not borne boys. Suzana bore two sons, one of whom died and four daughters. (She omitted the fact that Jacques' two other wives had borne four sons altogether.) Jacques' brother had not paid the bridewealth for his wives, and the family was not allowed to keep his sons. The family would not receive bridewealth from Jacques' daughters. Look, how they bore children without bridewealth! Nobody had quelled the anger of the family ancestors! Only now, years later, the family had started to talk about obtaining a sacrificial hen and drinking beer, the traditional way of appeasing the ancestors.

There was a long silence after her speech. Then Suzana's brother commented,

"It is a great sin, a great sin, to kill a person. God's first commandment was 'You shall not kill!'" I think he was referring to the Bible and simply happened to get the order of the commandments wrong, for the Fofu God had not given any commandments.

The serious part of our visit ended there. From then on Deta became merry; she joked and laughed as she had said she would, and occasionally dropped in at the neighbor's to get a drink. Suzana's brother continued making rope out of sisal fibres with his wife, and a sister-in-law brought food into the house. I was invited to eat alone in the house while everyone else ate outside. I knew that it was the fate of an honored guest but I still felt isolated alone in the house. It was a reminder to me that I was not one of "them."

Suzana saw us off for a few miles. She wanted to tell me what had happened to her during the past year. Deta had been dominating the stage during the visit, so that Suzana and I had not been able to talk. She had returned to her husband soon after my visit and her daughter Ana, then 19, had come to live with them. The husband grew grouchy about the step-daughter's presence because food was expensive in the city. Once after drinking he told Suzana that her daughter had to leave. Suzana was offended and retaliated,

"If you want her to go, you buy a ticket for her." He lost his temper and beat her until she lay on the floor, crying helplessly.

"Look, I got two stitches!" she showed me a scar on her chin.

Ana could not bear to see her mother being mistreated, so she grabbed a pestle, a heavy wooden stick used for pounding manioc, corn, rice etc., and relentlessly pounded his head with it until he too lay on the floor. She had caused an enormous gash on his head which bled profusely. She immediately ran away, fearing the consequences, and went to live with a man who was interested in her at the time. He had not paid her bridewealth yet. Soon they moved 50 miles away, perhaps to escape the stepfather's wrath. The affair was not finished yet. It was no small matter for a girl to injure her stepfather and his family wanted to sue Suzana through the official legal system. Suzana's husband did not agree, however. He took the view that she was after all his daughter and the affair should therefore be handled informally within the family. Suzana thought that her husband would arrive in her village any day now to discuss the case.

Suzana recounted her story without much emotion except perhaps to show some satisfaction at having such a loyal daughter who acted bravely for her mother. I was shaken by the brutality my friends endured. When we were about half-way to Nyanya, Suzana stopped at a market to buy something for the children back in the village. I bought bread for them and sent it back with Suzana. She turned to return home and Deta and I continued our journey.

On the way back, we visited Elisabeti, who was Deta's lineage member, and spent a few hours there. When on the road again, Deta spotted a sister of Jacques' first wife eating lunch while waiting for a bus to the city. They chatted a while. Then she saw her sister. I could hardly get her moving again that day, she was so pleased to see her.

While walking home Deta told me about her return to her husband after the death of her father. Her husband loved her and wanted her to stay with him but her co-wife tried everything to get rid of her. Twice Deta found a dead snake at the door, which was a sign of bad intentions on the part of the second wife. When that did not kill her, the co-wife tried to put poison into her food.

"God helped me and I did not die, did not die. I only had bad diarrhea." She looked at herself and commented victoriously, "I lost weight but I did not die!"

Her troubles did not end when she left her husband. She wanted to go to her home village Gangu, but one of her brothers' wives told her not to come unless she brought gifts from the "rich city." Deta had nothing to give since she had left empty handed, so she did not dare to go there. Instead, she had come to Nyanya to help take care of Jacques' children. To add to her troubles, the evil sister-in-law had caused her diarrhea to start again. So this was the secret of her slim figure, I thought.

Two days later I called at Jacques' house. His first wife led me to a neighbor where Desiree's fiance was having tea. I was asked to join him. Deta served the tea. She did not participate in the discussion, however. The fiance seemed excited and tense. He told me that Jacques' brother from Gangu had visited his place to see whether Desiree really meant to live with him and whether he intended to pay the bridewealth. The uncle was satisfied on both points. Now the fiance was at Nyanya to look for a witness to transport the three goats to her uncle. He assured me that he had the animals at home in readiness for the transaction.

"I am afraid that Desiree's father will come home, will come home, and I don't want to anger him."

The payment of cows had to wait but it appeared that paying goats would satisfy the uncle for the time being since the goats were thought of as being symbolic tokens for the right of a man to have sexual access to the woman and receive domestic services from her. The cows were valued as payments for the children the wife would bear. Although in a "proper" marriage all transactions should have been completed before the bride entered the groom's house, many people nowadays delayed some of the payments. Desiree had not borne any children yet, so the cows could wait.

I asked the fiance if he could not have retained his first wife while taking Desiree as his second. He replied in a matter-of-fact fashion that he could not because he was a Protestant church member. A man having two wives was not allowed to participate in the communion of the church. I inquired how the church would view his membership in the communion now that he had sent one wife away and taken another one. He admitted that he would not be allowed to take communion now. But once the turmoil about his divorce was over, he would repent and join the communion. Desiree would be taught the Protestant doctrine and she would be converted from Catholicism.

His cool calculation in the matter of the church rules was typical of the Fofu. While the missionaries intended the rules to induce sincere repentance, the Fofu followed them mechanically; they treated them as necessary steps on the way to advantages they wanted to gain. Observance had nothing to do with their convictions: the rules were there to be manipulated.

I happened to know the family of the fiance's first wife and had seen her at her parents' home with her infant. The family had seemed so distressed about the events that I had not bothered them by asking questions. I had felt sorry for them. I did not mention any of this to the happy fiance who proceeded to tell me that his first wife was a "bad" person and that her behavior had driven his mother away from her home — she had moved to Kisangani. He had sent a complaint about his first wife's misdeeds to her parents.

I asked if any bridewealth for the first wife would be returned to him in the divorce but he said not, because she had borne two children already.

I did not see Desiree nor her fiance after this but I heard that he paid the goats as he had promised. In a year the first wife returned to him and Desiree took the position of the second wife.

Deta came to greet me the following day and helped me to hang my laundry out. She was shaken by what happened to a Nyanya woman who had gone to a stream to wash clothes. "Satan" rose from the stream and caught her by the arm but she had struggled free. The beast avenged her by tearing her skirt in two. Its touch was like a bolt of lightning and one side of her body was now paralysed. Nobody knew if she would live. Deta talked about the woman on several other occasions; the matter seemed to bother her enormously. Without my suggesting it, she asked the woman if I could go and see her, but the idea of a white woman probing into the Fofu spirit world frightened the woman too much and she did not give permission for me to go and see her.

ALL-NIGHT SEX

Deta and I used to discuss various topics intensively while doing things together. I never knew what would come up when she was around. I did not think that a bundle of manioc leaves, which she brought me one morning, could lead us into the topic of Fofu sexuality but it did, in a round-about way. It was only eight o'clock that morning and she had already pounded the leaves in her mortar because she knew I did not have one. She helped me to chop onions and I started cooking the sauce under her instruction. Then she went home to take care of her chores returning in the afternoon with my other friend Georgette. They spent a long time at my place. We ate together and drank tea for hours that afternoon. Deta looked at me and shook her head,

"You are living in this house alone, alone, don't the men bother you, bother you?"

I was surprised and asked why they should. Deta explained that Fofu men would not leave a woman alone if she was living by herself. They would bother her all the time. I suggested simply that I would not let them in. Deta talked to me as if to a child,

"They would break your windows, even doors, doors, in order to have sex with you! Don't the white men here do so, white men?"

"No, I have not seen that yet," I answered not being able to imagine the white men behaving that way.

Deta told me that Fofu men desired women all the time, all men had women on the side, even if they had three or four wives. Jacques had always had lots of women on the side.

"Dear me!" I exclaimed, "Don't his wives get upset?"

Deta knew that his present wives bore it without complaining but when Suzana was his wife she found out who her husband's lovers were and went to beat them up. Deta told me that Jacques had a "wife" now in the distant city and that is why he was not returning. Apparently his wife was a white woman and he did not want to leave her to return to Nyanya.

"Can't the wives take lovers as well if their husbands are allowed to be unfaithful?" I inquired.

"Oh no!" both women declared, "because she is living in her husband's house, husband's house." I wondered how many did anyhow. We talked about Jacques' second wife who had become pregnant while he was away. Deta admitted that it was very bad of Jacques to leave his wives by themselves. He must have known that other men would take advantage of them in his absence. In the old days the husband's brothers took over the economic and sexual roles of an absent husband. If the custom had continued, Jacques' wives would now be pregnant by his brothers and it would be fine, Jacques would not mind. But the custom was no longer followed.

Deta and Georgette explained that Fofu men wanted sex many times a night. A wife might be tired after working all day in the garden but the husband demanded her to open her legs for him. If she refused, he would sulk for days or force his way anyhow. Men could interrupt their wives at their cooking and demand immediate sex and the wives had no choice. The women went on describing sexual relations and confirmed what I had heard also from others, that all couples had sexual intercourse every night and many times a night. It was hard for me to believe it literally but there was no way for me to check. The women told me that if their husbands did not have sex with them for a few days they immediately suspected the men of having other partners. Other Fofu confirmed this view. Deta told me that women sometimes were sore in the morning from a hard night.

Deta and Georgette shook their heads in disbelief when I told them about white people's habit of not having sex every night. Georgette told us that once she met a white man who knew the Fofu way of all-night sex and she was pleased with him. Georgette talked of sex as if it were great fun and this positive attitude towards sexual activity was generally born out by other women I spoke to. Deta, on the other hand, talked as if sexual activity was an obligation. I now regret that I never asked Deta about her prostitution because she probably would have told me about it. However I think that her somewhat negative views on sex were colored by her professional experiences.

That was the last time I saw Deta. Soon after this I went and lived in other villages. When I came back to Nyanya, Jacques' wife told me that Deta had left for a gold digging centre. Jacques never returned and many people commented that Jacques' family was suffering because of his absence: the father was a must for marriage negotiations. Also, the children seemed dirty and the wives miserable. Nyanya people condemned Jacques as an irresponsible person but he stayed away presumably enjoying an affluent life on Filippo's earnings and his white wife or wives in the city.

I saw Suzana twice on my journeys from one village to another. On both occasions, she was walking with long firm strides at three times my speed. Once she was going to a distant market and my companion who also knew Suzana explained to me that she was looking for medicine for her epileptic son. Another time she was returning from Gangu, where I was going. She had attended a funeral and told me about it. The widow, after becoming intoxicated, had started blaming her husband's family for his death. This angered the villagers, who were, of course, the husband's relatives and they chased her away from the village.

"Too bad that had to happen," Suzana said, and hurried homewards before dark.

Her statement was typical of what I had observed in villages. During the time of mourning, the bereaved spouse always suspected the partner's side of the family of witchcraft. It was a "default" pattern everywhere. If the person could hold back his anger and avoid expressing it, the funeral would pass peacefully but often bitter feelings were expressed with the encouragement of alcoholic drinks. If the trouble maker was a woman, she invariably had to leave the village because she was an outsider anyhow, having come to her husband's village from another clan on marriage. Occasionally old widows were allowed to stay in their marital villages usually with their adult sons. The village decided at the time of death. If she was pleasant and cooperative she was allowed to stay, if not, away she went.

I met Pascarine, Jacques' and Suzana's second daughter, near Yenyabo when she was going to a market with a group of women of her marital village. She was a dazzling beauty, especially when she smiled displaying a row of perfect pearl-white teeth. Her face was round as Jacques' and her smile reminded me of Suzana. She remembered me, although she had seen me last nine years ago.

I spotted Suzana's son a few times in a group of teenagers roaming around the market with slingshots in their hands. Each time he smiled at me and greeted me with a child's due respect towards an adult. He had been only an infant when I got to know his parents.

One day I passed Jacques' old store and I recalled my first visit there to buy matches. I had grown so used to seeing him treadle his sewing machine that I turned to see if he might be there bent over his work with a tape measure around his neck. But he was there no more.

2 | No Lack of Questions: Fieldwork at Yenyabo

Since I came to live in the area in August 1974, I wanted to get to know a village which would be more traditional or less "contaminated" by Western influences than the commercial area near Nyanya. But where should I go? Which village should I choose? Where would people accept an outsider and allow me to observe them in their everyday activities?

Figure 2.1 A rural couple returning home from their fields.

I asked other foreigners who had lived at Nyanya longer than I. Two German nurses who worked at the mission hospital had a mud hut in one of the villages. They spent their weekends there when they wanted peace after a hectic week in the hospital. They told me that the people were friendly in this particular village: they were somewhat used to seeing white people around. The nurses also told me that I was welcome to use their mud hut. I made arrangements to go for a day.

I will never forget my first trip to Yenyabo. It was November 1974 when the dry season was starting and the old tall grass of the savannah was being burnt. Tom was two years old when we ventured to the village together. A house helper of one of the German nurses came along to show us the road which would have been too hard to explain since there were many tracks criss-crossing on the plains.

From the higher parts of the plateau we could see smoke coming from a dozen places. We could hear fire crackling in the tall grass. Twice the fire crossed the road and I stopped the car to wait for it to pass. People were catching grasshoppers near the fires. They would dive into the grass and emerge holding green, kicking insects victoriously in their hands. They strung the grasshoppers onto a grass stem by piercing their bodies. There was a lot of laughter and excitement in the air. Later I was to taste these grasshoppers roasted in palm-oil. They were a delicacy and I, too, liked them. But at the time I was worried about getting to the village and was afraid that the gas tank of my car would explode if I went too close to the fire. Over the years I became far less cautious. It must have taken us two hours to get to the village that day, in favourable conditions it was only about a 30-minute drive.

At last, our African companion pointed towards a hill and said,

"That's it. That is Yenyabo." We saw a row of mud huts on either side of the road standing in bright sunshine. The road dipped once more before starting to climb the hill and the village disappeared for a moment. Then we were there in the village which I was to know best of all.

A group of children gathered around us. They recognized our companion, who had been to the village before: they knew that he worked for the German nurses. The children came with us to the nurses' hut at the edge of the village, near the church which was also made of mud. There was a gorgeous view over the savannah which now had countless fires burning.

The hut was cool inside because of its thatched roof. The main room contained a few simple chairs and tables, a paraffin burner for a stove, and some dishes. In addition, there were two tiny bedrooms with a narrow bed in each. There was no running water, of course, (I had been advised to bring a container of water with me). In the local fashion, there was an outhouse a little ways from the house. Tom refused to use it for fear of the round unstable logs over the deep pit. It required some practice to crouch on the logs.

After inspecting the hut and eating our sandwiches surrounded by gazing village children, we set off to see the village. We greeted people who happened to be at home and a group of women soon gathered around us. I told them that I was from Nyanya and would like to start visiting the village to learn about Fofu customs. The women looked puzzled.

"Are you a nurse, a nurse?" they inquired politely. They had to put a label on me and find out my true interests.

"No, I am not," I replied.

"Do you want to preach to us, preach to us?" they continued.

"No, I don't. I am not a preacher."

There appeared to be a third possibility, "Are you going to teach us?"

Again the answer was negative. I attempted to explain to them that I did not want to do anything other than observe their every day life and participate in it. I would like to go to the fields and for the water with the women, see how house chores were done and how children were raised. I had my own child, I pointed to Tom who was then getting acquainted with the children of the village and was kicking a football made of banana leaves. I strove to explain that I was taking a university course in different cultures and would like to write my assignments on the Fofu villagers. I don't know how much the women and the men really understood but they invited me to join them.

I told them my first name which they repeated but did not use. To them I was "Madame Pilote," Mrs. Pilot, on account of my husband's profession, which they learned from our guide. Only one man in the village ever called me by my name.

In this manner, my anthropological fieldwork commenced in Yenyabo. I do not know how much the villagers ever understood about my work. At first I did not keep a note book with me. I just participated in activities and chatted with people. I wrote my notes in the hut, on the way home in the car, or at home. I kept asking questions all the time which amused and sometimes irritated them. My interrogation did not follow the Fofu pattern which included questions about the well being of relatives, the food they had been eating lately, the destination of a walk, the absence of a family member and so forth. I learned to ask these questions, but I also needed to know many matters which seemed self evident to the Fofu.

"Madam truly truly does not lack questions, no lack of questions," they commented.

When I wrote the first sketch of the ethnography of the village, I translated the main parts of it for some Fofu who had gathered in the hut to greet me. The men exclaimed,

"Aha, madam has been doing real work here, real work! Yes, that is work, work. One can call it work!" as if they had been wondering all along how to classify my activity. When I did structured interviews about the families with a notebook on my lap, people looked at me with awe. Paper and pencil were highly respected and a rare commodity in the village. Over the years I heard children cry bitterly over the loss of a pen, worth a few coins, in fear of parental punishment. A woman stopped near me watching my feverish writing and stated,

"You must make a lot of money, a lot of money, because no one would work so hard without being paid." Another woman, whom I happened to be interviewing then, replied to her,

"But she is doing her university exercise, university exercise. Students are not paid, no pay for students."

Whatever they thought of me they treated me well. They were hospitable and friendly toward me and my family whom I brought to the village many times. Many of the villagers came to visit me at Nyanya when they had to spend time in the hospital and I served them drinks and cookies.

Interviewing was sometimes hard to arrange around their daily work, but most of the time people answered my questions while continuing their tasks. People usually conversed this way, anyhow. Once a woman told me that she was too hungry to have any coherent thoughts and asked me to postpone my interview. I though that this was tantamount to refusing to be interviewed but the next day the woman called me in and was ready to answer my questions. She had eaten that evening and felt good in the morning. When I started walking long distances I understood how overwhelmingly hunger could affect a person.

A couple of times the interviewees broke off the interview and I was almost literally kicked out of the house. I was devastated, offended and puzzled, wondering what on earth I had done wrong. The reason for the treatment gave me a very important insight into the values of the Fofu. The interviews were dealing with family trees. I had asked the subjects to name their siblings, their siblings' children, their parents, the siblings of their parents, and the children of these, and so on. In both cases the interviewees had very few relatives to mention. They grew nervous after stating that they had hardly any family and then they turned hostile towards me. After I realized the reason for their behaviour and did not bother them any more on the matter, both individuals became friendly again. This event taught me the importance of the family and kin in their culture and, conversely, the misery of not having any.

The families generally allowed me to take pictures, tape stories and conversations, and film them. Only a few times did they forbid me filming and then it was for what I thought a trivial reason. I was not allowed to film the muddying of a house and a funeral procession because the Fofu were wearing ragged work clothes.

"We don't want you to show us to your countrymen, to your countrymen abroad, in these rags," they protested.

I refuted this by saying that clothes were immaterial compared with the interesting topic of the pictures but they were firm in their refusal and I had to respect it. Perhaps clothes are immaterial only to those who can buy as many of them as they wish.

I used to go to the village by car, first a Volkswagen stationwagon and later a Volkswagen Combie. The first three miles from Nyanya was on a road which was usually passable. After three miles, one had to turn off and onto a track which was not really a road, only a pair of wheel tracks. During the dry season, there were no problems, apart from the fact that the track was bumpy. But during the rainy season one never knew if one was going to make it. If you saw a puddle ahead, you took your chances in going through it. The puddle might be deeper and softer than you expected.

I was once driving alone to the village and got stuck in a pot hole. I tried to drive forwards and backwards but could not get out of it. A local man carrying a garden hoe on his shoulder came from his nearby field to see what the noise was. I got out of the car, jumped over the puddle, and exclaimed with typically Finnish pessimism,

"I guess I will sit here until the sun dries the mud!" The man looked at me with surprise and then scolded me as if my utterance was sacrilegious,

"You must not say so, must not say so. God IS! God is!" He stepped into the puddle and started pushing the car. I hopped in and started the engine again. After a few trials we succeeded and I thanked him profusely.

This happened at the beginning of my studies and I could not understand why he was annoyed with me. Little by little the Fofu world view was revealed to me by similar spontaneous sayings and I came to understand his remark. The Fofu believe that God created everyone and is still sustaining the world and its people. Fofu would continually express their gratitude for this supreme being, or God, by statements like, "I live from the force of God," "God gives me life and livelihood." So when I declared my pessimism of getting out of the pot hole, I denied their basic tenet, namely that God keeps me and my car going. On the other hand, the Fofu view also acknowledges death and failure, for God has power to take life as he created it in the first place. However, Fofu would resign to it respectfully, not in annoyance, as he had interpreted me as doing. The Fofu's annoyance was never aimed at God but at other people who would harm a person with ill will or witchcraft. It is interesting that the man interpreted my "innocent" frustration as a statement against God and not against other people, or, as I had intended, just an expression of frustration with reference neither to cosmos nor people.

I had a favourite spot on the way to Yenyabo. It was soon after the pot holes: the soil became sandy as the road rose and turned towards a mountain range. From here, when driving to the village in the mornings, I could see the wide open savannah, the bluish green mountain range, and a blue sky. It was beautiful and I did not need to worry about getting stuck in the mud for a few miles. At that point I always dropped my Nyanya worries for the day and emptied my mind so I could receive Yenyabo into my consciousness. Conversely, on the way home, at the same point, I entered the troubles of pot holes and everyday life. To me, Yenyabo was a refuge.

Anthropological enterprise requires some measure of reciprocity, although I felt that I could not reciprocate everything I received from the villagers. But I tried as best I could. For instance, when asking about the Fofu customs, the villagers often asked me about the customs of my country and I shared the knowledge with them. Then we would discuss the difference in customs. Sometimes they would laugh at us, sometimes get annoyed, but often accepted differences as a fact of life. After all, they were used to living among people who followed different cultural rules from theirs, such as Hiha and Lelo. Through these discussions, I learned more not only about their culture but also about mine, as I compared it with theirs.

Almost every time I travelled between my home and the village, people on the road asked for a ride and I gladly obliged. Once there was a group of men carrying an old, very skinny man in a hammock made of a blanket suspended on sticks. The men explained that they had taken the old man to the hospital but had been sent home because there was nothing the hospital could do for him. Another time there was a group of men and women walking towards Yenyabo for a wake. I stopped and they crowded in: women at the back of the stationwagon, men on the seats. I told them that I could take only five people. Henry had seriously forbidden me from carrying more people because any heavier load on those horrible roads would damage the car. The women climbed out and the men continued to sit. I wondered if I should exert authority over them in the matter of gender relations but I did not. The men rode in the car while the women walked!

I transported patients to the hospital speeding over the bumpy road, sometimes mothers in the final stage of labour. I could not always remember the faces of those I had transported but sometimes years later, a passenger would tell me that, say, his son whom I had helped to get to the hospital, had recovered and was grown to such and such a height. On occasions, I offered rides to sick people at Yenyabo but they refused to go to the hospital in fear of a strange place. Some people thought the hospital was a place of death, so it was not worth going there.

Often women wanted me to carry their heavy baskets of sweet potatoes or manioc to Nyanya to be stored with acquaintances overnight. The women themselves would follow the next morning. Generally I was driving in the opposite direction to the one they wanted to go: in the morning I drove from Nyanya to the village while the women walked from the village to Nyanya and in the evening we moved in opposite directions again. But my delivery service on the night before their market day relieved them of carrying a heavy load the next morning. When the church was being built, Yenyabo people organized someone to send wooden planks with me to the village.

Once I gave an airplane ride to these women who had been my informants in the village. The men of the village were not happy that only women were invited but I explained that I was studying women and children and wanted to give some fun to those whom I had bothered with my questions. It did not satisfy the men, who believed that by favouring the women I was breaking a rule of nature. The four women wanted me to go with them instead of having an additional Yenyabo person in the plane with them. They felt more secure with me there although I told them it was the pilot who flew the plane, not I. My husband was on another flight that day so I chartered his colleague to fly us. The women walked to my house, had lunch with me first, and then we went for the joy ride.

Having lunch first may have proved hazardous but fortunately no one became airsick. The women had never been in a plane before and I had to help them buckle up. They took comfort from each other joking and whooping when getting ready for take off. I held hands with the two women on either side of me when we took off and for a while it was dead silent in the cabin. The pilot turned toward the village, which was only a five minute flight over the savannah. The women studied their village from the air and shouted to each other when recognizing their homes and fields. The pilot, whom some called a cowboy pilot, enjoyed entertaining us and dived down over the village several times thus making the women scream and the villagers run for cover waving their arms at us.

On the way back to Nyanya airstrip, the women competed to tell each other what they had seen. After the flight I drove them back to the village where they were the object of great jealousy and the centre of attention as they described their experience and imitated the sound and movement of the airplane. It was an experience they never forgot.

When I began my study, the population of Yenyabo was some 300 people but it grew steadily during the years through natural growth and also through the influx of new inhabitants. Yenyabo and three other villages belonged to the smallest clan of the Fofu people. The other four Fofu clans consisted of up to 20 villages. Old Catholic sources claimed that the Fofu had left their forest dwellings further south in search of food and came to the plains, one clan at a time, each by a different route. The Yenyabo people's account of themselves, which had been passed on orally, was that they had come from what is now Uganda and had crossed a huge river with the help of a monkey. This animal became their totem and was forbidden to be eaten.

Some cattle herders of the Hiha joined the Fofu in pursuit of new land and became and stayed friends with them until today. Yenyabo encompassed a few Hiha families who lived a few miles from the string of houses so that their cattle would not disturb the villagers. The Hiha exchanged their dairy produce for Fofu garden produce. A Hiha cattle compound may have several Fofu families as "their" Fofu, meaning partners, to whom they regularly brought milk and who gave them a sack of corn, beans, sweet potatoes, or peanuts at harvest time. No exact calculations were made, but each partner reciprocated with his specialty at the due time. Sometimes one-off transactions took place. The Hiha might for example exchange the harvest of a field for a cow, which the Fofu needed for bridewealth payments. Sometimes the Hiha looked after Fofu cows in their camp until the Fofu needed them. For this service, the Hiha received every other calf and the Fofu kept the rest. This involved much trust on both sides. In the beginning of my stay, cow raiding was still common, as it was all over East Africa. A Hiha man told me that he had lost at least forty cows to raiders. He did not mention that the forty cows might have been gained by raiding in the first place. Later, a German cattle raising project was established in the area and most of the cattle owners joined the association because it guaranteed medication and advice. Raiding ended because the association had a strict rule against raiding.

When the Fofu moved from the forest to the savannah, they met with another ethnic group, namely the Lelo, who were cultivating the land there. Furious fighting broke out and the Fofu were able to push the Lelo further north. But the latter always remembered the past and at times fought to regain their territory. In 1984, I returned to Africa soon after one such clash and heard Fofu whispering about the event. Government troops had been called to calm the situation. I will deal with this dispute in "Two Wives Who Left."

During the period of my studies, there were some Lelo living at Yenyabo and more of them at Nyanya, seemingly on good terms with the Fofu. At Nyanya, however, I gathered that there was competition for "Western jobs" between the ethnic groups. Of the three groups, members of the Hiha held the most prestigious positions, then the Lelo, and last of all the Fofu. Yenyabo, in contrast to Nyanya, was a Fofu village and was run according to the rules of the Fofu until the arrival of a Bible school in the 1980s.

Yenyabo had three parts which I thought of as the new, the secluded, and the colonial. The new section of the village had been established on top of the hill in accordance with the government order which stipulated that villages should be passable by road which in this case was only two wheel tracks in the savannah. Middle-aged and younger men had built their houses on either side of the road, from about 30 to 100 yards apart. When there was no more road frontage available, some men had built further from the road and made footpaths between their houses and the road. Some of these families started their fields near their homes.

A Protestant church and its personnel were situated at one end of the new section of the village. The Catholics, who formed the majority of the villagers, attended their church in another village, about a mile away. Protestantism suddenly took on a much higher profile when the Bible school was built in the village in 1982. It caused much trouble at first and will be dealt with in "Persevering Cecilia."

There were no shops, schools or dispensaries in the village when I first got to know it. However, in the early 1980s a Protestant elementary school was established with the help of an American charity organization which gave free uniforms and other gifts for the school children thus attracting them from the Catholic school of the next village. During my last year of field work, a retired Zairean nurse from Nyanya was building a dispensary in the village and thus contributing to the Westernization of the main part of the village.

The older folks lived in the secluded part of the village, in a fertile valley beyond the hill, where all the Yenyabo people had their fields. The homesteads were dotted about, up to several hundred yards apart, each being near large fields. The swept yards had bushes along the borders which gave each house its privacy, unlike those in the new part.

The third part of the village, the colonial, was about 4 miles away and very close to the rain forest. The colonial government had ordered the villagers to move there to guard a telegraph track from elephants. Now the track was no more, and most of the people had moved to the new section of the village; however, in the 1970s some of the older people were still living there. To most, the third part was only a memory of the colonial past which was fading away quickly.

So village life was concentrated in two parts of the village, the new and the secluded. I could feel the difference between these two sections. When I started descending from the hill to the valley, from the newer part of the village to the older, it was like going from time to timelessness. Everything was quiet on the path, except for the chirping of the crickets. I was only aware of the bright sun shining over the tall grass and the Fofu fields and huts, which blended in with the environment perfectly. I enjoyed the feeling of peace and oneness which totally encompassed me.

But if I walked this path early in the morning, the dew from the tall grass made me wet to the skin. It was a very hostile feeling, a complete contrast to that of the daytime. It made me realize how powerful the cycle of the sun was: people would look at the sun and plan their activities according to it.

Exact hours and minutes did not matter to the Fofu: only to me. I used a stopwatch for my infant observations when I timed how long a baby cried before it was attended to. I also timed the family observations in forty-five minute sections over the day. Modern science, so called objective measurements, and traditional timelessness met. Sometimes I felt a fool racing to the homesteads not to be "late" and I am sure the Fofu regarded me as one.

When I was doing the timed observations I hired young men to translate what the family members said to each other in Kifofu. It was hard to find a person who had enough leisure to tag along with me all day. Young, unmarried men had the most time. But they did not see the importance of the work and refused to work for me during the market at Sengi. They preferred to go and parade in the market dressed in their best clothes.

When I first arrived at Yenyabo in 1974, all the houses were made of either grass or mud and constructed on reed frames. They were either round or rectangular in shape and the roofs were made of thatch. The Fofu told me that their original houses were, as almost everywhere in East Africa, conical grass huts but colonial rule introduced the rectangular mud hut from the western ethnic groups of the country. Over the years, the rectangular mud huts became more common at the expense of the conical grass huts. Some families acquired corrugated iron roofs and used stones or cement in parts of the buildings. In "Persevering Cecilia" I will tell how Herabo built a more modern house after living in a mud hut for most of his life.

The conical grass huts had a place for an open fire in the middle of the house, but most families with mud huts built a separate hut with a place for an open fire to serve as a kitchen. In "Persevering Cecilia" we will see that little children sometimes fell in the fire and were seriously hurt. The grass huts were sometimes fire hazards. Over the years of my visits to the village, several burned down accidentally or by arson. Also lightning sometimes struck houses on the hill and razed them to the ground in minutes. Sometimes these fires resulted in fatalities. On other occasions people were shaken but intact.

Figure 2.2   Lightning struck the house and razed it to the
ground in minutes. The shocked survivors sitting
while passers-by stand in awe.

The village of Yenyabo was composed of three Fofu patrilineages which shared
a common ancestor. In the Fofu system, all children belonged to the father's lineage,
not the mother's. Although daughters belonged to their father's lineage their children
belonged to their husband's lineages. It was a very clear system and all knew where
they belonged. Furthermore, the Fofu followed a patrilocal residence rule. This
meant that a young couple moved to live with the groom's father.

The patrilineal and patrilocal system created a clear residence pattern which
determined the experiences of the two genders. The sons and daughters grew up
together with their parents in their father's home village. On marriage, the females
left their childhood villages and moved to their husbands' villages. Sons were valued
more than daughters because they were to stay in their fathers' place and continue
the lineage and occupation. Sons took care of their parents in their old age.
Daughters, on the other hand, stayed with their parents only until "their breasts
grew," i.e. started to grow, and then they were married away.

Fofu daughters could return, or, as the Fofu expressed it, "run" to their fathers'
or brothers' place, that is, to their lineage land, in the event of marital trouble and
be assured of a livelihood and moral support. The expression "a daughter of the
village" had warm connotations and implied that she had a right to the fields any
time she decided to return home and her male relatives would look after her well.
Although sons were valued more than daughters, the latter were important in
bringing in the bridewealth, three goats and three cows, at the time of their

marriage. Their bridewealth could be used to obtain wives for their brothers, so males were really dependent on their sisters and this dependence created a bond between siblings of the opposite sex.

Before colonial rule, the Yenyabo people did not have a chief, each of the three lineages took care of their internal conflicts by themselves. They probably had what Evans-Pritchard calls a segmentary lineage system with complementary opposition, a system in which different segments of the lineage divided and fused depending on how distantly related the two opponents of the disputes were to each other. The more remote the relationship the greater the number of people involved in the dispute; the closer the relation, the fewer the people involved.

Colonial rule, however, demanded that each village have its chief and that a group of villages have a higher chief above these village chiefs, and that there be one big chief over several groups of villages. Altogether, the Fofu area was divided into five districts, each with a big chief. Central government stipulated what kind of cases each type of chief could handle: the higher the chief, the more serious were the cases he could deal with. The Fofu numbered around 120,000 in the mid 1980's. The colonial courts outside the Fofu area, called Zone, handled the most serious

Figure 2.3 A Fofu woman hoeing her garden.

crimes. Above the Zone were sub-regional and regional courts. The independent state followed the former colonial organization.

The Fofu considered themselves horticulturalists although many of them also raised some cattle. They grew sweet potatoes, manioc and other root crops, beans, corn, some dry land rice, bananas, and occasionally millet. Men cleared the bush and dug the ground for the first time, both men and women planted, and women weeded and harvested. When I timed the work in the fields by gender, I noticed that men and women both averaged about four hours a day in their gardens. House building and maintenance were mostly men's work, although women helped by carrying the grass for the roofs and muddying the houses.

Women were actively involved in the local markets: they sold their garden produce in the markets in order to get money to buy such household items as soap, salt, sugar, coffee, tea, kerosene, and palm oil. They also clothed themselves and their children with the proceeds. Sometimes they also bought clothes for their husbands to show that they really cared for them.

Men owned some cattle and would butcher a pig or a goat if they needed cash. Household chores and childrearing were women's work. Women were busy most

Figure 2.4 Women selling their garden produce in the market.

of the time while men had more leisure time to drink beer and walk along the village road with transistor radios tucked under their arms. Although women worked longer hours, they could visit each other while working. They performed much of their work out-of-doors and chatted with passers-by while pounding rice or tending to their children in their swept dirt yards.

To me, Yenyabo was a refuge from four walls and a black box, the radio. At first I had a very idealistic view of village life, but over the years I learned that it was no different from life anywhere else: it contained tensions, contradictions, and hardships as well as having very positive and humorous characteristics. My friendships ranged from the superficial and casual to deep and intimate relationships. The most profound of these was with Cecilia.

Figure 2.5 Males were in charge of the cattle.

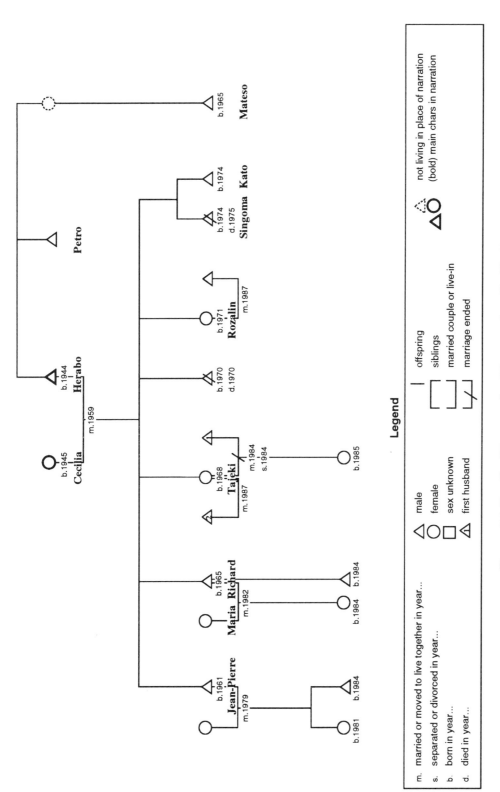

Legend

m.	married or moved to live together in year...	offspring	|
s.	separated or divorced in year...	siblings	⊔
b.	born in year...	married couple or live-in	⊐
d.	died in year...	marriage ended	⊐/

△	male	△ O ⟵ not living in place of narration
O	female	(bold) main chars in narration
□	sex unknown	
◁	first husband	

Figure 3.1 Family Diagram for "Persevering Cecilia."

3 PERSEVERING CECILIA

WORK BEES

Cecilia became a good friend, in fact, my best Fofu friend. Because "our bloods matched," as the Fofu would say, she allowed me to share her joys and sorrows over twelve years. I met Cecilia on my first trip to Yenyabo. She appeared from her house holding twins to her breasts. Soon one of her older children came to take one of the twins so Cecilia could shake my hand in greeting. For about a year, this was a typical sight of Cecilia, one or both of the twins on her hip, back or lap. She was busy most of the time when she was at home: cooking, sweeping, washing, or attending to the children. Her movements were swift and definite, she knew what she was doing and did it efficiently. It was amazing that she was so energetic despite having the twins to look after continuously.

She was about 30 years old when I became acquainted with her and 42 when I left Africa. I noticed her aging but one thing stayed the same: her face lit up with the most captivating smile, so friendly, genuine, and warm that people were drawn to her. She accepted people with kindness, even her adult children when they broke tribal rules. Her adult sons were drawn to her long after they were married. They would come and spend their evenings with her rather than spend time with their wives at home.

Herabo, her husband, was the same age, if not a year older. Neither knew for sure. Most of the time he wore big rubber boots which made him look bigger than he was, perhaps a calculated move on his part. His forehead was high, in contrast to Cecilia's, giving him an ambitious appearance, and ambitious he was. He wanted to do better than the average Fofu, to own a nicer house, a bicycle, a radio, and even a car which was unheard of at Yenyabo during the 1970s. Perhaps because of his ambition, he was furious when his children broke Fofu rules for marital arrangements, and drove them away from home. He spoke very clearly because he was a preacher and accustomed to public speaking. When he was excited, his voice became falsetto and sometimes he stuttered, too.

Although Herabo was very polite, he kept his distance and would not reveal himself. I found the same characteristic in many other men and wondered if this was peculiar to their dealings with white people. Since colonial times, white people had always communicated with the Fofu men. The Fofu kept the women away from white people as much as possible and tried their best to prevent the women from going to school so they would not be "contaminated." I think the men developed two levels of communication, one for white people and another for their own people.

For instance, I could not get anything out of Herabo about witchcraft. If I asked about it he stated flatly that no Fofu believed in it any more since they were Christian. However, if I asked Cecilia, she discussed witchcraft like any other topic, naturally and openly. I think Herabo was ashamed of many of the Fofu customs but Cecilia was not.

When I visited the village, Cecilia's was the first house I came to. If she was in, I would sit with her, often on a low, round stool in the kitchen hut separate from the main building. She would be busy with her household chores and feeding her babies. I would help her cut manioc leaves, peel peanuts, and hold one of her twins while we chatted. If Tom was with me, he would play with Cecilia's children somewhere in the neighbourhood. I would ask questions about her life, her past, about other families of the village, and about Fofu customs. She was happy to talk and offer her opinions. During the corn season in July and August, when everyone in the area was eating corn, she would throw a cob on the fire and roast it for me. Sometimes I would follow her to the fields where she worked. There she sometimes took a break and roasted sweet potatoes on coals under a small grass shelter built to provide shade. While resting she would talk about her future and her dreams.

Cecilia had borne seven children of whom one son had died as a baby. She talked about it without anxiety.

"God took one of our children but gave us two instead, Singoma and Kato, two boys."

The twins played a major role in family life. As was the Fofu and Hiha custom, the elder one was called Singoma and the other Kato. Tajeki, Cecilia's 6-year old daughter, was delegated to baby-sit the twins and did not go to school for several years because of this important duty. Cecilia's sons, 13-year-old Jean-Pierre and 9-year-old Richard, also carried the twins around. Rozalin, only three, was free from baby-sitting duties for a few years. Cecilia's husband Herabo often walked about at home chatting with his male friends with one of the twins in his arms. Neighbours who dropped by always held the twins on their laps for a while. Sometimes, when one of them was crying desperately, a neighbour, Katarina, would walk over from her house, pick up the crying baby and carry him to her home for a while.

During the first year of our acquaintance Cecilia was busy feeding a group of seven church builders. Herabo was one of the lay pastors of the Protestant church of the village. Cecilia always referred to him as *mwalimu*, a teacher, a term used for both school teachers and preachers. She continued to use this term even after Herabo gave up his position in the church. In those days, Herabo was a driving force in the small village church. He clearly enjoyed preaching at the Sunday services, when he had his turn. He would jump up and down and his voice would go up and down, too.

It was Herabo's ambition to see a new church built in the village. There was an old mud church with a thatched roof but he wanted a bigger church built of stone and with a corrugated iron roof, which would be a unique building in the village.

The Protestant villagers worked every Thursday on church construction and on church fields. One group tended the fields and sold the produce in markets to obtain money for the church building. The other group carried rocks on their heads from a nearby quarry. The mother church in Nyanya sent masons and carpenters to build the church.

Some other church women including Cecilia helped with the two meals a day for the workers. It was a big job above a woman's normal daily work load of tending fields and feeding her own family. I asked Cecilia who was paying her for her job, expecting the payment to come from a church fund.

"God will pay, God," said Cecilia busy peeling sweet potatoes.

She did not mind the work and planned it well. She cooked sometimes on one open fire on the ground, sometimes on two, in huge pots black with soot. Cooking took hours, especially if there were several kinds of food to cook, because pots had to wait their turn for the fire.

Cecilia not only cooked for the church builders but for all the many visitors her husband had because of his church business. There were also relatives who came to visit the family from time to time and expected hospitality. On top of this Herabo

Figure 3.2 A girl babysitting her siblings.

and Cecilia occasionally took care of strangers, old men and women, who, unusually, did not have relatives to take care of them. There were also children who needed boarding for school.

Once as I passed Cecilia's house during the latter years of my stay she told me that she was helping the chief to feed the official delegates to the meeting of chiefs, about fifty people. Cecilia was not nervous at all. She had everything under control with her daughters-in-law at her side to help.

Cecilia once showed me a handbag she had received from a soldier. She told me that nobody would feed the soldier because soldiers had a terrible reputation for harassing and beating people. This particular soldier had been sent to a nearby village to catch a thief and was begging someone to give him food. So Cecilia invited him to her home and gave him a meal. He was so thankful that some time later he sent the handbag. It did not seem to matter to Cecilia how many mouths there were to feed, she cooked with ease no matter what.

I did not stay in her house at first, only dropped in to chat. I cooked my own meals and slept in the German hut, not far from her house. Cecilia and other women would bring me gifts of sweet potatoes and manioc from their fields and I would

Figure 3.3 Cecilia winnowing rice.

serve them coffee. Men of the village would visit me for longer than the women because they had more time.

After five years, however, all this changed. There was a wages dispute between the field workers and the German nurses who were in charge of the hospital fields in the village and the hut was broken into. The church elders took the nurses' stuff from the hut to protect it from further thievery, so there was no furniture in the hut and I could no longer use it as my base. Although I felt that I was imposing on Cecilia, I asked if I could stay with her on my next visit. By that time I had already moved to Bululu and visited the village for a week at a time. Cecilia was very happy to have me. She had a small guest room which she let me use.

At first I brought petrol, palm oil, salt, sugar etc. with me but transporting those items was difficult in a small plane. Once the bottle of petrol spilled over my clothes, giving me a distinctive perfume for the whole week. I asked if it was all right for me to give her some money to send her children to buy these items. It was. I tried to lighten her burden of cooking the noon meal for me alone (this was not a regular meal for the Fofu) by bringing bread for myself and making my own snacks during the day. Cecilia could stay in her fields. Living with her turned out to be a much better arrangement for me. I did not need to stay alone in the hut at night and I learned much more about family interaction. It was more work for Cecilia but she seemed to enjoy it, too.

As I mentioned earlier, Cecilia used to cook for the church workers once a week. One such day I arrived at Cecilia's late in the morning. Cecilia was alone in the kitchen cooking corn in a big pot on the fire. The twins slept on a mat near her. Cecilia had gone to the fields for the food while they were asleep. Soon neighbours came to tell me that my son Tom and his friend had spilt all the drinking water that I had brought for us. I had to go and see but the damage was already done. Tom and Johnny followed me back to play in Cecilia's yard. By that time, some women had arrived, one of whom was delousing Cecilia's hair. Cecilia comforted me by saying, "Children always give us trouble, give us trouble. It is their nature, never mind! Singoma once poured a bottle of palm oil on the ground, and continued to play with the bottle."

I could imagine how messy it must have been because palm oil is a thick, red grease.

Singoma was playing on a palm mat. Soon Cecilia picked him up to feed him. Three women left for the stream to wash their laundry. Katarina, her neighbour, played with Singoma on her lap. She spoke softly to him, half singing, then laid him down next to Kato and Rozalin. Cecilia pounded coffee beans to loosen the husks from the hard beans. Tajeki, her daughter, came back from the stream carrying an open clay pot of water on her head. Some of it had spilled onto her face, which was shining with sweat. Three neighbouring girls used to join Tajeki to fetch water, since the work was more fun in a group. They would carry water to each others' houses until every container was full.

Figure 3.4 Girls fetching water.

The girls were now about to make another trip to fetch water and I followed them. I noticed that the way back was steeply uphill for about a mile. When we were nearly back home with the water, the girls stopped to watch Tom, Johnny, and some of the Fofu boys climb a tree. By now Cecilia was winnowing the coffee with a special tray. She worked rapidly and then lay the tray on the ground and let Katarina finish the cleaning by hand while she took another batch of coffee to pound. After putting the water pots away, Tajeki and her friend knelt down to help Katarina clean the coffee beans without anyone asking them to do so. Meanwhile Kato woke up and made a noise. A neighbour boy, about ten years old, picked him up and took him into the yard. The minute Kato started crying Cecilia took him from the boy and suckled him.

Next Cecilia prepared two bowls of food for the children: boiled manioc tubers in one and sauce made of manioc leaves in another. The children sat on a mat, took a tuber, dipped it in the sauce and ate it. They were quiet and seemed to concentrate on eating. In other houses, I heard parents scold children if they talked at all while eating because meal times were reserved for eating and not conversation. When Cecilia had roasted the coffee beans Katarina ground them with a hand stone. She knelt down by a flat rock on which she put coffee beans and then crushed them against it with another rock.

After the children had eaten, Cecilia carried a steaming bowl full of corn into the house for the men, although these were now going to the stream to wash after their work. The children got a bowl of corn, too, and Cecilia did not forget Tom and Johnny who stopped climbing trees and ate with pleasure. Cecilia herself sat down outside the kitchen in the shade of the overhang and ate corn with her legs stretched straight in front of her. Singoma was brought near us and Cecilia wanted him to demonstrate how he had learned to wave his hand when she sang a hymn.

"Heri jina lake, heri jina lake . . ." (Blessed is his name, blessed is his name), Cecilia sang while Singoma waved his hand. Everybody laughed.

Among the children and women, I counted five dogs but could not count the hens, as they were all running around trying to catch scraps of food. Whenever someone threw an eaten corn cob down, they all rushed towards it and fought for it. Nobody paid attention to the animals unless they were in the way. Then they just gave them a hefty blow or kick which caused them to squeal. Often there were pigs and goats in the kitchen as well but this time these had been tied further away in the yard.

The men returned from the stream. Cecilia hurriedly dished out the rest of the food for them: manioc tubers in a big bowl, sauce of manioc leaves in a small one. She placed the small bowl on top of the bigger one. I, inculcated with Western ideas of hygiene, noticed that she did not as much as wipe the bottom of the bowl although it had been standing on the dirt floor. Then she carried the bowls to the dining room inside the house.

Meanwhile more women had arrived and they sat on ground in the shade of the kitchen overhang. Cecilia carried out two bowls for the women to share. In the midst of laughter and joking, the women started eating. I did not understand them because they spoke in Kifofu, although they sometimes switched into Swahili because there were some Hiha and Lelo women amongst them. The men ate, laughed and chatted inside the house. By now, Katarina had Singoma in her lap as she mixed ground coffee with boiling water in a huge black pot on the fire. I thoroughly enjoyed the atmosphere of these occasions.

Sometimes I was invited in to chat with Herabo and the other men. If my husband came with me, we were always invited into the living room for coffee and a chat. Cecilia would serve the coffee. When Herabo gave orders to her, she would curtsey to him and go to the kitchen to fulfil them. She never stayed in the room with us. When I asked her why not, she told me that it would have been rude for her to stay.

"God gives each of us our work," she said.

A long time afterwards I learned that it was an old custom for the Fofu to segregate the sexes. Cecilia followed the old tradition. It took me years to realize that she never looked at her husband or other men directly but looked away or down. This was also the polite way for the children to behave towards adults. I learned this only during my penultimate year in Africa. Cecilia then told me that Tom was especially "bad" with his eyes as when he was small he would stare adults straight in the eye. Cecilia opened her eyes wide in imitation, which made us laugh, and said,

"Among us, a person who is angry at someone else behaves like that, like that!" The Fofu appreciated sociability and people did not show anger easily.

A man who was sitting with us then added, "We would spank, would spank our child if he used his eyes that way."

I put my head in my hands and did not know whether to laugh or cry. All these years I had been among them and never before had they straightened me out in this matter. What kind of messages had Tom given? How about me?

"Only a prostitute looks at a man straight in the eye!," Cecilia explained.

I was choking with laughter. "How can you stand us white people when we break all your rules?" I asked Cecilia.

"That's all right," she comforted me, "we know that you are different. You are not like us, not like us." Her tone implied that white people were not as smart as the Fofu.

I liked to take my husband to the village on his days off. To save gas, he mended an old motorbike, long since abandoned by someone, and we travelled to the village on that. Tom would sit in front of Henry and I behind him, with my hands around his waist. When we appeared like this in the village the first time, I could not understand the reaction of the villagers. Cecilia and Herabo were at their neighbour's with many other people. It was Sunday afternoon and people were chatting together. They came out of the hut rolling with laughter. I could not see anything funny about us. Cecilia took me aside and scolded me while still finding it hard to talk for laughing.

"Madam, you should never travel with your husband like that, never travel like that! He should be with men and you should be with women."

I shrugged her advice off as impractical. It would be ridiculous to travel to the village in separate vehicles just because it was funny to be seen together. We continued occasionally to use the motorbike. Years afterwards I found this statement in my notes. Having learnt so much more about the Fofu I can now understand their reaction. They were not laughing at us because we looked funny but because we were behaving outrageously. We were breaking their rules, and their sense of decency. I should have shown my respect for their customs and heeded Cecilia's advice.

Herabo was a busy man, he was on the go all day. He was often either coming or going on his black bicycle. Maybe there was a wake in a nearby village and he had to go to preach or pray. Or he might be supervising the workers in his fields and the forest. Often his living room was full of church elders discussing church business. And sometimes Herabo was hanging around with a long stick. That meant it was his turn to herd the cattle.

Four families had joined together in taking care of their cows. Since cattle were men's business, a custom acquired from the Hiha, only men herded and milked the cows. Each family was in charge of herding for one week at a time. The men found it boring and were always looking for an opportunity to sit around and chat with people. That was a good time for me to get information because they were hungry for company. Every once in awhile they got up to check where the cows were or they sent a child to take care of the animals while they continued talking to me.

Once I was sitting outside someone else's hut when Herabo returned from his fields. He had a machete in one hand and Kato in a sling on his side. Two Fofu women sitting with me started laughing when they saw him,

"Hi, Herabo! Are you a woman now, a woman? A true mother!" they yelled at him.

Herabo greeted them with a normal Fofu greeting paying no attention to their remarks. The women told me that in the morning Katarina, Cecilia's neighbour, had helped her carry one of the twins to the field. The twins were almost a year old and, until that day, Cecilia had not worked in the field a full day, only gone there to fetch food for a meal.

"How come Cecilia worked all day today?" I asked. Herabo stopped in his tracks and told me that her "maternity leave" was just about finished and she had to get on with hoeing their gardens.

About a quarter of an hour later Cecilia walked home from the fields with Katarina. No woman would be so indecent as to walk with her husband, of course. Both women had a basket of sweet potatoes on their heads and firewood on top of the basket. In addition, Cecilia carried Singoma on her back. When I dropped by her kitchen hut some time later, she was winnowing beans in the same way she did coffee. The husks flew away with the wind but the beans fell down in the basket. Then Cecilia sat down on the ground to finish cleaning the beans by hand. The twins and Rozalin were sitting behind her on a mat. Rozalin soon went off with some neighbour boys to watch her oldest brother cart dung away from the cattle enclosure a dozen yards from the house. As I took one of the twins onto my lap Cecilia told me that she still had to go down to the stream to get water to finish preparing the supper. It was a long hard day for somebody who had recently borne twins. Herabo was at that time sitting in the living room talking to his male friends.

Obedience of children to their parents was greatly emphasized in Fofu upbringing and I continuously observed that the children were submissive and helpful to their parents. When Herabo came home with his bicycle, he left it without a word in the hands of Richard or Jean-Pierre who unloaded it, put it away, and if it was dirty, washed it for him. Before he left on a trip he would send one of them to prepare the bicycle for him.

"Richard, bring my briefcase!" I often heard and soon Richard would hand it to him.

Sometimes if Richard was not in the view of the parents, he would pretend he did not hear and then his sisters were sent to get the object for the father. But if he was in sight, he obeyed immediately.

The children learned their pecking order. The boys could beat the girls and older children could bully the younger ones with the exception of babies who ruled the roost. Tajeki, for example, was often beaten by her older brothers. Once we heard her crying outside. I asked Cecilia,

"Aren't you going to check what is happening?"

"By the time I go out they'll have forgotten about it, forgotten," said Cecilia and continued our conversation. Unlike Western parents, Fofu parents did not continually mediate in their children's disputes.

Another time Cecilia, Herabo, and I were in the living room when we heard Tajeki crying outside and the boys laughing. Tajeki came in the hut and we could hear her sobs behind the partition wall. I would have rushed out to yell at the boys had they been my children, but Herabo and Cecilia merely listened solemnly to her sobbing and turned to explain,

"A girl's lot is hard. Her brothers can beat her up, beat her up." Tajeki did not seek their comfort but sobbed in the children's bedroom until she fell asleep.

Another time Tajeki had just come from the stream and was filtering the water through a cloth. Cecilia talked to her jokingly,

"I'm going to beat all the other children for beating you!" She was only mocking. I could tell that she was ridiculing the situation and had no intention of beating anyone. Tajeki continued her work with downcast eyes.

But Tajeki was not completely downtrodden. She herself was rough with her younger sister, Rozalin. Once Rozalin was playing with a corn doll. She had pieces of material in an old tin can. Tajeki was playing with bigger girls. They had leaves as cows and stones as a cow enclosure and as a cooking place. Spotting the tin can, Tajeki suddenly got up, walked over to Rozalin, tipped the scraps onto the ground and took the can. Rozalin burst into tears but did not resist or retaliate. She knew her place. Only I paid attention to her. Then to make matters worse, Cecilia came and took a piece of Rozalin's material and tied a hen's legs together with it. Then she took the noisy hen flapping its wings and gave it to me. "For Tom," she said smiling.

I looked at Rozalin whose feelings had been completely disregarded, but she kept looking down shyly.

"GOD TOOK HIM"

I became more occupied with my own family in the summer of 1975, and neglected my visits to Yenyabo for several months. In August, I had my second baby, Tania, and Henry, Tom and I were adjusting to the change in the family. I did not dare take the little one to the village when she was very young and I did not want to leave her at home either, so I saw only those Yenyabo people, both men and women, who came to the hospital and called in to greet and see the baby.

"Thank you very much, thank you, thank you," they said when they saw Tania, "So God helped you bear her, thank you very much, thank you very much."

Herabo was the first of the Yenyabo people to see Tania, when she was just a day old. Cecilia did not come until a tragic accident brought her to the hospital.

The twins, active little boys, were now a year and a half old. One evening Kato went too close to the fire in Cecilia's cooking hut, tripped and fell onto it. There was a big pot of boiling water on the fire into which Cecilia was about to mix manioc flour. Kato scalded his chest, stomach and thighs. He was brought to the hospital by his relatives that night in great pain.

As soon as I heard about the accident, I went to the hospital to see Kato. Cecilia was lying in bed with Kato, bandaged and asleep, on one side of her, and Singoma, the healthy twin on the other side of her. Family members were responsible for the non-medical care of patients in the hospital; they cooked for them, washed them, and so on. Cecilia slept in Kato's bed, and if other members of the family stayed over night, they were allowed to sleep under his bed on the floor. There was plenty of room there because the hospital beds were high. Kato's ward had about twenty beds and at least one child and one adult were in each bed. Cooking pots and pans were around the beds. Lots of people were coming and going. Some patients were moaning with pain and some people were talking and laughing.

Kato was slowly getting better in the hospital but when he had been there for about a month another tragedy struck the family. A couple of days before Christmas, one of the German nurses came to tell me that Singoma had died in the hospital the night before.

"Singoma! he was the healthy one," I gasped.

"We think he got typhoid playing in the hospital grounds," she said sadly.

The other German nurse had been awakened at three o'clock in the morning by Herabo and asked to transport the body and the family back to the village. She had done so and stayed in the village to participate in the funeral service.

I was staggered. How can a healthy child get typhoid in hospital which is supposed to heal the sick? Only later did I become aware that the danger of catching other people's sicknesses is inherent in hygiene- and bacteria-conscious Western hospitals, as well. The chances of it happening in Nyanya hospital were much greater. It had open sewers, no running water, and only pit toilets. There were, moreover, some two hundred beds and hundreds of outpatients visiting the hospital dispensary daily, to say nothing of the attendant relatives.

I left for the village as soon as I heard of Singoma's death. I took Tania with me for the first time. She was only four months old and sat quietly strapped into her baby seat in the car not knowing what I was taking her into. I wished her first visit could have been a happier occasion. My heart went out to the family but at the same time I was scared. How did one behave at an African funeral? How did one behave at a baby's funeral? Was the death of a twin baby different from other babies? What did one say to the bereaved? Was I allowed to cry? I was not used to funerals in my own culture, much less in the Fofu culture.

The funeral had already been going on for a few hours when I arrived. I stepped into the hut and sensed enormous tension. It was like the inside of an anthill. People behaved as if they were driven by invisible forces. They were not the jovial and polite people I was used to but furious people who paid no attention to me. I was glad that they would not, therefore, notice any inappropriate behaviour on my part but at the same time I was scared. I was holding Tania tight against me and her softness comforted me in the strange and hostile world.

Because it was a cloudy day and the window holes were small, it was very dark inside the house. The living room was packed with men, who were talking excitedly. Most of them were church elders from the village and Nyanya. Herabo was serving them coffee but there was no coffee for the women. He was excited himself, talking in a falsetto voice and very much involved with the conversation. They were speaking in Kifofu which I did not understand. Now an old man was speaking, waving his hands in the air and Herabo agreed with flushed cheeks. All the men nodded.

"No sleep over here, no washing ceremony, no sleep, no washing ceremony!," someone explained to me in Swahili. "God has taken his property and man has nothing to add, nothing to add. This is the very last occasion to commemorate Singoma. May the Lord be praised for such a wise decision, a wise decision!" said a church elder who had arrived here from the mother church of Nyanya.

I did not understand then what was going on. The meaning became apparent to me only afterwards. It was a Fofu custom to have a wake of four days in the case of a death of a male member of the society and three days in the case of a female. The body was, of course, buried as soon as possible because of the heat. Relatives and friends would gather in the home of the deceased, sit on palm mats on the floor, and mourn the dead. No one would wash during this time. When the set time was up, there was a ritual purification ceremony where everyone went to the stream to bathe and change into clean clothes. Church members also followed this custom but sang only Christian songs instead of indigenous songs.

Among the Fofu, the case of twins was different from an ordinary death. No wake was arranged if only one of them died because that would cause the other one to die. So in deciding not to have the wake for Singoma the elders were in fact following their tribal custom, although they presented it as a Christian decision.

Somebody led me to Cecilia who was lying in bed, weeping in utter despair. She seemed to have a bad cold, too, or perhaps she had wailed so much that she had no voice left. Village women were sitting at her bedside. One of them held Kato in her lap, another one grabbed Tania from me. I knew she was only being polite, for Fofu women always held each others' babies. So I should have been thankful that in this terrifying situation she remembered to be kind to me, but I was more lost than before without the comfort of Tania's soft body and calm spirit.

I expressed my condolences to Cecilia in the fashion I had learned from my country, feeling deep sorrow for her. She did not answer or react in any way and I did not know if I had said the right thing. One of the women was talking with a loud voice,

"God does what He wants and takes His own. A human being can do nothing about it, nothing about it, nothing."

Her tone of voice was as if she was scolding Cecilia who did not bother to answer or react to her either. I could not understand the vehemence in the woman's voice and the need to repeat this over and over. It was almost like a mental whipping of the mourner. Then the woman softened up and said,

"Yes, a mother has sorrow on a day like this. She has borne the child and fed him. She has rejoiced about him, rejoiced about him."

I remembered that some time previously I had been at the funeral of another Fofu friend who had lost her baby son. She had repeated vigorously,

"God took him. It was God who took him. There is nothing else to it, nothing else."

Why did they frame it that way, as if they were arguing? What were they arguing against?

I did not learn the answer to this question until a year later when I was again attending a funeral of an infant at Yenyabo. That time Cecilia walked next to me in the procession and explained what was happening.

When the father detached himself from the other mourners and kept his distance while walking to the grave, I asked her why. Cecilia explained that he thought his mother had killed the baby by witchcraft. I immediately connected this with Singoma's funeral and asked quietly,

"Cecilia, did you think that someone had killed your baby?"

"Not very much," she answered evasively.

"A little bit then?" I persisted.

Cecilia looked away and said, "I had those thoughts but Katarina helped me to repress them. God took him."

"Who did you think was responsible for the death of your baby?" I pursued.

Cecilia became nervous. "Leave it, madam."

I did not bother her further. It was dangerous ground and painful. By then Cecilia had gotten over her sorrow, why dig into it any more?

Gradually, over the years, I pieced their reaction to death together. Before the arrival of Christianity, witchcraft was always thought to be the cause of death. Now people were Christian and they had to try to find other explanations since missionaries did not believe in witchcraft.

Although the decision was made at Singoma's funeral not to have a wake for him, the matter did not end there. Some Yenyabo women passed by my home a week later and told me that Herabo had arranged an end feast for the wake after all.

"Why?" I asked.

His relatives had insisted on following the ethnic custom of ignoring the death of one twin lest the other one die, too. Herabo, after initially agreeing had decided to show that he did not believe in this custom by arranging a feast. After all, he was a Christian, not a "heathen."

Such dilemmas were not uncommon for Fofu Christians but Herabo was zealous in his new found faith and on this occasion Christianity won. He told me on several occasions that he had become a Christian while in Uganda after living a "bad" life. When he had returned to his home village an elderly Protestant missionary couple had spent time with him and Cecilia. Several Christians from the village talked about this foreign couple with great affection. The couple had spent months at a time in the village sharing their lives with the Fofu and walking with them on long treks. The villagers could drop in their hut or their home at the mission station any time and be welcomed. This was in contrast to the present missionaries at Nyanya who were not very approachable and who preferred an appointment for a visit. This missionary couple had taught Cecilia and Herabo to read but neither had learned to write. Both of them had a taste of European food in the home of these missionaries.

Some time after Herabo's return from Uganda, the pastor who was responsible for the village church had to leave his position because he took a second wife. Herabo was asked to take more responsibility in the church and he moved to live nearer to it. It was the ambition of every Fofu man to have more than one wife although many could not afford it. However, church members were not allowed to fulfil this ambition. Being a church elder or a pastor in a church was also prestigious, but not as prestigious as having two wives. So it was common for a man to give up his position as a church leader in order to take a second wife. This would be Herabo's fate as well, although it would take many years for him to come to that decision.

A HUSBAND-SNATCHER

After Singoma's death Cecilia was naturally depressed for a while, but she could not dwell on her sorrow because she had the other twin, Kato, to look after as well as her other household duties: hoeing the fields, carrying food and firewood home on her head, cooking, going for water, and the like. Kato was often seen on Cecilia's back when she walked through the village to her fields. Rozalin, two years his senior, sometimes cared for him, Tajeki more often, and the older brothers every once in awhile. Cecilia resumed her church activities and once again, noisy women filled her kitchen helping her fix the meal for the church working parties.

One and a half months after Singoma's funeral, I went to Cecilia's fields where she was busily digging sweet potatoes. Tajeki, Rozalin, and Kato had got themselves up and also walked to the fields. They were now sitting in the shelter and squabbling. Cecilia went to the children to breast-feed Kato. I sat next to her chatting about many things. At one point I asked about the future of the children. Cecilia first described how they would give Tajeki, now eight years old, to a man who would bring the necessary bridewealth payment of cows and goats. It did not seem to matter to Cecilia what kind of a man the husband would be, as long as this condition were met. Years afterwards when Tajeki and Rozalin were of marriageable age, I saw that Cecilia and Herabo did in fact try to arrange marriages that were in the best interests of their daughters. Indeed, in Tajeki's case they probably tried too hard. But we were happily ignorant of the future at the time we sat in Cecilia's fields dreaming about it.

Then Cecilia talked about Jean-Pierre's marriage, the thought of which excited her. Jean-Pierre, who was then 15 years old, would get married in a few years if he did not continue further in school. Herabo would take the goats and cows, which were demanded for the bridewealth, to the bride's family and the bride would be brought to their home. Then Cecilia and Herabo would enjoy life. The young daughter-in-law would have to get up at 5 o'clock in the morning to sweep the floors, fetch bath water for the parents-in-law, heat it up and then carry it to a bath hut. She would make coffee for them as well and do all the cooking, so Cecilia would have all the time in the world to sit around or work in her fields. If she saw that the daughter-in-law was not a good worker, she would simply send her back to her home, demand the return of their bridewealth, and look for a better daughter-in-law. The thought of her son's marriage warmed Cecilia's heart. She kept on smiling happily long after our discussion. But she came down to earth when she realized that it was time for her to take Kato to the "kilo," or well-baby clinic. (This was a mobile clinic from the mission station which was scheduled to visit the village once every two months to check on infants up to two-years-old, pregnant mothers, leprosy and TB patients.) We went to a stream which ran near the fields and Cecilia gave Kato a bath which he resented. A Hiha woman who joined us gave Rozalin a bath. Tajeki and the women then washed themselves in the stream, starting with their feet and toes and proceeding upwards, a typical order of bathing among the Fofu. I did not dare go in for fear of getting bilharziasis, a disease caused by a parasite which humans could pick up in fresh water in Africa.

Kato was to be Cecilia's last child. When she had borne the twins, an American doctor had advised her not to have any more children. The twins were her sixth and seventh children and in Cecilia's words, the doctor had told her that "her stomach was too tired, too tired to have more children." As another pregnancy would have been dangerous, a hysterectomy was performed on her. It did not bother her that she could not have more children but I think it bothered Herabo a great deal. He did not talk about their situation directly but he would remark in conversation that a man must leave a large family behind when he dies. He, as many other Fofu, criticized me for having only two children, and wondered if the pilot was not planning to take another wife. There was genuine surprise followed by disbelief and annoyance when I announced that my husband did not want more than two children either.

Figure 3.5 Cecilia and the children washed themselves in the stream, starting with their feet and toes and proceeding upwards.

Who knows how long Cecilia would have nursed Kato if she had not become sick and quit nursing him on the advice of the American doctor. Kato was then two and a half years old. Cecilia then smeared her breasts with pilipili, a very hot spice, to wean him, as was the local custom. A mother usually suckled a baby until she was pregnant again and then weaned the child immediately. It was believed that the fetus would poison the milk. The last child was allowed to suckle longer, well over three years.

Cecilia and Kato were very close. She still bathed him when he went to school at the age of six. When he fell asleep in the evening, she carried him around on her back while doing her chores even when he was seven years old, an age when he should have been, and occasionally was, carrying younger children around himself. Over the years Cecilia kept telling me that Kato refused to sleep apart from her, although he should have slept with his siblings by then. When she and Kato stayed at my home for a week, she told me not to make two beds for them because Kato would sleep with her. He was then 12 years old.

❏ ❏ ❏

Herabo had grown up in Yenyabo. His father died when he was still a child and his elder brother brought him up. When he was fifteen years old, his brother said that his cows would get stolen if he did not use them, so he might as well do something useful with them. So he sent word to his sister who was married in Gangu to find a wife for Herabo.

According to the Fofu custom, after the go-between found a girl, she arranged a viewing ceremony, called *lingana*, for the boy to see the bride-candidate. So Herabo arrived in Gangu to view his bride. Apparently she was so drunk that she could not stand up. Herabo did not care for such a bride and he told his sister to find him another girl. The second candidate was Cecilia.

Cecilia had just returned home from another village where she had spent several years taking care of her brother's family. Her father lived in Gangu and she was a member of the local clan. Her brother had moved away, against the local custom, to work for a white man on a plantation. Cecilia was so shy that she did not want even to look at the groom candidate. She looked down and ran away with shame. When Cecilia told me about the occasion she laughed happily as if those were her good memories. It was a sign of virtue for a girl to behave like this. Herabo had liked this virtuous young woman very much and so they got married. Cows and goats had been delivered to seal the marriage agreement.

Cecilia was about fourteen, Fofu were not sure about their ages, and was not menstruating yet. She did not know about sex but her young groom "of course," to use Cecilia's words, knew all about it and forced himself upon her as a good groom should. They had been married for a while when Cecilia had her first period. Having no knowledge about it she was panic stricken and thought she was dying. She stayed in bed crying. Her aunt, who was married in the same village, was then called to see her. She comforted Cecilia and explained women's affairs to her.

Herabo and Cecilia had one child when Herabo decided to go to Uganda to work for a while. He went with another villager, his great friend of even today. Cecilia, and the friend's wife were happy at first that their husbands would bring them a lot of money. But as time went on and the husbands did not return the disadvantages of their absence became more apparent. Cecilia remarked several times to me,

"If the *mwalimu* had not been in Uganda I would have one more child, one more child." She pointed out that there were four years between her first two children which is longer than normal. In the end the women became angry with their husbands and contemplated leaving their marital village. The in-laws agreed to this because it was the right of a woman to have children regularly. Before they followed their decision, however, the men returned and they resumed normal married lives again.

There were other troubles later in their marriage. Cecilia told me how she ran back to her brother when things went wrong between them. Her husband had to humble himself and go to her home village to reclaim her. Like other women, Cecilia talked about her husband's humiliation with pleasure. Wives had this one power over their husbands: although they had to be submissive as daughters-in-law in their husbands' village, they had their clan villages as refuges in times of trouble. Their parents and lineage members would protect them and challenge their husbands about their treatment. The boot was very much on the other foot if a husband ventured into his wife's clan area. When things got tough for Cecilia she threatened to run to her father or to her brother, and Herabo took the threat seriously.

In the summer of 1976, Cecilia and Herabo had been married about 17 years and life was getting back to normal again after Singoma's death when Cecilia fell sick. It was a peculiar sickness. Cecilia had been busy arranging a wedding for Herabo's brother's son. The preparations and wedding festivities were successful. I had attended but had hardly talked to Cecilia because she was busy as a hostess. A few weeks afterwards, I went to spend a day in the village and found Cecilia in a reclining chair outside in the shade of the house. She was weak and in low spirits.

She told me that the sickness had started after the wedding at midnight. Her lungs had hurt and she could not stop burping. The symptoms had persisted. During my visit she sat in her chair with a blank face burping continuously. Between burps, she told me that her husband had prayed that night and then taken her to the mission hospital in the morning. She had a check-up and was told that she was fine, the sickness was only a figment of her imagination. Herabo then brought her home, where she continued to be sick, although she had taken Fofu remedies. Two of her sisters had since arrived from her home village, Gangu, to help with the chores. They were now in the kitchen hut shelling peanuts. Smelling trouble, they wanted to take Cecilia home with them but Herabo would not let them.

After a short chat with Cecilia, Tom and I walked to her fields a few miles away, and saw a group of workers harvesting her peanut field. Cecilia's oldest son Jean-Pierre, was there as was Henrietta, a young woman to whom Herabo and Cecilia had recently given a home. The new bride whose wedding we had just celebrated, her young sisters-in-law, and some wage labourers were also helping them. Henrietta was a relative of and had been living with Cecilia's next door neighbour, Katarina. But there had been friction. Apparently, Katarina was mad at Henrietta for not helping her with the housework. She expected Henrietta to have a meal ready for her when she returned from the fields but she never did. When Henrietta's other relatives arrived from her home village to settle the dispute, Herabo offered to let Henrietta live in his house in order to calm the situation.

I recorded the above explanation in my note book without giving it a second thought. I was to learn, however, that there was much more behind the matter and that Herabo's kind offer would lead him into a lot of trouble. She was a dangerous girl, but I should not jump ahead.

On my following visits to the village, Henrietta was helping Cecilia both in her fields and in the house. All the children were in the yard helping with the peanut harvest. The peanuts had to be separated from the plants and the husks removed. Kato carried the empty husks to the garbage heap on a little plate on his head while bigger children used baskets. Cecilia had started doing some house work herself again and her sisters had returned to their homes. Sometimes I saw Cecilia tending her fields working side by side with her wage labourers.

One evening in September when I spent the night in the village, Cecilia told me that Henrietta had received a marriage offer but she had refused it. Instead, she had dreams of attending a mission school of home economics at Nyanya and after this prestigious school, marrying a rich man and never having to work hard in her life. She thought she would be like a white woman. Everyone whom I talked to in the village was angry with her for refusing the offer. Katarina even threatened to beat her if she did not get married. A village man explained to me that Henrietta was going against the Biblical commandment, especially that of Apostle Paul, to marry. This statement tickled me because I was under the impression that that particular apostle was really for celibacy and admitted marriage only as the last resort. At the time, I could not quite understand why Henrietta's refusal to marry caused such an outrage in the village. Afterwards I understood it very well.

Henrietta had been married when she was still a child "and had hardly any breasts," a Fofu way of estimating age and demonstrating the breast size by covering half the length of the fingers of one hand with the other hand. However, Henrietta had been sent back home because she had not been a good worker. Now there was no doubt that Henrietta was an adult. In fact she was somewhat plump with bulging breasts and looked older than her age. She looked solemn and wore a mysterious expression on her face. Now that I know what her intentions were, I hate to think of her because I naturally sided with Cecilia.

Despite all the help Cecilia was getting at home and in her fields her condition took a turn for the worse and in November Herabo took her to the mission hospital again on the back of his bike. The doctors decided to try electric shock treatment on her. While there, Herabo received treatment for his bad ankle which he had wounded when working in the field. Kato followed on to have the doctors check his thigh, which had been burned again in another accidental fall into the fire. This time the wound was superficial and did not require extensive treatment. While they were at the hospital, Herabo often visited my home and talked with me about the Fofu customs and the history of the village. It seemed to please him to talk about the familiar village while he was away from it. He admitted being anxious about the shock treatment Cecilia was getting. He went back to the village by bicycle to spend an occasional night there, to check the children and work, and to fetch food supplies because the patients were responsible for their own meals. During this time Henrietta was in charge of running the family affairs. I dropped by to visit Cecilia at the hospital but she was living in her own world, buried in sombre thoughts, and did not want to talk.

Cecilia stayed in the hospital almost a month but there was no apparent change in her until she returned home in December. When I went to Yenyabo after her homecoming she was in her fields. From far away I could hear her talking to her workers in a high pitched voice. A young Fofu man was walking with me and I asked him what she was discussing. The man stopped to listen and then said that she was talking about "the Henrietta matter." Everyone in the village knew about it, and gossiped about it. I, too, was soon to learn all about it.

Cecilia was a changed person. The quiet woman of the hospital was now a furious woman. She was full of rage and anger and had no intention of concealing her emotions. We sat down in Cecilia's fields under the manioc bushes. The young man took Tom aside and played with him while Cecilia opened her heart to me.

She had been happy in the hospital, very happy and far removed from everyday troubles, but when she came home she found chaos. Henrietta had not taken care of the home. Cecilia's children were dirty and smelly, and her house was a mess. The children complained that Henrietta had not fed them but had driven them out of the house. Furthermore, in the market place, Henrietta had spread a rumour that Cecilia had not been washing her husband's clothes and was a poor mother. Then Cecilia came to the main point: Henrietta had wished her to die of the shock treatment, so she could marry Herabo! Henrietta had been hanging around their family for this very purpose, to lure her husband. Then Cecilia went back to the trouble that Henrietta and Katarina had half a year previously. The real trouble in that house was, not so much the labour problem, but the fact that Henrietta had been fishing for Katarina's husband, too. Katarina had become enraged when her husband had asked her if he could take Henrietta as his third wife. Female relatives did not share a husband, according to the Fofu custom.

Cecilia had come out of hospital on a Tuesday. On the Friday she had exploded. She took a knife and tried to slit Henrietta's throat. Someone wrestled the knife out of her hand. With her weapon gone, she started beating Henrietta with her bare hands. Katarina came to her assistance and said that she would be more than glad to beat Henrietta for Cecilia. The two women vented their long suppressed anger on this husband-snatcher. The commotion was so great that someone called the village chief in. He was angry with Henrietta and told her not to disrupt any more families in the village. He ordered Henrietta to leave the house and the mother of the children to stay. He also fined Herabo for taking a girl into his house.

News of what had happened reached Henrietta's parents in their village the very same day and they hurried over. Cecilia yelled at them,

"Why do you let your unmarried daughter live in this village, live in this village, and not keep her at home where she should be, where she should be?"

Indeed, the proper place for an unmarried woman was her father's home in her own clan area.

The end result that day was that Henrietta was driven out of Cecilia's house but stayed in the village and went to live at Petro's, Herabo's brother.

Cecilia spent all Saturday and Sunday, both day and night, walking in the bush. She wanted to hang herself and be relieved of the pain and be with God in peace. On Monday she packed her clothes and decided to go to live with her brother, some 80 miles away. The children refused to go to school that day and insisted on accompanying their mother wherever she went. The younger ones hung onto her skirt crying desperately throughout these tense hours. Herabo knew that if Cecilia went, she would never return, so he locked all her clothes away.

Church elders talked to Cecilia and tried to calm her down. They reminded her that she and her husband had a great responsibility in God's work. Yenyabo's church was really dependent on them. She should not quit so easily. Cecilia claimed that she did not care, she was going to leave. She must, however, have taken notice of the elders because she stayed and even went to work in her fields and this is where I found her when I arrived in the village later that Monday.

Although she stayed she was extremely agitated. When I was at her home later the same day, Herabo asked her to do something in his customary fashion. Cecilia answered back angrily and ignored his request.

When I asked a church elder about the situation, he said Cecilia was a jealous wife with no grounds for suspicion and the fine, although imposed on Herabo, was really for Cecilia beating Henrietta.

When writing my notes in 1976, I did not know whose interpretation, Cecilia's or that of the church elders, was closer to the truth. Now the elders' views seem to be only excuses. I learned later when visiting numerous villages that unmarried women deliberately went to live with a relative outside their clan villages in hopes of getting a new husband. One woman even asked about me when I spent a week in a village, "What is she doing here anyway? Is she looking for a husband for herself, looking for a husband?" Women who knew my family history then explained that I already had a husband but that I was doing some university studies.

The average villager understood the situation: Herabo would like to take another wife but was afraid of losing his position in the church. I wondered why the church elders did not admit this. Herabo was a charismatic leader and a driving force in the church. The elders probably thought that pronouncing Herabo innocent would be best for the church. They accordingly put the blame on Cecilia. They did, however, ban Herabo from preaching while the trouble was continuing.

Cecilia went to her fields again, cooked for the family, and took care of her children. But Herabo's and Cecilia's relationship had not regained its former stability. In mid-December, for example I heard her answer him with an angry bark. Yet a few days later at Christmas 1976, she was all smiles. I asked her how she was.

"Fine!" she beamed back.

"No fights with Herabo?" I asked.

"Not yet, not yet," she answered. She added that the church elders had given her permission to go to her home village for a week's holiday. She would go after she finished weeding her sweet potato fields. Her private plan was to stay a month. I thought that she deserved it and nodded approvingly.

Herabo was a man who planned for the future. In 1977, he built a new house outside the church lot. I realized only afterwards that the turmoil must have prompted this plan. I wonder now if Cecilia understood the underlying motive, she probably did. He was then living in a church-owned house, which he would have to leave if found breaking church rules.

I happened to be in the village during the muddying of his new house and took pictures of it. It was done in the traditional way. The women carried water on top of their heads in pots and kerosene containers which were becoming more common in the village. They poured the water into the soil which the men had already dug. As the women poured the men treaded it with their feet, buried in mud to their knees. When the soil was of the right consistency, other men and some women threw it over the reeds until all holes and cracks were filled with mud. Afterwards the wall was smoothed out with fresh mud. Muddying usually took a day.

After the muddying, Herabo had his workers cement a layer of stones on both the outside and the inside of the walls. So the walls were about a yard thick. He also had a corrugated iron roof put on. He told me that his relatives were worried about the modern roof. They told him not to go for it because there was a danger that envious villagers would cause his death by witchcraft. Herabo thought about it and came to the conclusion that he would die anyhow, so he had the corrugated iron roof put on.

Herabo's house was the first building in the village, save for the church, to have a corrugated iron roof and stone walls. Even today there are few such buildings there. I stayed in his new house numerous times. It was huge and far from ordinary. It had concrete floors and real glass windows, as well as some pictures on the walls. The living room was full of wooden couches made by a carpenter Herabo hired especially for the job. The couches had cushions filled with dry grass. These features were all very extravagant for the village where the rest of the houses were built of mud, had thatched roofs, dirt floors, simple wooden chairs, and no glass windows. Although corrugated iron roofs were very prestigious in the village, I am not so sure that they are superior to thatched ones. Although iron does not rot like a thatched roof, it radiates the heat of the sun and makes the rooms very hot. It does not always keep the rain out either. Once I was in the house during a terrible rain storm. The rain poured in through the roof as well as the doors and windows! We and our beds got wet.

There was one more episode of the Henrietta affair even after the new arrangement of Henrietta living with Petro. A year later, Herabo gave Cecilia a key to his private storage room in the new house to get sugar for the guests they were hosting. Cecilia found sugar all right but she also found Henrietta's skirt. She confronted Herabo with it,

"What is THIS doing in the storage room, the storage room?"

This made the church elders change their attitude. They swiftly got Henrietta married to a widower in a far away village, a widower who was a preacher, had children, and was desperate for a wife. After that we never heard about Henrietta again and Cecilia was cured of her burping.

"SECRETLY IN THIS ROOM"

The following five years in the life of Cecilia and Herabo seemed to be calm and both individuals were productive in their work. Cecilia took pride in her fields and worked there relentlessly, sometimes alone, sometimes with her wage workers, and every once and a while with the help of her children. She sold some of the produce in the markets. Once or twice a week she would go to the Sengi market in the neighbouring village. Once a week there was a market at Yenyabo where most of the local women gathered and at least once a week she would go to the Nyanya market. The Yenyabo and Sengi markets took only a few hours of the women's time although the profits were not that great. The best profit was at Nyanya but it was two hours walking distance away. The women would leave early in the morning and return after dark in the evening. It was hard for the family, especially if there was no one to cook supper. The children would wait anxiously for their mothers to come home.

Often Cecilia was allowed to transport her sacks of potatoes in the mission truck which came to fetch food and firewood from the village once a week. The mission wanted to support the church leaders' families and bought food from Cecilia and Herabo and another church leader. Although the mission did not charge her for the transportation of her private potatoes, the driver wanted a little "gift." Cecilia calculated this gift worth paying since she could ship more potatoes on the truck than she could carry on her head, which the other village women had to do.

Herabo organized some of his workers to help Cecilia in the fields. Other workers helped him in the forest. His father had been far-sighted enough to lease one hundred hectares of forest from the government zone for 65 years. Herabo and his brothers tried to make money from it. They had workers cut trees for charcoal, boards, and firewood.

Once, on my husband's day off from work I took my family to the forest for a picnic. The forest was about four miles from the village. As I mentioned earlier, some decades ago the colonial government had asked the villagers to move closer to the forest in order to guard the telegraph line in the bush. At the time of our visit, some old people were still living in this location but eventually all moved further into the savannah.

My children found it exciting to be in the dark forest. It was cool and shady under the tall trees and the children munched their carrot sticks happily. The forest contained different sounds from those of the village; it was especially pleasant to hear birds singing.

Henry wanted to help Herabo fell the tall trees. In his youth, he had worked in logging in British Columbia and had felled thousands of trees. Now we watched the local method of tree-felling. It was not an easy matter to get a tree down in Africa. Herabo's workers made a fire under the tree to burn part way through it, so there would be less to cut with a saw. Two men had built a stand for themselves about a meter high and were sawing a tree with a hand saw, each holding one end of the saw. Later they would use axes. They worked several days to fell one tree.

Henry had his power saw with him and asked in which direction Herabo wanted the tree to fall. Everyone left the designated site. When Henry started the saw, the terrible noise of the motor pierced the rain forest and frightened the workers. Herabo looked on in a state of great anxiety. Several times he stopped Henry to ask if our picnic basket was safe. I tried to comfort him and told him that my husband was an expert in this business but it did not relieve him at all. In ten minutes the first tree fell with a great crash. Everyone was amazed. Herabo marvelled at the power saw and giggled with pleasure and relief. Henry felled three more trees because Herabo needed four trees for a batch of charcoal. It would yield 10 bags of charcoal, one half of which would go to the workers. Herabo would sell the rest for profit.

Marvellous as a power saw is in cutting trees fast and easily, it may not be so good ecologically. The large rain forest was already shrinking. If power saws became popular, it would shrink even faster, as it is in other parts of the world.

Not only was Herabo ambitious in the business of forestry but also in cattle herding. He was among the first villagers who became involved with a German cattle project which operated from Lemura. Its purpose was to improve the cattle in the area by giving information to people about new methods, providing a veterinary service and building dips for cattle owners. These dips were medicated water holes in which cattle were dipped to get rid of pests.

As a result of his involvement in this project Herabo had an opportunity to go to Bululu, where I then lived, and tour around the cattle country and the dairy industry with delegates from different villages. I invited him to stay at our place during his week in Bululu. He arrived in a very nervous state. Although he had been in Uganda as a young man, travelling made him anxious. It had been a long journey from Lemura to Bululu lasting several days. The roads were rough and the terrain was mountainous, something he had never seen before. Although he was used to a white man's house, from his experience with his favourite missionary couple, he did not eat much in my house, and this worried me. He did not want to eat anything at all in the morning as was a custom in his village. He ate only in the evening, and then much less than he would at home. I think that his unease in the strange surroundings simply suppressed his appetite but I was afraid that he would return to his village thinner than when he had left. Then the whole village would conclude that "Madam Pilot" had not taken good care of him.

Herabo visited us in the beginning of December and my children, who were three and seven at the time, were eager to get a Christmas tree. I bought one from a local salesman and was specially glad to have an evergreen, which were not obtainable in all parts of Zaire. Herabo watched us decorate it and asked why we were doing so. Suddenly it struck me that it was a heathen custom practised in Europe before the arrival of the Christianity. I thought it was ironic that I was telling him, a recent Christian, about white man's heathen customs! Unlike us, the Zaireans did not celebrate Christmas with gifts or trees. They arranged an all night Christmas service in the church. New Year was a greater festival for them. They often butchered a goat for the occasion and drank a lot of beer. Herabo did not seem to condemn our custom but found it peculiar.

Herabo's party made day tours to surrounding dairy farms in the mountains. He was impressed by the size of the farms and the methods they used to feed the cattle and make dairy produce. Yenyabo cows just roamed around eating grass, no extra food was given to them. Now Herabo saw that these European and mixed European-African farmers would give them supplementary food. Fofu only used the milk of their cows for drinking: they did not make anything with it. The Hiha pastoralists took care of the butter making and sold it in the same markets as the Fofu women sold their garden produce. Herabo began to realize the potential of cattle. Each day he returned home shaking his head with amazement.

Herabo had arrived with all his things in a wooden box built by his carpenter especially for the trip. However, he soon bought a bag in Bululu—probably realizing that the box looked too rural in the city. He had brought quite a lot of money to buy some dishes to take home but we decided that transporting them on mud roads was too risky and he did not use the money. It was too bad because he lost that money. Soon after his trip, at the end of 1978, the government suddenly annulled two kinds of currency notes. People had to change them at the bank for new ones within two days of the radio message, or they would lose the money. Herabo was then already back at Yenyabo where there were no banks and so his money became worthless.

When I went to Yenyabo the next time, he mentioned this loss but did not let it bother him.

"Thanks to God," he said. I did not think it was worth thanking God, on the contrary, I was astounded that any government could do such a thing to its people. Perhaps his attitude was the best in the circumstances, since only a revolution could have altered the situation and people did not want to plunge into that.

As explained in the beginning of this story, when I lived in Bululu I used to stay at Cecilia's for a week or so at a time in order to do an in-depth study of some Fofu households in Yenyabo. Cecilia's place was a haven to me where I could go to take a nap when I got tired from walking under the hot sun. Cecilia was often working in her fields during the day but in the evenings she was busily doing house chores and greeted me with a friendly smile when I went "home." By then I was familiar with the children and adults in the household and I was allowed to sit with them in the kitchen hut and participate in little tasks and the gossip. People were always coming and going, greeting Cecilia in the kitchen and chatting with Herabo who stayed in the front yard or in the living room.

They had a tiny guest room which barely had room for a wooden bed and my suitcase. I kept my toiletries on the windowsill and my clothes hanging on a string as was the local custom. I brought my mosquito net, not so much for the mosquitoes but for cockroaches which were everywhere. Usually I carried a bug spray with me and sprayed the bed and the walls the first day I arrived. I realized the true benefit of this when I once forgot to bring the spray and the net. The cockroaches crawled over my face at night trying to get into my nostrils and mouth. They jumped out of my tooth brush case and camera case when I opened them. There were lots of flies as well. When Cecilia served me coffee, five flies could be sitting on the brim of the cup. The Zaireans did not seem to notice any of the pests and I tried to hide my aversion to them. I believe the bugs resulted from the variety of domestic animals near the home, such as cows, pigs, dogs, hens, and cats. When Herabo was forced to move the cows further away, of which I will tell you later, there was a significant reduction in the insect population.

Some women let the dishes dry on a rack in the sun but in this household the dishes from the previous day were washed just before the evening meal. The dishwater was cold and the dishes were left wet while the whole selection of animals came to lick them. My stomach was not used to such exposure to germs. I took a handful of Tetracyclin every few days to fend off diarrhea which attacked me fiercely if I forgot to take them.

When I came to stay, I usually brought a gift from Bululu for Cecilia. Once I had spent a lot of time selecting a special piece of material for her, a type she could not find locally. I did not think anything of presenting it to her in the living room on my arrival. But when I went to my room to unpack my notebooks, she came after me, closed the door behind her and lowered her voice to a worried whisper,

"Madam, you should never do this!" she said.

"What?" I asked, wondering what on earth I had done wrong.

Cecilia laughed and scolded simultaneously, "You must never give me anything in public."

"Public? It was in your living room," I protested.

"Yes, but village children were present, they were present. Now they will tell the whole village what you have given to me and the other women will be envious of me, envious. 'Why is she giving a piece of cloth to Cecilia, why isn't she giving us some, too'?" Then she added, "If you want to give me something you must do it secretly in this room, secretly."

I had assumed that the villagers would accept our Western tradition of bringing a gift to the hostess. It was so legitimate in my mind that I found it hard to grasp why it should cause envy among the villagers. After all, Cecilia did special things for me. How else could I show my appreciation? I carried on my custom of giving gifts all my years in Africa, although I did remember to do it in secret.

Only afterwards have I come to think that, perhaps, I should have done something else. My gift giving followed an individualistic Western pattern but Fofu thinking did not. To them it was not Cecilia who did something special for me but the whole village by letting me live and do research there. So I should have done something collective. During the first few years, a Fofu villager had suggested to me that I kill a cow and arrange a feast for the whole village. When I asked Herabo about the suggestion he laughed and shrugged it off. It is possible he did this to please me and I should have arranged a feast after all.

A TWIN'S TEMPER TANTRUM

I grew accustomed to the daily routine in Herabo's house. In the morning I would wake up to Herabo's morning prayers. He prayed loud and long. He asked God to give him and his family strength to live the day, to do the work, and to evade sickness. Then he would turn the radio on and the whole family would awaken. Cecilia would soon be sweeping the floors and the yard energetically, sometimes helped by Tajeki, then eleven years old. Jean-Pierre, 18-years old, or Richard, 14-years old, would set off to guard the rice fields from birds, a monotonous job which the sons took in turn.

That year Herabo's sister's son, Mateso, was living with the family attending the school with Cecilia's children. He shared the jobs with the boys of the family. The one who did not go to the rice fields had to take care of cows. Jean-Pierre, being the eldest son, was temporarily excused from these jobs and given the errands which entailed cycling, a prestigious means of transportation, to Sezabo or Nyanya to buy soap or a toothbrush or the like. This year he also started building his own house about 100 yards from the family home. I saw him examining the posts for his house in his father's shed. Occasionally he would assist one of his father's workers with the house building which had started in June and was almost finished four months later. This meant that his marriage negotiations were under way and he would soon marry. Cecilia's dreams were coming true.

In the morning, the younger children would gather around the fire in the kitchen and throw corn cobs in the coals and wait for them to roast. Cecilia would make coffee for adults to sit and drink at their leisure, but she usually drank and ate while doing her chores, hardly ever while sitting still. Sometimes, she drank coffee while hurrying from the house to her kitchen hut or while scrubbing a pot. Once Kato, then five-years old, remarked when she had her coffee,

"You are having your coffee in vain."

I did not understand what he meant by the phrase but Cecilia thought it was funny because she laughed and offered him her mug. It had been Kato's round-about way of begging some coffee. Rozalin, Kato's eight-year-old sister, passed by and he promised that he would leave some for her. That was the last Cecilia saw of her coffee, but she did not mind.

Several incidents involving Kato gave me an insight into his character, which was more wilful than most Fofu children. Village women would often stop by Cecilia's place and gossip with her before going to their fields or the market. Sometimes, but not always, Cecilia gave them coffee, too. One day, a Hiha woman was chatting with Cecilia at the kitchen door while Kato ate his roasted corn near the fire. She asked for his corn cob but Kato did not give it to her. She kept her hand extended toward him, and, reluctantly, he gave it to her. She flung her hand in the air toward his face as if annoyed that he had delayed, although her smile showed that she was not serious. Then she pointed to two rows of the kernels and said,

"I'll eat these, look over here."

Kato nodded. She stepped outside to join a group of other women who were excitedly talking about a pig which had got loose and destroyed the neighbour's garden. Soon, she returned to the door, about three yards from him, and offered the corn back with the two rows of kernels eaten.

"Bring it here!" Kato told her. The woman looked impatient and shrugged her shoulders. An adult would not walk for a child. It was a child's duty to run errands for an adult. Kato would not walk either because he had done her a favour. The woman found a solution when a neighbour girl was passing by. She gave the corn to the girl to take back to Kato. He put it on a stone as if to show that he no longer cared about it, but soon he continued to eat it.

While still gossiping with the women, Cecilia carried water into the utility room of the house and proceeded to wash dishes. Kato went to stand by her, listening to the women. For a while he followed his mother step by step while she worked and gossiped intensely with the women. Then, perhaps to get attention, he played with a stick and dropped it near Cecilia. She got annoyed and said, "W-e!," an expression of irritation for dogs and children.

Some minutes later, Cecilia gave each of the women a banana and a sweet potato, left over from the night before. Kato received one as well. Then she rekindled the fire in the kitchen and started frying an omelette in palm oil. By this time Kato was crying aloud in the house. The neighbour girl who had brought Kato his corn informed her that Kato was crying. Cecilia told her that Kato would not get the omelette. Cecilia then got up from the fire, threw a few words into the women's discussion and went to the house.

We heard her talking to Kato, "There isn't much omelette, omelette, why bother to cry?" I'll cook some other food for you, some other food." The escalating screaming expressed Kato's protest.

Cecilia scolded, "Don't cry so loud. It is bad to cry loud!"

When he did not heed her words she said, "Rozalin is sick. Go and cry elsewhere!"

Rozalin had worked in the peanut field the previous day and had a headache. She was still in bed in the adjacent room. Kato increased the volume of his crying and lay on the floor. But when Cecilia walked out and ignored him his voice modulated and faltered, only to increase if his mother happened to go near him again. At one point Cecilia said, "W-e, w-e!" which quieted Kato's voice for a second. But soon afterwards, when Cecilia was sweeping the floor, he was screaming and kicking a wooden door in a temper tantrum. Cecilia ignored him, completed her work, changed to a clean blouse and followed the women to a neighbour's house. Kato's crying died out after this and he finished his corn cob.

My interpreter, a youth, who accompanied me during that week and translated everything that was said, explained to me that twins possessed more anger than ordinary people, a view later confirmed by other Fofu. I smiled to myself because I am a twin as well, but being unaware of this law of nature I have not tried to take advantage of it as Kato did.

When I went to my room at lunch time, I saw a covered plate on the window sill. When I lifted the cover, I saw a yellow omelette cooked in red palm oil. I observed that someone had nibbled one side of it. I had my thoughts about who the nibbler might have been. . . .

❏ ❏ ❏

Herabo often drank his coffee in the living room with me. If he had other visitors he would give them some, too, but only after I had had my share. Cecilia served mine in a special small china cup. I never drank more than two cups, which surprised her and Herabo. They thought that it was no amount to drink because any Fofu could have finished a whole pot alone.

After early morning coffee, Herabo's workers gathered in his yard and he would allocate them various jobs for the day. From time to time workers would lodge with him, sleeping on the couches or on the floor on straw. For some time a young couple lodged in a little side room in the kitchen hut. Once I saw Herabo butchering a pig and dividing up the meat for the workers. I asked why he went to the extra trouble and he said that he tried to keep the workers happy.

One morning he was preparing to leave for the field in the middle of the usual morning chaos. I was sitting in the kitchen with my interpreter making notes. Cecilia, busy with the chores, mentioned that the egg shells had been fragile lately. I did not know if I should intervene but I told her what we had been doing about it at home. Henry, who raised chickens near the airport, dried the empty shells, ground them, and fed them back to the chickens. I told Cecilia this and suggested that she try it. Herabo and Cecilia listened to me politely but, afterwards, Herabo turned and spoke to Cecilia switching from Swahili to Kifofu. I asked my interpreter what he was saying. He translated that Herabo was commanding Cecilia never to do as the madam had said. I kept a straight face and decided that it was not my job to make any suggestions. I was, however, slightly offended that my very reasonable piece of advice had been rejected.

Having organized his workers, Herabo would then set about his tasks in the fields, the forest, Nyanya, or with church meetings. Cecilia never knew when he would return. He could reappear at any time or stay away a whole day till late at night.

One day he happened to return before noon. He had been at the centre of the administrative zone in connection with a cow thievery matter that had been going on for years. It was pouring rain, one of those fierce storms. Jean-Pierre, Kato, and his friends were at home. There were also two boys who had been walking through the village and had asked for shelter from the rain.

Jean-Pierre was the first to spot his father and let out a surprised, "E-e-e-e-e!"

Herabo was pushing his bike which was useless in the deep mud. He was dripping wet. I was sitting with the children in the living room. As he went to the back he chatted with me through the partition walls, apparently unaffected by the wet clothes and muddy feet. He also chatted with a worker's wife who was cuddling her baby in the kitchen hut. He did not chat with his own children because a father is not supposed to have an informal relationship with his offspring. Jean-Pierre hurried to help him, by removing a hoe from the corner and helping to push Herabo's bicycle there. Although it was muddy, it was put in the house, presumably for safety's sake. Herabo inquired of the strange boys where they were heading and then disappeared to his bedroom to change his clothes, humming a hymn. Soon he called Kato who hurried to his father. His friend tagged along and I saw each of them carrying one of Herabo's boots and pouring water out of them.

Some minutes later, Herabo emerged from the back room in dry clothing and gave both Kato and his friend a banana, eating one himself. He asked his oldest son if the workers had reported for work that day and asked Kato's friend where his father was. The rain had subsided but it was still drizzling. Next Herabo told Kato to go to a house about 300 yards away to buy coffee beans. Kato left right away and his friend ran after him. Soon they returned and Kato asked his father how much coffee he should buy.

Herabo, who by then was sitting comfortably in an armchair, said, "One zaire's worth." Kato left again. But Herabo went to the door and, not trusting his young son's memory, yelled directly to the neighbour, "One zaire's worth!"

He went in the back room again, humming some songs. Meanwhile, Kato brought him the coffee, wrapped in big green leaves. Now Herabo sent Jean-Pierre to the neighbour to make sure that Kato had bought the right amount and went to the kitchen to give the beans to a neighbour girl who had appeared there. He asked her to grind the beans by pounding them with a mortar. The girl obeyed him. The worker's wife then cooked the coffee for Herabo and he sat again in an armchair enjoying his hot coffee after a long and wet walk home.

When I later interviewed children and adults about the right of an adult other than parents to order children around, they told me that all adults were like parents and should be obeyed.

I remembered this event later when I interviewed Herabo about parenthood and childhood. We were talking about what it was like to be a child at home and he was thinking of his own childhood. He said that he did not really like to be a child because a child could be woken up at night and sent on an errand, and there was nothing a child could do about it. One could see that now that he was an adult he enjoyed the privileges that his status gave him. He let his sons run errands for him even if it rained.

I discovered Kato's point of view five years later when I gave a questionnaire at his school about parent-child relationships. To my question "Why do the children need to obey their parents?" he wrote "because the parents gave birth to the child." To another question " How do you show respect to your parents?" Kato answered, "When they send you on an errand you go very fast and with happiness and you return happy." The Fofu see the parent-child relationship as one of reciprocity; parents have given life to the children and are now supporting them, therefore children owe it to their parents to obey them and run errands for them, not grudgingly but with a happy heart. I tended to see parents as ruthlessly exploiting their children until, through the interviews, I understood the Fofu view: parents only acted out their part of the reciprocity system. The other part was that they had given life to the children and took care of them. I admired the children for acknowledging the parental role gratefully, unlike Western children who take it for granted that parents bore them and take care of them.

During the morning, when Cecilia was in her fields for several hours at a time, the older children were supposed to be at school. But it seemed to me that they were at home more than they ought to have been. Various reasons were given: the teacher had gone walking (*mwalimu alitembea*); there was a holiday; a child was not feeling well, or had to help the mother in the fields. Tajeki had failed the first grade in 1977 because she had been helping her mother during exams. She repeated the grade. Cecilia was proud of her help in the fields, more proud in fact than she would have been of her passing the grade.

In 1979, Tajeki was in grade two, Richard was in grade three, and Rozalin and Kato had not started yet. Jean-Pierre had finished six grades, all that was possible in the village. He had asked to continue at Nyanya but Herabo had not agreed. "There is much work at home, work at home," he told him implying that school was not really work. Herabo told me that it was not really worth continuing education because the only job one could get around home was a teacher's job. It did not pay much, about 80 zaires a month. He could get the same amount of money for one bag of potatoes in the market. So Jean-Pierre stayed at home and helped with farming.

The children were at home early in the afternoon because school ended around noon. One such day, I came home for a snack and heard children reciting the multiplication table in unison. I peeked into the dining room. There Rozalin, Kato, Tajeki and Gilbert were standing at the huge table rhythmically chanting, "Three times one is three, three times two is six . . ." I went to my room and heard the girls take the lead, "Five times five is ten." Gilbert shouted at them contemptuously, "Don't you have a head?" He was older and knew the right answer. That broke up the unity of the children. Gilbert then started to examine Kato, "Five times one?" Kato answered, "Five." I was glad that the choir's performance was over, for I could then fall asleep after walking from house to house all morning in the hot sun.

One day Richard and Gilbert were reading the Bible at the dining table. They did it in the same fashion as the multiplication table, that is yelling mechanically, verse by verse. Nobody paid any attention to them.

Another afternoon the smaller children, Rozalin and Kato, were at home with eleven other children of their age or younger. They were sitting on the remains of the tractor, a souvenir from an ill-fated development project, which was left abandoned next to Herabo's shed. There were eight boys and five girls, all village children and it was not difficult to see that they were playing the *kilo*, the hospital clinic which often visited the village. Girls had "babies" tied to their backs. One girl stepped down and opened her cloth to tie it better. I saw that her baby was a piece of banana tree trunk. The children were starting the *kilo* by singing church hymns as they had seen happening in real life because the clinic that visited the village was from the Protestant mission station. The biggest of the girls was acting as nurse. She climbed down from the tractor and started giving them a lecture on child care. The others listened to her and then broke into loud singing again.

Soon the play was changed into a church service. The group moved to better shade next to the kitchen. My ear drums were again tried with their loud singing. But I was glad that they continued to play without paying attention to me. I sat on a stool a little aside from them in the shade, writing my notes and occasionally glancing at them.

Kato loved to play at driving a car. I often saw him with the neighbour boy about his age sitting on a mortar lying on its side on the ground. Kato had a battered bowl as a driving wheel. Making the engine noise through his loose lips he was totally absorbed in the fantasy of car driving. Another favourite game was playing the drums with his friends. Anything that made a noise such as pots and chairs, was used as a drum and beaten with sticks. The rhythm was fabulous and the excitement in the children's faces was priceless.

When the adults were not at home, I could observe the relationships between the siblings. Kato was bullied by his older brothers but he sometimes gave as good as he got without them retaliating. When with his mother he was protected from their bullying. The older brothers slapped Rozalin but every once in a while she and her girl friends attacked the brothers and, surprisingly, the brothers did not try to hit back. Rozalin and Kato, a couple of years apart, often teased each other and had a generally competitive relationship. But they were also friends. If I gave Kato a piece of bread that I had brought with me, a rarity in the village, he broke a piece for Rozalin without her asking. Once Kato was crying after his mother left him. Rozalin comforted him, "Don't cry, I'll give you a big sweet potato." That soothed Kato and he was soon absorbed in eating.

The children were fascinated by Western packaging. When Jean-Pierre had unwrapped a toothbrush he had bought for his father in Sezabo, Richard immediately grabbed the packaging and started playing with it. "Look at my glasses," he said and spread the wrapping over his eyes so that the transparent part

Figure 3.6 **A mortar lying on its side made an excellent car for the boys to drive.**

served as goggles. The others laughed at him. He manipulated the packaging into different positions for a long time. When he left off Kato picked it up and started examining it. The same thing happened with a plastic bag my bread had been wrapped in. Both girls and boys felt it with their fingers and modelled it on their heads in various ways.

As for Cecilia and Herabo, things seemed to be going smoothly between them. However, a remark Cecilia made to her neighbour may have indicated that trouble was brewing. Cecilia mentioned that Kato had been fighting with a friend who had yelled at him, "Your mother can bear no more children, children!" Kato had punched his friend's nose. I concluded from this incident that everyone in the village knew about Cecilia's hysterectomy and that the operation lowered her status in people's eyes, so much so that even little kids talked about it. Perhaps Herabo was battling with his desire to take another wife and to father more children, which was the greatest goal in life for the Fofu. Once when we talked about African polygyny he told me, "A human being is not a bull who has many cows." I wondered if he said this to convince himself.

Another time he was surprisingly open and told me that he was afraid of his blood. He feared that he might have the same blood as his older and younger brothers who beat their wives when they were angry. At the time I thought he was unnecessarily hard on himself but now that I know what followed I realize that his fears were justified—and prophetic.

A DREAM COMES TRUE

Cecilia's dream finally came true when Jean-Pierre received a wife at eighteen. His new house was finished and Herabo had found a young woman who pleased him. It was not a simple matter. I was in the village when he went to visit the parents of one prospective bride. Herabo's sister had suggested this family since she was married in the same village as the young girl. It was the Fofu custom for the women to look for a wife for their brothers' sons. One evening, when I was having supper with him, Herabo told me that the bride was not suitable after all.

"Why?" I asked. Herabo intimated that the parents were Catholic and did not really understand the Christian life the way Herabo's family did. He was determined to look for another one who was a Protestant. Being a Protestant pastor it was important for him to have his family and in-laws attend the church. I thought that it was interesting that Herabo talked to me about it and not to his son who was playing outside with other children apparently unaware of what was going on.

When I next visited the village in 1980, Herabo had found another girl and Jean-Pierre was married. The young couple spent their nights together in their new home but they spent their days in his parents' place. Jean-Pierre worked in Herabo's fields and helped his father with errands to Sezabo and Nyanya as before he was married. His wife worked under Cecilia's surveillance. She was a young girl, about fourteen or fifteen at the most; she was not sure about her age. She had big wide eyes and a shy smile. She was very slow in her work as if she did not know household chores very well. I commented on it to Cecilia and she agreed that the daughter-in-law was inexperienced. Tajeki, who was 12, could do chores better than the bride. Although Cecilia had told me years back that she would send a slow worker back to her parents, she did not do it. She liked the prestige of being a mother-in-law. She did not overwork the young bride either, although I had thought she might from the way she had talked about it. She was a considerate mother-in-law.

When the young bride had served Cecilia a few months, Cecilia took some utensils and stools, carried them to the young couple's house and gave them formal permission to run their own household. This did not mean, however, that they were entirely free of obligations towards the parents. If Cecilia or Herabo needed their help, they could call on them. They might, for example, be asked to help Cecilia in her fields when harvesting or take care of Cecilia's family if she was away. In addition, Jean-Pierre would continue to run errands for his father. However, Cecilia pointed out to me that the young couple could plan their work on their own and tell the older couple that their request for help was inconvenient. Cecilia would not be offended.

Jean-Pierre continued to come home often and sit with his siblings in the evening. I often saw him eating with Cecilia and his siblings and lying down on his father's couches. I knew that intimate sharing of ideas was not a custom between couples but this surprised me since I knew that his young wife was alone at home. Once I asked Jean-Pierre what he talked about with his wife and he said that he tried to teach her when it was the best time to plant crops. How unromantic, I thought. One day Cecilia told me, laughing with approval, that Jean-Pierre had been yelling at his wife because she had not washed his laundry. Cecilia was pleased that he had acquired manly ways and was acting like the head of the house.

Soon Jean-Pierre's wife was pregnant and everyone was happy to have the family expand. Herabo bought a maternity card for her to attend the maternity clinic and deliver the baby in the mission hospital. However, when the time to deliver arrived, it was too late to walk to the hospital. Cecilia and a female neighbour helped her to deliver a baby girl in Cecilia's kitchen. Here I could see that the in-law relationship worked both ways. If the young couple had to serve the older couple, the older and experienced couple in turn helped the younger and inexperienced.

Cecilia gave good care to her daughter-in-law at child birth. She had borne seven children herself, so her handling of the baby was full of assurance. In the mornings, when I came out of my bedroom Cecilia was busily exercising the baby on the dining table. She pulled the baby's arms and legs and massaged them. When I saw it the first time I asked why she did it. Cecilia smiled and explained that that way the baby would become a strong woman who could work well in the fields and carry heavy loads on her head. The young mother who was unsure of how to look after a baby stayed at Cecilia's, so that Cecilia could keep an eye on her.

Herabo's mother, the baby's great grandmother, also moved in for a while to help care for the baby when Cecilia was at the market. The great grandmother and the young mother shared a bedroom and the young husband, Jean-Pierre, slept alone in his own house. One night the baby woke me up. I heard the mother trying to comfort it, then the old woman's voice joined in. But the baby would not stop crying. This went on for quite a while. Then I heard footsteps hurrying from Cecilia's bedroom through the house to the women's bedroom.

"Give the baby to me!," she said shortly and walked back to her bedroom. The crying stopped immediately and there was no more of it all night. In the morning, I asked Cecilia how she had made the baby stop crying. Cecilia looked at me and said simply,

"The baby knows that she is well with me, well with me."

I remembered how my daughter Tania had known it too when she was under a year old. Cecilia's confident touch gave the assurance of well being to the young.

One month after the delivery, the young mother went back to work in her fields. Rozalin, then 10-years old, was designated to be in charge of the baby. Many a time I saw them walking through the village toward the fields: the young mother walking in front carrying a hoe and an empty basket on her head. A few steps behind her, was Rozalin carrying the baby in a sling on her front.

Richard was sixteen when we left Africa in 1981. He still looked half grown but he was also anxious to get married. He had made his own fields and was very excited when he was telling me about it. He explained that he was sending his mother and sister, Tajeki, to sell the products of his fields in the markets. He had already bought cloth with the money received and was going to have the village tailor make him trousers. When his father considered he was capable of supporting one, he would bring his son a wife. Richard clapped his hands with joy in anticipation of the prospect. He laughed without embarrassment and his sisters laughed with him.

HOUSE DIVIDED

It was three years before we had the chance to return to Africa. It was a joyous reunion for Cecilia and me. During the two months, we saw each other frequently, although I was busy visiting other families and villages as well.

The village had drastically changed its appearance. A Bible school had arrived from another village which had been unable to provide fields for the students because of land shortage. Although the situation was now calm and the people of Yenyabo claimed that all the difficulties had been forgotten, it was obvious that the arrival of a new and big institution was not an easy matter for the village. When I flew over the village, the Bible school with its roofs shining in the sun, stood out. They could be seen from far away across the savannah, too.

The Bible school buildings together with the huts of the students, most of whom were from far away villages, formed a large complex near Herabo's house. I noticed that the rest of the villagers had moved away and made their houses available for the school staff. A pastor had sold his house to the director of the Bible school, and other villagers had sold to school personnel. Herabo was alone in the middle of the Bible school complex.

Cecilia told me that Herabo had refused to leave his house. He was the only one who had not obeyed the Bible school's order to leave and he did not intend to give in. His brother had moved only after one of his cows came home with three legs, the fourth having been cut off by angry Bible school students. The school people said that the cows had destroyed the fields of the students and they had wanted to give their message to the cow owners in a more dramatic way than simply reporting to the chief, which they had done numerous times before. Although Herabo had not moved he did have a shed built for the cows down in the valley further away.

Village women were upset that they had to quit their old village market. The school was adjacent to the former market site. No noise was allowed so near to the school and the women were not willing to have their market elsewhere. The chief was also unhappy because he had not been given a gift for the permission to build the school there. All this had happened soon after my departure. Apparently there had been some talk about it while I was still there but I had missed it. Now when people were telling me about this change I could see that there had been much turmoil about the matter but that generally people wanted to forget it and go about their everyday lives.

This summer I did not stay overnight in the village but I frequently came to the village for a day. I left Nyanya early in the morning by foot and returned just before sunset around six. Cecilia's house was one of the first I came to and I always stopped there to have a rest after the long walk. Now I drank more than two cups of coffee at a time because the walking took its toll.

Cecilia's children had grown and developed. Jean-Pierre now had two children, the second one was a boy. Richard was a tall, handsome young man, now nineteen years old and married. He had broad shoulders and big muscles, a handsome face with a warm smile. I could not believe that he was the scrawny Richard who had been growing his first field when I left the village three years ago. I bet the girls were crazy about him.

Richard's wife had been chosen by Cecilia. She had spotted a young girl, Maria, in the wedding party of another village youth. She was a daughter of the village where a "sister" of a middle-aged Yenyabo man was married, an ideal category to pick a wife from. The formalities had been completed, the girl had moved into Cecilia's house and worked for her for five months and then the young couple had been sent down to live in a hut near Herabo's cows. It had not worked out well. Cecilia said that Richard was too young to take responsibility for the cows. So Jean-Pierre and Richard had switched houses and now Richard was living near Cecilia and Herabo while Jean-Pierre took care of the cows.

Maria had borne a daughter at Nyanya hospital. Cecilia had accompanied her and taken care of her there. According to Cecilia, the labour had lasted a week and the delivery had been difficult. It is hard for me to believe that a hospital would have allowed labour to go on that long without a Caesarian, but I never checked the records and don't know if this is what really happened. The child could not cry, feed, nor open her eyes for almost a month but was fed through a tube. When it continued to have trouble, Cecilia blamed an event during the mother's pregnancy: Maria had travelled to another city and seen a monkey and that's why her child now behaved like a monkey, not like a human.

Richard had also fathered another child in the village. A teacher had moved in from another clan area to teach in Sengi village school. Richard had taken a liking to his daughter. Herabo, however, had been very angry at this affair and had forbidden him to take a second wife. Herabo, as the father of the culprit, had to pay damages to the girl's father and maternity fees for her delivery. Cecilia was however looking forward to keeping the child once she was weaned. Because Herabo had paid damages and a cow for the child, his family was able to keep the child and Cecilia would be the guardian.

Tajeki, now sixteen, did not go to school any more because she looked like an adult and teachers made fun of girls with full grown breasts. About ten men had asked to marry Tajeki, but Cecilia and Herabo had refused after careful consideration of each case. Years back, Cecilia had told me that the only requirement for Tajeki's husband would be that he brought the bridewealth. But now it was evident that there were other considerations. Many of the suitors were drinkers or gold diggers. While gold digging was now legal and profitable, Yenyabo people did not accept it at all. They said that one neglected fields if one spent time digging gold and it was not good for a wife to have a husband away digging. Tajeki had already gone through the *lingana* or viewing ceremony once, which was interpreted by the Fofu as almost a certain marriage. However, Cecilia and Herabo had cancelled the marriage arrangements after the ceremony when new information indicated something negative about the groom. On my first visit to Yenyabo that summer, Tajeki was guarding rice fields from birds, apparently oblivious to her parents' plans.

Rozalin, age thirteen, was in grade five now. She was a well behaved young girl, always looking down when I glanced at her. Once when I arrived in the village after a long walk and no adults were at home, she opened the door to the living room curtsying to me and left right away, since children were not supposed to keep adult guests company. Later on when Cecilia came home and made coffee, Rozalin had to walk past me to the cupboard to get some cups. When passing me, she curtsied, then took the cups and exited not to disturb me. A Fofu man served as my informant and kept interpreting her movements to me and later Cecilia and I discussed the etiquette of children. That was when I learned the rules about the use of eyes, which I should have known from my first visit!

Rozalin now knew how to cook and I often saw her at that task in the kitchen. On my previous visits, the girls had helped pound and clean rice, but they had not prepared a whole meal alone.

Kato refused to guard his father's rice fields and his refusal was accepted. So Tajeki, Rozalin and some boarding children alternated in doing it. I observed that Kato had kept his special status as the youngest, pampered child and a twin.

Herabo no more preached but he ran the same businesses as before, except that now he also sold planks of wood from the trees he cut down in the forest. Richard told me that he helped his father to supervise the work.

On numerous visits I acquired much information. I seemed to get deeper into the customs of the Fofu and their underlying meanings. Conversation generally progressed more easily and naturally, without an effort. I was surprised myself and wondered why. First, I had done the ground work of establishing human relationships which is the most arduous and lengthy process and now at last I could reap the benefits. Secondly, I was now an old friend returning to the village, so I was appreciated more after my absence than before. The villagers were eager to talk to me. Thirdly, while away from the Fofu I had been able to view them more objectively and in addition, I had done more studying, so perhaps I knew better what to ask. Finally, I had no pressure to accomplish anything this summer, so I was relaxed. Doing anthropology was great fun!

I had visited Yenyabo several times before Cecilia started to tell me about her relationship with her husband. Henry, Cecilia and I were walking to Cecilia's from a wedding feast not far from her house. Most of the village had gathered at the groom's home and they were to stay there all night. We were walking in single file on a narrow path surrounded by high elephant grass. Cecilia who was in front suddenly turned around and asked me very seriously,

"Did you notice that *mwalimu* did not sit with the church elders any more?"

I nodded, Herabo had sat among other men, not the "dignitaries." Cecilia poured out the news,

"He has left the elder's work and the church, he has secretly married another woman, and now there is no peace in our house. Look at my hand . . ."

Cecilia stopped and stretched her hand out. Henry almost knocked us over because we had stopped suddenly.

"Look, *mwalimu* beat my hand so bad that bones broke," Cecilia showed me how one of her fingers was twisted. Then she told me quickly the string of events. I could not quite grasp the details because she spoke fast and with vehemence. I only understood that Herabo was running after a terrible woman (not legally married to her), that Cecilia had then gone to her home village, and Herabo had come to get her back. She was only sleeping at her marital home because her children cried if she was not there, but there was no harmony at home.

She looked sad and old at forty, shrivelled, without the spark she once had. We did not have time to talk more then, but on other occasions she told me more about what had happened. The next time I was at Cecilia's I was sitting in her living room with Richard and a young teacher. Cecilia was serving us tea and pineapple. The teacher was telling me about the beginning of the Yenyabo school when Cecilia flared up and joined our conversation,

"Now, the very first teacher, the first teacher, was the Lelo girl. She seduced my husband with the help of her mother! She came here from Nyanya after having an illegitimate baby. Her mother was with her and was an excellent evangelist, an excellent evangelist, indeed. Oh, did she ever speak beautifully to the sick, to the sick! She walked around in the villages and preached the gospel. But when she arrived in a house she started whispering to the husband, whispering to the husband, in order to turn his heart from his wife to her daughter, 'Your wife does not know how to cook.' Then she served the husband coffee with b-r-e-a-d (bread being special in the village) by kneeling down before the man, kneeling down before the man." Cecilia knelt down in imitation of the woman and she put on a humble smile on her face. Richard and the teacher were laughing heartily. "The husband's desire for his wife's food is gone, is gone, that food is too simple."

I turned to the teacher and asked if Cecilia's description was true. He stared at me blankly and did not answer. Cecilia interpreted his silence to me,

"He cannot comment because he is my husband's close relative."

I marvelled at her ability, typical of the Fofu, to take politics into account when judging people's words. The young teacher did not comment on this either.

I asked if the girl had been a good teacher. Again Cecilia hurried to answer that she never taught anything because Herabo hung around her during school hours. The children went home because she turned her back on them to talk to Herabo through the windows.

Herabo had spent some nights at the girl's house before bringing her to Richard's house, who had to move elsewhere. At that point, the church elders had kicked the girl out and told her that she was not allowed to stay in the village. Herabo had built himself a house at Nyanya and settled the girl there. Then she had been moved from one village to another, and finally to Lemura. Herabo had tried to set up a fishing business in one of the places she was teaching, but had lost his boat and nets. Now Herabo frequented Lemura denying that he had any other women, but Cecilia knew different and there was no harmony in the house.

"I want to go home, go home," Cecilia moaned with exhaustion but then perked up to add that first she would buy some fish for Maria because she was weak and could not carry much to the market. After that she would go to her home village. My head was spinning with all the moves Herabo had allegedly made but I hung onto the bit about buying fish because I was going to Lemura after that week with Henry. I accordingly invited Cecilia to come with me to Nyanya the evening before our trip, stay over night at our home and go with us to Lemura the following day. There she could buy fish for Richard's wife. Cecilia became interested in the plan. We would have fun in town together.

The day before the planned trip. I drove to the village and spent the day there talking to many families as usual. Before leaving I stopped by Cecilia's house. She confirmed our plan but then Tajeki arrived from the fields with a message from Herabo: she was not to leave because he had two men from Lemura as business guests to buy planks from him and she was to cook a meal for them.

"Richard's wife knows how to cook," Cecilia said and went to get her wallet. Unfortunately, Herabo had hidden it. Cecilia told me that she would come to Sezabo in the morning and meet me there. Her children would help carry her bag of potatoes on the bicycle.

Sofia came to see me at Nyanya that evening. She too was going to Lemura with us to sell a basket of mangos in the market. When she heard that Herabo had not let

Cecilia come that day she predicted that he would not let her come the following day either.

"Herabo is a very bad man, very bad man. He and Cecilia have been fighting a long time, trying to hide it from outsiders but the villagers know it, know it." Then she changed her tune, "But Herabo is a good man too; when my child died, he gave me a coffin to bury her. Herabo has always been helpful to the villagers. He is a good man but he has only departed from God." Then she added a promise, "I'll pray that he will return to God." I did not know if it was a cliche or if she intended to do so.

Sofia was ready first thing in the morning. On the way to Sezabo she predicted again that Cecilia would not come. I insisted on waiting for her at the agreed place. We waited and waited. Sofia told me,

"I know Herabo, he will not let her come." I had to insist on waiting a little longer, Herabo had always been so jovial in my presence that I could not believe he would actually prevent Cecilia from coming. No Cecilia came however, nor did any other women from Yenyabo. We decided it was time to go if we wanted to accomplish our tasks in town.

We spent the day in Lemura doing our errands. On the way home somewhere between Lemura and Sezabo, we spotted Herabo with his bicycle on the roadside. It was raining and he had a flat tire. We took him, his bicycle, and his load of fish to Sezabo for which he was very grateful. He told us that he had helped carry Cecilia's potatoes to Sezabo that morning but that they had arrived too late, I did not know whether to believe him or not. Cecilia denied it when I checked with her later. The next time I saw her at Nyanya market I invited her for a meal at my house. She told me that Herabo did not want her to go to Lemura lest she met his mistress. Cecilia had told him many a time to bring the girl to Yenyabo as an official wife so she could help hoe the gardens. But Herabo denied having anyone.

Just before our two months were over Cecilia agreed to come and spend a night at my house. I was so happy to have her for the first time, after countless nights I had spent in her house. Kato came along too. She had not dared to announce her intention to stay over night at Nyanya but pretended to leave only for the Nyanya market. Rozalin would have cried had she known that her mother would not return and that's why Cecilia had told her that she would be back at night. I realized that mothers did this to the children all the time to make them feel good at the moment.

Kato became restless while we were chatting and asked to go to the washroom. I showed him ours but he looked terrified at the white man's toilet and wanted to go to a Zairean style outhouse. I had to think fast to remember where the nearest one was and gave him directions, I could see that he was in agony by then.

The house that we were living in had only waterbeds. We did not mind them but Kato was again afraid. He said that it was like a lake. Cecilia insisted that they would be all right. At night there was a thunder storm and I went around the house closing all the windows. I knocked at her door apologetically and told her that the window should be closed. She had made a bed for herself and Kato on the concrete floor by putting her wrap-around cloth under her. I did not say anything, only hurried to close the windows, but I was disappointed that I could not offer her a "proper" bed.

When we departed, her future seemed uncertain. I was going to return in a year to do the fieldwork for my doctoral dissertation but she did not know if she would be at Yenyabo or Gangu, her childhood home. As I had visited her relatives in Gangu I knew where to find her in either case.

On the last morning, Henry took a picture of us three together, Kato, Cecilia and me, in front of a huge flower bed in our yard. During the year in Canada, I sometimes looked at the beautiful picture wondering how Cecilia was doing.

PERSEVERING CECILIA

When I arrived at Nyanya in 1985, I immediately heard about Cecilia from several people. Although her future had seemed gloomy a year before I had not expected it to be as bad as it was. It was a horror story and Cecilia had almost lost her life.

I met her after a week, when she came to the Nyanya market to sell manioc and sweet potatoes. She confirmed the stories and told me all about it when she came over to my place for lunch after finishing selling her garden produce. I noticed again, as many times before, the Fofu capacity of talking about their own disastrous situations with detachment.

During the past year her relationship with her husband had deteriorated and there had been much fighting. Herabo had ripped up most of her clothes, including the ones she was wearing in the picture of the previous year, which I brought for her now. He had had affairs with village women, including Katarina, who had been one of Cecilia's trusted friends. Cecilia was so angry that she created a scene by beating Katarina in public. I could not but think of the time when these two women had joined together and beaten Henrietta. . . . Finally, Herabo had brought a new mistress into Richard's house but the church elders had chased her away. Cecilia was so fed up that she wanted to go to the village where she was born and the church elders gave her permission to do so. When she was at her father's place, Herabo came humbly to fetch her home, as Fofu husbands were supposed to do. Cecilia was so mad that she would not return to her marital home. Herabo made three futile trips and on the fourth one he was determined to show that he was serious: he refused any food and slept on the ground outdoors. He also promised to pay a goat to her father to soften his heart towards him. These were all signs of a humble, repentant husband. Finally, Cecilia had returned to Yenyabo in February 1985.

In May, Herabo had visitors, a young woman with her mother and sister who stayed as guests. Cecilia was hosting them as a dutiful wife should do. After a while,

Herabo let them live in one of his houses and told them to guard his fields. He told Cecilia that he was glad that someone was there to frighten wild animals and thieves away. Cecilia had no knowledge then that the young woman was her husband's new mistress and that Herabo had given her and her relatives the right to eat food from the fields Cecilia had cultivated.

One day in June, Cecilia went to her fields to get some sweet potatoes. While she was digging them up the young woman appeared and asked,

"What are you doing, doing?" Cecilia did not answer because it was obvious what she was doing. The woman repeated her question but when she received no answer she went to get her mother and sister. Cecilia saw them coming with pestles but did not pay attention to them. Suddenly the women said,

"Let's kill her, kill her!" and they started beating her. Cecilia was so surprised that she did not resist at all and soon lost consciousness. When telling me about it, Cecilia compared herself with Jesus: both were innocent, had no fault, and both suffered.

The commotion caught the attention of an old woman at a neighbour's. She had heard the women talk about killing and had run to see what was going on. The women attacked her, too, but her screaming attracted more people who were working in their fields near by. Soon a group of people gathered and the women were subdued. Everybody thought that Cecilia was dead because she did not react to anything and they carried her body to the chief's place in Sengi. There she moved when cold water was thrown over her and one of the women hurried to make tea for her. She was then carried home where her body swelled three times its normal size and her eyes were closed with swelling. Now, three months later, she had a black scar under one eye, one tooth was missing, and one of her knuckles was huge.

The day after the beating, Cecilia's sons Jean-Pierre and Richard, and Herabo's brother's oldest son found the three women and beat them the same way as Cecilia had been beaten. In addition, the young men took the faeces of the women and smeared their eyes, faces and mouths with them. The young men were pleased with themselves, Cecilia was very proud of them, Herabo thanked them, and the whole village praised the young men for their just deed. That was the end of those women in the village. Cecilia laughed contentedly when telling me about the youngsters and added that a woman who had adult sons had it made!

The village was outraged by Herabo's behaviour. Taking a legal second wife was all right but taking a secret mistress was not. Furthermore, Cecilia had a right to her fields. The chief inspected the site of Cecilia's beating, i.e., where she had been digging potatoes, and declared that it was in one of her own fields. Everybody considered the beating to be Herabo's fault. He could not prevent his legal wife from using her own fields and he had no right to give them to a mistress. A legal second wife would have been a different matter. In pre-colonial times, the matter would have been handled privately between Cecilia's and Herabo's lineages. Now in the post-colonial era, it was taken to a formal court in the zone. Herabo was ordered to pay three cows to the judge and one to Cecilia's family. I never heard anyone mention if the women or Herabo's sons had to pay anything for causing bodily pain to others.

Cecilia's family were very angry with Herabo and threatened to kill him if she died. They repeatedly asked her to live with them, saying she had no obligation to stay with a husband like that. But Cecilia did not go.

Everybody's sympathies lay with Cecilia and church people flocked to her house to comfort and give support to her. Eventually she got better and told Herabo that it was best to terminate the marriage, but Herabo refused. He said that it was only Satan that had made him do such things and he would turn over a new leaf. He did in fact repent in front of the church elders according to the custom of the church. The elders then told Cecilia that she should try to continue the marriage, since Herabo had repented, and see what happened. Nobody outside the church believed in the sincerity of his repentance and Cecilia's family declared that she would be a fool to stay.

Cecilia, however, decided to stay — she would persevere with the marriage. She believed that it was God's will because the church elders had told her to do so. She was comfortable with her decision although it made her family mad and other people shake their heads in disbelief.

"Every person has his own grave, own grave," Cecilia said repeatedly. I was amazed at this statement of individuality in such a communal culture. Cecilia added that God would judge each person individually and she felt that her decision was right for her.

That not all church elders thought alike, was proven by the fact that Nyanya church elders approached Cecilia and told her that if she ever wanted to, she could move to Nyanya and the church would find her a house in which to live.

Her fate brought her increased popularity but without the envy which was the cause of much tension in Fofu villages. No one wanted her role, that was for sure. She was so well known that she never had any trouble selling her garden produce in the market and she finished her bags before any other women, as she had done earlier that day. I had arrived at the market just as she was putting her sweet potatoes and manioc in tiny piles on a burlap bag on the ground. I tried to chat with her but customers kept coming and interrupting. So I left and told her to come for lunch when she was finished. She had three full bags and she sold them in a couple of hours. The other Yenyabo women were still trying to get rid of their produce while Cecilia was now happily lunching with me. She believed that her friendliness and interest in people made her successful in addition to God's blessing. It was true that she was friendly and kind to everyone and had a personal word for each customer, but I think that her unfortunate experience also made people sympathetic towards her. She had become a celebrity.

I never discussed the matter with Herabo. I assumed he would not want to and so I pretended to know nothing about it. He was as jovial and hospitable towards me as before. Cecilia told me, however, that he did not give her any money to run the household or to buy clothes but she managed with God's help and by busying herself with trade. Surprisingly, when I came to visit, Herabo gave her money for hospitality. Cecilia used that money to buy necessities from the market. She bought herself clothes with the money I gave her for my keep.

During my last year of fieldwork, I did not hear any more talk about new mistresses and affairs. Perhaps Herabo was coming round to the idea of taking a legal second wife.

There had been another disappointment for the family during the year of my absence. Although I had thought that Tajeki was oblivious to the marriage proposals rejected by her parents, she in fact, became frustrated and took the matter into her own hands. One day, unexpectedly, she eloped with Herabo's shepherd and went to live with him in his clan area, about 10 miles from her home village. Cecilia sent Tajeki's brother, Jean-Pierre, to investigate and he returned with the news that Tajeki was dirty and hungry and lived in misery. Cecilia sent him back to bring her home. She was pregnant and Herabo was furious. He declared that he would never accept any bridewealth produced by her and she would only enter his house over his dead body. So Cecilia sent her to live at Jean-Pierre's house.

When Tajeki's labour started, Jean-Pierre accompanied her to the Nyanya hospital. On the way there the baby was born. Tajeki cut the umbilical cord herself but the placenta stayed in. With Jean-Pierre's help she continued to the hospital where she had to stay several weeks because of the complications. Her abdomen swelled and she needed a blood transfusion. Cecilia had recovered from her beating enough to take care of her in the hospital. There were some other Yenyabo women who were looking after their daughters-in-law in the maternity ward at the same time, so Cecilia and Tajeki had company for the meals.

Cecilia told Herabo that Tajeki's troublesome delivery was caused by Herabo's curse over his daughter. The church elders tried again to mediate and bring father and daughter closer together. Eventually, Herabo saw that he might lose her forever and apologized. When Tajeki was better she apologized for shaming him and spoiling her chances of a good marriage, i.e. one producing substantial bridewealth. Tajeki moved back home and all seemed to be forgiven, although I once heard Tajeki tell some church elders that she still had a little bitterness in her heart toward her father.

At seventeen, Tajeki no longer looked like a young girl but more like a middle aged woman, with her plump figure and huge breasts. She carried her baby on her back and played with her. Cecilia let the baby suck her breasts to pacify her and the baby was calmer with her than with her own mother. Rozalin and Kato helped Tajeki with child care by holding the baby or running errands for Tajeki. I asked what chances there were of Tajeki marrying. Cecilia said that right then no men would want her because the baby was so small but when it could stand, men would ask to marry her. Such men would be those whose first wives had not borne any children, because they could be sure that Tajeki was able to bear children. Mature men who could not afford to marry earlier would also consider marrying her.

Another development during my year away was that Jean-Pierre had built himself a house further away from his father's house. He was no longer guarding his father's cows although he spent quite a lot of time in his father's house. Many a time I saw him and Richard eating at Cecilia's, joking and laughing with their mother and siblings. If I needed help to transport my suitcase, Cecilia always told Richard to help me. He obeyed her like a lamb. He was strong with big muscles and peddling my suitcase to Nyanya was no problem for him while I walked behind him admiring his youthful appearance.

A year ago, before leaving Africa, I had heard rumours that Richard's baby was not developing normally. By now it was obvious that the child was permanently disabled. At sixteen months she could neither sit nor crawl and still only took her mother's milk. Her head was covered with bed sores because she could not move at all. Rozalin and Kato helped carry and care for the baby. Cecilia had suggested that Richard's wife take Richard's illegitimate child, who had developed normally, to her house, but she had refused. She claimed to be satisfied with her own infant. I was sure the little one would die if Maria became pregnant again because it could not eat.

One day while spending a week at Cecilia's, she was going to harvest beans in her distant fields. I wanted to see those fields and prepared to go with her. It was going to be a fun day for us. I saw her packing a sheet and a pineapple. Cecilia's daughters-in-law and a couple of female day workers came along, too. Richard's wife carried her baby on her back because it could not have survived a long separation, but Jean-Pierre's wife left her children in Rozalin's care at home.

It took us two hours to walk to the fields which had been carved out of the rain forest. Cecilia explained that such virgin fields were far more fertile than the Yenyabo fields which had been in use for a long time. Cecilia paid some Mbuti Pygmy women, who had a permanent camp at the edge of the forest, to help with the harvest: the wages were bundles of beans. So we harvested the beans to the rhythmic chanting of the Pygmy women. Fofu women did not sing when working. I have to admit that by 10:30 I had wilted under the sun and had to go in a small mud hut near the fields and have a rest while the other women continued to work. Cecilia had anticipated this and had spread the sheet on the bed for me and left a cut pineapple for me to eat! I felt ashamed of my weakness but I could not help it. The two hour walk and two hours' work in the fields had finished me until I had lunch which Cecilia had cooked for me. After lunch the women brought the beans where I was and I helped to husk them. On the way back home, the women carried loads of beans, rice, and firewood, while I carried only my notes and water bottle, which became lighter the closer we came to home. That day was a practical lesson for me in how arduous an apparently simple task of harvesting beans could be.

A less exhausting way of learning Fofu values was by observing the interaction between Herabo's family and their visitors. One day, there was excitement when someone spotted a red pick-up truck far away in the savannah on the way to Yenyabo.

"Mugegere is coming, Mugegere is coming!," the children yelled excitedly. The villagers recognized every vehicle from afar since vehicles were still a rarity. I was curious to see this "Mugegere," which was a name of an ethnic group further north. The pick-up truck roared and rattled up the hill and stopped at Herabo's. Two men got out, of whom one was obviously the owner. He was a bald man with some teeth missing and wore a leather jacket. He behaved as if he owned the whole world, talking in an assertive and loud voice and looking around with authority. There was much commotion around him. People from other houses ran to see him, the children stared at him whispering, and Herabo talked in falsetto, excited by the honour of receiving such a distinguished guest.

It was Sunday morning and I was writing my notes in Herabo's living room, when the guest entered with his adjutant and Herabo trailing behind him. So I had an excellent opportunity to observe what was happening. Whatever the man said, his adjutant agreed and repeated the latter part of the sentence. After a while the man expressed the purpose of his visit: he asked for permission to bring one of his ten wives, her children and about 30 cows to Yenyabo. He came to Herabo because he was the president of the local cattle owners' association.

I was fascinated by the size of his family and asked him more about it. He explained that he had 40 children. I inquired if it was a common custom among the Gegere to have ten wives. Herabo turned to me, explained that it was a pan-African custom, and after a while added that the Christians took only one wife. The Mugegere man corrected Herabo,

"But I, too, am a godly man. I fear Satan and God." Then he added, "I am only joking."

I asked him, "Does one need to fear God?"

"Yes," he answered simply.

"Why?" I persisted.

"Because he punishes when you do wrong."

"How does he punish?" I asked.

"He burns us in a fire in the end," he said and laughed.

I bombarded him with these questions because I was in the process of investigating the influence of Christian teaching on Fofu thought and actions. I was coming to the conclusion that they knew the teaching by rote but that it did not have much internalized meaning among them.

Changing the subject I asked him if he knew the names of all his children. He said that sometimes a child had to come very near before he recognized him. He bragged that he had enormous tuition fees to pay, high piles of exercise books to buy, and had to have lots of clothes made each fall. Herabo and the others listened spellbound.

Next I inquired if his wives got along with each other. He answered simply,

"If they don't they better return to their fathers."

He gave the impression that he ruled his house with a rod of iron. Herabo tried to joke and stuttering in a falsetto voice he said,

"It is a-a-a-a-amazing, amazing that that th-th-that that, if it be God's will, God's will, even one wife, one wife, is like the s-s-s-spout of a t-t-t-teapot and she is able to feed l-l-lots of guests, lots of guests."

The Mugegere went on to brag about his many businesses: a saw mill, coffee plantation, ranches, and gold digging. Herabo fawned on the man and praised him excessively.

After my interrogation, he returned to the purpose of the visit. Would he be able to move into the village? Herabo was in a bind: he badly wanted to please the man but there was a shortage of pasture land. The pastures would support 5000 cows and there were about 6000 using them now. The cattle owners were scared of overgrazing.

"Never mind, God will show you new pastures," the Mugegere comforted.

His remark amused me because it was so typical. The Fofu always referred to God as giving life and sustaining it. I concluded from my research that their concept of the Christian God was greatly influenced by the idea of the Fofu traditional God, Mbali, whose role was almost exclusively that of the creator and sustainer of life. Everyone was thought of as living from the force of God. However, I thought that no God could provide them with enough grass if they kept on accepting outsiders.

Herabo promised to take the man's petition to the association meeting and discuss it also with the chief who was ultimately in charge of the land. Then he asked if the man had recovered from his car accident of earlier that year.

"God left my wit, that is what counts. Everything will be O.K. if only the wit stays intact. I have my life force and I want to take more wives and bear more children."

Some time later I heard that the man had been granted permission to move his wife into the village and he was building a cattle camp for her. His camp was to be somewhere in the savannah away from the village. Herabo told me that the man would be the very last to be allowed to move in, anyone else who requested permission would be refused. I asked, if they were not afraid of the shortage of pastures, to which Herabo replied simply,

"The world is God's."

Cecilia told me a few months later that the Mugegere had asked to marry Rozalin. Herabo and Cecilia had seriously considered the possibility. If they had known one of his wives they could have been sure that she would be well supervised and looked after. But since they did not know any of his huge family they thought it was unsafe to send Rozalin to him. She was so young and inexperienced in housekeeping that she would have needed good supervision. I did not say anything but I was glad they had not given their sweet little fourteen-year-old daughter to this boasting man who could have been her grandfather! Here I obviously had my cultural bias.

During the year, Herabo bought a pick-up truck for himself. He did not know how to drive or to take care of it but hired a driver-mechanic from Nyanya. I happened to know this man and talked to him about his work. Herabo got him to drive the pick-up as a bus between Nyanya and a village in the rain forest some fifty miles away. Such "buses," whose official capacity were ten people, were often loaded with thirty people plus their luggage and trade items such as sacks of charcoal, wood, flour, baskets of tomatoes, and fish.

Drivers were suspected of putting some money in their own pockets so Herabo sent Richard along both to learn to drive and to take the money. However, according to the driver, Richard had pocketed some money for himself and used it to buy alcoholic drinks. Herabo became angry with Richard when he found out and forbade the driver from taking him with him any more.

After a while, the truck broke down. The driver worked on it for a long time, bought spare parts, and got it running again. But the truck stayed put in the driver's yard because Herabo had not paid him. I suggested that Herabo would get money from his wood sales to pay his bill but the driver did not put much faith into it. He said Herabo did not get along with his workers and they kept stealing planks from him. I asked if Herabo could pay with his cows. The driver answered that he had none left. I never walked to Herabo's cattle enclosure to check if there were any cows so I do not know if this was true. I remembered, however, Cecilia telling me that Herabo had used his cows to pay for his clandestine affairs and illegitimate children. I had not taken her literally but perhaps it was true after all.

Cecilia had not seen my children for eight years as I had always come to the village without them since we had moved to Bululu. Whenever I visited the village, however, I had to give an account of them. Now Cecilia insisted that I bring the children to her house. She had a right to see them! So when the children had a long weekend off, they and Henry joined me in Nyanya and we all went to Yenyabo together. Cecilia had her wish come true.

Tom had been five and Tania two, when we moved away. Now they were thirteen and ten and they did not remember their friends any more. Cecilia showed us her old pictures of her with the children. In one of them she was cooking with one arm and holding Tania in the other. Now we took some more pictures of Cecilia and my children, and of Cecilia's and my children together. I knew she would save all the photos and reminisce over them in the future. She asked me to write to my parents and ask for their pictures, too. That I did and Cecilia was enormously pleased to have a complete set. As my parents had only briefly met Cecilia in 1975 it amazed me that she wanted their pictures. But on second thought I realized that her request reflected African collective thinking: a person is not regarded as an individual apart from one's family.

On one occasion during that year, Cecilia upset me very badly. It happened like this. She had heard that I was going to do fieldwork in Gangu and offered to accompany me because it was her natal village. We arranged a date and I notified Sofia in Gangu. The day arrived, I packed early in the morning, and waited in Nyanya for Cecilia. She was supposed to arrive with the women who were going to the market. At ten I went to the market; no Cecilia. As some Yenyabo women were there I left a message for Cecilia that I was waiting at home. Still she did not come. Finally, I sent a boy to the market and he returned telling me that Cecilia was there selling her wares. At sunset, I walked to the market and found Cecilia happily chatting with another woman with no intention of going anywhere.

"Let's go, Cecilia," I said to her.

"I can't come," she said. I was dumbfounded.

"Herabo told me I cannot go until I have finished harvesting the beans, harvesting the beans," she said and continued chatting.

I walked away furious. Why had she not let me know? My schedule was tight so to waste a whole day made it even more annoying. I did not appreciate then the Fofu custom of making a person feel good with a friendly promise which was never intended to be kept. Was I mad! I arranged the trip by other means and arrived in Gangu late when the moon had already risen. But I never told Cecilia how cross I had been.

Most of the time, however, I enjoyed being with Cecilia. I also enjoyed the evening talks with Herabo. Cecilia did not join us for meals because it was not a Fofu custom for a wife to eat with her husband. I, as a white woman, had the status of man in this case. When we were eating together we always philosophized. We talked about Fofu customs and values and Herabo asked me about my culture. He sometimes kidded me about it by saying something like,

"We Fofu pity you white people. You eat your supper at six in the evening. By the time you go to bed, go to bed, your stomachs are already empty and you toss restlessly, you toss restlessly in bed because you are hungry. We Fofu, we eat just before going to bed, just before the bedtime. Our stomachs are full and happy and we sleep calmly through the night."

I laughed and told him that our doctors thought our way was better but, of course, he thought our doctors were wrong.

It was Herabo who pointed out to me that the Fofu tradition demonstrated a balance of power between men and women. I tended to view Fofu society as very much male-biased. However, as he said, the men were in charge of the ancestors and the women in charge of the witchcraft. Both were respected because of the fear of what they might do if they became angry.

I asked him about the Sakana cult which was no longer practised and which I had read about in an old book. Sakana was supposed to have been a combination of all the ancestor spirits and its function was to control the morality of the village. Herabo had been introduced to Sakana when he was about fourteen years old, together with other village boys of his age. He remembered how they were blindfolded before the Sakana started biting, scratching, clawing, beating, and kicking them. It was so terrible that he almost died. Then they were unblindfolded and they saw that there was no Sakana, only the men of their lineage who had divided into two groups: those who attacked the boys and those who defended them. They were warned under the threat of death not to tell the women. It was the men's secret.

One evening there was another guest at the table. He was a soft-spoken man from the capital. To my surprise he was an army officer who was spending his holiday in the area. Herabo explained that the population disliked soldiers so much that no one would talk to him if he wore his uniform. I took my chance to ask him why the soldiers behaved cruelly. He calmly stated that people were so hard-headed that they would not learn anything unless they were treated harshly. Harshness was part of their job. Herabo then remarked,

"Soldiers are today's Sakanas."

This was a clever insight, which I had not thought of, although the two categories did have some differences. In the first place, whereas Sakana derived its powers from the moral consensus of the people the soldiers were imposed on the people by the government. Secondly, today's soldiers were believed to be corrupt while Sakana was not.

Another subject I raised with Herabo at one of our meals together was the traditional right of a younger brother to share the wives of an older one. When the older brother saw a spear stuck into the ground near the door he did not go in because he knew his younger brother was there with his wife. I tried to ask Herabo about it. He admitted that it had been a custom but it was heathen and now forgotten. He seemed to be ashamed of it. However, I thought that perhaps the present custom of having adulterous affairs all over the place — now that every one was a "Christian" — was more barbaric than the orderly sharing of certain wives without jealousy . . . Later I was to find out that Richard had an affair with his older brother's wife and Jean-Pierre was angry about it.

These philosophical meal times, therefore, often gave me an opportunity to raise a topic which puzzled or especially interested me. But we also discussed whatever subject the day's events led us to. Much about the Fofu was revealed to me which I would never have discovered if I had turned up with prepared questions. I appreciated Herabo as a host, friend and teacher.

During my second time in the village Cecilia suddenly said that she wanted to come and visit me at my home in Buva. I was surprised. Although she had once stayed with me at Nyanya, that was a small place and quite near her village. I had never managed to get her to visit me in a city. When I had lived in Bululu I had repeatedly invited Cecilia and promised her a royal welcome. Once I had got her to promise to come and I had arranged her a flight. To my great disappointment, she arrived at the airport late and missed the flight. Now she admitted deliberately missing the plane because she had been too scared to fly. This time she was ready to go.

I did not know if I was ready to receive her, however. Henry had recently moved to Buva and set up a household there but I had not even seen our home yet. On the other hand, this was my last chance to pay Cecilia back for her hospitality to me over ten years. I wrote to Henry and he agreed to arrange a flight for us together. Then Cecilia suggested that Kato should accompany her. At first I thought it was impossible because it ran to quite a bit of money but after counting my pennies I agreed.

Cecilia almost did not make it this time either. She and Kato arrived panting and sweaty just as Henry landed. Richard was somewhere behind bringing her bag but he was nowhere to be seen. Henry was upset that we were not ready because other passengers had to wait. Cecilia said,

"Let's go without the bag, without the bag." To me, a Westerner, it was unthinkable that a person could manage two weeks without a change of clothing. So I decided we should wait a while although the other passengers were restless — this was a special stop only for us. At last, Richard appeared dragging Cecilia's bag and we were ready to start our adventure.

Kato, Cecilia and I shared the back bench in the airplane, a two-engine Italian Partenavia. Cecilia and Kato held hands to give each other moral support. They were curious about everything they saw. I asked Henry to fly over Yenyabo so they could see their home from above, which made them giggle. Cecilia recalled her first flight with me and some other village women ten years ago when we had flown over Yenyabo. Then we entered an area about which Cecilia had only heard stories. She kept asking me where we were. There was the village where Richard's wife's parents were now living, there were the Rwenzori Mountains, Lake Edward, and the volcanoes of which I had told Cecilia. Then we flew over Bululu where I had lived for four years; then we were again above a lake. Our flight lasted two hours and she and Kato had great fun from beginning to end. When we arrived at Buva Cecilia told me that she had no identity papers. I was very frightened because that could cause trouble. The national officials were strict about permits to travel, even to transport a chicken between two villages. Cecilia went confidently to the office with me, and I tried to explain her breach of the rules. For some reason, the official was not interested in the lack of papers and let us go without penalty or bribes.

Cecilia had mentally prepared herself for this trip so well that she enjoyed every moment of it. She adjusted to the schedule of our family and ate three meals a day with us. Although she claimed in the beginning that Kato did not like meat, I kept on giving little pieces to him as I knew that in Fofu families the fathers ate the meat and the children had no chance to try it. Toward the end of their stay he was eating meat happily. This time Kato had to get used to the Western toilet because there were no Zairean ones in our compound. Kato and Cecilia shared a bedroom and a bed. Every evening I ran their baths for them and as I did so I thought of Cecilia, Tajeki and Rozalin carrying my bath water up the hill for a mile.

During their stay, I and my children enjoyed doing things with Cecilia and Kato. Sometimes we went to the market where Cecilia helped me to bargain. Now it was her turn to make observations about the strange life she saw. She compared Buva with her village and Lemura and kept on commenting about the differences and similarities. She would listen to people talking and spot those who were from her geographical area. I was not able to detect any difference in the way Swahili was spoken but she was. She also made friends with the Zaireans in our compound and spent time chatting with them. One day I asked her to help me make *bugali*, local food made of manioc flour and water, since Tania was extremely fond of it. Cecilia mixed it in a hot cooking pot which she set on the floor and held between her feet. I laughed thinking of Western health regulations in food preparation.

Our house was in an ideal situation overlooking a beautiful lake. Cecilia spent much time marvelling at the lake and the passenger boats which passed by. Kato joined my children in their activities and especially enjoyed the rides on the back of a motorcycle with Tom. Cecilia and I had a great time discussing all kinds of topics and I tried to use the opportunity to interview her on anything I might have forgotten before. Unfortunately, I fell ill with malaria and had to stay in bed for four days which was not pleasant. I was still weak when they had to return home. Tania and I went by car to see them off in Bululu where they were to take a mission plane back to Nyanya. Cecilia was pleased to see where I had lived before although I was not well enough to show her around very much. Our American friends invited us for supper and Cecilia and Kato saw their first television. In fact, while eating their dinner, they almost broke their necks trying to watch it in the adjacent room. It was also the first time they saw their president speak.

Cecilia was very courageous and did not worry about the complicated return trip; the little plane was to land on several small airstrips before reaching Nyanya. She waved good-bye and off she went with Kato.

When I saw her at Yenyabo a month later, she was beaming. She told me that the journey had gone well and everybody was asking her about Buva. The trip was something she would savour the rest of her life.

She soon came down to earth, however, as another scandal hit the family. I learned about it when I went to Yenyabo by bicycle to give a questionnaire to the school children. Afterwards I called at Herabo's house and found Cecilia hosting fifty guests of the chief of the neighbouring village. The yard between the house and the kitchen was full of people and I could not make out who everyone was. Cecilia came over to me and pointed out a young girl shyly standing beside Richard's wife,

"Have you met Jean-Pierre's wife yet?"

I looked at her in confusion, I did not know what was going on. The young girl bore an amazing resemblance to Jean-Pierre's wife but she was not her. Everybody was laughing and Cecilia explained,

"Now Jean-Pierre has two wives."

Jean-Pierre was nowhere to be seen nor was his first wife. I did not ask questions then, but when Cecilia walked me to the road on my way home she told me what had happened.

Jean-Pierre's wife was having several affairs with Nyanya men. At first he had forgiven her, but when she continued he became so angry that he beat her unconscious. When she came round she disappeared without trace. Cecilia thought she had gone to her parents. Jean-Pierre said he did not care about such a wife and he sent Herabo's sister to find him another one.

I asked why Jean-Pierre's wife had affairs. Cecilia answered me as best she could but she was convulsed with what I can only assume was nervous laughter, caused by her extreme distress.

"We black people, when we see money, money, we forget everything else. Money spoils us."

Then she continued, "She already has three wrap-around skirts, she didn't really need another one."

This reminded me of something I had been wondering about and I asked Cecilia,

"Do the men bother you, too?" She looked away and said,

"Yes they do but I don't let them." I did not know whether to believe her or not. The fact that she did not get any money from her husband made her very vulnerable to offers of money by men. Furthermore, it was the Fofu's view that every adult had the right to a sex life. If Cecilia's husband was not interested in her, would she really resist other men?

When I stayed in the village the last time, the first wife was still absent and the second wife was taking care of Jean-Pierre's children. An old man, Herabo's lineage member, gossiped some more about the affairs in the family. He told me that Jean-Pierre's first wife had also had an affair with Richard which was very bad, almost the same as sleeping with your father. His condemnation of the affair indicated that the Fofu had forgotten the traditional right of brothers to share a wife. In his view, Jean-Pierre had been wrong to beat his wife so hard. But maybe he said this only because his wife was a relative of Jean-Pierre's wife. The affairs seemed to be so tangled that I could not follow who was with whom, who owed a chicken or goat to whom, who was wrong and who was even more wrong.

When I looked around me I marvelled at how the Fofu could go about their every day tasks as if nothing had happened. The women walked to their fields and to the market with both serenity and determination. In the evenings, they cooked for their families. The men hoed their fields and strolled through the village with transistor radios tucked under their arms, as if nothing was amiss. Yet I knew, that they all experienced traumatic events in their lives. How could they cope with it all?

The last month of my fieldwork was hectic as I rushed from one village to another to complete everything. But whenever I passed the Nyanya market, I dropped by the place designated for the Yenyabo women and chatted with them for a while. Sometimes Cecilia was there and sometimes the other women told me that Herabo had forbidden her to come. On one occasion Cecilia took me aside and told me that her husband had asked her if he could take another wife.

"And what did you answer?" I asked.

"Fine. Take her so I get help with the fields, help with the fields," she said.

I was glad that Herabo had finally come to terms with himself and followed his cultural tradition rather than pretend to be something which he was not. Cecilia seemed to be happy about the decision, too. A legal second wife was no problem to her; what bothered her were the clandestine affairs which drained the family economy.

The day before our departure my children arrived from their school and we packed our luggage, weighing everything several times trying to keep within the weight limit. Fofu people came by to bid farewell and to receive their gifts from me. When it was already dark Cecilia came with Kato. They sat a little while and drank coffee with me. Then Cecilia told me that she must return to cook supper. Rozalin would be waiting for her at home. My tears started rolling. I had participated in her life events and I had liked her so much that parting was painful. I did not even try to hide my tears and Cecilia was very pleased that she was loved.

I wrote to Cecilia some months later from Canada and told her the news of my family. I had to wait a long time before I received a self-addressed letter which I had left with her. I knew that Kato had written it for her. It was brief, as most Zairean letters are, and did not give much information. After the greetings and some comments about my letter she wrote,

> "I am left alone at home. There are no girls left at home any more, both of them, Tajeki and Rozalin have married. I am alone at home with Kato and my husband. I remember your mother and your father, and you and your husband and your children and I am very sad, I miss you, very, very much. Kato is continuing his school very well, now he is on a holiday because the teachers are having their training day."

I had a thousand questions: Whom did the girls marry? Are they the first or second wives? What are their husbands like? How are Jean-Pierre and Richard? Does Cecilia have a co-wife? What is her relationship with her husband like now? I wrote a letter to her a few years ago but I have not received an answer yet. Perhaps she never received my letter.

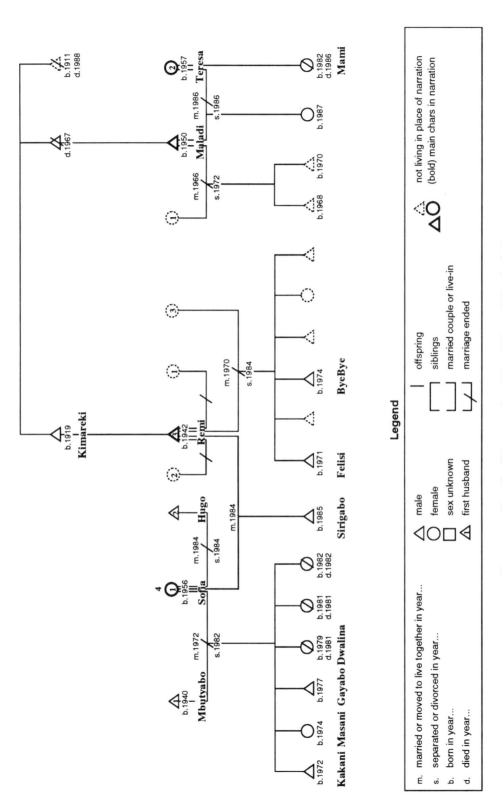

Figure 4.1 Family Diagram for "Two Wives Who Left."

4 TWO WIVES WHO LEFT

STILLBORN

Sofia lived at Yenyabo, six houses down the village road from Cecilia's. For the first few years of my visits to the village, I was not particularly welcomed in her house. In fact, the first time I went there in 1975, I was not even offered a chair, the significance of which became clear to me only years afterwards: it was a sign of rejection and I would have been wise to have left immediately. In ignorance of this, however, I chatted with Sofia's husband until I got tired of standing and talking. Over the years I felt I was received in a more friendly manner but there was always a distance between us.

When I returned to Africa in 1984 after a three-year absence, Sofia had left her husband and her marital village and her attitude to me had completely changed. Now she actively sought me and invited me to visit her childhood home and her sister's home; she joined me on my visits to Yenyabo and Lemura. When she remarried, she insisted that I stay with her. I could not quite understand this change from rejection to embracing friendship. Why had she suddenly overcome her uneasiness about me? Did she hope to gain some advantages by attaching herself to a white woman? She often referred to Cecilia, who had been invited to my house. I had also given Cecilia a piece of cloth. Perhaps Sofia hoped I would treat her to one, too.

Sofia was a person I could never trust. She would tell me one thing and then blurt out an opposite story to others half a minute later. She would invite me somewhere and when I was ready to go, she would cancel everything without a good reason. Although I was occasionally frustrated with her, I liked her, because she was friendly and enabled me to learn Fofu customs by observing her family. I especially admired her perseverance in starting a new life after disasters in her family, which would have left me depressed for the rest of my life. But not her!

From 1974 until 1981 Sofia lived with her first husband, Mbutyabo. He was a brother of the village chief and both of them drank excessively. The chief was said to wet his pants after drinking bouts but Mbutyabo did not have that severe symptom. When I passed by I used to ask where he was, as was the custom. At least once I knew that he was in another hut drinking, but Sofia told me he was working in his fields. His mud hut was in bad repair all the years I knew him and he patched the holes in the walls with grass instead of going to the trouble of muddying the holes. During the early years of our acquaintance, Sofia was not much at home when I passed by. She was said to be in the market, in her fields, or at the dispensary. I now wonder if these explanations were given to discourage me from dropping in. On the other hand, they could have been true, for Yenyabo women did criticize her for being out of the house too often.

Mbutyabo's old mother lived with the family after her husband died. She was a skinny old lady, dressed in rags, who limped and complained of pains in her hip and leg but worked diligently in a field near the house. Although she normally walked slowly, I saw her run once. This was after she had discovered someone had stolen sugar cane from her field. In her fury she ran from hut to hut telling the whole neighbourhood.

The villagers used to joke about the old woman's wish to get married. They thought it was funny that she had such a strong desire for a man that she would approach men assertively in the hope of getting one of them to marry her. Years afterwards, when Sofia's third husband's old father lived with her family, Sofia told me how frustrating it was always having to put up with her husbands' relatives. Only then did she admit that it had required a lot of self-discipline on her part not to answer back to the old mother of her former husband. She had been a senile, irritating person. As a daughter-in-law, Sofia had to be submissive and serve the old people humbly no matter how rude they were to her.

Once during the early years, Mbutyabo came to ask me to give Sofia a lift to the hospital because she had bad toothache. Sofia was sitting motionless on a stool with one hand on her cheek. By the time I was ready to go, the toothache had disappeared and she no longer wanted a lift. Villagers went to the dentist only for the extraction of aching teeth: nobody would "waste" money on fillings or other dental work.

Sofia had a hot temper and once the whole village was entertained by it. I heard many tell of this event. A goat of a neighbour had strayed into Sofia's field behind her house. When discovering some of her corn and manioc plants stripped of leaves she stormed to the neighbour's, blaming him for not taking care of his animals. The man was not willing to be told off by a woman and he raised his voice and a finger at Sofia. At that moment she could not care less about the respect a woman was expected to show towards all the men of her husband's village and she attacked the man with all her might. He fell down like a feather with the angry Sofia beating him up. Fofu women were strong after all the physical work they did, although most of them let their husbands beat them.

Sofia kept having children all through the years she lived at Yenyabo. When I became acquainted with them in 1975, Sofia and Mbutyabo had two children, a three-year old boy Kakani and a girl called Masani. The younger one was a year old and she was terrified of me. I wondered what they had been telling her about me. Later I heard that little children were told that the white woman would take them with her or eat them: horrible threats for a child. I remember that my son Tom had been very shaken as a three-year old when the villagers frightened him in a similar way ("We'll cut your ears off"). As Sofia continued to bear children, the youngest child, around its first birthday, always started fearing me. I was not happy about being a bogey woman for the family, but neither smile, nor peanuts nor candy helped the situation while the parents wanted to maintain the status quo.

Both Sofia and Mbutyabo had lived with other sexual partners before their marriage. Mbutyabo had lived with several women before taking Sofia as his wife, but the others had not borne him children. The woman previous to Sofia was actually legally married to someone else and Mbutyabo decided to let her go because her husband was dangerously jealous about her. And Sofia, while still living at home, had borne a son by a man who had paid no bridewealth for her. So her son had stayed with her father's family. Sofia mentioned him in a matter of fact way and did not offer any more information about her affair of long ago.

I was interested in ordinary household activities so in 1979 I spent twelve periods of 45 minutes at different times of the day observing the household activities at Mbutyabo's. I noticed that Sofia was at home six times and Mbutyabo was at home only twice. Their children Kakani, Masani, and Gayabo (born in 1977) were usually playing together in the yard, sometimes with other village children. When Gayabo saw me he would always walk into the house looking at me sideways and suspiciously. Kakani was at school a few times but he did not attend school regularly which was typical of Yenyabo children. Kakani and Masani were often taking care of their cuddly baby sister Dwalina (born in 1979) by holding her while the mother pounded corn, chopped firewood, or did other household chores. Masani, as a girl, was required to do more babysitting than her brother Kakani, but he was very tender to his baby sister. When no adults were present he acted as if he was in charge of his three siblings. When Sofia was around, she sent him or Masani on errands all the time,

"Go and buy palm oil!"

"Take this corn to the neighbour!"

"Go and get some beer for me!"

Sometimes he delayed in the hope that she might forget but she was persistent and he had to go. Once she promised that I would give him peanuts if he obeyed. Luckily — or maybe she had checked my bag — I had peanuts in my bag that day.

In 1980, Sofia quarrelled with her husband and went angrily to her home village with all her children. She stayed there for three months. The villagers were gossiping about her and Mbutyabo. Later that year she went to her home again and stayed three weeks. But it was to help her parents harvest rice and not in anger.

In 1981, when her youngest child was two years old Sofia was expecting another baby. The delivery happened when I was in Bululu but I heard about it during my following visit to the village. Sofia went to the next village, Sengi, which had a government dispensary with a *mademoiselle*, a Zairean midwife. Because Sofia was not in labour, although weeks overdue, the *mademoiselle* sent her home to wait, because the dispensary was full of patients. Sofia's labour started at home and she experienced difficulties. Her husband hurried back to the dispensary for the midwife.

She told Mbutyabo that her job was to help mothers at the dispensary, not to run around the villages. By that time Sofia was incapable of walking there. In desperation, Mbutyabo looked for other village women to help but they were all in their fields. So Sofia delivered a still-born baby alone: the umbilical cord was wrapped around his neck.

I saw her three weeks after the tragedy and was devastated by the news. I thought such things should not happen, something should have been done to prevent it. To lose a life like that seemed a needless waste to me! I could not understand the resignation of the villagers and Sofia when they talked about it. I now see that it was not as easy as they let me think. Although Sofia sighed then that it was God's will, this event was the beginning of strife between her and her husband, as in so many other marriages. Sofia thought that someone in her husband's lineage had caused this tragedy by witchcraft.

I chatted with her at her home just before moving away from Africa in 1981. She was still weak from the unfortunate delivery and was sitting by the door out of the sun. Sofia wondered where her husband was. I had seen him in another hut enjoying beer and told her so. She got excited and asked Kakani to run and get some beer for her too. "I wish my husband was here, I need him for something," she sighed. I suggested that she send word with Kakani for him to come home. Sofia did not like my suggestion, "It would not work. It would be very shameful for a wife to send such a message with a child in front of other people. But I do wish he was here." I could not understand her bashfulness in this situation when she could beat another man up in front of the villagers.

When I left Africa, I thought she would never bear other children after such a bad experience. I thought her life did not hold much in store for her. Little did I know what was going to happen.

Sofia actively sought me out when I returned to Nyanya for the summer 1984. All dressed up and with her hair braided she looked young and attractive. She was smiling broadly when she appeared at my house at Nyanya and I noticed that she had beautiful white teeth and an attractive dimple in her cheek. She was a little plump which was rare and coveted among the Fofu. At Yenyabo she had always been dressed in work clothes and been so busy with childcare and household chores that she had taken no time for herself. That day I was going to drive to Yenyabo to visit old friends and she said she would come with me. Before leaving we had a leisurely snack of bread and jam with coffee and I learned what had happened to her.

After my departure, Dwalina had died. Having coughed up blood she was taken to the Nyanya hospital but to no avail. Another time Sofia said that Dwalina had died of tetanus. I don't know if she really knew the cause of death.

Then Sofia had become pregnant again. She delivered her baby at Nyanya hospital but it died after a month and a half in the hospital despite a blood transfusion of Sofia's blood. She talked about the matter with detachment but I knew that it must have been an emotional event at the time.

She had fought with Mbutyabo so much that she decided to go home again. "I saw that things were not working out and I decided to leave Mbutyabo for good. You see what a drunkard he is anyhow. Ask his present wife and she will tell you what kind of a man he is!"

She had to leave her children with her husband because he had paid the full bridewealth for her. When I asked if she did not miss her children, she said, "Yes, I do, but then, what can I do when my husband has kicked me out of the house?" I never knew whether her husband had sent her away or she had left him voluntarily.

Sofia asserted that she would never marry again. She had had enough of men and she would live without them by hoeing her own fields in her father's village.

When we arrived at Yenyabo, we called on Cecilia. Having only just told me about her decision to live without men, she turned to Cecilia and bragged to her in Kifofu that she had a wonderful new husband. She did not even bother to explain this contradiction. When we later walked through the village, Sofia spent a long time telling a village woman that her new husband had a big new house with good furniture. The other woman seemed very impressed.

Sofia's children heard that their mother had arrived and they ran to her. "Come!" said Sofia to Gayabo, her youngest, and from that moment he was glued to her. He sat on her lap at Cecilia's and walked hand in hand with Sofia when we made our way through the village. It was a hot and sunny day and the little boy had beads of sweat on his forehead after walking with us. Sofia sat down on the roadside and wiped his brow. I was glad that Gayabo was not afraid of me any more. When it was time for us to leave the village, Gayabo's face twisted. He held on to his mother's hand tightly. Sofia spoke softly to him that she would come back again soon. The boy cried and nodded his head. The older children seemed to be adjusted to the absence of their mother. Their father's sister was taking care of them while their new step-mother was at her home village awaiting the death of her child from a previous marriage. The child was suffering from *kwashiorkor* (undernourishment caused by protein deficiency).

When I visited Yenyabo another time without Sofia, the villagers gossiped about her. Their version of what had happened was different from Sofia's. Her former neighbour explained that Sofia left the village because her husband drove her away accusing her mother of having caused Dwalina's death by witchcraft. Furthermore, he thought the stillborn baby was not his, although the neighbour herself thought it was. Sofia's children were present listening to this gossip without any expression on their faces and the neighbour made no effort to censor her speech because of them. Here I saw once again that Fofu children witnessed adult life without any "screening."

Cecilia criticized Sofia by saying that Sofia had been a bad wife but Mbutyabo a good husband. During the last year of her marriage in the village, she had gone to the market every day leaving her home and children uncared for. Her poor husband had to do the cooking and childcare. I doubted whether Cecilia's criticism could be taken literally, especially with regard to Sofia going to a market every day. I realized, however, that they were from different clans, so Cecilia would tend to speak ill of Sofia, especially if she wanted to show loyalty to her husband's village and his clan members.

I heard a third explanation for Sofia's divorce a year later. Sofia's contemporary husband Remi told me that her former husband had been suspicious of the body lotion I had given her and thought that Sofia was practising witchcraft with it. What? I was flabbergasted. Was I the cause of all the trouble? I had innocently given her a small bottle of lotion and this had caused furious fights between her and her husband, and finally divorce! For a while, I was afraid that I might get into trouble but neither Sofia nor her former husband seemed to bear a grudge against me. I wondered whether Sofia had told her new husband the lotion story just for fun.

Nor did Sofia appear to bear any grudges against her former husband, his relatives, and his new wife. I once walked by Mbutyabo's house when he was cutting grass in his yard. He greeted me with a friendly smile and said that Sofia had been very glad that I had visited her at Gangu. I gathered from this that they were on good terms and discussed their activities with each other. Another time Mbutyabo's sister told me that Sofia had given her a blouse as a gift. Sofia herself told me that she invited Mbutyabo's new wife for a beer whenever they met at market places. I saw that she went out of her way to erase hard feelings against her. This was clever of her; it meant that she could go and visit her children and they could come and visit her. It was also easier for her to start a new life without emotional baggage. And, I assume, she and the children were less likely to be the victims of witchcraft.

Sofia invited herself with us to Lemura when she heard that we were going to drive there one day. She brought two huge baskets of mangos with her which she asked us to drop at the Lemura central market for her. I had to smile at her manoeuvring. She was a good business woman; this way she did not need to pay any transportation fees. On the way home from Lemura, Sofia was holding her head complaining about malaria. It was through her headache that I became acquainted with her new husband.

The next day Sofia's new husband, Hugo, arrived at our door. He was a soft-spoken man dressed in a suit, the kind that office workers wore. Sofia was still suffering from her headache and she had sent him to get some pills for her. I thought that she had malaria and told him that I did not have very many malaria pills left; he should go to the hospital to get some. He explained in a smooth manner,

"The hospital requires money and I don't have much these days because we are not allowed to imprison people until after the elections."

I could not believe my ears. Here was a well-mannered, well-dressed man talking about the cruelties and injustices of Zaire as if they were normal procedures. He was apologizing — not for the injustices — but for not being allowed to perpetrate them now! We all knew that government officials imposed fines, accepted bribes, and imprisoned people whenever they needed money but that a person talked about it openly, as if it was an accepted procedure, really bothered me.

Hugo told me that he worked as a census officer at the Nyanya chief's office and he would show me the statistics of the region one day. I was very pleased because statistical information was hard to get in Zaire. I could make a dozen trips to the chief's office, only to hear excuses why it was not convenient for me to see the information that day.

I sent a few malaria pills for Sofia and Hugo bowed politely as he left. At that time, I felt sorry for Sofia because I thought she had a tendency toward malaria. Now I know better: she was probably suffering from a hang-over and a couple of Aspirins would have been much more appropriate to send back to her than malaria pills.

Hugo kept his word and showed me all the books I wanted to see and also let me copy the information. He had carried the books from his office, about seven miles away, to his house to show them to me. What courtesy!

I noticed that Sofia acted shy in the house, more like a guest than a hostess. This was very different from her behaviour at Yenyabo, but I thought that with a new husband, she had to behave in such a fashion. Cecilia, however, put me right. She was from Gangu, where Sofia was now married and I trusted that she knew. Cecilia told me that Sofia was not living with Hugo because his first wife could not stand her. He had taken Sofia as his second wife, or, rather mistress, without asking for the permission of the first wife, as he should have, and it infuriated the first wife so much that she had beaten Sofia up. Sofia was now living with her sister up the hill who was married to another man of the village. That explained Sofia's shy behaviour in her husband's home.

Sofia kept telling me how much her husband "needed" her and "wanted" her. I asked why and Sofia said proudly,

"Because I am a hard worker in the garden."

She told me that she was waiting for her fields to grow to the point where she would be self-supporting. Then she could have her daughter come and live with her for a while. She could not invite her now while she was living off her husband's fields.

One Sunday Henry and I went by motorcycle to Gangu to visit Sofia's parents in her home village which was not far from there. To our disappointment, when we arrived in Gangu, Sofia was waiting to tell us that it was not suitable to go to her village. Why had she invited us then? We were very upset. To make up for the disappointment, Sofia asked us to go with her to the market place on the mountain. Half-heartedly we drove up there. It was a huge market: a large open space in the village was so crowded with people and merchandise that one could hardly walk around. I met many women familiar to me from Yenyabo, Nyanya, and other villages. I also met Cecilia's sister who asked us to go and greet her father at home. So we drove to Cecilia's birthplace and met her relatives which was compensation enough for the trip Sofia had cancelled.

Another time, Sofia insisted that I visit her sister's house up on the mountain. I drove to Gangu by car and then walked up the path to the mountain. I spent the day at her sister's, where Sofia behaved like the hostess, leaving her sister and her sister's husband as minor characters in a play. She served me a big meal and acted as a tour guide telling me what was worth seeing. She arranged a meeting with a village chief and a tour to a gold digging site outside the village. As a good tourist, I took many pictures and brought them back to her a year later to take to the young men who were digging for gold. Sofia's brother-in-law rented rooms to gold-diggers. When sitting in the living room, we heard loud snoring from one of them. Sofia explained that one of the prostitutes was taking a nap before the evening and the return of the young men. Her snoring seemed to entertain the household.

Physically, it was a difficult day for me because I forgot to take drinking water along with me from home. After climbing up the mountain and walking around as a tourist in the hot sunshine, I was very thirsty. Sofia offered me water but I did not dare to drink it. I had suffered from intestinal amoebas several times before and did not want the experience again. Neither did I want to bother her to boil water for me. So I stayed thirsty. Sofia did not take offence at my refusal to drink her water but laughed and asked,

"What is there in this water that you fear, you fear?"

"We white people are such softies that we cannot take unboiled water without getting sick," I answered.

When walking in the village, I started asking questions about the tribal clash that had taken place in the village the previous year. Sofia hushed me up right away and when we came back to her sister's place she scolded me for being so stupid as to talk about the delicate issue in public. She walked around the house outside, came in and told me that her sister would have been killed during the clash had the attackers not been friends of her husband. Although he was not at home that night, they showed her mercy because of him. She said that many other women had been raped and killed, but I don't know if it was true because the deaths were never admitted officially. The national army had been brought in to calm the situation and by the time of my visit, everything seemed normal. It was unwise to discuss the matter, however.

The clash was a result of long-standing tension between the Fofu and the Lelo, stemming from the fact that when the Fofu arrived in the area in the distant past, they had conquered the land from the Lelo. The village was on the border of the two tribal areas: to the north, the area was occupied by the Lelo; to the south, by the Fofu. In this village, there were some Lelo living among the majority of Fofu, and there were a few mixed marriages. Apparently, the Lelo area was not sufficient for the growing population and that is why the fighting had broken out. Now people were carrying on their every day activities as if nothing had happened, although a similar attack could occur at any time.

Some time after my visit to the mountain village, Sofia came to my house. She had been looking for me the day before to ask me to transport her sick sister to the hospital. I was not at home and Sofia's relatives had carried her there by foot in a sling made out of a blanket. This was the sister who lived at her father's. Afterwards it dawned on me that perhaps she had been sick when I was to go to visit Sofia's parents and they did not want me to see her at that stage.

I felt sorry for her sister and asked what was wrong with her.

"She has trouble with her pregnancy, trouble," Sofia replied evasively.

"Is it a miscarriage?" I inquired.

"No. My dad is mad at my sisters-in-law because they are not helping with her situation at all, at all," she added. She explained to me that her sick sister's husband was in prison 200 miles away.

"In prison!" I exclaimed. Sofia belittled the gravity of the situation by saying that her brother-in-law happened to be guarding the collective money of a group of gold diggers when the cash was stolen and, unluckily for him, he had to go to prison. He had visited home a month ago and now her sister was sore from the pregnancy. Her casual voice calmed me down and I promised to come and see her later that day.

Cecilia dropped in that day, too, and we went together to the hospital. Sofia and her mother were arranging pots and pans near a bed where a young woman lay motionless. She opened her eyes and appeared to be in great pain, on the border of consciousness. Sofia and her mother looked worried; gone was the casual tone of voice. I did not know what to say but Cecilia chatted with the two for a short while, appearing to be fully at ease, and then said we had to go. We walked out quietly and when out of earshot, Cecilia analyzed her observations.

On the way to see the patient, I had told her Sofia's explanation. Now Cecilia compared her observations with Sofia's story. She had not seen any people from the husband's side in the hospital. If the pregnancy had been by her husband, they would have certainly been there. Nor did Cecilia believe in the husband's visit home. A man who was jailed in a far away city would never be granted parole. Cecilia happened to know that he had been there for three years already. And he was not accused of petty thievery either, but of a murder! Thievery was a matter for local courts, not regional ones. Cecilia had heard that the sister had many lovers and assumed that she was now pregnant by one of them. She must have tried to abort the fetus and became sick. In these circumstances her in-laws naturally did not want to help her.

Cecilia, like many others whom I observed, let a person present the front she chose to, as in this case Sofia presented her sister as a virtuous wife of an unjustly condemned prisoner, having troubles with her pregnancy. Yet Cecilia made her own independent evaluation. She was tactful enough to keep her thoughts to herself and let Sofia feel good about herself and her family reputation.

When my summer visit in 1984 ended I left Sofia and her family in the hospital not knowing how her sister would fare.

A MODERN MEDICINE MAN

About a month after my arrival for the final year in Africa, Sofia managed to find me. She was carrying a tiny baby on her hip in a sling. It was two months old, born at the Nyanya hospital. I assumed Sofia was still with Hugo and asked about him. Sofia told me that she had left him because his wife was too jealous of Sofia's plumpness. Soon after my departure, she had married another man, Remi, from Gangu and the baby was his. He had recently returned from a town, about 60 miles into the rain forest where he had grown up, although he was of the Gangu clan. His wife had borne him 12 children but left him because he stayed away on a gold transportation trip too long. Two of his children were living with him and Sofia at Gangu and respected her well. She told all this at one blow.

When I bent to admire her little baby, Sofia told me that he was born with four teeth and according to the Fofu custom, these had been pulled out.

"Why?" I asked horrified at the idea of someone putting dirty tools in a little baby's mouth.

"If you don't pull the teeth out, they will rot and the baby will die," Sofia said knowingly. Sofia had not asked white doctors to do it because she knew they would refuse. A relative had done it and the baby had become sick, lost weight, and cried a lot. He had been given injections and native medicine and was all right the day I saw him. I was appalled that the belief in the danger of teeth at birth had caused so much pain to the poor child. Sofia only seemed relieved that the supernatural danger of the teeth was over. Later she showed me the teeth which she kept at home in a worn-out plastic bag.

"What happened to your pregnant sister?" I asked, remembering that I had left her in a critical condition.

"She is fine. She had a baby during the past year," Sofia replied happily. I assumed that the pregnancy had gone full term but I did not ask for particulars because I was not supposed to know about the attempted abortion. Later I learned that this was not the case.

The other news was that another of Sofia's sisters, the youngest, whom I had met once on a trail with her mother, had been taken to the rain forest to marry someone there and Sofia's parents were well.

When Sofia came I was leaving for the Nyanya market and Sofia walked with me to the shops. She insisted that I go and greet a relative of Remi, her new husband. This relative was a church elder at Nyanya. Sofia informed me that Remi's family were Protestant whereas Sofia's family and her former husband were Catholic. I was studying the Protestant Christians at Nyanya, so I was glad to have Sofia introduce me to such a family. We went into a house built by the Protestant mission for its African staff. Although church elders were lay people and were not paid by the church, the church provided some of them with houses. As we entered I could hear our footsteps echoing off the concrete walls and floors. The building also had a tin roof which added to its "superior" quality in the eyes of the local people.

A woman was sitting with outstretched legs on a palm mat on the floor. She greeted us in a friendly way and then continued eating sweet potatoes and sauce made of manioc leaves from a bowl on the floor. Sofia appeared submissive in front of the old woman and kept her eyes lowered. There was a strong smell of urine in the house. Sofia explained to me that the woman was the wife of the church elder who was Remi's father's brother, or *baba mudogo* (little father). The wife had been paralysed from the waist down for nine years and had to be lifted up to sit. She could do no work. Her husband had to do everything for her, including garden work and housework.

Now that was a surprise to me! An African man doing women's jobs. Unbelievable! Sofia told me that most African men would have taken a second wife, especially because this one had not borne any children, but he did not because he was a church elder. Sofia said all this in front of the old woman who, of course, understood everything.

I thought this was insensitive. I had similar experiences later when Protestant pastors told me, in the presence of their wives, that "ordinary" Zairean men would have taken a second wife in their situation e.g., where a wife did not bear children or was incapable of working because of an ailment. On each occasion the wife did not react. I would have been embarrassed and in tears if I had heard my husband speak of such personal matters to a stranger but these women did not seem to mind. I wondered if the rules of their society were so clear in their minds that it did not bother them to hear them spelled out. I noted that their husbands did not brag about their Christian virtue of staying with one wife but stated it as a matter of fact.

While we were standing near the paralysed woman, her husband came to the yard from the field, threw his hoe in a storage room, and greeted us. He was an old man with grey hair and slow movements. It was hard to think that he kept the household going. Although stern, he had a humorous twinkle in his eyes, and a missionary commented to me later that he had a great sense of humour. This humour must have helped him survive his home situation.

Next, a teen-age boy came in and handed the old woman a glass of water, curtsying to her as he did so. Sofia told me that he was Remi's nephew who was living with his relatives in town. His true father was at Gangu and I would meet him there. Later I became well acquainted with him as I stayed in his home.

When we were out of hearing range, Sofia told me that the youngster had a tendency to steal. His brother had also lived here previously but had been kicked out of the house because he was a worse thief. I had an idea of thieves being tough looking people but the youngster I had seen looked as tame as a lamb, especially when curtsying to his "grandmother." During the year of my fieldwork, these brothers got into serious thieving, causing the old man terrible stress and shame as a church elder and making their real father at Gangu furious.

During the year I spent at Nyanya, I had to pass the old man's house on my way to the market. Often I saw the wife sitting at the door or in the yard in the sun and the husband spreading laundry to dry on the grass in the yard. I used to chat with them for a while as other passers-by did. I also interviewed both of them. When I left Africa, I kept in contact with Sofia at Gangu through the old man because unlike Sofia the mission had a post box.

I was looking for an additional village to do my studies in and Sofia wanted me to go and stay in her new village. I thought it would be as good as anything else. At first, she presented it as an invitation and then added demandingly,

"When are you coming to stay with us at Gangu?"

In fact I was glad to have an offer of a place to stay. I told her that I had work at Nyanya first but would certainly come in a few weeks.

After two weeks, she sent me a letter by Remi's son asking the same question. I sent back an answer giving a date and gave the shy boy a couple of bananas and pieces of candy to chew on his way back to Gangu, some six miles away.

Persevering Cecilia's story tells how she had promised to walk with me to Gangu the first time I went there and how the plan fell through. I also mentioned how angry I was at her for not letting me know frankly that she could not come. However, another acquaintance showed me the shortcut to the village and during the six-mile walk, I forgot my frustration and had a good conversation with my companion, better than we ever had when he was busy in his home.

Sofia came to the road side to meet us when she heard shouts through the village that her guest was coming.

"I thought you would not come when it was getting late," Sofia said holding her baby on her hip. "Now you have to go to bed hungry because I did not know whether to cook food for you." My stomach was groaning with hunger after the walk but I said in a Fofu fashion,

"I'll persevere, never mind."

Her husband, Remi, came to greet me. He was a sociable and friendly man with whom it was easy to talk. A crowd of children surrounded us in the yard and Sofia chased them aside so she could carry my suitcase into a neighbour's house.

"We don't have much of a house," Sofia apologised. Her husband had bought an old house from someone when he returned to his home village. He was slowly building a new house.

"Where are you taking me?" I asked as Sofia took my suitcase. She muttered that her husband's brother would accomodate me but she was planning to cook the meals for me.

I did not question her, I was only a guest, satisfied to have a bed under a roof. Although Sofia had not promised food that night, she brought me some and I was left alone to eat in her brother-in-law's living room by the light of an oil lamp. Then Sofia told me that my bath water was ready, and took me behind the house where a small pot of warm water was waiting for me. She stood next to me while I undressed and chatted with me all the way through my bath in the moonlight. I would rather have had company for meals and bathed alone, but what could I say as a polite guest? And the warm bath felt heavenly after a sweaty walk.

I kept up this politeness even when I realized that Sofia had arranged for me to stay in the house with her brother-in-law alone. He was called Maladi from the French *maladie* meaning sickness: apparently, there had been much sickness in the family before his birth. Anyway, Maladi was a divorcee and lived by himself. Sofia installed me in one bedroom and he was to sleep in another one behind the mud wall. He was a well-mannered middle-aged man and told me that he was always asked to host village guests for the chief because he had a guest room. I trusted that the villagers would view me only as one of those guests. With hindsight, I could well have requested a couple of Remi's children to sleep in the living room to protect my reputation in a society where the spheres of men and women were strictly segregated.

Maladi was a modern medicine man. The Nyanya mission hospital was organizing health care by training local villagers to take care of the most common ailments of the local people. Maladi had been chosen for Gangu and he had to attend training sessions a few weeks at a time at Nyanya. He was still in the midst of his training program but he already treated patients. In the morning, there were patients waiting for him before I was up. He got up before dawn and went to hoe his gardens for an hour. Then he treated his patients. I grew accustomed to seeing children, women, and men sitting on a stool complaining about their health. Maladi would heat up water on a charcoal burner, drop a huge syringe in the water to sterilize it and prepare an injection for them. He owned only one basin which was used for his medical work, cooking, and other needs. When I washed my face in it in the morning, I wondered if I would get his patients' diseases.

Maladi worked with confidence and told me that he had never made a mistake and that he had helped crowds of people. I did not know how much he charged for his services, but he mentioned that some patients paid in kind: either by giving him a chicken or hoeing his gardens for him.

One day a half-grown girl walked in the living room as I was combing my hair. She let out a cry of astonishment and ran back outside. Maladi laughed mischievously: the girl had thought that I was his wife and she was startled at the thought. Looking back, I honestly cannot understand why Sofia made such a strange arrangement for me unless her ambition to have a white guest made her blind to the social rules.

I stayed in the village a week and each night before falling asleep Maladi and I chatted through the dividing wall. He told me about his life and I noticed that his voice was dry and colourless regardless of the topic he discussed. I thought that it expressed his deep-rooted bitterness. He was 35-years old, born in Gangu and a member of one of the four local lineages. Although he called Remi his "brother," in our terminology they were cousins, since their fathers were brothers. When he was six-years old, his father sent him to Nyanya to live with his uncle, the old man with the paralysed wife whom Sofia had introduced me to. The uncle had no children and as it was considered bad to be childless, he was treated as his uncle's "child" and the uncle paid for his education at the mission school. When Maladi finished the six grades he was sent to Lemura for the upper grades because Nyanya had no further education at that time. However, the struggle for national independence took place around that time and the school was dissolved for a few years because of the political turmoil. Maladi, therefore, returned to his uncle who arranged for him to get married. Maladi himself did not want to get married and cried at the thought, but he could not do anything against the wish of the family elders. They told him it was important to have many descendants to carry on when the older generation died. The elders brought him a wife.

Maladi had enormous difficulties in adjusting to marriage. Having been a student most of his life he did not even know how to hoe gardens. When the independence struggle was over, Maladi went to Lemura to look for office work, for which he was more fitted. He was sent several hundred miles away on a government job and was gone for about a year.

Meanwhile, his wife went to live at his uncle's house at Nyanya, because the uncle was responsible for her during Maladi's absence. She learned to run around with men from her sister who was living near-by. Maladi was worried about her all the time. He visited her when he could but it was not often. Once, having been away for seven months he returned to find his wife six-months pregnant. (I could not believe the Fofu counted the time that carefully). He immediately suspected that the child was not his but she insisted it was. When he went to see her next she was in the maternity ward after having a baby boy. He noticed that her mother and sister left through the back door so they would not have to face him. He knew then that the child was not his. Subsequently they had another son and Maladi doubted that he was the father of him too.

Maladi was angry with his wife and divorced her. That was about fourteen years ago. Since then she had been married to seven husbands but had borne children to only two of them. She was now married to someone who lived along the Gangu road.

"Do you greet her when you see her?" I asked.

"Yes, but I never shake her hand, her hand," Maladi declared in his dry voice. Refusing to shake hands showed much hostility in this culture, shaking hands was a must when greeting people. Maladi had never remarried but had lived alone in his house, which he kept in meticulous repair, and cultivated his land while his two sons lived with his uncle at Nyanya causing him much shame with their thievery. He was disgusted with his sons and had nothing good to say about them. His suspicions about his fatherhood must have caused the basic division between him and the sons, although legally they were his because he had paid the bridewealth for his wife.

Although he never mentioned it to me, it was common gossip that Maladi had been involved with many women since his divorce — and before it, too, one of them with a woman from his own clan (Georgette, who appears in "Anastasia, The Focus Of The Fofu"), which was considered an incestuous relationship. I never met his former wife and could not hear her side of the story. No doubt it would have been very different from his.

Now after about fourteen years of bachelorhood, Maladi was engaged to be married again. As he spoke of his engagement his voice lost some of its characteristic bitterness but it was still far from warm and enthusiastic. He told me in great detail how Teresa had arrived at Gangu to spend her summer vacation from her teacher's job with her sister, who was married in this village. As a semi-official guest entertainer, Maladi had shown her around the village and brewed her tea after the tour. When she spent her second vacation in the village, he had asked her to marry him. She told him to contact her brother for approval because her father had died. She had borne a child by someone else out of wedlock and she wondered if he wanted her to leave the little daughter but he agreed for her to bring the little one along.

"It is a hard situation for a step-father," he pondered, "because he will not be awarded with any bridewealth when the daughter gets married, gets married although he has fed and clothed her for many years until then." So I realized that his future marriage was not to be without problems either.

One day Maladi took me to his fields and showed me his avocado trees. He had twelve of them and they provided him with a good income during the fruit season. He sent some of the girls of his lineage to the market to sell them since men were not expected to sell garden produce in the markets themselves. Maladi was modern in this endeavour as he was in what he planted in his gardens: he was experimenting with cabbage which was not very common among the villagers at that time.

Maladi's younger brother lived on the opposite side of the village road. The same night I went there, he brought home a second wife to replace the first. It happened without great ceremony and I only heard about it afterwards when Sofia mentioned it. Maladi had not got along with his brother's first wife because she spread it around the village that Maladi was "sleeping on money," or as we say, rolling in money, because he was a "doctor." Maladi was offended because he did not want to give the impression of being rich, an open invitation to witchcraft caused by envy. He was therefore glad that she had gone. I chatted with the new wife one day and asked if the first one was coming back. The young woman held her eyes politely down as she answered,

"I don't know. It is none of my business."

I was surprised. "Whose business is it then?" I exclaimed.

"It is between her and my husband." she replied and continued peeling manioc. She behaved as if she had always lived in the house and her new husband's children were helping her as if she was their mother.

BOYS ARE EXCUSED

Remi was my informant at Gangu and as I needed to know more about his background, I interviewed him and his family members about their past. Remi's father and uncle, the Nyanya church elder whom I had met, were the first Protestants in the village. In fact, the uncle had been the first person to tell the villagers that the tradition of Sakana was a lie. The villagers warned him that he would die after this blasphemous statement but he was still alive.

Remi's father, Kimareki, was now living with Remi and Sofia. He was an angry old man, and was bitter about his wife having left him a couple of years ago — unreasonably, in his opinion. His favourite topics were the injustice of his being deserted by his wife and his greatness as the first Protestant preacher in the village. He went on and on about these topics to anyone who would listen. Sofia and Remi treated him with deference because they were expected to do so. Remi never complained but Sofia lamented her fate of always getting overbearing old in-laws in her marriages.

About thirty years ago, an American missionary had moved Kimareki to another mission station, about 60 miles west of Gangu, to preach the gospel to another ethnic group. He had worked there many years and had his family there. Kimareki boasted that he had worked hard as a preacher and had done a good job. He could not understand why he was no longer allowed to preach in church. He could not care less: he preached in the markets instead because he was a preacher and he knew how to do it.

Remi and Sofia fed the old man because he had back trouble and could no longer hoe fields. He earned some money for clothes and other personal expenses by selling used tin cans for a few pennies each in the markets. He obtained his cans by begging from the missionaries at the mission station. I put all my cans aside for him after learning about his need. He was not the only one who went around begging for them. There were many other old men who had noticed this possibility for trade. Whenever there was a market in Gangu or a nearby village, Kimareki collected his cans to torn plastic bags and tied some of them to his belt with string. With the cans dangling, he left for the market. This unruly collection of cans added to his unkempt appearance. He was quite a spectacle!

Kimareki had two ambitions: to preach and to find a new wife. He tried to reach these two goals while in the market places. He was constantly scouting for a new wife there. Sofia told me he was crazy about women and ran after them offering them money but none liked him. He drank a lot and preached in the markets while intoxicated thus bringing shame to his family and to the church. The local pastor of the church verified this story. It was only out of their respect for an old man the church and his family left him alone and did not try to change his behaviour.

Because of his peculiar habit of speaking in an angry tone and literally spitting contempt out of his mouth, children sometimes laughed at him. But not offensively. On the other hand, he was very kind and tender towards Remi's baby and often held him while Sofia pounded food.

Remi, now 44-years old, was the oldest of Kimareki's sixteen children. Eight of them had died either as babies or when a few years old. Remi, like Maladi, had attended Nyanya school whilst living with his uncle. He continued his schooling at the mission station where his father was working. After a total of five years schooling, he quit and some time later started a store with a school friend. They sold soap, salt, flour, cloth, clothes, etc., i.e., the sort of things all the local stores handled. After many years of hard work, they were so successful that they started another venture. They bought a Volkswagen van and ran a regular passenger service between two busy towns in the forest. Remi acted as the driver for several years.

About ten years ago the presidential order came to annul the currency and Remi lost everything. Just like Herabo in "Persevering Cecilia," he was unable to find banks to change his old money in a few days.

"Tulibakia ku zero" (We stayed in the zero), he said and laughed. He had a broad smile and a round happy face with big eyes. He also had a very carefree attitude towards life which allowed him to talk about his financial disaster without any bitterness.

After the loss of his store and bus service, Remi went into the gold trade. He travelled about a hundred miles to buy gold and then sold it in another place. Unfortunately, someone stole both his money and the gold and Remi was left penniless far from home. By the time his friends helped him to travel back home, a year had elapsed and his wife, tired of waiting for him, had returned to her home. This was his third wife. Remi had had two other wives before her but both those marriages had failed: his first wife threatened to kill him with a knife and the second one had children by other men. He got rid of both of them. This third wife had given him six children (five sons and one daughter), and he tried hard to get her back.

Sofia told me that he had made three trips to beg her to come back from her parents who lived twenty miles from Gangu. Her parents had asked for a goat and a cow from him because he had made her go through a delivery all by herself when he was away on his gold business. He had taken a goat to her parents but insisted on his wife's return before he brought the cow. The wife, however, stayed at her parents and Remi's begging did not help him to get her back. So at last he started to look around for another wife.

When Sofia was Hugo's second wife at the other end of Gangu, Remi heard that her marriage was not going well. When Sofia left Hugo, Remi hurried to ask if she would marry him, instead. Sofia agreed and Remi took two goats to Sofia's parents. These animals were regarded as payments for a man's sexual rights over a woman and his rights to her domestic work. He should pay a cow soon and another one some time later, he told me. The cows were for the children she was expected to bear him.

Remi and Sofia took pride in their fields. Often in the morning when I got up, they had already left for the fields. Sometimes, I would go there to admire their work. I saw Remi's 14-year-old Felisi and 11-year old Bye-Bye hoe with him. Bye

Figure 4.2 Sofia took pride in her fields.

Bye was so named because when they lived in the rain forest he used to say "bye-bye" to tourists eagerly. These two boys lived with Remi and Sofia. Sofia bossed them around as if she was their true mother, and the boys usually obeyed humbly. In the evening when Sofia was cooking the meal for the family they would hold the baby. They also ran errands for the adults and carried manioc leaves to the pigs which were tied in the bushes near the house.

One evening I noticed that Felisi had been holding the baby for a couple of hours before Sofia took it from him and fed it. Felisi instantly turned around and went outside to roll a used bicycle rim with other village boys. Bye-Bye was running errands for his father. When Sofia had nursed the baby, she called Felisi to look after the baby again but he ignored the call. I wondered what Sofia would do and was ready to record it in my note book, since the main topic of my study was the obedience of Fofu children. She dumped the baby on me saying,

"Why don't you hold the baby, since you have nothing better to do?" I put my note book aside and took the baby and Sofia scolded me for not picking up the village babies more.

"How come you let Felisi get out of this? It is the siblings' duty to carry the little one, isn't it?" I retaliated. Sofia was already pounding manioc flour when she replied to the rhythm of the pounding,

"Felisi has been carrying the baby a long time, a long time, today. He has worked patiently like a girl and deserves time off." Had he been a girl, however, he would not have received time off: girls were expected to have even more patience with babies and house chores.

Remi and all his children had big round eyes and round faces. The little baby was no exception and was so cuddly that everybody's heart melted at the sight of him, especially when he smiled with his toothless baby mouth. Remi enjoyed holding the baby and in the evenings he would often walk around the neighbourhood with the baby in his arms or sit on a stool near Sofia's fire playing with him.

On my second visit when Sofia was away from home over night with the baby, Remi told me that he missed the baby. When Sofia returned Remi slept the night with the baby on his chest. He loved being close to his baby son. Never before had I heard fathers express their emotions this frankly and was amazed at his openness. I don't know if other fathers cuddled their babies in privacy. I did see fathers holding their babies in the evening when their wives were busy but Remi was the only one I saw playing with his baby.

One evening when Sofia went to fetch water, she assigned Felisi to watch the fire and the beans which were cooking over it. When she came back, the beans had burnt. Again, I waited to see her reaction. She noted what had happened and investigated the degree of waste but did not say anything to Felisi. When Felisi disappeared to play, I asked Sofia, if she never got angry at children's mistakes. Bending down to chop wood she admitted,

"Had it been a girl I would have beaten her severely but being a boy I do not get mad, no I do not. He does not know better, he is a boy." I was amused and scribbled notes on the differential treatment of boys and girls.

Although boys were excused from household chores they could be subjected to at least one duty which was much more unpleasant than babysitting or watching the fire, military service. I got to observe the hostility young men felt towards military recruiters. One day, when Richard and Mateso, a son and nephew of Cecilia dropped in on their way to greet Richard's grandfather. A warm feeling went through me when I saw them sitting in Sofia's yard. I almost felt as if I was seeing my own children and was happy about their visit.

After a while, the youngsters left for the older part of the village on top of the mountain and we did not expect to see them any more. But by noon, they had returned shaken. They had gone by the market place and seen soldiers capturing young men, about twenty years old, as Mateso and Richard were. The boys knew what it meant, for the word had been spread that the president needed volunteers for his army. These "volunteers" were captured by force and sent by plane to the capital for training. Richard and Mateso turned around and ran as fast as they could to avoid a horrible fate. In the turmoil, Mateso lost a shoe but he did not intend to go back to look for it. He was glad that he was spared and free. After relaxing and joking for a while, the boys left again. That time they took a round-about route. They knew that their relatives would hide them once they arrived at the grandfather's place.

□ □ □

After getting to know Sofia's family, I wanted to become acquainted with the village and Remi volunteered to show it to me. Gangu was comparable to Yenyabo having about 1,000 inhabitants in addition to those who lived on the top of the mountain which was the old site of the village. Some old men still lived there, one of them being Cecilia's father. These old men did not want to uproot themselves and move to the new site. I wondered if they were guarding the ancestral shrines, although the existence of shrines was never officially admitted because of colonial and mission opposition to ancestor "worship." In fact, Cecilia had told me that when her father had destroyed the ancestral altar in his house, he had fallen ill with epilepsy and had suffered from it ever since.

The village comprised of four patrilineages, the physical location of which were in the form of a cross. One could, therefore, tell the lineage of a person by the location of his house. Remi had been asked to be a sub chief of the village for his lineage but he tried to fend off this responsibility because it would involve litigation between quarrelling parties and would be very time consuming with few returns. I observed that it was hard, almost impossible, to fend off responsibilities decided by the consensus of the people because the others would threaten a resistant person with supernatural sanctions.

On our village tour, we also visited Sofia's previous husband. The two husbands were cordial towards each other — both seemed untroubled by the past.

It was Sunday and I wondered which church Sofia would attend: Catholic or Protestant. Her family was Catholic but her husband's was Protestant. She attended the Protestant church which was having guest speakers from Yenyabo that day. Sofia tiptoed into the church as if she was not sure how to behave in it, being more used to a Catholic service. Although her husband and his father told me that she would change her denomination she never admitted this to me.

Protestant missions strictly forbade drinking of alcoholic beverages while Catholic missions only forbade becoming drunk. Sofia was used to making money by distilling liquor and was not going to bow down to this Protestant rule of temperance, although married to a Protestant. It did not take long for her to notice that it was good business for women to distil liquor and sell it to the gold diggers of the village. With their pockets full of money, they were glad to buy drinks at the end of a hard working day. A Catholic school teacher told me with pride that the alcohol sales had greatly improved the income of the villagers. He did not pay attention to the increasing numbers of drunkards in the village. Every single night, I heard drunken singing in the village and one moonlit night a drunkard was streaking through the village. Poor Remi tried to prevent me from seeing, not knowing that, as a Finn, I was used to seeing nude people. He only knew that Americans were touchy about nudity.

Sofia may have intended to hide her distilling activity from me but I found out accidentally. One morning I heard Sofia at work in her living room. Without further thought I walked in and startled her. Obviously she did not want me there that day but it was too late, for I had already seen. She was busy distilling her liquor. I did not react. I knew that all the Fofu women in Bululu were earning their livelihood from distilling. I chatted with her while she continued to work with the help of her Protestant husband who put wood on the fire for her. Both of them seemed relieved that I did not criticize them.

Jacques, who featured in "The Dissolution Of A Marriage," belonged to the same lineage as Remi and Maladi. So on this visit I had the pleasure of calling on people whom I had visited eleven years earlier. One of Jacques' brothers was busily sewing in front of his house when I went to greet him. "Much work," he excused himself and did not talk to me. Later that day another man explained to me that the tailor had a bad conscience over something that had happened years back. I scanned my memory but it was blank. He told me that on a visit to his old father I had left money with the tailor for fifty eggs but he had never brought me the eggs. I did not remember it. On second thought, I remembered Suzana, Jacques' wife, coming to see me with another of Jacques' brothers and bringing me many eggs. The behaviour of the tailor intrigued me. I did not think the Fofu had bad consciences or guilty feelings about anything. Usually the fault was put on another person or witchcraft. Clearly I was wrong. I found it very interesting that he sent a mediator to bring the "confession" to me. I sent a message back that I forgave him whatever had happened years back. There was no face-to-face discussion about the matter, but from then on the tailor smiled and his work did not keep him from chatting with me. Later he sent his children to me with the gift of a hen.

During my visit to Sofia, the nights were gorgeous with the full moon shining so brightly that no petrol lamps or candles were needed outside. Adults stayed out of doors doing their chores and chatting with each other while the children played noisily in the neighbourhood. I wrote my daily notes in the moonlight. One night, however, the bright moonlight suddenly dimmed. I turned to see if clouds were passing in front of it but there were none. Instead, I saw a huge red shape of the moon which did not light the earth at all. I could not find an explanation for the phenomenon and an eerie feeling grasped me for a moment. Then it occurred to me that it must have been a lunar eclipse. Since there were no newspapers, I had not read about it ahead of time. I was relieved to find an explanation and was curious to see what the villagers would make of it.

People kept turning their heads towards the moon. Then they walked to the road where the view was good, congregated into groups, and gasped with amazement. Remi's old father announced in a strong voice,

"Look at the moon! It is red with blood from the many wars in the world, bloody wars. People are killing each other, killing."

Others asked, "Does this mean famine?" and "Does this mean that the sun will be burning this season and there will be no rain for our fields, no rain?"

People were scared and excited. I heard the famine interpretation the most. Then Remi came from the centre of the village where he had been listening to the men's talk.

"It is the shadow of the earth on the moon," he explained.

"How do you know?" asked the others.

The Protestant pastor of the village had told the men what he had heard on the Lemura education radio program. It amused me that a Protestant pastor favoured a Western scientific explanation while his congregation preferred the more "spiritual" explanation of a connection between nature and human destiny.

I told the villagers about white men landing on the moon years back and doing more research on it since then. This received unanimous disapproval. A human being was not to tamper with something that belonged only to God's realm.

In an hour, the moon started lighting up little by little as the shadow moved across it. The people sighed with relief and went back to their chores shaking their heads in amazement.

"GOD LEFT US EMPTY HANDED"

I wanted to see Sofia's home village and meet her parents, since the visit had been cancelled the previous year. I wished not only to meet her parents but also to walk in Sofia's clan area just to get the feeling of distances. Years back I had hiked to the waterfalls which were close to Sofia's village and I must have walked through her village not knowing it. Sofia arranged a day and said she was coming with me. In the morning of that day she cancelled everything saying that nobody would be at home. I do not know where and when she received the message because we were both ready to go when she changed her plans.

I was very disappointed. Why did Sofia do this to me again? My mind was so strongly set on going that I could not think of doing anything else. I told her that I would go anyhow; just to look at the village. I did not need to meet anyone.

"Fine," said Sofia, "Let's go!" She already had the baby on her back and Remi joined us.

We visited Sofia's father's place and her brother's home. All of her relatives, except her father, were at home and we had a good day together. Perhaps she had wanted to shield me from the liquor distilling her sister-in-law was doing that day, but I did not pay any attention to it anyway. Sofia and her sister — who had been in serious condition at the hospital a year before — held each other's babies on their laps and braided each other's hair. It seemed, therefore, that Sofia was getting something out of the visit, too. I became attentive when the sister talked about the previous year. She was looking at her baby and remarked,

"God really helped me to bear this baby, he helped me. I was so scared during the pregnancy because the doctors had told me not to get pregnant for six months but I became pregnant after one month."

One month from what? I wondered and decided it must be from her abortion. So the abortion had worked, she had recovered and become pregnant again right after it. Nobody alluded to any particular man nor mentioned her husband in prison.

We spent a long time at the brother's place and I asked some of Sofia's relatives about the old times. Everyone seemed willing to talk, especially after entering the hut and coming out with glazed eyes — the sister-in-law's liquor must have been good. Sofia's mother started to tell me about the Sakana tradition from a woman's point of view. I had already heard the male point of view from Herabo at Yenyabo. She trembled when she talked about it. This conveyed to me the emotions connected with the tradition, while Sofia's young brother explained it in more philosophical terms.

"In the old days there was a force, it was like God. God could not be seen, neither could Sakana, neither Sakana," he narrated dramatically while his mother nodded her agreement.

Then she continued, "When we (women) heard the horrible voice of Sakana, we were so afraid that we ran in and covered our eyes."

She told me that young men of the village surrounded Sakana and banged on the roofs and walls with a terrible roar thus pulling thatch off and causing damage to the walls. Sakana sent some of the youngsters in to ask for salt or tobacco. If a woman told them that there was none, they declared her a liar and pulled the items from their hiding places.

"Sakana knew everything, knew everything!" whispered Sofia's mother. These young men would then take a bracelet from the woman as her fine and continue their havoc in the next house.

It was clear that the fear of Sakana kept women in line. Sofia's brother explained how children were also kept in line with threats about Sakana. He confirmed what I had already heard from Herabo, i.e. that youngsters were taken to the bush to meet Sakana. Sofia's mother summed it up,

"It was a lie but it worked, worked!"

An uncomfortable silence fell upon us when I mentioned that years back I had walked through the village to see the waterfall.

"Why do white people want to go to the water, to the water?" Sofia demanded aggressively.

"We admire the beauty of a waterfall; we get refreshed at the sight of it," I replied and tried to think other explanations of a recreational nature. I could see that they did not believe me. Then Sofia's mother inquired point blank, "Do you go there to watch it or to take it, watch it or take it?"

"Take what?" was my innocent question.

"See, you do not want to let us in on the secret," Sofia's mother said with resignation.

"Take the magic, take the magic, of course," explained Sofia's brother. I was astounded at this revelation. So they believed that white people got their magic from the waterfall! And they thought I knew the magic, too, but was withholding it from them, like all the other white people. Now I understood why an American friend of ours hadn't been allowed to build a cabin near the waterfall. The excuse had been that in the empty wilderness outside of this village there was no land available!

Sofia's mother spelled out the Fofu view of us Europeans, "You have magic, you have pens, radios, thermoses, bicycles, cars, houses. . . . Tell me does your God give you whatever you ask for?"

When I hesitated, Sofia's brother gave an example, "If you want a bicycle, does your God give it to you if you pray?" I tried to explain that we get those things by working and getting money for our work.

"We work, too, we do work.," they all said in unison, "but we don't get bicycles!"

They were right. They worked. They hoed their gardens, they distilled liquor, some of them worked for the government or for the white people. But few Fofu had been able to obtain the items they mentioned.

"You must have a secret agreement with God because you get so many things. We gave up everything, we gave up our ancestors and now we pray only to God. But God has left us empty handed, empty handed," one of them said.

"Truly, you are God's favourite children!" they decided but added, "Fofu fathers have favourite children, so God may have them, too. We have favourite children, why not God then?" They nodded their heads, satisfied with this explanation.

I could not comment, because this way of thinking was new to me. The more I thought about it afterwards, the more have I understood it. The Fofu explanation for the difference in wealth between themselves and Europeans makes sense. Max Weber (1947), the sociologist, hypothesized the wealth of the Western world as a result of "the Protestant work ethic." That would not have made any sense to the Fofu who did not think we were working. God gave us money although we did not do anything while he withheld it from the Fofu, who worked hard.

Now that we had created an atmosphere of intimacy where we could talk about topics not easily discussed with white people, Sofia's mother decided to discuss one more sensitive subject. She leaned forward, lowered her voice and said,

"We black people respect you white people very much." I looked at her almost toothless mouth and waited for what was to follow. "We tell our children that the white man will eat them and they will cry!" She laughed mischievously and the others joined in. I did not. I hated that custom. Maladi had told a crying village child when we passed him, "Be quiet or madam will eat you!" A school principal told a class of children in his introduction to my questionnaire, "Don't be afraid of madam, she won't eat you!" I thought such threats were in poor taste.

Others elaborated on the theme by telling me about the origin of the habit. When the white man had come to the country, he started eating black people.

"How do you know?" I asked, trying to keep calm although my stomach turned over.

"We know all right, know," said Sofia's mother mysteriously. Sofia's brother, who had worked for the white people, explained that the Fofu knew it because the colonial overlords gave their houseboys one afternoon a week off work.

"The white madams locked the doors, closed the curtains and cooked human flesh for supper for their families."

"How did they get the flesh?" I inquired. He explained that the white people drove around at night with their Landrovers and captured anyone who was outside. Then they transported the black people into the rain forest (he named a particular place) where they threw the Africans into a pit, dug out for the purpose, and fattened them up. They checked to see when the fingers of the victims were fat enough and then shipped them to Europe in huge planes. In Europe they were butchered and their flesh canned and sent around the world for consumption.

All this had been told with a mixture of delight and awe which I could not share. Then someone concluded the discussion by stating, "That was then but when we became independent the white men did not eat us any more. Now we are all Christian and love each other."

I was stunned by the story and thought about it for years afterwards, trying to make sense of it. I connected it to the stories from the more distant past when Fofu clans were feuding with each other. Herabo had told me that the local men always ate their dead enemies.

"Now we marry from where we used to eat people, eat people," he mused. Other historical tales described Lelo chiefs drinking beer out of a skull of a Fofu chief. I concluded that cannibalism was an expression of power over another clan or tribe. The story of white man's cannibalism was only an allegory for colonial power.

At the time, however, I reflected on the difference between these tales and those we learned in our childhood. How much more pleasant were Cinderella, Sleeping Beauty, and Little Red Riding Hood. But wait a minute. Wasn't there a kind of cannibalism involved in the last tale? Didn't the big bad wolf disguised as the grandmother devour Little Red Riding Hood? How about Hansel and Gretel? Didn't an old woman fatten the two children up to be eaten and actually check the progress by the size of their fingers? Our stories were not so different after all.

So the visit to Sofia's home village which nearly did not take place, turned out to bear much fruit. I learned a lot about Fofu thought.

The week's time limit which I had set for my visit to Gangu, was soon over and it was time to leave Gangu. I tried to borrow a bicycle from someone in the village but I could not get one. Those few who owned bicycles were not willing to lend them.

When Maladi saw me running around he stopped me and said, "It is not the duty of a guest to worry about transportation, it is the host's duty." In fact, I am not sure if it is so or whether he only said it to please me. However, he went on to boast, "When I was young, I would carry 130 pounds of mangos to markets in a basket. I am still a strong man, don't worry." Remi reinforced his cousin's words and said if Maladi did not help, then he would. I no longer worried.

In the morning we were ready to leave at seven o'clock. I carried my suitcase out into the bright sunlight. The one who took it was neither Maladi nor Remi. It was Sofia. Without a word, she lifted the suitcase on top of her head and gave orders to Bye-Bye to carry my camera and a gift hen. Remi handed me the baby and I made a sling on my side to carry him all the way to Nyanya. The three of us started our hike with Remi accompanying us as far as the stream which marked the boundary of the village.

The baby was content on my side and did not cry or wet himself. In fact, he slept most of the way with his head leaning against my arm. People along the road exclaimed at the sight of a black baby and a white woman and I fuelled their astonishment by telling them that he was my baby. Sofia went along with me, nodding her head. When we were almost at our destination, we heard footsteps behind us and saw that Maladi was catching up with us. He was carrying half a dozen of eggs tied in a cloth and my empty water container. There was the strong man who used to carry 130 pounds in his youth!

When we arrived at my home in Nyanya, I sent someone to buy two loaves of bread. They were freshly baked, steaming hot and tasted delicious with tea and margarine: a treat for my company, after an hour and a half walk. It was nice to relax and savour the familiar taste in one's mouth. After tea, Sofia wanted me to go with her to the stores and I guessed she wanted me to buy her something. She pointed to a baby bottle which she wanted. I did not want to buy it because I knew artificial feeding caused problems in Africa: dirty bottles, contaminated water mixed with milk powder, dirty nipples etc. But Sofia insisted on getting one and promised to boil the water — as she had been doing for me — and to clean the bottle. In the end I bought her the bottle and a can of milk powder. When I went to the village subsequently I never saw the bottle, so perhaps she sold it to someone else. Bye-Bye was ever so glad when I bought him a bar of soap, since children were not often allowed to use soap even if the family had some.

"I DO NOT KNOW HIM YET"

During the following weeks I saw my Gangu friends occasionally when they came to the hospital or to the market at Nyanya. I enjoyed seeing them and served them coffee or tea. On one such visit Maladi offered to arrange for me to stay with his fiancée at the Catholic mission station where she was teaching. I thought it was brave of Teresa to accept me as her guest not knowing me at all. Maladi told me she was worried about being able to be a good hostess.

When I arrived at Teresa's house, it was empty. A neighbour came to keep me company while I waited for Teresa and her colleague to return from fetching water. When they arrived, each carrying a "gallon" container on top of their heads, they scolded me for not entering the house. I said that as a guest I did not dare to go in. They told me that as a guest I should have gone in. This gave me an insight into the privileged position of guests.

Teresa lived in a brick house built by the Catholic mission for school teachers and shared it with another single mother who also had a daughter. I spent a week with them and we three women had a good time together. The women left for school every morning and returned early afternoon. Meanwhile, a half-grown girl, a relative of Teresa's colleague, baby-sat the two little girls, and I went around the station interviewing people. In the afternoon, the women did their housework, went to the local market, and prepared their lessons for the next day. I helped them with the chores, went to the market, and attended station events with them.

Teresa had completed twelve years of schooling, which was more than most Fofu had. The last four years of school consisted of a teachers' training course. One day I mentioned that we usually took a Lufthansa flight from Nairobi to Europe. Teresa said, "Lufthansa, a German Airline." I was surprised. How could she know it when she had only seen national airplanes at Lemura airport? She also listened to European radio programs with a girlfriend who had received a radio from a Catholic father. Her schooling seemed to have been very Western orientated. Teresa had digested her learning better than her colleague who seemed to have learned by heart but with little understanding. Teresa quietly helped her with school questions she could not answer.

As Teresa's maternal aunt had been a Catholic sister she knew many Catholic fathers and sisters personally and had observed their private lives. She told me wild stories about the Catholic sisters' life behind the scenes. But, of course, I could not know if they were true. I suspect that the Africans simply could not understand the celibacy laws of the Catholic faith and made up stories which indicated an exaggerated amount of sexual behaviour.

I remembered that Maladi had once stated, "A woman has no denomination," implying that she would follow her husband's. So I asked Teresa if she was going to change from Catholic to Protestant. She answered, "Can I really?" In Fofu this was a polite way of saying, "I cannot." She added that her whole family had always been Catholic.

During my stay with Teresa I couldn't help noticing that she had a very close relationship with her daughter Mami, who was then three years old. Teresa carried her on her hip or back whenever we went out. Mami followed her mother everywhere at home and often moved her little stool near her mother's to eat, although Teresa set her up to eat near the baby-sitter in the corner of the house and we adults ate at the table together. On a few mornings, she tried to block her mother's way when she was ready to leave for school, and once Mami cried for ten minutes after her mother had left. She babbled all the time to her mother who talked softly back to her, except when she wanted to keep her in line. Then she yelled at her, "Mami, I'll hit you!" At this threat, Mami obeyed. I could never get over this habit of adults changing their soft attitude into a harsh one very suddenly and the fact that little children bore it patiently.

One Saturday, Teresa and I went to her home village, which was an hour's walk from her school. Mami was pampered by all her maternal relatives and she ran from one to the other sitting on the lap of each. She was dressed up for the photos I was going to take of her and the family and she looked very cute in her white pleated skirt and shiny black shoes. Everyone's heart melted at the sight of her.

Teresa had experienced a Western type love affair with a man from the Hiha tribe while she was teaching at another Catholic school. Traditionally, village girls did not even see their fiances before the wedding except once at a formal meeting, but Teresa's relationship with her boyfriend had been much freer. He had promised to marry her if she got pregnant but fled to another corner of the country two days before Mami was born. Teresa was very ill after the birth and recovered only after a long period of treatment first at Nyanya hospital and then at a native doctor's. She believed that the native medicine healed her, not the European. A native healer had claimed that her illness was a result of witchcraft by a member of her own lineage who was angry at not receiving any bridewealth for her, since her lover had abandoned her. I appreciated Teresa's openness with me and her ability to respect her cultural heritage despite many years exposure to Western thought.

While I was at her house, Teresa was very much looking forward to her new marriage. She let me read her letter to Maladi, which was in French (perhaps Kifofu and Swahili did not suit courting because the tribal customs forbade it). In it she said that she would be lost if the "decided agreement" fell through. She told me that she was tired of teaching and wanted a break. Perhaps later she would teach in her new village. She also told me that she was not going to take any of her dishes or furniture to her marital home but leave them at her lineage place with her mother. If the marriage was unsuccessful, there would not be disagreement as to who owned what. She would take only her clothes with her. A couple of times she pondered, "I do not know if this marriage will succeed. I do not know him yet."

THEY DANCED ALL NIGHT

I was keen to attend Teresa's wedding as it was to be a traditional one and I was very excited when I was invited to the great occasion. I did not see Teresa again until her wedding several months later because soon after my visit she quit teaching and went to Lemura to stay with her sister and earn money for a new wardrobe. With her older sister's help, she baked bread and sold it at the Lemura market. This way she made much more money than by teaching.

I wanted to buy a wedding present for Maladi and Teresa in accordance with my own custom. Once, when Maladi was at Nyanya, I asked him to come with me to the stores to choose something he would like. He said that he would like a thermos to keep coffee warm. I bought one for them but I noticed later that Maladi regarded it as his sole property. Remi and Sofia kept me informed about the wedding preparations. Maladi had paid three goats for Teresa so making her mother and brother very happy. Her relatives permitted the wedding although Maladi had paid no cows as yet. They were to follow if the marriage was successful and if Maladi could afford them. When the great day arrived, Remi brought Felisi to Nyanya because of his toothache but the day being Saturday they could not get any help. I gave them some Aspirin and Remi took my tape recorder and camera to Gangu when he returned home. I was to follow later with Maladi's sister.

It was the only traditional wedding I was able to observe and it made a deep impression on me. Sofia warned me that there would be no meal all night and fortified me with food before the festivities. Maladi was busy doing something but I could not make out what. Perhaps he was only restless. While I was still eating, shouts were heard, "They are coming!" I rushed out to be ready to see everything, record, and take photos.

A long file of women from Teresa's village was approaching the village after several hours of walking from home and visiting her relatives and friends on the way, eating in each place. With great assurance they entered the village, singing at the top of their voices. The married women came first, carrying beer in calabashes and hens tucked under their arms. In their baskets were fish, salt, and palm-oil. Their songs praised themselves for bringing an excellent bride and a truckload of fish and barrels of beer. The villagers receiving the bridal party lifted the pots and baskets off their heads and mocked at them, "Why did you not bring any fish? Why do you only bring clothes?" This kind of praising and mocking went on for a long time. Teresa walked in the latter part of the procession, covered from top to toe with cloths, her head hanging down in sorrow at the impending change in her life. Someone else carried Mami.

Teresa, her mother, and accompanying women were ushered into the home of one of Maladi's brothers. The bride was led to the furthest corner of the furthest room in the whole house. There she sat all night on a new palm mat while others noisily celebrated. I was amazed how well everything was organized. The master of ceremonies, Maladi's older brother, had the guest list. From this he announced into which room each guest was to go. Fortunately, I was allowed to walk around to make my observations.

Before midnight the Fofu traditional drums started in the yard of the house. Maladi's brother announced that it was time to dance. I went out with others and tried to learn to dance, that is, shake my hips and arms in rhythm. The women were in the middle and the men outside in a circle shaking to the rhythm of the drums and singing as loudly as they could. The groom's side sang,

"The mother of the bride promised us a truckload of fish. Where is it now?"

The women repeated over and over, "One single fish in the basket!" or "Half a fish in a basket!" Everybody laughed at these songs.

Next, the bride's party sang, "What do you think the groom is anyway? Our lineage is superior to yours!"

The groom's party retaliated, "We eat rice! You people are good-for-nothing, you do not eat rice!"

Teresa called me to the back room where she sat quietly with Mami sleeping in her lap. She had clearly internalized the ritual competition between the lineages, for she complained to me, "My party is not happy with the liquor they serve here. There isn't enough."

Outside the two parties continued to sing in praise of their own side. Teresa's side sang, "Maladi is marrying a white woman."

Maladi's side replied, "Teresa is marrying a doctor!"

Teresa's side continued with an insult, "Poor Maladi, he owns nothing, not even a belt. He ties his pants with a banana string!"

The participants laughed as the insults got more and more outrageous. It was all good humoured. This custom allowed the unavoidable conflicts between in-laws to be expressed healthily in a ritual fashion.

The dancing and singing lasted all night long. I could not understand how people could be active so long. I almost fell asleep at one point but was awaken by another round of the shouting match between the two lineages. Teresa and Maladi did not see each other all this time. Teresa kept quiet in the back room and I did not see Maladi at all.

At sun rise I was pulled to see a ritual in one of the rooms. It was hard to see through the people crowding into the room but someone explained to me what was happening. Teresa with a female relative and Maladi with a male relative were crawling on the floor on their hands and knees with their heads covered. They went to greet Maladi's male lineage elders and Teresa's mother. As they humbly approached, the elders accepted the young couple by marking their foreheads with their saliva. I learned that saliva was a sign from the ancestors and it would serve as a blessing if the young wife stayed faithful to her husband — and as a curse if she left him. I failed to check if it demanded any responsibility on the part of the groom, but no one mentioned it. I also failed to inquire if the mother's side of the bride has always participated in the ritual. Only now do I notice that I have always been biased towards thinking of the Fofu as patrilineal and patriarchal: I have failed to see the actual participation of the matriliny in rituals.

Unfortunately I had to leave the wedding at that stage in order to do fieldwork in Lemura. Afterwards Teresa told me that the wedding party then had a nap until the afternoon when she, accompanied by her village women, went to bathe in the river and change her clothes. Then there was a huge meal for the party, after which Teresa formally entered Maladi's house and her party returned home. She told me that she cried all the following night and day while doing chores for her in-laws: fetching water and sweeping the celebration house clean. Initially she was under the supervision of her husband's relatives: she had to work a couple of weeks for Maladi's older brother before she was allowed to start her own housekeeping at Maladi's.

I learned all this two months after the wedding when I went to stay in the village for another week. This time it was better because I knew both Teresa and Maladi well, and I stayed in their house without the apprehensions I experienced on my first visit. The first evening I played the tape of their wedding and the newlyweds listened to it four times, laughing all the while.

Afterwards, Teresa smiled and told me that she was relaxed about life. Before, she always worried how she could make ends meet for Mami and herself. But now she did not worry any more.

Maladi looked at Teresa and asked proudly if I had noticed that his wife was getting fat. It was rare and coveted to be fat and people evaluated marriages by looking at the figures of the couple: if the couple were skinny, the marriage was thought to be suffering, if they were on the heavy side, the marriage was successful. I had heard from others at Nyanya that this marriage was successful. I also learned from Teresa that she was expecting a baby. So everything seemed well.

The next day I started my work of interviewing people and doing a census of the village, house by house. Remi's son Felisi accompanied me; he was a useful informant about the families in the village. I was in the swing of fieldwork and forgot about everything else.

When I dropped in at home to get more paper, I heard the noise of a motorcycle approaching. All motor-vehicles were rare and, like everyone else, I went outside to see who it was. Of all people, it was Henry and he was coming to see me in the village! I was in a daze because it was rare to see him. I missed him very much and always hoped he would have a flight to Nyanya but there were not many. I embraced him warmly and gave him a kiss in front of everybody. I was glad that he could meet Teresa and Maladi, of whom I had told him. Teresa gave us lunch and Henry and I sat holding hands.

As Henry had to return to Bululu the next morning, we drove back to Nyanya to have some private time together at my base there. The following morning he drove me back to Gangu. Half an hour later, we all heard an airplane approach the village and rushed out, knowing it was Henry. He dipped the wings of the airplane and roared the engines to say good-bye and was gone. We waved to him. How I missed my family although I enjoyed my fieldwork! Later I heard that those villagers who did not know about Henry were very frightened when he flew low and kept on asking each other what it meant. I don't think any anthropological fieldwork manuals would recommend such behaviour: they talk of anthropologists being inconspicuous.

No one had laughed at or commented on my loving attitude towards my husband although such behaviour was unheard of in the Fofu culture. The next day, however, when Sofia returned from an overnight trip to a wake, Teresa shouted to her from her house,

"Sister-in-law, hug your husband as madam did yesterday!"

Sofia ignored her advice as a good wife should but the others burst into laughter and mimicked me embracing my husband. I was the laughingstock of the neighbourhood.

Sofia was away most of the week I spent in the village. At the beginning, she was about 20 miles away at a wake for a man who had drowned in a river. She had been there about a week. Remi was anxious the day she was to return and I noticed him glancing at his wrist watch all day. I was more surprised when he frankly admitted that he missed Sofia very much. I did not think a Fofu man would ever say it aloud even if he felt it. To Remi's joy she came home but almost immediately heard that her sister was vomiting blood at her home village. So she spent only one night at home before leaving to see her sister. Later on in the week, she stayed at home for another night before going to another wake and then again to a third one. Teresa criticized her for leaving her family so much,

"Poor kids, they are not properly fed. Poor Remi, has to fend for himself." Then she added, "Remi is a patient man, many men would not put up with that kind of wife."

One day when Sofia was not absent Teresa returned home from the village store out of breath and very annoyed. "Remi's door is closed and the baby is crying desperately inside!"

Maladi was ironing his shirt (an iron represented modern technology and therefore belonged to the realm of a man) but he interrupted his work immediately and ran to the house. Soon he returned carrying the crying little Sirigabo and talking to him gently. He told us that he had found Sofia fast asleep and the crying baby sitting next to her. He had tried to wake Sofia up by slapping her and pulling her by the arms but she had continued her drunken sleep. Teresa commented that she had seen Sofia returning from a wake in the morning drunk and that she had still drunk after it. Both Teresa and Maladi were full of condemnation for such a mother.

Maladi even told the infant, "A woman must not drink like a man. She must keep her senses."

I was worried that the baby might have alcohol in its blood after feeding at its mother's breast. But I didn't know how to test it.

"I drink only beer," said Teresa as if exonerating herself. Sirigabo continued to cry and Maladi continued to hold him for half an hour until Remi came from his field and took him. Maladi told us afterwards that Remi went home to scold his wife but she kept on sleeping, blissfully ignorant of the condemnation she received.

I thought it was interesting that Teresa did not enter the house or have anything to do with the baby, although she saw it as her job to deplore the situation. The reason was that as she was not a member of either Sofia's or Remi's lineage, she could not safely take care of the baby: she would be accused of ill-will if something went more wrong. Maladi, on the other hand, was of the same lineage as Remi and the baby and therefore an acceptable guardian for the little one when the mother was incapacitated.

Although, if we can believe what she said, Teresa drank only beer, she was going to distil liquor to sell. She told me that I would not see her the following morning because she was going to get up very early to collect firewood for the distilling. Her sister, who also lived in the village, would come and show her a good place to get wood, high up on the mountain.

I did not hear her leaving in the morning but when I got up she was gone. Maladi served me some tea and poured the extra into the thermos for Teresa's return. Mami chattered to him all the time and Maladi replied with good humour. I thought of the time when he had lived alone. How much more life there was in the house now! He also seemed to have a good relationship with Mami. At one point, for example, Mami dropped some food on the ground.

Maladi asked softly, "Why do you throw food away? I'll give the next food to Remi's children." Although his words were quite harsh I don't think Mami took them as a rejection. Later Mami got too close to Maladi when he was preparing his medicine.

Maladi warned her, "I'll prick you with this syringe if you don't behave!"

Mami drew back but stated in a confident voice, "You are not my father! You go out!" It only made Maladi laugh and he didn't carry out his threat.

That day I took Mami with me when I did my census work. Hand in hand we walked on a narrow path through grass and bushes. Mami chattered to me all the while and I was glad that she was at ease with me at last. Teresa told me that Mami called me *muzungu yangu*, my white woman. Because Mami felt comfortable with the people at Teresa's sister's, I thought I might as well do the census of that particular household that morning. The husband was at home and some of the children were too. They were bigger than Teresa's because the sister was much older. Teresa had told me that her sister was a remarkable woman as she had mustered the courage to leave her first husband when she had already borne him four children. Something had gone wrong in Teresa's sister's marriage and she started anew with another man in this village and bore him three children, one of whom had died. The husband was a widower and had five children alive from his first marriage; some of these children were already married. She was a tremendous support for Teresa in the village. Mami was often sent there if Teresa needed a baby-sitter, for example, and now the sister was helping Teresa find firewood. Mami played with her maternal cousins while I interviewed their father who was a quiet older man.

When we had gone to a few houses, we returned home and found Maladi tending Teresa's toe, which she had hurt. A huge bundle of firewood was lying on the floor. I tried to lift it but was not able to move it an inch.

"How could you carry this so far?" I asked Teresa.

"She is not a child," said Maladi, implying that I was.

Maladi wrapped a clean white bandage around Teresa's toe and poured tea for her. She was exhausted but determined to continue with the distilling. This was to take place under her sister's roof and supervision and with her equipment, too, since Maladi would not permit such an activity in his Protestant house. Nor had he lent Teresa any money for the ingredients. This was a source of irritation to Teresa.

Teresa spent all afternoon distilling and I continued the census with Felisi. The villagers liked his respectful and quiet manner and I appreciated the information he was able to give me. He would tell me afterwards if the people had not told me the truth and for what reason, so I learned more about Fofu thinking. Also, while interviewing people, I had a splendid opportunity to observe parent-child relationships which was very interesting. I noticed, for example, that parents often ordered their children to run errands. Sometimes I saw parents beating their children or heard them yelling at them. Once I observed a father requesting the chair his son was sitting on: he moved away without opposition.

That evening Teresa was annoyed. The distilling had been successful but something else was bothering her. Remi's father and some other lineage elders came to her and said,

"You killed an elephant, an elephant, why did you not bring us any meat?"

Out of respect for them Teresa had not let them see her displeasure. But she complained to me that she could lose all her liquor as gifts. And she wanted to make money. In the end, she decided to give one bottle out of ten to the old men to share and no more. As a new daughter-in-law in the family, she did wisely to keep the elders happy.

Maladi bought one bottle to give to a village household who were having a wake. Teresa would pay her sister for the ingredients but would not give her any money for her help. A female neighbour promised to sell the rest of the bottles in the market on the mountain. She would get one bottle as her commission. Her husband was of the same major lineage as Maladi and Remi, but not from the same minor lineage. In other words, he was more distantly related to Maladi than Remi was. Relatives from the same minor lineage helped each other for nothing but relatives from the major lineages had to be paid.

Teresa did not like Maladi's negative attitude towards her way of making money. She said she chose this because she was ashamed to walk to the market with a basket on top of her head to sell garden produce in the Fofu rural fashion. She told me she could never do it. I did not understand why she felt this way when she had walked miles with a heavy load of firewood with no shame. She continued to criticize her husband by saying that he himself drank all the time. Maladi denied this and Teresa had to admit that she had never actually seen him drunk.

Despite this friction, however, Maladi and Teresa generally seemed contented. They teased each other in the evenings and laughed a lot. Teresa reminisced about her "wonderful" single life and Maladi praised her appearance as a married woman.

"She is relaxed because I give her salt, palm oil, and everything. There are no bad thoughts here." He then proceeded to iron Teresa's blouse and they continued to tease each other with Mami running between them until she fell asleep on the floor.

When the week was over Teresa walked me back to Nyanya carrying my suitcase on top of her head. I carried a lighter load. The same day, I flew to Buva to be with my family for Easter.

WHY IS MAMI SICK HERE?

While on holiday, Henry was able to buy me a bicycle. He had tried all year but none of the cities to which he flew had one. When I returned to Nyanya therefore, I was much more mobile. The trip to Gangu only took half an hour by bike. I went there twice to give the school children a questionnaire and dropped in at Sofia's and Teresa's. Sirigabo was a cute chubby baby who was crawling on the ground reaching for any object in sight. Bye-Bye and Felisi were busy protecting him from the fire. I learned that Mami had been sick and the results of a medical test were awaited.

My second trip to Gangu school was quite eventful. It was raining and I wondered if it was wise to go because the mud on the road would make cycling difficult. However, the rain soon stopped and I decided to try. But unfortunately the mud built up under the mud guards until there was no space between them and the wheels. As it was impossible to ride the bike like this I left it at a house about half way there and continued on foot. After I had finished at the school, Sofia invited me to lunch. While I was waiting for it I heard thunder in the distance. Seeing I was worried Sofia comforted me by predicting that it would not rain at Gangu but at Bilibali, her home village. In the middle of the lunch, however, Sofia was proved wrong and my heart sank. I knew I would have a tough trip home.

Maladi accompanied me to where I had left my bike and I started riding back to Nyanya. I had proceeded only one hundred yards when the mud under the mud guards prevented the wheels from turning. I took a stick from the road side and scraped the mud off. It was very sticky and heavy and my legs and clothes were covered with it, too. When I rode on, the mud collected faster and I made hardly any progress. I was determined to get home and cleaned the mud guards every few yards. I must have been going three hours and was still about a mile from home. I cycled down a hill and stopped at the bottom. The mud was so deep it reached half way up to my knees. I tried to push the bike up the hill but I could not move it. I was tired and the mud was heavier in the valley than elsewhere. Just then a husky young man appeared, asked if I was having difficulty and offered his help. He took the bicycle and carried it up the hill on his shoulder. The muddy bike made his clothes dirty. On top of the hill he continued to push the bike and I trailed behind him concentrating on lifting my mud-heavy feet step by step. I was very grateful to reach home that day. I thanked the young man and gave him a bar of laundry soap to wash his muddy clothes with. After that experience, I had a friend take off the mud guards and was consequently less vulnerable to the weather in the future.

A couple of months later, I cycled to Gangu with my suitcase on the back of the bicycle for my last visit of the week. This time it was a pleasurable ride. I stayed at Maladi's again. Remi and Sofia had moved to live in a relative's house further down in the village, so I could no longer observe their family life directly from Maladi's house. Remi was busy acquiring the building materials for his new house. When I saw Sofia, she was distilling liquor and serving it to customers. Little Sirigabo was crawling on the ground dirty from top to toe. Sofia picked him up and nursed him while doing her chores. Sofia's daughter from her first marriage, Masani, was staying with her for the school vacation. She smiled at me as if I were an old friend and stretched her hand to touch my hair, commenting on its softness.

"She wanted to do that long ago, long ago, at Yenyabo, but did not dare to," Sofia explained. I was glad she was not so shy of me as she had been.

Maladi's old mother, who had lived with his uncle during my previous visits, was now living at Maladi's as was his sister, whom I had never met. She had come to visit her lineage relatives but was planning to return to her husband very soon. The women slept on banana leaves in the living room.

When I arrived Teresa was subdued because Mami had a high fever. She slept most of the day, not waking until late afternoon. When Teresa saw that she still had a fever, she sponged her down in a bath of cold water. Mami whimpered. Maladi gave her a shot of quinine and I comforted Teresa by telling her that children often had malaria but recovered from it all right. I was thinking of my own children who went through it many times when growing up in Africa. In the morning Teresa carried Mami all the way to Nyanya hospital. Maladi followed behind on my bike.

I launched my last phase of fieldwork in the village. Again, Felisi helped me and in Teresa's absence, Sofia fed me. I felt the pressure of time heavy on my shoulders because I was going to leave Africa for good in less than a month. Consequently, I did not pay much attention to Mami's ailment, which I now regret.

In the evening, Teresa returned exhausted having carried Mami all the way back, too. Teresa was angry at Maladi who had insisted that they return home for the night because of their guest (me!). They had quarrelled on the way home and Sofia had heard them as they passed her house. The next day, Sofia expressed her concern about it. Apparently they had quarrelled several times before and she and Remi were worried about their young marriage. I felt badly that my presence caused friction between them and wondered if I should go somewhere else but Sofia comforted me by saying that she had already told Teresa that she would look after me whenever Teresa was away. Also, Maladi's mother and sister were helpful in the house, so I thought it was all right to stay.

That evening everyone was low in spirits: Teresa tired and depressed about Mami; Maladi silent; and his female relatives sympathetic and worried. Gone was the happy babbling of Mami. She slept all the while.

In the morning, I woke up to the sound of Maladi's mother praying aloud, "Please God, let Mami get better because a little child has no fault before you, no fault before you."

Teresa set off for the hospital once more and Maladi followed her after a decent interval. Later that day he came back to get clothes and food for Mami and Teresa who were going to stay in the hospital. I was glad that they were staying there.

My host and hostess gone, I got to know the other two women better. Maladi's sister swept the floors and his mother cooked. At night she carried a tiny pot of hot water outside for me to bathe. It was very hot and I did not dare to use it. I asked if it would be all right for me to wait a little for the water to cool. It was. The mother paced up and down the living room. That night Maladi's sister went elsewhere to sleep. The mother's bed was made and she was yawning.

At last she got angry with me and said in her normal loud and harsh voice, "Hurry with your bathing, so I can get to sleep, get to sleep!" I rushed out and splashed the hot water quickly over my hands and feet and came in. She pulled the bamboo door in front of the opening and tied it with a vine. Her movements were jerky. She had run out of patience with me.

When I kidded Teresa afterwards about my being a nuisance to Maladi's mother, she laughed and explained to me that old people were like that, they had no patience. This set me thinking about other instances of bad temper I had witnessed. Remi's father and Sofia's first mother-in-law were two good examples. They were cross and grouchy people.

Another day I witnessed that Maladi's mother tried to keep a check on her own behaviour. I was chatting to her when Felisi came in. She immediately turned on him and inquired in a demanding voice, "Where is the change?" Felisi had run an errand for her and explained humbly with downcast eyes that his father had the money. The old woman turned to me and said, "I better not yell at him or I will be accused of witchcraft if a child should die in the family." Then she carried on the conversation with me. I also recall talking to an old man at Yenyabo, who blamed young men for all the evil in the world. Afterwards, my young companion laughed and said, "Those old men are funny. We often suspect them of witchcraft." I could easily believe in witchcraft instigated by them, they were seething bitter people condemning everyone around them!

I also saw how easy it was to believe that the ancestors were angry, since they were only an extension of the old people. No wonder it was thought that ancestors kept an eye on family life and punished any breach of custom with thunder bolts or sickness.

As Teresa had decided to stay in the hospital over the weekend, I thought I would visit her on the Sunday and see if there was anything I could do. I found Teresa sitting on the bed in which Mami slept. She was clearly very depressed about Mami. Fortunately her own mother, a small, frail woman was there to look after them. Teresa told me that Mami had not held any liquid for 30 hours and that the nurses did not do anything about the diarrhea.

"Have you told them?" I inquired.

"Many times but they do not care, do not care," Teresa answered. I was alarmed. I went to a nurse, a tall black man, who was walking through the ward and asked him to do something about Mami. He was annoyed at my interference and looking down at me, said,

"We know what we are doing, we are nurses, nurses." I told him that surely something should be done about a little child being dehydrated. He went to a junior nurse and told him to give Mami diarrhea medicine. I protested that diarrhea medicine would not be adequate but he slammed the cupboard door and told me to shut up.

Teresa watched me following and challenging the nurse.

"We don't know him, so he does not care for us, care for us. If we were from his tribe, he would do something." I stood at the foot of the bed not knowing what to do. Teresa decided to give Mami another cold bath. She shook Mami and shouted,

"Mami, your white woman is here!" She did not wake up. She did not even react to the cold water when Teresa bathed her but looked dangerously quiet and limp. Her arms were as thin as straw. I grew very alarmed.

"Should I appeal to the doctor?" I asked Teresa.

She looked at me imploringly, "Please, madam, do it!"

She was normally a calm person and seldom raised her voice, but now I detected a note of panic in it. I ran to find out who the doctor on call was, and ran to his home. It was a hot and sunny day, and the mission station was on a hill side. The doctor was not at home but his house help told me where he was visiting. Again, I ran on a path through thick woods to the other side of the mission station and arrived sweaty and panting at the house. He was just coming out after a leisurely lunch. He was a young blond man, still in medical school in Switzerland and spending his summer months practising in this hospital. A Zairean hospital must have been quite an experience for him.

Although still out of breath, I managed to explain to him that I was extremely concerned about my friends who had come here from Gangu to get medical help and were not getting it. He listened to me, asked the exact location of the patient's bed and told me he would go to check her.

A few hours later I went back to the ward and met another nurse at the bedside trying to put a tube into Mami's stomach through her nose. It looked revolting and he did not succeed. Then he decided to give her an intravenous drip. He was a relaxed and friendly nurse and patiently tried to find a vein in Mami's thin and dehydrated arm. Teresa watched his activities with a serious face and her mother walked outside not to be in the way. When the drip was installed and the liquid was going into Mami, we were all relieved. I was absolutely sure that she would recover. Teresa told me in a quiet, even voice about the tests they had been doing. She did not think they were thorough enough and was not satisfied when I told her that the doctor in charge knew what to do.

I saw the doctor again and he told me that he thought Mami had meningitis, although the test results were inconclusive.

"I have ordered her two kinds of antibiotics and our medicine is good. I hope she will pull through." I was sure she would and I walked to the market happily to buy ingredients for a big meal for the Teresa and her mother. I cooked it at home and took it to the hospital in the evening. Teresa managed a faint smile. Her mother was quiet and kept her eyes on Mami.

On Monday morning I went by the ward. Teresa told me that Mami was a little bit better. She was still asleep. I had only optimistic thoughts as I pedalled back to Gangu. On arrival the villagers asked me about Mami and I told them that she was getting better. They seemed to be very concerned about her.

I continued with my work and walked through the village. But the dark side of African life seemed to haunt the village and taught me a lesson about death being an ordinary, almost everyday, event in the lives of the Fofu. On my way back to Maladi's later that day I heard wailing. I noticed that there was a big crowd of people around a neighbour's house. The mother of the house was the woman who had sold Teresa's liquor on the mountain. I had interviewed her a few days ago. Her eight-month-old baby had coughed endlessly during the interview. It must have been whooping cough, although the people diagnosed it as "a bird's sickness," i.e. when a child's eyes roll around in convulsions and the child dies. I thought that she must have died. When I approached, however, someone told me that the child was still alive but the people were waiting for her to die. They stood motionless in the yard staring into the house. I joined them. Someone else told me to go in and I did. The living room was dark because people's heads were blocking the light from the windows. The mother was sitting on the floor wailing. The child was lying stiff on another woman's lap. The house was packed with silent people. Among others I spotted Sofia with her two children.

The mother's bitter chant pierced the silence and gave me shivers. Sofia took the child from the woman who was holding her. The mother wailed,

"If she dies, I will leave this house. My husband's father has bewitched our family!" She repeated this and then went on to describe other deaths in the family, "He has already killed four children of mine, one by one!"

Later I referred to my household census, and sure enough, she had lost four daughters in infancy.

I had to go out of the room. The darkness, the sight of the dying child, the silence of the people, and the heart-rending pain of the mother were too much for me, not being used to death. The air was heavy from the human bodies filling the room and the smell of the dying child. For courtesy, I should have stayed longer, but I slipped outside where the bright sun greeted me. As I took a deep breath, I spotted the father of the dying infant. He was sitting on a low stool holding one foot in the air. On the sole of the foot was an open wound which was bleeding. The foot was very swollen. As he got up with great difficulty someone handed him a set of home-made crutches. They seemed uncomfortable and too short for him but with their help and that of a male relative, he managed to hop to the outhouse. Then he hopped back through the crowd of visitors and went to a bedroom to sleep. I could not comprehend how these people were able to handle so much misery at one time. He did not mourn or complain.

Maladi had joined the crowd and quietly explained the family situation. He spoke in a dry voice like a lecturer. He criticized the man for not taking care of his family when they were sick. Not only had this daughter been sick for a long time but his son's ears were rotting. Despite this he had spent no money on medicine. The mother had come to Maladi to beg for injections and he had given them without charging. Although she had used Western medicine she did not want to take the child to the hospital where Teresa was. Over Maladi's monotonous voice we could hear her piercing shout, "I am not going to go to Nyanya to waste money, waste money! My children have died there, too!"

Maladi also enlightened me about the accusation of witchcraft by the husband's father. He had not gotten along with his son for a long time and had often wished his son's family ill with curses such as,

"May your sewing machine bring you no happiness, may the profits go to liquor!" Also, when his daughter-in-law had not brought him a hen after returning from her home village, he forecast, "Trouble will come to this house!," it was Maladi's view that these curses resulted in the daughter-in-law bearing mostly daughters rather than sons, and four children having died. This would be the fifth.

The old man had fled when this child was deteriorating because he knew that he would be blamed. Had he stayed the crowd would have captured him, beaten, and speared him for all his curses.

Maladi finished his explanations and walked home with me. I saw Sofia coming out of the neighbour's and walking home with her children. People were starting to disperse. Maladi prepared to go to the Nyanya hospital to see Mami. Again, he took my bike and was off.

I was still at home writing notes when he returned. I looked up from my writing, "Did you forget something?." He did not answer. He put the bicycle away, walked in, threw a bag on the floor, and sat down.

"God has taken Mami. There is nothing for me to do, nothing to do," he said in a lifeless voice. He had met a runner on the road with the bad news.

It could not be true! I had left her recovering, she was getting better! I refused to believe it. No, no, no! I did not understand. How could it be possible?

"There is nothing one can do now, do now," Maladi said quietly. His old mother agreed, "It was the Lord's will, the Lord's will. There is nothing to do now, nothing to do." We sat in silence, they with resignation and I with rebellion and protest in my heart. Then Maladi said, "It is so quiet here." Gone were Mami's happy chattering and laughter.

"What will Teresa do now?" I asked after a while.

Maladi explained mechanically that members of Teresa's lineage would carry the body to her village and bury it there. Teresa would stay there three days until the bathing of the sorrow ritual and then return to Gangu.

"Are the folks from here going to attend the funeral?" I inquired.

"No need to, no need. They'll go for the bathing ceremony," said Maladi.

Later that evening, Maladi and his mother discussed the cause of Mami's death. Perhaps Mami's father's lineage, who had never paid anything for Teresa and had shown no interest in the child, bewitched her because she was a smart girl. Or perhaps Teresa's own lineage was angry at her for taking the child to Gangu, to her step-father's lineage, and not leaving her to live with Teresa's brother, to whom she rightfully belonged. Maladi was content that he had done everything he could to save the child.

"Nobody can blame me, blame me, for anything," he announced with satisfaction in his dry voice. Maladi's mother said, "Teresa will be very angry about the death of her child." Maladi agreed, "Yes, Teresa is a very angry woman, angry woman." I did not understand them. To me, Teresa was a calm and gentle person. I wondered what was going on and asked Maladi,

"Why do you say she is an angry woman?"

"Because she holds a grudge for a very long time, very long time, but I will not give in," he replied sternly.

I gathered from this discussion that there would be a dispute about the cause of Mami's death. Teresa's family would surely have a different view from that of Maladi's. I had sensed it already during Mami's illness. At the beginning of the week, Teresa's sister had posed a question,

"Why is Mami always sick here in Gangu? When she lived with her mother at the Catholic station, she was always healthy, always healthy."

"Could it be that someone here at Gangu does not like her?" I ventured.

She latched onto this excitedly, "That's it! We have been thinking that, thinking."

"Who is it?" I continued, but she backed off.

"That is impossible to know, know. Witchcraft works at night, not daytime." Then she added, "Our brother will take Mami to his home, to his home, when he gets leave (from Lemura)."

Quite late on the evening of Mami's death, Teresa's sister appeared at Maladi's. She was wailing and sobbing rhythmically. She had come for Mami's clothes so they could be buried with the little body. While she waited for Maladi to gather the belongings, she kept on sobbing in rhythm. I stood near her and felt like joining in but did not know how to. I remembered that five months previously, she had been the first in the married women's file to lead Teresa to the village with joyous songs and clapping of hands. When Maladi had made a bundle of Mami's belongings and handed it to his sister-in-law, she left, increasing the volume of her wailing.

Maladi commented, "I cannot see how she can keep up the wailing all the way from here to Nyanya, from here to Nyanya. My, some people start early!"

I was shocked by this remark. Wailing was a Fofu custom: why did he criticize a person for following it? I wondered if, in fact, he was relieved at the death. Although he had allowed Teresa to bring Mami with her, he resented the fact that he would not receive any bridewealth for Mami's marriage although as her step-father, he would have fed, clothed and generally cared for her throughout her childhood. Indeed, he had already given her numerous injections during her illnesses and paid her hospital bills. Some time before Maladi had told me that he had ordered a new bed for Mami at a carpenter's but had not paid for it yet. He was not very happy about Mami sleeping with him and Teresa in the same bed. After hearing the news of Mami's death, he had immediately gone to the carpenter's to cancel his order. His swiftness surprised me.

If Mami had lived, her natural father would not have gotten any bridewealth on her marriage either because he had not paid bridewealth for Teresa. Thus Mami was viewed as belonging to Teresa's lineage, not the lineage of the natural father, and Teresa's brother would have legally received the bridewealth on Mami's marriage. No wonder Maladi felt that he would have cared for her for nothing.

The news had spread in the village. When I walked through it again, women were exclaiming with astonishment. One woman said to another,

"Perhaps God showed us an image through Mami, a vain image in this world, an image!" I could not understand what she meant except that, in her own way, she tried to make sense and see a meaning in Mami's death. Then the women expressed their fondness for the happy, talkative little girl.

The next day was scheduled to be my last day in the village and I wanted to leave early to be able to attend Mami's funeral. Unfortunately, however, I had to meet a group of village elders whom I had been trying to see ever since the very first day of my first visit. The chief had always postponed the meeting and finally we had rescheduled it for the last morning at eight. I packed my belongings early in the morning and waited for the elders to arrive. Sofia, Maladi, and some other relatives left for the funeral on foot early in the morning. I told them I would catch up to them on my bike after my meeting. Remi stayed to attend the elders' meeting with me.

Two hours passed and still the elders had not arrived. I was very upset, although I knew that the elders would not have watches and that they never kept time, anyway. I was restless because I wanted to go to the funeral but felt that I could not give up the meeting because it involved ten respected elders. Eventually the first elder arrived at 10:40 and the others after 11 a.m. We had an hour's meeting during which they told me the history of the village and the lineages. Then they asked me to repair their identity cards, which were torn and worn (from rubbing in their pockets). I did this with transparent Scotch tape and they were very pleased.

When they had left, Remi told me that the funeral would be over by then because the child was not a full human and would have been buried before noon. I said,

"I'll go and give Teresa my condolences, at least."

Remi shook his head, "There is no use going today, no use. Go when they wash the sorrow away in three days." I was surprised at his suggestion but trusted that he knew what was proper. So I rode slowly to Nyanya and waited until the next ritual in a few days.

I did not take my bike to Teresa's village because I knew that the path was narrow. It was only an hour's walk away and I enjoyed the peace. Half way to the village, Teresa's sister's husband from Gangu caught up with me and we went on together. He had been away when Mami died and like me had missed the funeral but his wife and children had been at the wake since the death. He informed me that Maladi's neighbour's child had also died. The mother had finally taken her to a native healer but to no avail. I asked how the mother was doing, remembering her bitter wailing before the death. He explained that he had consoled her and enabled her to bear her sorrow without protest and thoughts of witchcraft by telling her,

"Other children in this village die, too, you are not the only one to lose your child. That is the Lord's will, there is nothing a human being can do about it, nothing." How many times had I heard this cliche before?

When we arrived at Teresa's brother's place, the women were leaving for a stream to bathe, the men having already returned from their ritual bathing. I was going to join the women but Teresa forbade me.

"Don't come, don't, madam!" I promised to stay aside and not disturb anyone, but she was firm and did not let me join them. I was disappointed. Despite having spent ten years trying to gain the friendship and confidence of the people, I was still not allowed to see their bathing ritual. Much was still withheld from me. At that moment, I felt a failure as an anthropologist, forgetting how much I had learned and how many parts of people's lives I had shared.

While the women were away, I walked to Mami's grave which was near the house. It was marked by a little heap of gravel. I stood there alone with tears in my eyes remembering my visit to this house before Christmas. It was tragic that the vivacious and happy three-year-old was dead less than a year later.

The Catholic sisters told me that in fact Mami's funeral had been held around 2 p.m.: only infants were buried before noon because they were not considered truly human yet. So I would have made it to the funeral had I set off immediately after the elders had left.

While contemplating the grave, Maladi came over to tell me that his neighbour's foot was more swollen. Apparently he could not move around even on crutches and had to be carried to the toilet. He badly required a penicillin injection but had no money. I gave Maladi the money and begged him to give him the injection as soon as possible. Maladi was in a good mood. He appeared very satisfied with himself having done all he could to save Mami. He even smiled when he talked.

When the women returned from the stream, a short service was held. I was ushered under a temporary shelter erected for the occasion. The men, a few black Catholic sisters, who had come from the Catholic mission station where Teresa and Mami had lived, and I sat there on chairs. Other women and those men who arrived late found places further away in the shade of the house or under a tree, and sat on the ground. Teresa's brother led the service: he read prayers from a Catholic book and gave a short sermon stating that a human life did not end in death as "a hen's life ended" but continued after death to eternity. One day, we would meet Mami again.

A rainstorm interrupted the service and we all ran into the houses for cover. Teresa's brother's house was full of women, most men having run to the neighbour's where the men were expected to gather. Two men, however, remained among us women and they appeared uncomfortable. Remembering the rule of the segregation of sexes I observed their behaviour with interest. They spotted an empty room and moved there. Soon someone told them that the other house was for men and they left immediately, regardless of the heavy rain.

During this interruption, Teresa and I had a chance to talk. I told her about the meeting of the village elders and my intention to come to the funeral late but that Remi had advised against it.

Teresa was offended, "They over there have ill will, don't listen to them!" She told me that her colleague from the Catholic mission station could not attend the funeral either but she had come before and after it to greet her and be with her in her sorrow. "That is the right way to do it, the right way." I was sorry that I had not followed my intuition.

Teresa had nothing good to say about her husband. One reason was that Maladi had not been in the hospital to help her when Mami's condition deteriorated. If she had not had her mother, she would not have known what to do, especially when the child died. Apparently, Mami had been transferred to intensive care soon after I had left on Monday morning. A few hours later, her body ceased to accept the serum and Mami's life ebbed away. When she died, her mother knew what to do: she started wailing and they carried the child's body home. Her mother knew the rituals and took care of everything. Teresa only had to follow. All her siblings had now arrived home and were giving her both moral and physical support. I could see that her family was a fortress for her at this time of deep sorrow. Even now her frail mother, assisted by her daughters and daughter-in-law, was busy preparing a meal for the funeral guests.

Another friend of mine, related to Maladi on her mother's side, had been in the hospital at the time of Mami's death. She told me that the moment Mami died, Teresa's mother started her wail with the words, "They killed my child because she played and rejoiced, played and rejoiced!" My friend could not decide if there was an accusation against Maladi's family or her own family in the word "they."

Teresa also blamed Maladi for not talking to her before the funeral and not bothering to view Mami's body before the coffin was opened for general viewing. Other complaints were that he had not given her money for Mami's hospital expenses and did not really care about her sorrow. I wondered why she was so critical of her husband. Then I remembered that in our culture, too, death puts enormous stress on couples. Here the lineages of the husband and wife were often historically hostile ("Now we marry into the clans that we used to eat"), so it was understandable that they accused the spouse's lineage of witchcraft. Of course, in this particular case, Maladi's complacent attitude did not help either. When Teresa was looking to him for empathy and comfort all she saw was his self-satisfaction.

Another factor which, it seemed to me, led Teresa to thoughts of witchcraft was that she did not believe Mami had meningitis because the blood samples had been taken only from her fingertips and not from the elbow. Teresa was agitated but tried to calm herself down by repeating,

"That was the Lord's will, the Lord's will. There is nothing one can do, nothing, nothing."

Late in the afternoon the meal was ready. The men, the Catholic sisters, and I were served first. The other women ate afterwards. This was not the first time I had been given the status of a man among the Fofu. I left an hour before dark to allow myself time to walk back in daylight and promised to come and see Teresa once more before I left Africa. The rest of the mourners stayed.

I had finished my fieldwork in the villages but I still had to wrap up my interviews at Nyanya. I was busy till the end. Two days before I was due to leave Africa, I arose early and set off at six o'clock to see Teresa. It was my last opportunity to enjoy African landscape. I walked on a lonely path from Nyanya to Teresa's village. The elephant grass was tall, about three meters high. From a hill top I could see far away over the savannah, the green grass sprinkled with trees and bushes and, of course, villages with brown mud huts which blended in with the landscape. The birds were singing, the sun was rising and the air was cool and fresh. I breathed deeply. Back in Canada, I would miss my long hikes — there I would be driving a car in the city!

Teresa was surprised that I arrived so early but was nonetheless glad to see me. She was wearing a dark blue wrap-around skirt and a top made of the same material. I knew it was customary to wear dark colours until the string around the neck was cut in a big feast. I asked when she would arrange the festival but she did not know.

"Whenever I will get the money together to arrange it, after three months, after two years, whenever," she said. "But the sorrow will not end even then, not end," she reminded me. I had heard other Fofu mothers say the same thing when their children died. She said she kept on thinking of Mami all the time and sometimes called her by name until awaken by the harsh reality.

"How can I continue to live alone, alone?" she asked me but I had no answer. I remembered that she was pregnant and hoped she would have another little girl.

Again, she blamed Maladi for not bothering to come and see her. He had not even sent her a letter. I asked if it was customary for a husband to visit his wife at her village during the mourning period.

"It varies, varies. Some men mourn a lot."

She was not sure whether she would like living in Gangu any more but thought that she would try it for a while.

Her old mother made us coffee. Her brother was still on leave from his job in Lemura. He spent his time here painting pictures, calabashes, and post cards for sale by the road side. Some missionaries had taught him these skills and he made more money from these sales than by his regular job. Her sister-in-law was washing dishes and I noticed that she was wearing a red watch which I had given Teresa as a gift at Gangu. I was amused that my gift was being used by somebody else because in our culture that would have been considered impolite. But I knew that family reciprocity was behind Teresa's sharing of her gifts and her possessions, such as the dishes which she had left at her mother's house when she got married. Now her family was reciprocating by offering her shelter, food, and comfort. There was no guarantee she would receive such services from her husband's family: indeed, she was at this very moment blaming his side for not providing them.

I left her some self-addressed aerograms so she could easily write to me and asked her to wave when we took off from Nyanya in two days time. The plane would fly over her home on the way to Lemura.

On the day my children and I were to leave, Sofia with the baby, Remi, and Maladi came to bid us farewell. They sat with us in the house waiting for the plane. I gave Maladi a set of aerogrammes, too, because there was no guarantee that the two would write to me together. He promised to keep me informed about Remi's family. I also gave Maladi my umbrella so Teresa could use it as a parasol when she bore the baby. Fofu mothers protected their newborn babies on their backs with parasols. The four came with us to the hangar when it was time for the plane to arrive. They felt out of place in the hustle and bustle of a white man's hangar and sat quietly on a bench. Sofia looked as shy there as she had seemed a year ago in her husband's home.

I told Maladi that I had gone to see Teresa and she had complained that he had not come to see her.

"Only a few days since I saw her, a few days," mumbled Maladi.

"And so much work, much work!" added Sofia, nursing her chubby baby. I calculated that it had been six weeks since the funeral when they had been in Teresa's village. Their coldness hurt me as it must have hurt Teresa. I wondered if my parasol would ever reach her . . .

The airplane took off and flew above Teresa's brother's place. I looked down and could barely see Mami's rounded grave, a heap of dirt. People were waving to us in the yard. I identified Teresa, her brother and mother. My last farewell to Teresa!

A year later, Maladi wrote to me that everyone was well. Sofia's baby had been sick but had recovered by the time of writing. Remi had agreed to be a sub-chief in the village and was living in a new house (in a new location) near a road. The villagers had built a medical hut for Maladi's community health work and he no longer needed to treat his patients at home. He had not been able to pay more bridewealth for Teresa and her brother was preventing her from returning to him. He also told me about his old uncle at Nyanya via whom he received my letters. His paralysed wife had died and he was diagnosed as having diabetes. Later I heard from others that he also died.

After two years, Teresa wrote to me, as well. I was astonished to hear that she had moved away from the Fofu area and was living with her cousin who, as principal of an elementary school, had arranged a teaching position for her there.

"I saw that I could not get along with Maladi. He never helped me with the baby, not even with a bar of soap." Instead of returning to him she had run far away from him. To my delight, however, she had borne a daughter and I was sure she was happy to have a baby girl again.

PART II

WHO CAN SURVIVE IN THIS CITY?

5 WHERE ARE THE FOFU?

A TWO ROAD TOWN

In 1977 we moved to Bululu, a city situated about 230 miles south of Lemura on the northern shore of Lake Kivu. When we visited the city over the years before moving there I thought that the scenery was gorgeous both looking toward the lake and looking toward the volcanoes surrounding the city. The volcano, called Nyiragongo, was especially majestic. Most of the time it was capped with clouds but often in the mornings the weather was clear and you could see its black cone with a flat top standing solemnly against the blue sky. The other volcanoes were smaller and less spectacular, but nevertheless contributed to the overall picture.

Bululu had been founded in colonial times as a government post near the game reserve and it had been an active tourist centre before Independence, as had the Rwandese city just across the border. When I lived in Bululu, cross-Africa safari trucks and Landrovers could still be regularly seen in town, and sometimes individual tourists, too. But neither Zaire nor Rwanda was as friendly to tourists as Kenya. In Zaire, tourists could expect hassle with immigration officials and the army, bandit attacks, thievery, and general hostility from the people of the country.

The foreigners who had lived in Bululu before Independence remembered the town as well kept and neat. When we moved there, it was run down. True, there were flower baskets hanging from the lamp posts in the middle of the main street but nobody took care of them. Nor were any of the public flower beds tended. Sidewalks were cracked and worn out and many steps were broken or missing.

Bululu was not a big city. The population was below 100,000 in 1977 growing to 120,000 by 1985. Most people lived in tiny houses in slum areas, while the few wealthy people and foreigners (the latter numbered about 1,200 in 1985) occupied the big villas between downtown and the lake. In 1985, I noticed that the upper class was moving out of town into lake side villas with their own water and electricity supplies.

When we first lived in Bululu there was only one surfaced road. It ran from the Rwanda border through the shopping section of the city to a point about 15 miles south. It was old and rough and was repaired by filling the numerous holes with loose sand just before the president arrived in town, once every two or three years. Subsequently another road was surfaced about four miles long, running from the airport to the lakeshore, or more exactly, to the President's villa. This was a great improvement on the bumpy and dusty old road but it was not repaired any more frequently than the larger road.

The main downtown shopping area consisted of small shops, about 15 on either side of the street. They were more specialized and a bit bigger than the rural stores at Nyanya. Many of the shop owners were Asians but some were Zaireans. There was a butcher's, a baker's, several pharmacies and grocery stores, a hardware store etc. There were a few similar shops in other streets downtown and closer to the slum areas there were many more shops. The slum shops reminded me of rural ones as they sold a wide range of goods. Some Bululu stores were stocked with dairy produce, such as cheese, butter, cream, and yogurt from the farms in the surrounding mountains. Elsewhere in Zaire these items had to be imported, so Bululu was a privileged town in this respect. However, the majority of the population could not afford these products.

The downtown section contained various institutions as well as shops. There was, for example, a post office, a zone administration centre, a regional administration centre, a military police office and a court room. In 1977 there were two hospitals in the city but in 1985 a huge new hospital was being built with foreign aid. In addition, there were several private dispensaries around town. There were about ten major hotels in the centre of town, countless small ones scattered around the slums, and one really big one outside the city on the lakeside.

The biggest employers in town were a truck transport company, a coffee factory, Air Zaire, and an air charter company which flew between the capital and Bululu. Each employed between 200 and 550 people. Employment was very insecure as everywhere in the country. As an example, the coffee factory had over a thousand employees in 1975 and ten years later only half that number. In 1978 a tea factory employed over 200 people but in 1985 it had only about sixty employees. Shortage of packaging material was then said to be the cause of lay-offs. I had no figures of the unemployed but there were crowds of them everywhere in town begging for employment. There was, of course, no redundancy or unemployment pay from the state. A large portion of the population of the town was engaged in smuggling manufactured goods from Rwanda to Zaire and selling them in Bululu. Smuggling coffee across Lake Kivu in the opposite direction was also a large scale business. When we went for picnics on the lakeshore, we used to watch dug-out long boats making their way toward Rwanda, loaded so full that their sides were deep in the water. On top of the smuggled coffee beans, which everyone knew was the bulk of the cargo, were thrown a few hands of bananas.

There were three major market places in town. The location of the downtown market place was changed at least three times between 1977 and 1981. The petty traders were treated like pawns by the rich builders who needed the land for their more profitable businesses. The traders had no say in the matter.

European vegetables were sold twice a week by farmers who grew them some thirty miles from town. This was the best place we had lived in Zaire: we could buy strawberries all year around! It sounds good, but there was a catch. At first we ate the strawberries only after rinsing them in boiled and filtered water — and we soon developed amoebic dysentery. The disease was terrible, it drained us of all energy. After that we either boiled the strawberries with sugar to make strawberry syrup or soaked them in a poisonous solution and then rinsed them in boiled and filtered water. We had to soak lettuce, too. We realized that our supposed paradise had parasites!

Electricity and running water which flowed by the power of electric pumps, were a problem in the city for years. There were unexpected cuts in the supply of both, sometimes for several days. Our washrooms stank after a few hours without water and our fridges, freezers, and stoves caused us headaches. We foreigners thought it was an awful hardship to endure although we could go to the lake with our cars — our houses were near to it — and fill our containers with water. Many of us bought gas stoves as reserves and some even installed private generators. We complained although we had the financial means to overcome the problem. The Zaireans, especially those in slum areas, had to walk several miles to the lake or across the border to Rwanda to get water and carry it home on their backs or heads. When there were cuts it was common to see the two asphalt roads full of people hauling water and the lake shore crowded with people washing their laundry and swimming. Once, during a long "drought" a cholera epidemic swept through the city. One child of the Fofu lost his life together with many other people, mostly either very young or very old.

I wonder how much it helped that the city sent health officials to teach people to cover the holes in their outhouses and boil their drinking water. My own househelp, a woman, who daily boiled the drinking water for my family as part of her work, told me that she did not do it at home because if you were on God's list you would die whether you boiled your water or not. The Fofu told me that it was too expensive for them to use their hard earned firewood just for boiling water and they continued to drink water unboiled as before.

In 1984 a new power line was built from Buva to Bululu some 120 miles. The source was a huge hydroelectric power station built by Belgians and later expanded with the help of the World Bank. After that, electricity and water supplies were more reliable, although not impeccably so. The better houses in the centre of town had running water and electricity but the slum areas did not. The slum families had to send representatives, usually women and children, to line up at private pay-taps scattered around town. During a political election campaign, a candidate installed a free tap in the slum area to win votes. That tap was the most crowded of all and the Fofu told me that fights often broke out if somebody tried to jump the queue, and children were in danger of being beaten and robbed of their containers. I will often refer to the duty of water hauling in the stories of the urban Fofu families because it was an essential part of the daily routine.

As I said earlier, Bululu was surrounded by volcanoes. Although most of them were extinct, some of them continued to erupt every few years and new ones appeared. The inhabitants of Bululu lived in constant fear of eruptions because one never knew when they would occur. Europeans told stories of eruptions several decades ago that had covered their homes. Six months before we moved to the city, the foot of Nyiragongo erupted and the hot lava flowed toward the city covering huts, fields, and the main road leading to the game park. About 75 people lost their lives. A government program offered new farms to people whose land was destroyed by the lava. Although these families had to move to the rain forest about 60 miles away, people were so anxious to go that some of those who lost nothing in the eruption gave false information in order to get new farms elsewhere. My family went to see the lava a few weeks after the eruption. Although it had solidified by then and we could walk on it, albeit with difficulty because of the rocky terrain, hot flames and gases were still rising to the surface. I could feel the heat through my shoes. Here and there a scorched black tree stood lonely in the midst of the black lava. Zaireans chopped the remaining trees for firewood while observing the vegetation regain control over the lava.

They talked a lot about the event over the years and recounted how panic had taken over: everyone had wanted to get out of the city which they expected to be covered by the lava but escaping was not easy as the smoke and fumes made visibility poor. Even in their rush to leave, wealthier Zaireans were wise enough to take their most treasured possessions with them: their goats, doors, and roofs! The border with Rwanda was kept open without customs inspection and the people filed through to the sister city and climbed the Rwandese mountains until they felt safe. The lava, however, stopped in the outskirts of Bululu and the people were able to return to their homes after a few days.

While living in Bululu, we witnessed several eruptions but in each case the lava flowed away from the city. We flew over and hiked near these eruptions to photograph them. They were some of the most memorable events in the whole of our time in Africa. While doing fieldwork in 1985 there was fear of another eruption. Japanese and European scientific research teams arrived in the city and recommended its evacuation. Some inhabitants left, most did not, but a general hysteria reigned in the city. Bandits took their opportunity. One night they blew up an electricity transformer station yelling that the smoke was from an eruption. Much confusion resulted and while people were trying to decide what to do, the bandits plundered their homes. After a month or two the foreign teams left saying that an eruption in India had released the pressure inside the earth's crust and there was no longer immediate danger of an eruption.

I wondered how people could live under the continuous threat of an eruption. I remember having nightmares about lava flowing toward our house and us trying to run to the lake to be safe from the hot lava. Tom stayed awake crying for nights because he had heard people say that the next eruption would be at a hotel near his school, half a mile from our house. He was sure we would be buried in lava because we lived downhill from the hotel. I could not comfort him very convincingly because I was not sure myself that it could not happen.

The danger of the volcanoes was not the only threat the inhabitants of Bululu were living under. There were two others.

The lake was the first one. Although it was a source of beauty and recreation for the foreigners in Bululu, the Zaireans disliked it. Indeed, some of them systematically avoided going near it. It was believed that a mermaid lived in the lake and that she captured bathers, sucked their blood and brains out, and after a few days, abandoned the bodies on the shore. The Fofu used to laugh at me for taking my children to the lake for picnics and swimming.

Although we viewed the lake as a positive phenomenon, we realized that it was a great danger to us, too. There were spots where people kept on drowning and it was thought that volcanic gases rising from the bottom of the lake were responsible for these deaths.

For us there was also a personal tragedy connected with the lake. Two of Henry's colleagues crashed their small plane in the lake. Although it was only about fifty yards from the shore, the plane sank to the bottom which was also about fifty yards deep and it took months before appropriate equipment was obtained to recover the wreck and the bodies. During those months the shores were filled with crowds who watched the recovery attempts and talked about the accident.

The other threat the inhabitants lived under was the bandits. Nobody was ever safe from them; neither the foreigner, the wealthy Zairean, nor the poor slum dweller. We had a Belgian neighbour who was an honourary British consul and a coffee plantation owner. I used to admire his compound for its safety. He had a twelve foot wall around his yard, a thorny hedge, a high gate which was always locked, iron bars in the windows, four night watchmen and several big dogs. Surely nobody would break into his house, I thought. Amazingly we heard one morning that a gang of bandits had broken into the house, beating the night watchmen and the dogs and entering the house through a pantry door which was not as strong as the other doors. The bandits had demanded the money they had seen the man take out of the bank the day before. Unfortunately for them, he had used it to pay his plantation workers out of town. The bandits then demanded their valuables, beat the whole family up so that they were bruised and swollen for a long time, and took their clothing, jewelry, televisions, tape recorders etc. I saw the wife after the event. She had tried to shelter her children from the blows with her body and she was badly bruised. I asked her if it made her think again about her living in Africa. She answered calmly that an event like that had to be accepted as part of living in Zaire.

Our security was less comprehensive than our Belgian neighbours. We had only an evergreen hedge around our house and a low gate. Furthermore, as I had planted some new bushes where there had been gaps, it was very low in places although some sections were about six feet high. We had a German Shepherd who, having been stoned over the hedge by Zaireans, was very fierce at nights. We also had a night watchman who fell asleep on the job so soundly that when some Fofu tried to wake him up one night because they wanted me to help them, he could not be roused. We also had iron bars in the windows but these were ineffectual as Tom showed that he could slip through them. In the beginning, I used to lay awake worrying about the bandits but then got used to it.

One evening a thief walked in without any hindrance. As we had company for supper we had tied our dog at the back of the house so he would not disturb our guests. Our watchman was also at the back, our front door was closed but not locked. The thief was rummaging in our living room while we were having our dinner the other side of a partitioning curtain. I heard a noise and thought it was our cat. Suddenly I remembered that we had given it away the same day. Henry got up to look and found himself face to face with a well-dressed young man who had picked up our big tape recorder but could not free the wires leading to the speakers. He threw the recorder at Henry and ran through the door, dropping a tire iron on the floor when Henry slammed the door on his wrist. Then the young man jumped over the six foot hedge and disappeared into the darkness. We were fortunate that time and remembered in the future to keep our front porch gate and door locked at all times.

When I became acquainted with the Fofu, I learned that many of them had been robbed. I will mention one case in Chapter 6, "Anastasia, The Focus Of The Fofu." Another Fofu family who lived at the back of a small store were broken into and beaten several times. On one occasion the wife lost half a dozen teeth. My househelp, a single mother, lived with her children in rented rooms in the slums. She told me that the first person who noticed burglars were about, would start drumming on a tin roof in protest. Others would gradually follow suit until eventually the whole neighbourhood was drumming. That was a sign of a united front and the burglars would often go away.

Soldiers were robbers, too. They frequently arrested men for not carrying their identity cards in their own yards. One would think it permissible to take a leak without identification papers but the soldiers used any excuse to scare people into offering them bribes. If no bribes were forthcoming, they beat them up. Recovery from such beatings sometimes took months.

In some of my stories, I will refer to the "Red Berets." When Tanzania declared war against Uganda in 1978, the president of Zaire sent special troops, the "Red Berets," to monitor the situation in the east, since Zaire had borders with both countries. These troops wore a fancier uniform than the regular army soldiers. Their red berets in particular aroused admiration and fear among the population. These elite soldiers had a reputation of being very cruel and they kept the population under their rule by harassing people, beating them, and stealing their money. Instead of rebelling against them, which would have been suicide, or criticising them behind their backs, the population of Bululu treated them with respect, fear, and admiration. They had power! All people wanted the power to force their will upon others and these soldiers had it! Little boys imitated the "Red Berets" by wearing miniature berets and epaulettes and pretending to beat their playmates up.

But this admiration of the elite soldiers was mixed with bitterness. After a Fofu man was severely beaten by them, I heard his wife and other Fofu women discuss powerful curses to kill the soldiers. They lamented that they did not know such curses and comforted themselves by recalling occasions when soldiers had met with sudden deaths in accidents. When a soldier, who was married to a Fofu woman, ran into a rock on his motorcycle and was killed, I heard people mention witchcraft as the cause of his death.

WHERE ARE THE FOFU?

When we first moved to Bululu in 1977 I had no time for anthropology. My husband was starting a new air charter company and was very busy building the business up. In the beginning, there was hardly any help or equipment and I had to drive barrels of fuel to the airport for him to refuel. The lack of equipment meant that I did not need to spend time on a radio, which was good. But the bad side of it was that I did not know where he was and when he would arrive at the airport. Consequently I spent hours waiting in the van with the barrels of fuel. Eventually he got organized, rented premises, bought communications equipment and hired adequate staff, including somebody to tend the radio. I was free to start looking for the Fofu in the city.

When my domestic duties permitted me to take up my studies again my first task was to find the Fofu. But where were they? I had no addresses nor other leads as to where I could find them. Sporadic questioning was unproductive. I decided that the most likely place to find them would be at the central market because everybody went there at some time or other. I therefore started attending the market, usually with five-year old Tom, leaving Tania, then two years old, at home with my househelp.

I shopped at the market place at least twice a week and at other times I just walked around there chatting with people. It was busy, the heart of the city. Crude tables were arranged in rows with little space between them for buyers to pass between. The selling women would arrive carrying their merchandise on top of their heads and then organize it in little piles on the tables. Each woman would sell one thing: either tomatoes, onions, pilipili, eggs, mushrooms, sweet potatoes, manioc, flour, or palm oil etc. Men sold meat with pre-adolescent boys as helpers. They also sold imported goods. It was exciting to mingle with the crowd and talk to people. I forgot the time until Tom got tired and we had to walk or drive home. I got to know some women traders well. One of them asked me to help her write letters to her daughter in Belgium because she herself was illiterate. I acted as her secretary for some time and learned something about her as well. A Rwandese woman whose house overlooked the market place recognized me after a few visits to the market and invited Tom and me into her house. We remained friends throughout the years I lived in Bululu.

These contacts were very interesting but I had still not met any Fofu although I had been going to the market for a long time and constantly asking about them. I concluded that there were not many around. Most traders were Nandi and the others were mainly Rwandese, Nyanga and Nyali people. Then one of the egg traders told me that she thought she knew a Fofu woman near her home. I became excited and asked her to take me to see her. I would have been ready to go there and then but understood that I should not be too pushy. She promised to bring the woman to the market place. I thought that she would bring her the next day, after all I was anxious to meet her, but a week passed before the woman came. I could see that the Fofu woman looked worried and not exactly delighted to meet me. I am sure she could not imagine why a white woman wanted to meet her.

I came to know this woman well over the years. She was *Mama* Avion, Mother of Avion, an elderly woman with Fofu markings on her cheeks and sharply filed teeth. I also learned that her worried expression was caused not only by the stress of meeting me but by her home situation: her two adult sons were Bululu's most infamous burglars and caused her a lot of heartache. The younger of her sons was later shot by the military police in the act of thievery. The older son, Avion, spent most his time in prison. *Mama* Avion took food to him every other day.

At our first meeting I explained to *Mama* Avion that I had lived in the Fofu country near Lemura and knew many Fofu there. Now we were living in Bululu and I wanted to get to know "my people" in the city and learn how the urban Fofu lived. These concepts were totally outside her experience and she did not show much expression. I hoped that my Zairean outfit and my status as the mother of Tom who was speaking to people loudly in Swahili would make a favourable impression on her. She promised to take me to see her home and introduce me to the other Fofu.

I thought that I had it made and I would now get acquainted with the urban Fofu quickly. It did not happen that way, however. *Mama* Avion allowed me to visit her in her home but she was in no hurry to introduce me to the other Fofu. I assume that she wanted to check me out first. I wondered what I would have done if I had only one year for fieldwork. Four months had already passed and I knew only one Fofu. Fortunately my time was not limited to one year, so I tried to be patient and make her feel that I was trustworthy. While visiting her in her "townhouse," a long brick house with five families each having two rooms, I also observed her neighbours of different ethnic backgrounds. Then one day, when she was not at home, her neighbour led me to the place where she was drinking beer and I met the other Fofu with her. After that she introduced me to two more Fofu families who lived very near her and each of them introduced me to a few more. To my surprise, the mother of a family one block from my own house, was a Fofu. I had lived near her for four months without knowing it. I learned that her father had been the first chief chosen by the white administration in Lemura. *Mama* Avion took me to her house and sometimes sent messages to the woman through me.

Although I met several Fofu through *Mama* Avion I did not feel that I was generally accepted by them until Anastasia had given her approval. Without telling me ahead of time, *Mama* Avion had arranged for several Fofu women to assemble at Francoise's house to meet me. Francoise's husband was a customs official and she lived in a decent house. There was Anastasia sitting in the most comfortable chair in the middle of the living room dressed in her best clothes. She looked in command and everyone agreed with what she said. *Mama* Avion introduced me to everyone saying that she and I had become friends and that there was nothing to fear from me. Anastasia fixed her piercing eyes on me, asked a few questions, then nodded. I was accepted. From then on I paid regular visits to Anastasia's house and realized that she was, indeed, the central figure among the Fofu. The first story is about her family. Francoise's story is included in "The Survival of the Dependents of a Civil Servant" and "A Carpenter's Family" will be about the family of another Fofu woman I met at this get together.

I had been right about the number of the Fofu: there were not many of them in the city. The adult Fofu population was around 30, and with their children, there were about 100 Fofu in the entire city. This included people who were only half Fofu. In the local way of descent reckoning, children were classified as belonging to their fathers' ethnic group. So some of the people I classified as Fofu were not Fofu according to the local criterion. Some Fofu died during the years I lived there and a few moved away. On the other hand, new Fofu babies were born and a few new Fofu immigrants moved in. In sum, I studied about 100 people who had Fofu blood ties.

After about a year I heard in a round-about way that the Fofu had invented a myth which rationalized my interest in them. It was a good myth, even I could not have thought of one like it. The story went that my grandfather had been a Fofu and had lived in the Fofu country. That is why I looked for my brothers in Bululu.

Although I was generally accepted by the Fofu there was one exception, a Fofu man whom the Fofu considered extremely wealthy. I tried to become acquainted with his family but I was systematically shunned and I had to drop them from my sample. Perhaps because of his wealthier position, he kept aloof from the Fofu. He had Nandi wives and in many ways lived like the Nandi. There were only two other Fofu, who were better off than the rest. The family living in my street and another Fofu woman who was a bank clerk. The rest of the Fofu belonged to the poverty stricken part of the population of Bululu.

WHO CAN SURVIVE IN THIS CITY?

Unemployment was common among the Fofu as in the city in general. Even when the men found work, their wages did not cover the actual cost of living. Fofu men worked as bellboys, yard caretakers, night watchmen, house-helpers, carpenters, or office clerks. Those who had no work, would repair shoes or pots to make some money. The Fofu wives tried to add to the family income by distilling illicit liquor. My investigation showed that all Fofu women, even the better-off, had engaged in distilling or selling alcoholic beverages at one time or another. Several Fofu women were arrested or fined for this illegal activity. In fear of similar punishment, some women switched to legal activities, such as selling baskets, charcoal, flour, or sugar. However, the Fofu all agreed that no other trade was as profitable as liquor.

Figure 5.1 An urban home distillery.

The Fofu of Bululu would have liked to cultivate fields for their livelihood but there was not much land available. On the edges of their lots, they could grow some beans or squash, but it did not amount to much. Some families had bought small pieces of land for cultivation, or had relatives or friends who let them use a strip of land. In 1979 I timed how long twenty families in Bululu and twenty at Yenyabo spent in their fields. The result showed clearly that urban people did not spend as much time in their fields as the rural ones and that cultivation was an insignificant part of their livelihood. Rural Fofu women spent an average of four hours and twelve minutes a day on cultivation while urban women spent only forty minutes. Rural men spent four hours eighteen minutes while urban men spent five minutes.

Just as the rural Fofu derived their economic security from their fields so the urban Fofu derived their economic insecurity from their lack of fields. Difficulties particularly arose with regard to bridewealth. Without fields it was extremely hard for urban parents to help their sons to obtain bridewealth. This changed the traditional relationships between adolescents and parents.

Nearly all the Fofu in Bululu had spouses from other ethnic groups and Swahili was the conversation language in every family: none of them used Kifofu. Children would tell me that their fathers might talk to them in Kifofu when they were drunk but not otherwise. Some children understood Kifofu but none of them spoke it. Even the family where the husband and wife were both Fofu, conversed in Swahili. I could therefore understand the urban Fofu and never needed an interpreter.

All the Fofu had been raised as Catholics and most of them continued to attend Catholic churches. However, a few had changed their religion. One woman was converted into a Moslem when she married a Moslem man. A young couple became Protestants because the husband's family converted to Protestantism. It seemed that in religion, as in descent reckoning, it was the husband's family that counted. In one case, however, a young Fofu man married a Protestant girl who did not embrace the Catholic faith, not at least while I was there.

In addition to the government school, each religious group had a school in Bululu. The Fofu, however, enrolled their children in any school they could afford. The religious affiliation did not seem to matter much. "Mungu ni moja," there is only one God, was heard often.

The houses of the Fofu were made of various materials and the state they were in also varied. Some lived in hovels, ready to collapse any time. Three Fofu houses did literally collapse. I will describe one of these events in "The Survival of the Descendants of a Civil Servant." Some Fofu lived in better houses, but only one of them, Angelika, my neighbour, lived comfortably in a European type house.

There were seasonal health hazards in town as well as the constant ones. During the dry season, for example, the black volcanic dust on the dirt roads was blown about and many people suffered from jiggers which lived in the dust. Jiggers were insects which buried themselves under human skin near the toe nails or on the sole of the foot. They laid eggs in the skin which caused terrible itching. The egg sac could be removed with a toothpick, and one often saw friends performing this service for each other and parents for their children. During the rainy season, on the other hand, parts of the slums were flooded. I observed as much as a foot of water in some houses for weeks. The long-term puddles and floods harboured mosquitoes which caused malaria.

When my brother came to visit me in Bululu, I took him for a walk in the slum area where some of the Fofu lived. I had grown accustomed to it because I walked there almost every day but he was horrified. He commented on the stench which came from the open holes in the outhouses, garbage heaps and open sewers. I did not take my brother to the worst area, near the slaughter house, because I thought he would have fainted.

The outhouses in Bululu were on higher ground than the buildings because the lava rock was too hard to dig deep pits. Instead, people dug a little, then heaped the dug-out rocks around the pit and built a platform on top of the rocks, leaving a hole in the middle. Woven mats were wrapped around poles to provide walls for the outhouse. Of course, the mats did not protect the neighbourhood from the odour. There were many outhouses in the densely populated slums. During the cholera epidemic hygiene officers ordered people to cover the holes, but not everyone did.

Everywhere in the slum area there was considerable infestation of rats and mice, especially during the time of fermenting corn for liquor. When I was chatting with the members of a household a mouse would often run across the floor. Sometimes rats climbed up and down the walls or banged dishes in another room. The Fofu claimed that rats as big as dogs would come to their houses and take cutlery and clothes which were lying on the floor. Westerners have told me that rats cannot grow that big. I do not know about the size, but I certainly had a sense of their frequency.

The Fofu did not complain about their living conditions and seemed to be well adapted to their habitat. However, I believe that the stressful urban life caused their enormous intake of alcoholic beverages. The Fofu had a reputation for heavy drinking in the rural areas and were often mocked for it by other ethnic groups. I observed even more drinking in Bululu than in the rural areas. The Fofu who moved into the city also noticed this increase. When I went to find *Mama* Avion one morning, her neighbour commented that she was out drinking with the Fofu. Then she added, "Your people are an odd type, starting to drink early in the morning!"

Alcoholic beverages were also given to children and babies in the city. "Give her some joy," said a mother, as if life was joyless without it. I even saw adults joking about drunk children.

There was a remarkable difference in the clay modellings produced by urban children compared with those of the rural children. When asked, for example, to make a human being, the rural children modelled well-formed, rounded, and smooth figures whereas the urban Fofu modelled irregular, flat, and rough creatures. The proportions were way out, parts of the body were missing, the figures were twisted, and the surface was not worked but left rough. I interpreted the difference as being a consequence of the stressful urban life. Some of the children, although around ten years old, had difficulty in concentrating on the tasks. I wondered whether alcoholism had anything to do with it but had no way of measuring it.

I used to feel guilty going from my nice colonial house to the Fofu shacks, eating well when the Fofu ate poorly and having money while they did not. The contrast was highlighted by the European feasts in the city. When my children started attending the Belgian school and kindergarten, they were often invited to the birthday parties of their classmates. One particular time sticks in my mind as disturbing. I had just come home from visiting the Fofu. I was wearing a Zairean outfit and suspected I had some fleas in it. However, I had no time to change and had to take Tania to the birthday party dressed as I was. It was a "fancy dress" party. Tania went as an angel because she already had an outfit from a Christmas play. When we entered the yard of our neighbour, I was astonished to see the European children wearing the most fabulous costumes. Some of them had French court outfits from the 18th century, complete with wigs and shoes! The mothers had been busy sewing and buying outfits for their children. They themselves were wearing European clothing bought in Brussels or Paris and of course shoes with high heels. The tables were covered with cakes ordered from a European bakery and the guests could help themselves to any kind of European liquor they liked.

The European families probably had no idea about the poverty in the slums of this city. Some of them had made remarks to me like, "The Africans had as many years as us to develop, how come they did not?" Some of them belonged to charity organizations. I attended a women's organization for a while and noticed that it collected money for a Catholic orphanage. I was not sure if it was a worthy cause because the orphans would have difficulty in readjusting to Zairean life after being reared in the European way.

I did not know what I could do to alleviate the poverty. One person could not do much. As a matter of fact, my early attempts to help people turned out to be useless and only served to highlight their poverty rather than to decrease it. I continued, however, to give personal gifts as to friends, not as to poor people. I did not expect them to lift the poverty but to brighten the mind. For example, when *Mama* Avion was making herself a wrap-around skirt out of old clothes, I gave her a piece left-over from my skirt which then became a section in her skirt. When my children grew out of their clothes, I gave them to smaller Fofu children. When we went to the mountains to get a whole butchered cow, I gave pieces of meat and bones to my Fofu friends.

I thought that the life of European women in Bululu was very boring. The men were deeply involved with their jobs which gave them challenge, satisfaction, and a lot of money. The women, however, were left at home with nothing to do. We had servants who did the menial household chores. Some of us hired cooks while other European women preferred to do their own cooking. We had gardeners and, if we wished, nannies. Companies often paid all the wages for house employees. Some of the European women developed alcohol problems, some carried on secret love affairs to brighten their lives, and others arranged parties. Those who had children visited the mothers of other children. I took my children and their friends swimming and on picnics very often. But I was not satisfied with the European lifestyle. It seemed purposeless and futile, especially when contrasted with the extreme poverty of the main population. I would have gone crazy had I not been able to leave my sterile and eventless compound and mingle with the Zaireans whose lives were full of activity, noise and laughter, although they contained misery as well.

Before my children started school, they sometimes came with me to visit the Fofu families. This pleased the Fofu. However, my children were the centre of so much curiosity and attention that it hampered my "unobtrusive observations." Furthermore, some children (not Fofu) were violent towards my children. When I was not looking they would knock my children over. That annoyed Tom very much. Once there was an unfortunate incident with a Zairean woman who was carrying a load of firewood on her back. In a narrow path between houses, her load accidentally hit Tania's head. Tania screamed furiously and the woman was so embarrassed that she did not know what to do or say. With all these difficulties, the children soon preferred to stay at home. When Tania was ten years old, she volunteered to come with me again to visit Fofu. It was not a good experience for her. We were sitting in somebody's yard with a group of Fofu people when a strange man appeared. Being drunk, he started wooing Tania, stroking her cheeks and hair and begging to marry her. To avoid a fight, the Fofu never opposed a drunken person. They tried to make the man leave with gentle hints but it was a long time before he went. Tania was determined that she would never again go to be tortured like that. The Fofu lamented that I did not bring her with me again and failed to understand why she stayed away.

Henry never accompanied me to the Fofu homes, except perhaps once or twice in the beginning. He also stayed out of the way when the Fofu came to perform tests for me. If we were simply conversing, however, he would join in. But as the women did not feel at ease with him this was not always a good thing. Although he had little contact with the Fofu, they always asked about his health and his trips. They would recognize the company planes he flew and tell me in which direction they had seen him take off earlier that day. If they saw his plane coming in to land, they would suggest that I went home to cook for him. Sometimes children imitated him in their play and pretended to be pilots.

In Bululu I carried on with my anthropological work much the same as in the rural area. The difference was that I did not live with any families in the city and I did not spend full days among the Fofu, except at funerals. I usually took about four to six hours a day to do participant observations among the Fofu. Sometimes I drove near a Fofu house and walked from one Fofu family to another. The car was often scratched and covered with finger prints where children had climbed all over it. Sometimes bits of the car were stolen. Later I went by bicycle or, as during my last year at Yenyabo, I simply walked the few miles to the houses.

If I did not feel welcome at a Fofu home I left after the greetings. Otherwise I might stay an hour or two. Sometimes I joined women on their shopping trips to the markets and on their water hauling expeditions. Often the women carried on their household chores while chatting with me. I was allowed to hold their infants and husk the beans, but they did not let me help with other work.

As in the rural area, I interviewed women and men in their homes and sometimes in mine. I gave the same psychological infant tests and projective tests to children in both the town and the village. I experimented with the urban children by inviting them to my house and arranging games for them. They were happy to come and I made an interesting finding, namely that the smaller children were not competitive when playing games. Teenage children, on the other hand, were extremely competitive and the teams would be very noisy, encouraging their side to win. I thought that the increased competitiveness could be a result of Western schooling. When I invited the Fofu to my house for the tests and games I provided a meal or refreshments afterwards. I also photographed them at their tasks and gave each a picture as a souvenir. I noticed that our conversations were freer at my home with no interruptions than at their homes where strangers were constantly passing. During my last year, I invited all the Fofu to my home in ones and twos so that we could have a final long interview and a big meal together.

In 1981 we moved to Finland and Canada, having lived in Bululu for four years. In 1984, however, Henry and I spent two months at Nyanya, from where we flew to Bululu for one day. I spent that day with the Fofu catching up with their life events while Henry visited his Western colleagues and friends.

I had a frightening experience during this short visit. On my way to the Fofu houses I decided to take a picture of a young girl carrying water on top of her head. That day was one of those unlucky ones when there was no running water in the entire city and the street was full of people hauling water from the lake. I asked a girl for permission to take her picture and promised her a copy in a year's time. No sooner had I taken the picture when a group of husky young men approached me and told me in an aggressive manner to give the film to them. They claimed I had no right to take pictures and threatened me with prison. They surrounded me and yelled at me, soon attracting a crowd. I tried to tell them that I had permission but they did not believe me. Then a small, friendly looking man stopped and questioned me. He reasoned,

"If she has a visa to enter the country, and a passport, then she is allowed to take pictures."

I nodded profusely although I did not have my documents with me. The man asked to see my documents and as I was fumbling through my bag, a car stopped. A big official looking man came out and asked what the matter was. The youngsters had stopped harassing me by then because the friendly man, although small, had an authoritative manner. When he told the official what had happened, the official said I was entitled to take pictures. The crowd then dispersed but I was too frightened to continue to see the Fofu. I turned around and walked back to our guest house happy that nothing worse had happened. Anybody could be thrown into jail for no reason at all. Earlier the same year, for example, a group of tourists had been snorkelling in the lake. The inhabitants thought they were spies looking for colleagues arriving by foreign submarine and were so afraid of an invasion that the tourists were imprisoned and later transported to Kisangani.

In 1985 we returned to Africa for a year. Henry was based in Bululu and later in Buva and the children attended an American boarding school elsewhere. I spent most of that year studying the rural Fofu near Nyanya but I also spent about three and a half months with the urban Fofu in Bululu.

I chose the families for this section on the basis that I knew them the best. Only later did I notice how many members of these families had died. The other Fofu families did not lose as many members as these although death was known in all of them. I hope these stories will give an insight into urban African life which has many joys despite its harsh reality.

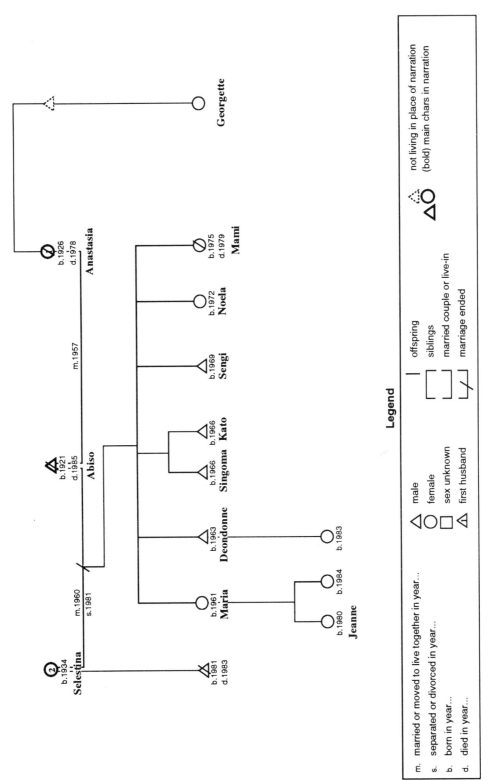

Figure 6.1 Family Diagram for "Anastasia, The Focus Of The Fofu."

Legend

		offspring
		siblings
		married couple or live-in
		marriage ended

m.	married or moved to live together in year…		male
s.	separated or divorced in year…		female
b.	born in year…		sex unknown
d.	died in year…		first husband

not living in place of narration
(bold) main chars in narration

6 ANASTASIA, THE FOCUS OF THE FOFU

THE DIGNITY OF AGE

Mama Avion who was the first Fofu I became acquainted with in Bululu told me that I should get to know Anastasia. All the Fofu knew her and talked about her. After meeting the solemn old woman at the memorable gathering where several Fofu women came to meet me I visited her home regularly. As she lived in the centre of the slum area with easy access to other Fofu homes, I often passed by her house. Usually I stopped by for a chat.

Little did I know that Anastasia was in the last year of her life. I thought that I would have many years in which to study her family. In reality she was ailing fast and her life and her relationships with others were greatly affected by her illness. Only afterwards have I been able to understand how seriously ill she was.

I almost always found Anastasia sitting on the same spot in her yard. She sat like a queen with a straight back and her head raised high. Slowly and solemnly she would perform her task which was always the same: frying manioc cakes for sale. She sat on a low stool according to the local fashion and I marvelled that she could look so royal on so lowly a stool. In a quiet voice she would command the children to help her. One of them, Kato, the younger of the eleven-year old twins in the family, was especially faithful in attending to her needs while the others slipped off to play. Although she could easily reach a palm oil bottle, Anastasia would tell Kato to hand it to her. Kato could be standing twenty yards from the bottle but he would obediently walk to the bottle and hand it to Anastasia. Another task which he repeatedly performed for Anastasia, was kindling the fire. He would take a long hollow pipe, a discarded car exhaust pipe, and kneeling down on the ground blow air into the fire. I never heard her thank him but she may have conveyed her gratitude somehow.

The preparation of manioc cakes was a long process. First of all the ingredients had to be bought. Kato or his sisters, Maria and Noela, would often help with this by going with Anastasia and carrying what she bought. Sometimes her female Fofu friends helped, instead.

When Anastasia returned from her daily shopping trip, she started preparing the dough for the cakes. First she peeled the bananas, throwing the peels in the yard and putting the bananas in a big wooden mortar. Then she pounded the bananas into a pulp. In a huge bowl she mixed manioc flour and banana pulp together until the dough was firm enough to be shaped into flat round cakes about two inches in

Figure 6.2 Anastasia drank beer slowly and solemnly.

diameter and less than an inch thick. Sometimes she made the manioc flour by pounding manioc roots, but often she bought the flour ready made. Kato, Maria or Noela usually helped with the pounding. The longest part of the process took several hours and consisted of frying on a huge round metal sheet which lay on three stones above a fire. She used rich, red palm oil for frying the cakes as was the local custom. Anastasia always did the frying herself; after all, she could do that sitting down.

Gradually, the dough diminished on one side of her and the pile of fried cakes grew on the other side. She put the finished cakes in another huge white bowl and covered them with a dirty old piece of plastic to keep them warm. Passers-by would see what she was doing and stop to buy some cakes at a few cents a piece. Kato, or whoever was handy had to deal with the sale, while Anastasia kept to her post and continued frying until slowly but surely all the cakes were done.

Then one of the children would carry the bowl to the road side and play nearby so as to be able to serve customers. Anastasia stayed sitting in the yard keeping a wary eye on her precious cakes and the money, which the children brought to her after each sale. Although Anastasia belittled this income I noticed that it was important because she used it to buy daily food for the family.

I was amazed that the children did not beg for the cakes. It must have been made clear to them that the cakes were for business and not for them to consume. I admired their self-control especially when they were hungry. Anastasia only gave a cake to a child very rarely, when she was exceptionally pleased with it.

Once she gave me a cake. It happened when I used the proper form of address to her. I had been calling her Anastasia for months not thinking anything of it because other Fofu always referred to her as Anastasia. I did not notice that they used another term when addressing her. Then I read in an anthropology book that in many kinship systems, terms of address were different from the terms of reference. One day I asked her if I was right to call her Anastasia. She answered that she would be extremely pleased if I called her *Mama* Maria, Maria's mother. A Fofu man who was sitting with us added that I could also call her *shangazi*, father's sister, which was another respectful term. In the city, Fofu immigrants had few real relatives, so they enjoyed making up a fictive network of relatives. Not being a Fofu I did not dare to use such a kinship term. Anastasia explained that if a Fofu child called her plain Anastasia, she would hit it. I went near her and asked her to hit me for the breach of etiquette. She laughed and refused to do so. After all, she would not hit a white woman.

The next time I greeted her, I called her *Mama* Maria and crouched down before her to emphasize my respect for her. She was so pleased that she took one of the cakes she had just finished frying and handed it to me.

Palm oil is a heavy fat and ordinarily I did not care for it. But at that moment, I was hungry and I gobbled it up. The manioc flour made the cake heavy and the mashed bananas gave it a sweet taste. One cake filled me.

After that incident I always remembered to call Anastasia *Mama* Maria. I noticed that the other Fofu also called her by this term or *shangazi* and wondered how I had not noticed it before. Anastasia called me *Madam Pilot* or *Mama* Toma.

On another occasion Anastasia gave a cake to Tania. I had taken her with me to see the Fofu. She was two years old then and attracted much attention in Anastasia's yard. All her children and the neighbours' children gathered around Tania staring at her and neglecting their duties. Anastasia probably regretted giving Tania the cake when she realised that Tania's presence was undermining her authority. Apparently Anastasia had been trying to catch the attention of her children for a while. Finally she lost patience with them and said in a slightly louder voice than usual,

"How many times am I to call you? I'll call you twice, on the third time I will spank you!"

All the children started. There was something in her voice that was sharp although there was not much volume. The fire was going out and Kato was asked to blow into the fire with the exhaust pipe. He obeyed immediately and then returned to stare at Tania.

Anastasia made much of her age. She was about 51-years old and proud of it. Once a man was passing the house on the road when she was pounding bananas in her mortar. He was a bit intoxicated and shouted,

"Let me pound your bananas, mama!"

Anastasia leant on the pestle and ignored him. The man repeated his offer but did not get an answer. Soon he continued on his way. I asked Anastasia why she had not answered him.

"I am not a child," Anastasia said proudly. Then she added that the man had shouted to her from the road which was rude. There must have been more to it because Anastasia often had exchanges with people who were walking along the road. Perhaps she was insulted that the man had offered to do a woman's job. Perhaps she was ashamed that she looked too tired to do what was considered a basic chore for a woman. Anastasia was a very private person and I did not dream of pursuing the question further.

Another time she taught me about the dignity of her age. It was when she came to visit me with my Fofu neighbour Angelika. She had walked all the way to the harbour and bought a boat ticket to go to Buva to visit her brother's son the following week. I knew about this trip because Anastasia and her family had talked about it for a long time. After buying the ticket she had first visited my neighbour, who was a distant relative of hers, and then the two of them came to visit me. We lived near the lake, so visiting us fitted with her trip to the harbour. I was delighted that the two Fofu women had come to my house and thought that they might do so often in the future.

Some time later, on a rainy day, I was sitting in Anastasia's living room and helping her clean rice together with her children. I asked when she was going to see my neighbour again. Anastasia told me that she was not going to visit her for a long time.

"Why not?" I inquired.

"She is a child as you are, too. An adult is not to go to see a child but the child must come to the adult." In this way she let me know that it would be some time before she honoured my home again, too. She also intimated that it was not good for her to go to my neighbour because Anastasia "feared" her husband.

"Why do you fear him?" I asked puzzled.

I now realize that I must have sounded worse than a child because every Fofu child would have known why. Although distantly related, Angelika counted as Anastasia's daughter and her husband as Anastasia's son-in-law. In Africa adult women often "fear" their sons-in-law. It is what anthropologists call an avoidance relationship. Because of such a relationship it is better for a daughter to visit her mother rather than the mother visit her daughter's house and risk meeting her son-in-law.

Anastasia never went to my neighbour's nor to my house again.

She emphasized her age whenever it seemed advantageous to do so. One day, for example, I observed her buying firewood from a woman who was passing by.

"Give me a big pile, I am a *muzee* (an old person)," she told the woman and critically threw some pieces away complaining that they were green. The woman put some other pieces in place of the discarded ones, and after a long inspection Anastasia accepted them. Being grouchy was also the privilege of an old person.

Anastasia and her husband lived in a long mud hut on a corner lot. The house had seen better days and was now leaning slightly to one side. In the local fashion, the roof was made of flattened oil drums, which were held in place by rocks. They made the house look untidy. Bundles of firewood, clothes, toys, and pots were sometimes stored on the roof and this added to its untidy appearance. Unlike other lots in the neighbourhood, this lot was large, and at times, there was a small strip of beans and corn growing in one corner. A collection of sackcloth and woven mats attached to four poles created an outhouse in another distant corner of the lot. Most activities of the family took place under a huge tree in the middle of the yard because it gave comfortable shade.

Abiso, Anastasia's husband, some fifty-six years old, was not a Fofu but a Logo, an ethnic group in northeastern Zaire. He told me that he had been married twice before when living in other cities and had left his wives when moving with his white patron. He had two children from his second wife who were now adults living elsewhere. He did not know much about them. Abiso had arrived in Bululu in 1944 and Anastasia some years later. When her previous husband had deserted her after a quarrel, Anastasia planned to go back to Lemura, her ethnic city. But Abiso told her to marry him, instead. Anastasia agreed and Abiso sent her bridewealth to her relatives in Lemura. They were married about 1957.

Anastasia had born three children by her first husband but only one of these children grew to be an adult, the other two died as infants. She had no children by either her second or third husband, Abiso. When she did not produce a child, Abiso secretly took another wife hoping to beget children by her. She was a younger woman and, according to Abiso, had worked as a prostitute after her divorce. He made arrangements for the bridewealth without Anastasia's knowledge. When he went to see Selestina, his second wife, he would lie to Anastasia that he was going to visit a relative. After a while, Anastasia learned about her husband's second wife from gossip. Wanting to show her generosity she went to see the second wife and invited her to live in the same house with her, each wife having her own bedroom.

I pieced the information about the relationship of the co-wives together from the gossip circulating among the Fofu, remarks made by Anastasia and Selestina, and from what Abiso told me. At first the two wives got along well. Anastasia was like a mother to Selestina (although there was only about seven years difference in their ages) and delivered the seven children Selestina bore Abiso. Despite the harmonious relationship people warned Selestina about the possibility of the first wife becoming jealous.

Although Selestina bore the children, they belonged to Anastasia, the first wife. Anastasia emphasized that they were her children, she even used the expression: "I have borne them." They were marked in her identity card as her children. Abiso's identity card had only Anastasia marked as his wife, there being no mention of Selestina. When I asked him about the information on the cards, he simply said that the card was cheaper if it was for a man with one wife. The identity card system was inherited from the colonial government which always made sure that a polygamist was punished with extra dues. Colonial government offices and businesses allowed benefits to one wife and her children only: their policies did not recognize multiple wives.

I found it interesting that Anastasia not only claimed to have borne the children but she put it at six children, instead of seven. She counted the twins as one delivery. Selestina, on the other hand, told me that she had borne eight children, counting also a miscarriage as a delivery. Her way of counting was more common among the Fofu than Anastasia's.

The Fofu told me that it was customary for the first wife to keep all the children born to her co-wives because the co-wives generally lived in the same house in rural areas. All co-wives then interacted with all the children. If the mother left her husband, the children stayed with their father and the remaining wife or wives would take care of them. So it was by no means unusual for a first wife to regard all her husbands' children as her own. To my knowledge, however, nobody had ever made such a strong claim to a co-wife's children as Anastasia.

Over the years the relationship of the two wives became sour. Anastasia was the first and more prestigious wife, she was regarded as the official mother of the children, and had greater power over her husband than Selestina. On the other hand, Anastasia was jealous of Selestina's fertility and feared losing her husband's love. Some Fofu friends told me that Selestina's oldest daughter Maria spied on her own mother for Anastasia and had observed her practising sorcery against Anastasia by spreading poison under Anastasia's bed.

Anastasia had lost her health about four years before I met her. This was attributed to the second wife's sorcery. In the hope that peace would be restored if the women did not live together, Abiso moved Selestina out by renting her a room further away.

When I first got to know the family Maria was Selestina's (or Anastasia's) oldest child, sixteen years old. The second oldest was Deondonne, a fourteen-year-old son.

The twin boys, Singoma and Kato, were eleven years old and a fourth son, Sengi, eight. The second daughter, Noela, was aged five and the youngest daughter, Mami, about two. The children spent their days at Anastasia's place under her supervision but some of them, Deondonne, Noela and Mami, and occasionally Sengi went to bed in their biological mother's house. Anastasia was proud that she fed and clothed the children.

Anastasia had managed to give three of the children Fofu names: Singoma, Kato, and Sengi. That was remarkable because normally the children followed their father's lineage and received the names of his ethnic heritage. I think that the naming, among other things, showed the unusual power Anastasia had for a woman.

There was a further child, Tabo, living at Anastasia's whom Anastasia also referred to as her child. She was about fifteen years old and had a Fofu mother who also lived in the city but was an alcoholic and not capable of caring for her. A long time ago Anastasia had taken her in and brought her up as her own child. The mother had borne other children after Tabo and was raising them herself. This led me to think that Anastasia wanted to use every opportunity to gather children around her to enhance her status as a mother.

A relative woman, Kristina, was also living in Anastasia's house. Anastasia told me that when she had become ill, Kristina had arrived from Lemura to help her. I did not quite understand the arrangement between the two women. Kristina herself told me that she paid rent to Anastasia. She occupied one end of Anastasia's house with a separate entrance and two rooms for herself. She did her own housekeeping although she sometimes helped Anastasia with her household chores. She never gave the children any of the food she cooked but went to her own quarters to eat it. The children did not seem to expect any food. Yet, she bossed over the children and sent them for errands as if she was part of the family. Her unsharing attitude intrigued me because it was common to see neighbours sharing food let alone somebody living in the same house. Perhaps the family of nine was too big to share one person's food with!

Kristina was secretive about her background. She had left her husband in Kisangani. "My spirit refused him," was her explanation. She never told me but it was rumoured that she was a mistress of a man who sometimes came to see her and gave her money. She was well dressed and groomed and ate much more often than Anastasia's family. In fact, she was cooking for herself almost as often as Anastasia was frying her cakes. Good appearance was important to her and once she criticized my appearance,

"That scarf does not suit you, madam. Please, don't wear it!" she told me.

I was a little offended because I tried to dress in the local fashion and wanted to wear a scarf around my head as the Zairean women did. But my hair was not as stiff as theirs and fell flat over my head instead of being supported in a high vault. I quit wearing the scarf after her remark.

One day Kristina looked awful herself. She had a big gash on her head and bruises all over her body. The children told me that a bandit had broken into her quarters, beaten her up, and stolen a sewing machine which she had borrowed from a friend. She had to pay her friend compensation.

IRON RULE

About the same time as the wives separated or soon after it Abiso was laid off work. He had worked as a driver in a white man's company but, according to Abiso, after a native owner took over the company, the majority ethnic groups made life difficult for him. Nandi people, who were one of the most populous ethnic groups in Bululu, played dirty tricks, such as putting stones and water in the gas tank, so that Abiso would lose his job. Abiso told me that he saw it was not worth fighting against a large number of people alone and gave up. He emphasized that the white men hired people regardless of their ethnic origin but the Zaireans gave preference to their relatives. With the exodus of the white men since Independence, it had become increasingly difficult to stay in work if one did not have relatives in influential positions. Although Zaireans sometimes criticized white people they generally acknowledged that whites were impartial when hiring workers.

At first Abiso talked to me about finding another job but then he gave up the idea. He seemed to be resigned to his destiny of being unemployed. His hair was white, he moved slowly, and he was suffering from one ailment after the other. Anastasia's manioc cakes and liquor distilling kept the family going.

However, Abiso did help feed the family. He had acquired fields on the plain about five miles outside the city and worked there diligently during the planting season. I once drove to see him at his work and brought him tea in a thermos. I could not believe that anything would grow in those fields: they looked rocky with hardly any soil showing. About thirty years ago lava had flown over the area from one of the many volcanoes outside the city. Abiso insisted that he was going to get a good harvest and kept on putting beans in the ground between the rocks. Sure enough, the harvest yielded basketfuls of beans for the family. Anastasia sent the children to carry them home. Some dispute arose between Anastasia and Selestina over the beans and in the end Selestina took some for herself because she had helped Abiso in the fields.

Anastasia distilled liquor as all Fofu women in Bululu did at one time or another. I was never allowed in when she was distilling but sat outside watching the smoke come out of the cracks in the walls and the roof. The bigger girls, Maria and Tabo, did the heavy labour while Anastasia supervised them. The girls were busy going in and out of the house, carrying firewood in and implements out and coming to ask for Anastasia's advice.

The whole process was extremely hot and heavy work with a hardwood fire burning for hours under a big metal drum where the liquor was distilled. It was heavy work carrying cool water to pour into a second drum where the steam of the liquor turned back into liquid before going out in three pipes to three bottles. Anastasia would inform me how many bottles a session produced, sometimes seven, sometimes nine, and if they were very lucky, eleven. Maria would carry them in a covered basket to a bar where Anastasia had a sale agreement.

"I would have been dead a long time ago," said Anastasia, "if I did not have these girls to help me, to help me."

Maria and Tabo not only distilled the liquor, helped Anastasia with the manioc cakes, cooked for the family, did the washing, swept the house and the yard but they also took personal care of Anastasia. They braided Anastasia's hair, treated the sores on her feet, and kept her company.

When I called one day, Anastasia was at a wake at another Fofu house. Maria was in the middle of cooking but had broken off to look at her face in the mirror and paint her eyebrows with charcoal. Tabo lounged in a chair chatting with me. Kato and Sengi were playing in the yard with an old bicycle rim.

Then a shout was heard, "Mom is coming!"

That was a signal for everyone to go back to their tasks. Maria attended to the fire, Tabo resumed washing clothes, Kato rushed to sit near the manioc cakes on the roadside. When Anastasia entered the yard, Tabo and Maria hurried to take the basket down from her head and without a word Tabo started peeling the bananas in the basket. Maria brought a chair for Anastasia and set it under the big tree. Anastasia sat on it heavily with a sigh and wiped the sweat from her face.

I tried to understand Anastasia's relationship with her children. It seemed to me that she aroused fear rather than love. But if I ever questioned the arrangement of Selestina's children living with Anastasia, the Fofu always replied that the children loved Anastasia. Kato often told me so too. He was like a faithful dog to Anastasia.

"I love my mom," said Kato, meaning Anastasia.

I saw a great discrepancy between the so called "devotion" and "love" that the children were said to feel toward her, and her attitude toward the children. She was stern with them, there was no softness in her. In fact she seemed to enjoy instilling fear in the children. One day, Mami was sitting between Sengi and Noela on a bench under the tree eating corn, when Anastasia turned to her and commanded angrily,

"Take your foot out of there!"

One of Mami's feet was folded under her other thigh. Sengi pulled her foot free with a quick movement. Mami stopped eating and stared at Anastasia fearfully.

"You won't learn to walk!" growled Anastasia and turned back to fry cakes.

Mami was then about two years old. I was not exactly sure of her age because nobody remembered it and her date of birth was smudged on Anastasia's identity card. She had suffered from measles which had almost killed her and left her cross-eyed and with weak limbs. Sengi and Noela carried her and entertained her all day long.

After a while I asked Anastasia softly why she had acted so angrily. She replied dryly that a child should fear her mother, that was all there was to it. I wondered if the children were obliged to say they loved Anastasia and they did not dare to say otherwise. Perhaps emotions were also culturally formed and you felt what you were supposed to feel. Another time, Josefina, a recent widow of a Fofu man, came to greet Anastasia in her yard with her three-month-old baby. Anastasia sat near Josefina and reached to the child, hit her on the head hard, several times repeating "Jambo!" (hello) each time. I was shocked but nobody else seemed to be. Kristina then joined Anastasia in teasing the baby. She took the baby and holding her tightly by the feet shook her upside down. The baby did not make a sound. I was flabbergasted and asked Josefina if she was not afraid for the baby.

"They are part of my family," she said trustingly, referring to Anastasia and Kristina.

Another time Anastasia held the baby in a manner I was more used to seeing babies treated: in an upright position and smiling to her. There was some softness in Anastasia, after all!

WHO CURES THE SHAMAN?

I wondered why Anastasia wanted to arouse fear in her children. Could it be an expression of bitterness for not having children of her own and of the strained relationship with the biological mother of the children? Then I heard something else which could provide a better explanation: Anastasia was a shaman. I knew from personal experience that shamans were feared. I had gone to see a Ugandan shaman who lived not far from Anastasia. He had shown me his paraphernalia and let me attend sessions with his patients. Once when I walked down the road with him I felt that people were shunning us. Fofu friends greeted me hastily and did not come to chat with me — I assumed that this was because I was with the shaman. I wondered if Anastasia was wanting to create the atmosphere of fear and awe to enhance her reputation as a shaman. Many sick people came to Anastasia for help and she had the knowledge to cure them. It seemed strange to me that she could not help herself if she was a shaman. But the Fofu explained that it was well known that even shamans were unable to cure themselves and their own families. Several questions, however, came to my mind. Did it not, for example, show a lack of power to fall ill from sorcery caused by a co-wife, whose status was lower than Anastasia's? Was it not a sign of a powerful shaman to fend off the malign intentions of other people?

I did not ask her about shamanism at the time but I thought that perhaps I could gradually approach the topic. Anastasia never hinted at her skill as a shaman and I never saw any clients at her house. I think that she wanted to hide this side of herself from me since white people were assumed not to know anything about witchcraft and magic. My questions remained unanswered as hopes of interviewing Anastasia on shamanism fell through with her death. I believe, however, that it was her ability as a shaman that made Anastasia the focus of the Fofu. There were many other old Fofu in Bululu, both men and women, but none of them was as widely known and respected as Anastasia.

Anastasia was moving more slowly than before and doing fewer housechores. I did not quite believe in the seriousness of her illness. I thought she exaggerated it to manipulate her family. There was no doubt that she did manipulate her family but the illness was serious, too.

As Anastasia grew worse the family began to look neglected. The children were dirty and in rags. The youngest of them, Mami, seemed miserable with her crossed eyes and weak limbs. Kato, the younger of the twins looked the worst. He had sores all over his body, an itch between his fingers, and much of his hair had fallen out because of the mould growing on his scalp. He scratched himself and aggravated huge sores.

I felt sorry for the children and tried to help them in clothing and health matters. Perhaps I should not have tried because it did no good. Once, for example, I had an extra piece of red-and-white checkered material. I thought that I could adapt Tania's dress pattern for Noela. Although she was three years older than Tania, her arms were no thicker than Tania's. So I made a dress for her and gave it to Anastasia for Easter. I was pleased with how the dress looked when Anastasia had Noela try it on. In two weeks, however, it was as torn and dirty as her other clothes had been and I could hardly recognize it. I was unable to hide my shock as I stared at the remains of the dress. Anastasia must have felt the shame of her poverty, for she said defensively,

"What good does one dress do in this neighbourhood, in this neighbourhood?"

How right she was! I looked at the rows of disintegrating houses around Anastasia's and the children playing happily in torn and filthy clothes. Indeed, how much did one dress help the situation? I reflected how I had given it with a good heart, out of love for Noela and she had indeed appeared happy trying it on. But now she was ashamed of herself. This gift of a rich white woman had only highlighted her poverty. I felt helpless and guilty.

Another example of a vain attempt to help was when I tried to improve Kato's skin. I took him to an American nurse who diagnosed eczema. I bought a lotion to rub on the sores after a good bath. The nurse told me that the mouldy sores should be removed with a brush after a bath. I took Kato to my home and gave him a hot bubble bath, rubbed his sores and put ointment on them. He came for treatment regularly and seemed to enjoy the bath which he had never experienced before.

Then I thought that he should learn how to take care of himself and told him that he should give himself a sponge bath at home in the Zairean fashion. He promised to do it regularly.

He did not bathe, however. He told me later that Anastasia did not permit him to use the family water for bathing. When I asked Anastasia, she denied it and made a point of commanding Kato to bathe in my presence. I saw that Kato was being double faced and could not understand why he did not go to get water from the free taps in the neighbourhood. Although water carrying was a job for girls, boys could do it without stigma. When I urged Anastasia to put pressure on Kato to take care of himself, she answered lamely,

"I am a sick mother, I have no energy for it, no energy."

I thought that she was making excuses but it was probably true. Frying manioc cakes took all her energy and the children had to be neglected.

Anastasia's weakness put an extra burden on her husband, Abiso. He was a kind man and helped Anastasia with female jobs. His behaviour contrasted with that of a Fofu friend, Filippo, who came to greet the family. Anastasia asked him to chop wood for her because she was too weak to do it herself. Filippo refused saying he had walked so far that he was too tired to do it. Anastasia asked a second time with the same result. When she asked for the third time he got up and went home.

Anastasia chuckled, "He is running away from me!"

Anastasia had not asked Abiso because he had hurt his foot with a hoe when working in the field. Although he was talking to his male friends on the other side of the yard he noticed what was going on and came to help Anastasia. He limped painfully and Anastasia said,

"Leave it. I'll buy from those women."

Some women were passing by with loads of firewood for the market. Anastasia bought twigs from them which did not need chopping. Abiso hopped to a chair to sit down.

Abiso appeared to be very devoted to Anastasia. He was in a difficult position between two quarrelling wives. He, like people generally, believed that the second wife had caused Anastasia's sickness. Anastasia told me that as she did not want any sexual relations with her husband when she was sick, Abiso slept with the boys in the middle room. Anastasia occupied another room and the girls of the family a third room. Although Abiso insisted that he did not see his second wife, he must have done so.

Abiso felt bad about not being able to pay school fees for the children's education after losing his job. He himself claimed to have completed twelve grades at school while neither of his wives had any schooling at all. The older children, Maria, Tabo, Deondonne, and the twins, had been to school for a few years but had to quit. I found it interesting that Maria told me she went to school long after she had quit it. I was not sure if it was wishful thinking or desire to please a white person, who would presumably favour education.

If the poverty caused the parents stress one could not see it bothering the children in their every day activities. They looked happy and were often absorbed in their play, which they nevertheless interrupted easily when called to help adults.

Once I arrived in the yard when Kato was roasting peanuts for himself. He had four round lids from shoe polish tins, two covering his ears and two in front of his mouth attached with a wire around his neck. When I inquired what he was supposed to be, he laughed and Kristina answered me from her apartment,

"Can't you see, he is a pilot?"

The planes flew by all the time, big ones and small ones. They knew that my husband was a pilot and it brought the fascinating profession closer to them. Kato had told me several times that he would like to be a pilot or mechanic.

I found Deondonne several times sitting on a chair, surrounded by younger boys, making a football by wrapping dried banana leaves around and around until a ball was formed. Then he would go to the street to kick the ball with the boys until the ball disintegrated.

Several times I found the twins busy building trucks. Singoma had got three shoe boxes from a downtown Bata store. The boys sat on the ground with outstretched legs and cut the boxes with discarded razor blades into three-dimensional trucks. They drew the windows and doors and other details with a Bic pen. It intrigued me that Singoma wrote the year 1929 on the side of a truck he made. Did he not know numbers or did he value old trucks? I should have asked him.

The boys often played with marbles. They would get them from young adult Fofu or neighbour men by doing errands for them. When the boys played marbles they were told to go away if they happened to get too close to the adults. Otherwise nobody paid attention to their games.

Noela occupied herself mostly with taking care of Mami. She carried her around, sat with her and fed her. Maria sometimes did this, too, but she was generally more involved with household chores. Anastasia told me that Noela's main job was childcare. Sengi frequently helped Noela. Both of the children were very tender to the little one. Mami liked them both and often smiled happily at them. Sometimes Noela would play with other girls, including Sengi, while babysitting Mami. Once I spotted her playing house: she was cutting the heads of tiny fish Kristina had bought for herself and saving them in small tin cans, which she then put on the fire to cook for her "babies."

I wondered if the children suffered from the tension between their mothers. I did not know how to broach the subject tactfully so I left well alone. I knew from the other Fofu that Anastasia used Maria as a spy on her real mother. I don't know whether it was because of her divided loyalties or the tension between the two women, but Maria rarely smiled. She wore a sombre expression and her voice was gruff: she bossed over her younger siblings in a harsh way. Abiso once remarked that no man would marry Maria because of her sharp tongue.

Deondonne was another one who might have been adversely affected by the home situation. Both Abiso and Anastasia told me that he had once raised his hand against Anastasia by throwing stones at her. Abiso distanced himself from the event and stressed that he had not witnessed it. Anastasia talked about it as being shocking and shameful. She and Deondonne did not interact when I was present but kept aloof from each other.

Figure 6.3 Noela and Sengi babysitting their little sister Mami.

I did not get to meet Selestina, the second wife, until a few months after becoming acquainted with Anastasia. I don't think Anastasia particularly liked the idea of me befriending her. She did not forbid me from going there but she had forbidden the Fofu from doing so. She was not easy to catch because she left for the bush early in the morning to collect twigs and branches to sell as firewood in the market. She would not return until the afternoon after selling her merchandise.

She lived a few blocks from the rest of the family in a rented room which had a roof made of leaves which leaked. There was no furniture at all in the room. She slept on the floor on a palm mat. She looked sullen and apathetic and wore very dirty clothes. She kept herself distant from me, never volunteering any information. I could understand her attitude since I came from her competitor's household. However, my status as a foreigner gave me some neutrality, so she did talk to me. Once she even came to my house for an interview about her mothering and breast fed Mami several times during the interview. Each time she saw me she begged some food or money and I felt uncomfortable, although I gave her what she asked for.

Selestina confirmed what others had told me about the relationship between her and Anastasia. She blamed Anastasia for having a bad spirit toward her after she fell ill. Apparently they had gone to the formal court about it and, according to Selestina, Anastasia had to pay Selestina a goat for her accusations of sorcery.

Selestina maintained that Abiso loved her because she had borne children for him and that he spent the nights with her instead of Anastasia. Selestina did not like going to the other house but she did sometimes to greet her children whom Anastasia had taken from her. It seemed to me, however, that she had not completely lost the children because they often went to her house and Maria and Noela frequently carried water for her. Mami spent every night at her place.

❏ ❏ ❏

As mentioned earlier, Anastasia bought a ticket to go by boat to Buva and some time later she did go. She was to get some medical care while staying with her nephew but I did not know the details. She had several outfits made before the trip and she looked regal in a matching top and skirt with her solemn expression and upright posture.

She stayed away longer than planned, because the boat was out of service for at least a month due to lack of fuel. Anastasia sent a letter to her family stating that she would return when the boat service resumed. While she was away the family's life continued as before except that Maria bossed over the children instead of Anastasia.

When she finally returned she looked refreshed and happy. Her nephew had taken good care of her and given her yet another outfit. She even forced a faint smile when talking about the trip.

It soon became evident, however, that her condition was deteriorating. She kept giving herself enemas with a solution made of the herbs she grew at the side of the house. Once she had just prepared a potful when we heard her desperate protests. The children came out of the house to see what the matter was. Ducks had found the liquid and were drinking it. Anastasia made no attempt to chase them away herself but called the children to guard the solution until she was ready to administer it to herself.

Another time I observed that Anastasia was very tired after returning from her morning shopping trip a mile away. Although another Fofu had carried her bananas for her, she was feeling miserable and vomited near the house. Then she sat down and held her hand over her heart. She said that it was pounding fiercely.

The next day she was in bed. Her body had swollen. Anastasia complained that she hardly ate and yet became larger. When I thought of it, she had been a bit bloated as long as I had known her. Until then I had thought that she was stout, a rare phenomenon for a Fofu, but now I connected it to her heart condition. From Western nurses I gathered that she might be suffering from a heart condition which often caused water retention. Abiso told me that some years back Anastasia had received Western medicine for her condition but it had not helped.

I went to see Anastasia in bed. The room was dark for, as a precaution against thieves, there were no windows in the room and the only light came in through the half open door. Kato was waving twigs over her face to keep flies away. Poor Anastasia, although she was a powerful shaman, feared by her family, friends and enemies, she lay there helplessly like a child. I knew that a swollen body was regarded by the Fofu as a sign of witchcraft. The Fofu thought that the co-wife's witchcraft was working.

On my way there the next day I heard a child screaming from far away. When I looked towards the yard I saw Noela being beaten by a strange woman. As I got nearer I could see that the woman was beating Noela on the head, back, arms and legs with a bundle of nettles. Noela was jumping and screaming on the top of her voice,

"I am dying, I am dying!"

"Go right ahead!" answered the woman passionately. "I will beat you to your death today! Go right ahead and die."

Kristina was pounding manioc a few yards away with her back turned to them. She paid no attention. Deondonne and Singoma stared ahead pretending not to see or hear. Neighbours also ignored the incident and got on with whatever they were doing. A man who was passing by stopped to watch but did not intervene.

I thought it was cruel but did not say anything, just walked in. As soon as the woman stopped Noela ran to the other side of the house howling miserably.

When I asked the woman why she had beaten Noela there was a long outburst of reasons: Noela was a bad girl, constantly hitting her siblings and so on. This time she had hit Sengi so hard that he was bleeding. I wondered aloud whether she would have beaten Sengi if he had hit Noela. She assured me that she would have because it was very bad indeed to hit another child. I did not believe her because I had seen Sengi hit Noela with no interference on the part of the adults.

I discovered that Anastasia was not at home. She had been taken to a medicine place but I was not able to get more information. I knew then that she was in the hands of a shaman in the hope of fending off the terrible witchcraft that her co-wife was thought to be causing her.

The woman who so ruthlessly beat Noela was a Fofu woman, Georgette, who called Anastasia her *shangazi*, father's sister, and had arrived from Lemura to help Anastasia while she was ill. She was a plump and energetic woman who immediately took control of Anastasia's family. No sooner did she see a child misbehave than she administered the punishment. She continued with the household chores confidentially while chatting with me and remained in charge of the family over the coming weeks.

One day she came to visit me with two other Fofu women. She did all the talking and told us about her past. Buva was not a new city for her, after all. She had lived here before. In fact she had borne children here a few years back. That seemed odd because she had told me earlier that she had no children. Then she explained that she had borne two rats in the hospital and the doctor thought they were so special that he hung them on the wall. They were on the wall of the hospital to that day if I wanted to go and see them!

At first I thought that there was no truth in her story but on second thoughts I realized that she may have been referring to a miscarriage of twins. In the early stages fetuses look more like rats than humans. However, I did not believe that the doctor had put them on the wall and never went to verify it.

Georgette believed that someone had bewitched her to deliver the "rats." She thought it happened when she was dancing happily in the yard. A passer-by may have been jealous of her happiness and given her witchcraft to make her unhappy.

Georgette went on to tell one unbelievable story after the other. With time I learned that she took delight in shocking people. She spoke easily and lightly, as if she were discussing trivial matters. One of her taller stories was that she had gone to Kenya to see the grave of the recently deceased president Yomo Kenyatta. His body was in a glass mausoleum. According to Georgette, on payment of a fee, visitors were allowed to press a button which caused Kenyatta to get up and shake their hands. When we shook our heads in disbelief, she assured us that she was speaking the truth.

The worst shock was yet to come. We were sipping tea while sitting comfortably in our arm chairs when Georgette suddenly asked me if I was interested in buying diamonds which her friend had smuggled out of a diamond mine in Kasai. She put the price at several million dollars. She repeated the price so as to make it clear that this was not an everyday transaction in the local market.

I quickly told her that I was not the least interested. She should not even suggest it to me. She volunteered to show me the diamonds which she had hidden between her breasts but I begged her not to bother. I thought of all the complications which such dealings would bring to me. We had lived in Kasai where diamonds were mined and knew several foreigners who had been deported after being accused of smuggling. She did not seem particularly disappointed by my refusal. It was as if I had only refused to buy bananas from her: no big deal. The faces of the other two women did not show any reaction either.

Henry's Zairean boss was very cross with me when he heard about the incident through the grapevine. He gave me a lecture explaining that I should have never let such women into my house. Zairean dealers were canny and this woman could have hidden diamonds in my house, then called the secret police, who would have found them and deported me. This scenario shook me but I was pleased that my Fofu friends had shown some loyalty towards me by not playing such tricks.

Some time later when I visited Anastasia's house, Georgette casually mentioned that the diamonds had proved to be fake. When I stared at her speechless she must have thought that I had not understood because she explained again that the diamonds had not been real. She continued to talk about the matter as she would talk about bananas which were not ripe enough to eat. I thought of all the millions I could have lost in the deal but it did not seem to concern Georgette.

SHATTERING SORROW

Anastasia had been away a few weeks, during which time I had not seen her at all. Nobody would tell me where she was although they knew I wanted to visit her. Then one Monday morning my househelp, who lived half a mile from Anastasia, told me on her arrival at work that Anastasia had died the day before.

I was hurt that no Fofu had informed me about it. I wanted to know more but my househelp did not know the details. She had only heard that the relatives were very angry about the death.

Wondering if Angelika, as a relative, knew more about Anastasia's death, I hurried down the road. She had just returned from Anastasia's wake where she had been since the day before. Someone had brought news of Anastasia's death to her, but my house, although only at a stone's throw from hers, had been left uninformed. When Angelika told me the events of the previous day and night I understood that my presence had not been wanted.

Angelika recounted that the relatives had grown tired of keeping vigilance at Anastasia's sick bed and had sometimes left her unattended. She had been under the care of a shaman but this had not helped and Anastasia had been only semi-conscious for a long time. When she was finally found dead her eyes and mouth were covered with flies.

At that moment, loud wailing erupted and Anastasia's relatives carried the body back home. The news spread fast among the Fofu who ran to join the wake. The second wife also joined the mourners. When Fofu women spotted her they attacked her and started beating her violently to avenge Anastasia's death. Her blouse was torn during the scuffle and the co-wife cried with pain. Angelika's relative, who had spent the night at the wake with Angelika, stated that she did not think the co-wife had killed Anastasia because she came to mourn. A murderer would not join mourners but would run away. The two women told me that Abiso and the children had cried all night. Where they would go to live was a major concern for Abiso because the house belonged to Anastasia and her relatives would take the house from him.

Having spoken with Angelika I hurried to the wake myself. The yard was full of people. I was told that the corpse was inside. I pushed my way into the middle room. Anastasia's body was lying on the floor covered with a white sheet leaving only the head exposed. I recognized her familiar solemn and sullen expression, now solidified making her seem many times more fierce than when alive. Everyone in the room was wailing and the atmosphere was very emotional.

Abiso was lying on the floor next to Anastasia supporting himself with his elbow. His eyes were red and swollen and tears were streaming down his cheeks. He wailed rhythmically,

"What did you do, what did you do, Anastasia?"

He kept on repeating this phrase.

The mourners had not washed themselves since they heard the news about Anastasia's death and a strong smell of sweat filled the room. Not washing themselves during the wake and sitting on the dirty ground and actually rubbing dirt on themselves was symbolic of the decay of death. The mourners were decaying in dirt in the same way as Anastasia's body was to decay in the grave. It was also an acknowledgement that the living would die in due time. This was intended to placate Anastasia's spirit.

Georgette appeared dramatically from the adjacent room. Her hair was all over the place, giving her a wild look, she was nude from the waist up and her breasts were bouncing up and down. She threw herself onto her knees near Anastasia's head, bent over and, stroking Anastasia's face and forehead, lamented,

"*Shangazi* (father's sister),
you sent for me.
'Come quickly,
come to take care of me!
I am sick.'
I came.
I came.
Now you left me!
Oo-o! Oo-o!"

There was a pause while she shook rhythmically and sobbed. Then she continued.

"Your brothers
will receive you.
There will be no trouble.
Rest assured.
No trouble."

She put her cheek against Anastasia's and sobbed. A Fofu man, who worked as a cook for a Greek family, sat on the floor near Anastasia. He was crying openly, also rhythmically although more slowly than Georgette. He wailed in a deep voice,
"There is only one road,
we will follow you.
I will follow you.
Where should I throw
this fifty makutas?
Outside?"
I later heard that he had given money for Anastasia's medical treatment. Perhaps that was what he was referring to. His financial help was no longer needed.

The room was filled with familiar Fofu women. They sat quietly on the floor facing Anastasia. Tears were running down their cheeks. I sat among them and felt the enormous impact of the wake. I felt like sobbing, too, but tried to control myself so I could observe as an anthropologist. I coped better than when I had attended a twin's funeral at Yenyabo some years before. Then I had been almost paralysed with fear.

I noticed that Kristina was nowhere to be seen. I heard that she was on a trip and a message had been sent to her about Anastasia's death.

After a while someone brought in a big bowl of hot water and we all left the room so that Anastasia could receive her last bath before burial. Five Fofu women stayed with the corpse while the rest of us went outside.

I drove back home to get a camera and tell my family that I was going to attend the funeral. I returned to the wake but did not dare to take pictures, after all. I thought that the family might be offended if they were photographed in such an emotional state. When I mentioned it afterwards Abiso was disappointed that I had not taken pictures. He would have liked to have seen himself in the fury of the wake. The children would have liked to have been photographed as well. I noticed that people were not sensitive about being emotional as they would have been in my country.

When I arrived back at the wake, I found Maria in Kristina's apartment standing in front of a display of photographs on the wall. It was prestigious to have family members photographed in a studio. There were several pictures of Anastasia, standing stoutly and solemnly in front of a fake background. Maria's upper body was naked and her hair untidy. She was either smeared with clay or she had rolled in the dirt. Her skin was covered with sweat. She looked fierce staring at Anastasia's picture and, shaking rhythmically, chanted,

"I lost my milk!

I lost my milk!

I lost my mother's milk!

I left school

that my mother would heal.

Now you left me."

She repeated this over and over with sweat running down her skin. I was surprised that she had internalized Anastasia's role as her mother to the point of talking about the mother's milk, although Anastasia had never nursed her.

Meanwhile in the other room Anastasia's body was being put into a coffin. There was an hysterical outcry as the coffin was being nailed down. This was occasioned by Abiso and the children trying to prevent the final closing of the coffin. Maria stopped her wailing and rushed to the other room. I followed her as closely as I could. She threw herself over the coffin and howled and twisted her body in a frenzy. Kato, Singoma, Sengi, and Tabo were pounding the coffin with their fists in protest of their mother's departure. Kato cried,

"Tati, tati, tati, tati!" (Grandmother)

Maria was by far the loudest and most prominent mourner. Despite the protestations of Anastasia's relatives, the Fofu men who were officiating went about their business in a professional manner and finally managed to get the coffin onto a truck. By that time Abiso had joined his children and was also pounding the coffin and crying loudly.

A rich Fofu had lent his company truck for the funeral. He did it for most Fofu, although he kept aloof from them otherwise. I thought that it must have been quite a drain on his finances since the Fofu were too poor to pay him back in any way.

The truck filled with people and started a slow drive toward the cemetery. I followed with my Volkswagen Minibus which was also full of people. Anastasia was so popular that all the mourners did not fit into the two vehicles. The rest walked behind the truck.

There was only one cemetery in Bululu and it was situated off the road leading to the airport. There was at least one funeral every day and the procession slowed the normal traffic down. The mourners would use the whole width of the road, caring little about mundane cars. White people especially and the rich Zairean businessmen hurrying to their flights were terribly annoyed about having to slow down to walking pace. The drivers peeped their horns and tried to overtake the funeral processions. This was considered very rude by the local population who always respected funeral processions. Passers by would stop at the sight of a procession and stand to attention while it passed.

A group of Fofu men had been at the cemetery digging the grave since early morning. It was a tough job because the ground was mainly lava rock. Consequently the graves were not very deep. I could not see very well what was happening at the graveside because of the crowd in front of me. I did, however, see Abiso being led away by two men. He had tried to jump into the grave with Anastasia. I heard that all the children had attempted the same and they were also led away. Maria was as limp as a rag after the energetic mourning. After attending many other funerals I learned that trying to jump into the grave was a ritual. It was something that family members were required to do to show their devotion to the deceased.

After the burial a Fofu man, Dudu, who always performed the official tasks at Fofu gatherings, wrote down the dates of Anastasia's birth and death on a wooden cross which was then planted on the grave. I noticed that the birth date was two years' different from the date I had copied from Anastasia's identity card. It was just another example of the unimportance of exact dates to the Fofu.

Back at Anastasia's home, Georgette went from one personal item of Anastasia to the other lamenting,

"This was her stool,
she liked her stool."

The other women of the family helped her go through the items: Anastasia's stool, her mug, bowl, and her favourite cooking pot while Abiso sat on the floor with outstretched legs wailing and crying. Soon the three rooms of the house were filled with people sitting on the floor. The rooms were hot and filled with strong body odours. Each time new people entered the house they put some money in a bowl set on a chair and a bookkeeper wrote down their names and the amount of money they donated to the funeral.

Later that day Georgette led some Fofu women back to the grave to take Anastasia's personal belongings there for her spirit to use in the after life. According to the city custom, they broke each utensil so that it would not be stolen and set them upside down on Anastasia's grave. Later on I heard Fofu saying that when they had looked for Anastasia's clothes to bury them with her, they had found only a few. The clothes were buried with her to prove to Anastasia's spirit that nobody wanted to get rid of her for the sake of her clothes. The rumour went around that Anastasia had sold most of her clothes to pay for her treatment.

The mourning period lasted three nights as Anastasia was a woman. The next morning I dropped in and saw that many participants had gone home for the day. Some men were sitting on chairs around a fire outside indicating that they were more distant relatives. Women were inside. Kristina had received the news and hurried back home the day before. She had stripped her top off, undone the braids of her hair and she lay on the floor with Georgette. The women no longer wailed.

The atmosphere was lighter than during the previous day. The women were conversing with each other. One, who was drunk, was telling the others that she had been pregnant for two years and wondered when she was going to deliver her infant. Board games were lying on the floor: apparently the men played them at night to keep awake. Everyone had been drinking liquor during the night.

I did not stay long that morning but I made up my mind that I wanted to be at the wake the following night. I had never attended a wake during the night and wished to take this opportunity. I packed a rucksack with some food, camera, and note paper, and went to my neighbour Angelika to ask what time would be best to go.

Angelika burst into laughter when she heard about my plan. She did not think it was wise at all. When I insisted, offended by her laughter, she took a deep breath and started explaining at length why it was out of question for me to go. People would be drunk and behave obnoxiously and I, being of a different colour and a woman, would be mistreated. It would not be safe for me to be there. If she could go with me, it would be all right because she could protect me from harassment. However, her back was aching from the night she had already spent there and, being pregnant, she could not take another strenuous night. Furthermore, she had no more money to donate for the funeral which was mandatory should she go there again.

I walked home and asked my househelp what she thought about me going. She agreed with Angelika. Henry was noncommittal. I sat down and thought it through. I knew that Anastasia's housing area was dangerous at night. White people did not dare to drive through it even on the main road because gangs of criminals would attack cars, pound them, smash windows, and beat people. I considered walking to the wake before dark to avoid undue attention. But in the end I gave up the idea altogether. Although the warnings of danger were undoubtedly justified I suspected that the Fofu did not really want me there.

The next morning was the great day of the ritual cleansing and the end of the mourning period. I did not want to miss it and luckily nobody objected to my presence. I drove to the house before dawn to find that the menfolk had already bathed and changed their clothes. The women and children were still bathing by the house. I noticed that Deondonne did not change his clothes and only splashed a little water on his feet. I wondered whether it was an expression of the antagonism between him and Anastasia.

A young man clad in soldier's fatigues was sweeping the floor and throwing the rubbish out of the house. The mats which the mourners had sat on had already been thrown out. They seemed well worn. The rooms smelled awful. No wonder, many people had been living in them three days and nights. The soldier paused to drink some liquor then he went back to his sweeping. He swept all the rooms and the yard. I heard Abiso say that the soldier would receive some money for his labour after the wake.

This soldier was a relative of Anastasia. He later led the others in the funeral rites. I had never met him before and failed to discover why he had been chosen for the honourable role. After he had finished the sweeping, he cut the hair of the immediate family as well as that of Tabo, Kristina and Georgette. I assumed that the criterion for hair cutting was whether one was a relative of Anastasia. The soldier used big scissors and cut the hair so short that the head looked almost clean shaven.

While the Fofu women were preparing food for the mourners, I drove back home for my breakfast and for more film. I thought that I would not miss anything important but when I returned an hour later I regretted having left.

I missed a ritual where a relative of Abiso accused the second wife of witchcraft against Anastasia. The second wife had denied the accusation. Then Abiso's relative had told her to return to live with her husband in his house now that the first wife had died. The second wife refused to do so.

I understand that Abiso's relatives had to clear his side of the family of any suspicion of witchcraft. The spouse always was a prime suspect. In this case the second wife had already been suspected of witchcraft so it was easy to put the blame on her. Of course, the second wife did not want to take the blame and to show it she refused to join her husband. Had she agreed to move in with him she would have symbolically admitted her guilt. People would have interpreted that she had wanted to remove Anastasia by witchcraft in order to live with her husband.

Although Selestina did not accept she was to blame people generally considered she was guilty and she was left to sit alone in a far corner of the yard holding Mami on her lap. Nobody spoke to her. She wanted to prove her innocence by staying because her absence would have been an admission of guilt. This way, at least, people could not be absolutely sure about her.

The whole point of the crying of the mourners, rolling in the dirt, accusing the second wife, as well as the libations, dancing and singing was to appease Anastasia's spirit and the spirit of other ancestors. Each death was thought to be caused by someone and this aroused the anger of the spirit world. If the living tried to find the culprit the deceased's spirit would not vent its anger on the family members. By crying vigorously, they protected themselves from the revenge of the spirits.

By the time I returned, the yard was full of people. Most of them were members of ethnic groups from northeastern Zaire but there were many others whom I had never seen. Anastasia was famous all over Bululu. This was a great occasion to be remembered long afterwards.

People were drinking all the time. Early in the morning Fofu women had brought more liquor to the house and they were now giving it out in bottles and in cut calabashes. People poured some of it on the ground before taking a sip and passing the bottle to the next person who did the same. At first I thought in the Western way and supposed that they were cleaning the mouth of the bottle for hygienic reasons. Then I switched to the Fofu thinking and realised that they were giving libations to Anastasia and the other ancestors. The idea was to share the drink with all the living and the dead, thus uniting everybody. In addition Abiso sprinkled liquor all around the circle of dancers in order to "scare Satan away," as one woman put it.

In the middle of the yard, people were dancing in the African fashion by shaking rhythmically. Kristina had just finished playing on a big drum and sweat was streaming down her face. The soldier drummed for a while, then Anastasia's neighbour took over. The climax of the dance was when the Fofu relatives, led by Georgette, came out of the house dancing and singing. Their song, which was in Kifofu, accused the second wife of killing Anastasia. The melody was very sad, bringing tears to the eyes. The dancing Fofu invited Abiso to dance with them. He refused at first but then gave in and joined them sobbing rhythmically, with tears running down his face.

I noticed that Maria was not among the dancers and someone told me that she had burned her foot in the fire and was not able to dance. When the Fofu tired of dancing and the feast was slowing down I took Maria to a clinic to have her foot bandaged. When we came back people were still drinking but the dancing was over. I was tired and went home.

A few days later Abiso appeared at my house. He was wearing a clean new shirt and looked relaxed and happy. He had slept well for a couple of nights and was smiling. I thought that none of my compatriots would have been smiling so soon after the funeral of his spouse. But then none of my compatriots would have mourned so intensively as Abiso had. He told me that after his mourning seclusion of three days, he wanted to go around town visiting his friends and relatives.

Within a month two other Fofu died. It was a sad time for the Fofu. The wakes of the others confirmed Anastasia's special status in the community. One of the deaths was of a child of a Fofu man and his Rwandese wife. It had died of cholera, which was sweeping through the city killing the very young and the very old. A wake of only one day was held for this child and when I visited the home I noticed that only the immediate family members were mourning energetically and following the ritual rubbing of dirt onto themselves, etc. The other guests kept away from even the dirt floor and sat quietly on chairs inside the house. The mourning period was short because the deceased was a child and therefore not considered an established person.

The second death was of an old man, a common-law husband of an old Fofu woman who had left him some months previously. The old man had kept on returning to beg to be taken back by the woman, but to no avail. One of his friends told me that the man did not eat properly after the separation but lived on the scraps other people threw away. The woman herself explained that another man had given her estranged husband the disease he died of, by putting poison in his food. Because the deceased was only a common-law husband and not, therefore, so important to the Fofu, his estranged wife held only a two-day wake for him. Another Fofu woman agreed to distil liquor so the wife could sprinkle her yard with it. His spirit would then not pester her any more but it would happily drum in heaven together with Anastasia's, as the woman put it.

It was interesting that the man did not have the customary four day wake because he was not important in the community. So cultural rules were modified according to the situation. It would be worth examining whether the urban financial situation influenced this particular modification: people had less money and food for wakes in the city than in the rural areas where traditions were followed more closely, even when children had died. In the city, a less important person had fewer people bringing in supplies for a wake: a more important person gathered more support from a wider circle of acquaintances.

Unfortunately Anastasia's spirit caused some disturbance despite the careful precautions of her wake. Years afterwards Georgette revealed that a persistent sore on her leg appeared shortly after Anastasia's death. After a while she "knew" that it was caused by Anastasia's spirit which appeared to her in dreams telling her to go back to the Fofu country. After discussing this with Abiso, it was decided to follow the Fofu tradition. Abiso erected a little hut for Anastasia's spirit and sacrificed a white hen for her. After the ritual Georgette's leg healed and she was free from spirit dreams. She stayed in Bululu a few more years, cohabiting with a Rwandese man but then decided to move back to the Fofu country.

MARIA TAKES COMMAND

The family had to carry on although the central figure had died. The yard looked empty to me with no Anastasia frying manioc cakes. Nobody continued that trade. Maria, however, took the position of Anastasia as the one in charge of the household chores. She distilled liquor to earn money for the family, she cooked, and commanded her siblings to help her in the chores. She had done these tasks earlier as well, but now she had more authority than before. I thought it was rather comical for an eighteen-year-old girl to talk harshly to her siblings. Once I entered the yard when she was twisting Singoma's ear, then thirteen years old, as punishment for not helping to pound flour. On another occasion I heard her threatening to beat Deodonne who, at sixteen, was getting to be her size. "Tonight you will not eat!" was another threat when one of her brothers did not obey her. Denying disobedient children food was a common punishment both among the rural and urban Fofu.

Maria acted very much like Anastasia but lacked the latter's mystical aura. Anastasia did not need to raise her voice to terrify the children whereas Maria screamed and yelled at them. Being young, robust and healthy she was much more energetic than Anastasia; she physically chased her siblings if they disobeyed her.

Maria also worked hard herself. She carried water on top of her head in a thirty-litre plastic canister. Once when I was at their place for about an hour, she brought water in three times from a tap half kilometre away. I heard her complain of headaches after carrying the heavy loads but nobody paid attention to her. To make the work more enjoyable she went water hauling with a neighbour girl and chatted while walking and lining up at the tap.

Maria's life was not all work, however. She observed life unfolding in the neighbourhood and gossiped with neighbours and her siblings. She often sang the latest records on the radio while working. So she was not isolated from the rest of the world. She even spent time on beauty care, smearing her skin and hair with palm oil and keeping her hair braided. As she had no mirror, she walked over to the neighbour's yard to gaze in theirs.

Noela, seven years old, continued to be in charge of Mami, who was about three years old at the time of Anastasia's death. I often saw her with the child. If Noela was not actually carrying her, she would be somewhere nearby, keeping an eye on her. Abiso scolded Noela if she left Mami alone and ran off to play in the road. Once I heard her begging to go to play without Mami but her father did not allow it. She looked disappointed but then tied Mami to her back and ran to play. Mami's head rolled from side to side as Noela ran. Noela was always kind to Mami and Mami liked her.

All the other members of the family paid a lot of attention to Mami, as well. Many a time I found Abiso sitting on a chair under the big tree holding Mami on his lap. All the boys played with her, carried her around, and talked to her gently. But the difference between the boys and Noela was that the former could generally abandon her whenever they wanted to, while Noela could not.

Noela was sent to run errands all the time. Maria, Kristina, Georgette, and even women whom I had never seen came to the yard and told her to go and she went. She literally ran for them. The younger boys, the twins and especially Sengi were sometimes sent to buy peanuts for Mami or charcoal for Kristina. Once Kristina was in a bad mood and criticized the charcoal Kato brought her. She ordered him to return it to the trader and get another kind, called "Rutshuru charcoal." I saw Kato walk down the road a hundred yards, stop to talk to a friend, and then return home pretending he had changed the product. I thought that he behaved cleverly. The trader would not have changed anything for a child anyway. Yet Kato pacified Kristina by appearing to obey her. On that occasion Kristina was satisfied, she did not even look at the charcoal.

After Anastasia's death, Abiso spent much time at home sitting on a chair or on the grass. Often he was not feeling well. For several months he complained about sore eyes. I noticed that red blood vessels criss-crossed his eyes and wondered if he was suffering from filaria, a common disease in Zaire caused by parasites invading the bloodvessels. It frequently attacked the eyes. He had seen a lemon tree in our yard and asked me to bring him some lemons. I did and was horrified when he squeezed the juice of the lemons into his eyes. They stung even more than before but Abiso believed that the juice helped him!

Despite his ill health Abiso still went to work in the fields sometimes. At the appropriate time Maria and a neighbour girl were sent to carry the harvest home. One day there was a huge bundle of beans in the yard. Abiso, Deondonne and Noela were sitting around it husking the beans. Another time Maria, Georgette, and Sengi were added to the work crew and a third time Selestina, Abiso's second wife, sat among her children smiling happily while steadily husking. She would come to the yard for a few hours on such days but did not move in with her husband.

Deondonne worked in the slaughter house on a hill about half a mile from home. It was a huge green building, one of the biggest in the city, a land mark to be seen from far away. It was surrounded by grass where the cows grazed before being slaughtered. The cattle was brought in from the mountains and had to endure a long walk before reaching the city.

Soon the twins joined their elder brother in helping with the butchering. They did it irregularly and they had no steady wages but they would get some money every once in a while and always some meat or bones to take home. Several times I saw the twins proudly carrying heavy, blood stained plastic bags home. They were helping to provide for their family. Deondonne was not so keen to do so, however. Abiso complained that he did not want to share his earnings with the family but bought himself toys and locked the rest of his money in a chest under his bed. Nobody knew how much money he kept there.

I passed the slaughter house on my way to the Fofu families and I knew it had a distinct and strong smell. This kept my curiosity in check for a long time but

Figure 6.4 The slaughter house was situated on top of a hill.

finally, having heard so much about the boys' work there, I decided to go to see them in action. After all, anthropological research was supposed to be empirical.

The stench as I approached the building was awful but I went on in spite of it. I opened the huge doors leading to the hall where the slaughtering was done. It is difficult to find words to describe what I saw. A swarm of bluebottles came out like a cloud, but there was another thick cloud of them left in the hall. They were angry and as noisy as bees, buzzing in my ears. I could not breathe because the smell of blood, faeces, flesh, and intestines was so revolting.

The floor was filthy and covered with blood, droppings and bits and pieces of animals. The walls were splattered with the same ingredients. Men were busy hacking carcasses. Boys of all sizes were helping them and running back and forth carrying animal heads, stomachs, legs etc. The hall was like a busy anthill. I spotted Sengi. He and some other boys had climbed on to something and were reaching to get pieces of carcasses to stuff their pockets with and take home. Sometimes they threw a piece of an intestine at each other. They were having a good time. Sengi noticed me and pointed to Kato and Singoma who were holding onto a cow that was being hacked to pieces. They waved to me and smiled, pleased to see that I had come. I did not see Deondonne anywhere.

I could not hold my breath any longer and ran outside feeling sick. I was sure I would catch something from the billions of bluebottles buzzing in my ears and feared for the health of the workers. I could not imagine how anyone could get used to that unbearable stench although those inside seemed comfortable enough. That was the last time I entered that horrible place but the men and boys carried on their work daily.

Then some time later the city department of hygiene ordered the building to be closed for a clean up. I never saw it reopened, nor did I see anyone working to clean it up. The slaughtering continued under a shelter a few hundred yards away. This arrangement did not seem to be an improvement for the surrounding population as the shelter was even nearer to the heaviest populated area of the slums. When passing by, I turned my head away from the butchering, held my breath for a hundred yards, and jumped over a ditch running with blood. The ditch ran into a little pond in the middle of the pasture area which stank more every day. Scavenging birds and flies circled above the carcasses. Nobody seemed to mind. On the contrary, women queued to buy meat directly from the slaughterers and the little boys continued to dive to the ground to steal a few pieces to take home for their families.

The twins were among these little boys. They often brought meat for Maria to cook for the family. Sometimes they only brought animal skin. This was cooked for the family dog, a skinny lazy animal, kicked by everyone.

From time to time the boys were sick. During one of my visits, the twins sat on a bench the whole time. Abiso had removed several jiggers from their toes and the boys had to sit still the rest of the day because their feet were sore. Another time Singoma was sitting on the ground quietly with an expressionless face. Abiso told me that his stomach was hurting and that's why he did not go to play. A third time I heard Singoma mention a pain but nobody paid any attention to him and he returned to his play.

When the twins were not working they played. One form of play was building toy cars. When the fashion of using cardboard died out the boys invented a new way of making their cars. They used wire which they stole from the fence of the international airport. This fence, which was originally three metres high and encompassed the whole airport, was soon stripped for the Zairean needs, the least of which was probably the boys' home-made cars.

Figure 6.5 Boys playing with home-made wire cars and trucks.

The boys bent the wire into the shapes of cars and trucks. They were so detailed that one could recognize different makes of cars. They made suspensions from elastic rubber bands and wheels from cut-up thongs and beer caps. They then attached six foot long sticks to the cars by tying them to steering wheels. So by turning the sticks the boys could control the direction of the wheels. The twins, as all boys I saw everywhere in town, loved playing with their cars. They would run in the road with their rags flapping behind them with total enthusiasm. One of the twins' friends exchanged his car with me for a packet of chewing gum and I have that car to this day. Sometimes they built roads, hills and garages in the yard for their cars.

Girls did not play with cars. On the contrary, Noela went and destroyed their garage one day and the twins beat her up for it. Poor Noela, she was often slapped by her brothers, but at least, for a while, she could have her revenge when she saw their garage smashed to the ground.

Figure 6.6 Children playing with an abandoned truck.

When the twins were not playing with their miniature cars, they were somewhere in the neighbourhood playing with an abandoned real car. There were abandoned cars and trucks all over the place in the slums. Having one in the yard gave a family prestige, although everyone knew that it did not work. Once Noela led me to her brothers who were playing with such a car. Half a dozen boys were in it, including Kato, who was bouncing up and down on the seats. The car was also bouncing to the rhythm of the boys. Singoma and another boy were lying on the roof of the car. When Noela arrived, she jumped onto the trunk and joined in with the bouncing. Kato's eyes were closed in ecstasy. The movement of something with springs was a new experience for them as none of their furniture was either upholstered or sprung. I stood and watched until one of the boys opened his eyes and saw me. They straight away stopped playing although the smiles were still on their faces. I gave Kato and Singoma chewing gum for interrupting their game. They immediately divided the gum between all the boys and started chewing it.

Although Georgette had moved to Bululu to take care of Anastasia she did not leave after Anastasia's death. However, she no longer lived with the family but rented herself a room nearby. She started living with a man, whom I never met. She often called on the family and asked for the children's help. Generally she had a critical word for their efforts. Once Noela brought her a mug of water as she had requested. Georgette examined the mug and remarked,

"This mug, you don't wash it at all, not the least bit!"

Another time she asked for an axe and checked the blade with a sour face. Someone had dulled it by hitting a stone with it. Although Georgette constantly asked for help, she herself assisted the family when they needed more workers, when Abiso harvested his beans, for instance.

Kristina continued to live in her apartment in one end of Anastasia's building. Her housekeeping was still separate from the family's but the children went freely in and out of her quarters as before.

Tabo, the girl whom Anastasia brought up, left the house after Anastasia's death. She moved in with her mother who lived nearby. I went to see her several times and chatted with her and her teenage girlfriends who were continuously singing the new love songs they heard on the radio. It surprised me that Tabo actively sought little babies to care for. She often played with neighbours' babies and tied them on her back when working at home or going around with her girlfriends. I thought that girls of her age in my country would not be as interested in infants.

Once Tabo's mother came home drunk and gave a spontaneous dance performance outside her door. An audience gathered around her crazy dancing which Tabo tried to ignore although it was hard to do so. Her mother was famous among the Fofu for her drunkenness. Although all Fofu drank a lot, everybody agreed that she drank too much.

After about a year, I heard that Tabo had married a teacher. Although the proper bridewealth had not been paid for her, her mother had received a length of cloth and was extremely happy with the deal. Later Tabo moved to Butembo with her husband. After being away from town for a few years, she returned with a child, having left her husband. She remarried and had two more children.

With Anastasia dead the family members did not feel as tied to the house as before. Sengi for example visited his maternal grandparents in another part of town for several weeks. Selestina also went away for a while and Kato was sent to his father's brother in Beni, and never returned.

I sometimes travelled to Beni and after about a year decided to use the opportunity to go and see Kato. Abiso explained how I could find him. I was to go to a person working in a certain office and ask him to take me to Abiso's brother. The advice worked and suddenly I was in the yard of Abiso's relative, surrounded by strange faces, except one face, that of Kato's. He looked reborn. He was wearing clean shorts and a shirt. His terrible eczema had healed; his skin was a rich brown colour as smooth as a baby's. Because his scalp had also healed his hair had grown and looked healthy. He too had grown and gained weight. He smiled broadly and looked happy in his new environment. His uncle told me that he had taken Kato to a native healer and it had helped immediately. Kato seemed content with his new home and ran errands for his uncle in the same way as he had done at home for Anastasia, his father, and Maria. His uncle had sent him to school again and everything was fine. I was very happy for him although I missed him in Bululu because he was a friendly child who was pleasant and open to talk to. Of all the members of the family I felt closest to Kato.

Not everybody prospered, however, for almost a year after Anastasia's death, Mami died. It happened when I was in Canada for an annual vacation, so I only heard about it on our return. Abiso told me that she had died of "a rib ailment" and did not elaborate. The other Fofu were gossiping that Mami's mother had taken the child with her to visit her relatives and returned it to Abiso in a sickly condition. As her body was swollen the Fofu concluded that she had given the sickness to the child by witchcraft. Not long afterwards Mami died. She was four years old.

The family was considerably smaller without Anastasia, Tabo, Kato, and Mami. When Tabo married, I asked Abiso if Maria was getting married soon. He told me that nobody had asked for her yet and probably would not because she had a big mouth. He added that Maria was like a wife to him because she did all the cooking for him which was a good thing, since his own wife neglected him. He also told me that he himself was planning to take another wife soon.

That Maria was not passively waiting for a husband was proven when she was thrown into jail for one night. The whole neighbourhood treated it as a joke although Abiso himself looked embarrassed when he told me that Maria had scratched and bitten a girlfriend so badly that the friend's father brought in the police. Maria had apparently lost her temper over a boyfriend but I was not given further details. The neighbours collected enough money to set her free.

Although Maria was not getting married it was soon obvious that she was pregnant. In 1980 she bore a daughter whom she called Jeanne. Abiso was both annoyed and happy. He put out feelers to see if the father of the child would be interested in marrying Maria. However, he had already three wives and was not interested in taking a fourth one. He promised to pay some damages but the money never came. This caused annoyance although Abiso realised it was not rare for a father in Bululu not to get bridewealth for his daughter. On the other hand he was happy to have someone to replace Mami. Noela and Sengi looked after baby Jeanne although the other family members also gave her a lot of attention. Maria continued to be in charge of the family as before.

Before Anastasia's death, Abiso had been worried about losing the house. Apparently Anastasia owned it and he feared it would pass to her relatives in accordance with the Fofu and Logo tradition. This was that spouses did not

Figure 6.7 Abiso with his daughter's daughter.

inherit from each other but the inheritance went in a patriliny from father to his sons or his brothers. A mother's inheritance went to her patrilineage, her brothers and their sons. Anastasia did not have true brothers in Bululu but her ethnic "brothers" could have claimed her property. I do not know why they did not. In the rural area of Nyanya, I noticed that a new rule was being increasingly observed. This followed the Western pattern of the surviving spouse inheriting from the deceased spouse and the children inheriting from the last parent to die. I assume that Abiso was allowed to follow this rule since he had been a "good" husband. After all, Anastasia's relatives did not accuse him of killing his wife.

The Fofu of Bululu spoke fondly about the Fofu country. In their memory it was the best place on earth. However, very few of them actually moved back to their home area. When Abiso had talked highly about the northeastern Zaire over the years I had taken it with a grain of salt. Some time after Anastasia's death, however, Abiso surprised me by showing definite plans to leave Bululu.

In 1980 Abiso put his house up for sale. He attached a small handwritten paper note to a wall of the house stating his intent to sell. Nothing happened for a long time. When we were leaving the country in 1981, however, Abiso told me that he was hopeful of selling it and was negotiating seriously with someone. He told me that he would move to the Ituri forest at Komanda where his "brother" was living. He had corresponded with him and the latter had agreed to take in Abiso and his children and give him a field and a lot to build his house on. He would live much better there than in Bululu by cultivating large fields. He was looking forward to the move. When I asked if he was taking Selestina along, he shook his head vigorously. Only he and his children were going and he would remarry in the new area. Selestina had killed his wife and his daughter and was not wanted any more.

DASHED HOPES

When I returned to Zaire in 1984 I heard about Abiso's family even before flying to Bululu for a day. The reason was that, to my surprise, Georgette was living at Nyanya. She had finally left Bululu because the spirits had told her to. Her common-law husband had stayed there and he had since died.

True to Georgette's nature, she had lived a colourful life after leaving Bululu. She had attempted different businesses with various boyfriends. With one of them she had tried to establish a bar only to be left high and dry by him when he fled with all the cash. With another she had attempted to trade in so called "wax cloth," special good quality cloth which was very coveted by women. Again she was cheated by her boyfriend and left empty-handed. There was mention of a third boyfriend who had been a bus driver between Lemura and Nyanya. However, Georgette was wise enough to leave him when his wife found out about her and threatened to kill her with a knife.

Georgette did not tell me about any other boyfriends she had accumulated in the three years I had been away but there was at least one more because Cecilia informed me that Georgette had returned to her home village of Gangu and had an affair with Maladi, who features in "Two Women Who Left." Because they were clan siblings their relationship was considered incestuous and Georgette had been expelled from the village.

There was also another failed business which Georgette had apparently managed without the help of a boyfriend. Before settling down at Nyanya, Georgette had lived on top of the mountain near Gangu, where she had run a restaurant for the gold diggers. Then one of her customers had died after eating her food and she had been accused of "poisoning" him with witchcraft. The Nyanya chief had been called to deal with the case and he had acquitted Georgette with the logic that other men had also eaten Georgette's food at the same time and had not died. Georgette told me that having lost some money over the case she closed her restaurant and moved to Nyanya. I was surprised that she had to pay anything as she was acquitted but Georgette enlightened me by saying that if government officials dealt with anything they would "eat" everyone's money, both that of the guilty and the innocent.

Again she omitted juicy details which I gleaned from the grape vine. These were that during the court case, the Nyanya chief had made eyes at Georgette and had taken her to live with him as one of his mistresses in one of his many houses near his office. This was her position when I met her again in 1984.

To my delight Georgette had news of Abiso and his family. I was particularly anxious to hear if he had moved. Yes he had, although he had come close to death before moving. His body, like that of Anastasia and Mami, had swollen and he had been ailing for a long time until finally he was well enough to travel in a bus to Komanda. Maria, Singoma, and Noela were with him at Komanda. Sengi had stayed with his mother in Bululu and Kato continued to live with Abiso's brother in Beni. Deondonne had gone to dig gold.

As Komanda was only about thirty miles from Nyanya I asked if Georgette thought she could help us find Abiso if we drove there one day. She became excited and told me that she would find him by asking at Komanda, since she knew his brother's name and the approximate location.

Henry, Georgette and I accordingly drove to Komanda one Sunday afternoon. True to her word, Georgette kept on questioning passers by until we were finally at Abiso's relative's house.

Abiso and the children were at home with the relatives. We had not been able to give advance notice of our visit and the children let out screams of surprise and joy. "*Dada, dada, dada* (elder sister)!" they yelled and threw their arms around Georgette. She was the celebrity: Henry and I were greeted more officially with handshakes.

When the chaotically enthusiastic welcome died down I could take note of the family members. Maria was there with her two daughters. The younger one, who had been born earlier that year, was sitting in the yard on a goat skin and looking scared of the wild shouting. Jeanne was now about three years old. Singoma and his sister Noela had both grown. Everyone looked neat, clean and well fed, and Abiso bore no trace of any disease. I could not tell how well they got on with the relatives because they did not know how to deal with white people and kept away from us. I only saw two small mud huts and wondered if there was enough room for everyone.

The family did not have very recent news of Kato but they had stopped by Beni on the way to Komanda and seen he was thriving at his uncle's place. Nobody had heard of Deondonne since he departed to dig gold.

Abiso was keen to show us his fields. Georgette was not interested in seeing them and stayed with the children and the relatives at the house retelling her adventures, while Henry and I walked with Abiso a few hundred yards to his fields.

Komanda was in the Ituri rain forest which started near the Fofu area further north. The air was noticeably more humid here than in the savannah. Abiso's relative's homestead was surrounded by a lush growth of grass, bushes and trees. When we reached a clearing in the forest Abiso stood aside and proudly explained how he had created it. Apparently he had paid some Mbuti Pygmies to fell trees for him. After the trees were felled, Abiso burnt them using the ash as fertilizer. The preparation of the ground for planting was different from that in the savannah, where I had observed Fofu cultivation. Instead of hoeing the ground Abiso had just made holes with a sharp stick and planted a seed of corn or beans in each hole. That was all. The corn was about a foot high and was growing well. Abiso was all smiles in anticipation of a good harvest. He was planning to enlarge his fields, to build a house for his family, and enjoy a better life. Everything would be fine. He urged me to visit him in a year when I was going to Nyanya again and I promised him I would.

Although Abiso said the children liked living in Komanda I could not tell during such a short visit, if it was true. Everyone seemed very happy to see Georgette but one could not tell whether they were normally happy. The change was extreme for everyone, among other things there was a lack of entertainment in the rural area compared with the city.

By the time we returned from the fields Georgette had arranged to take Noela to live with her in Nyanya. Abiso did not oppose the idea. As the relatives had daughters to look after Maria's daughters, Noela was not indispensable. She, therefore, gathered a few clothes to take with her and Maria prepared a bundle of sweet potatoes and local charcoal as a gift for Georgette. Soon we were ready to drive back to Nyanya.

In the car Georgette filled us in with the family gossip. The first piece of news was that Deondonne had fathered a daughter in Bululu but had not paid bridewealth for his lover and could not, therefore, keep the baby. Anyway, his lover was a prostitute who did not want to get married. Both Georgette and Noela giggled when talking about Deondonne's affair.

The second piece of news was that Kristina had died in Bululu. Her body had swollen badly and she died quite soon afterwards. I was surprised because she was a young person who took good care of herself. As soon as Georgette mentioned the swelling of her body I knew that the Fofu would blame witchcraft for her death. Georgette did not want to go on to speculate who her killer was although Maria must have told her about that, too.

The third piece of news was that Abiso's second wife Selestina had borne another child a couple of years ago but the child had died a few months later. The child was by a man with whom she was then living.

Soon after our trip Georgette had a dramatic experience with ancestors "entering her head" in a trance. Georgette's sister came to tell me about it one day and asked me to visit Georgette again soon. While other Fofu were very secretive about trances induced by ancestors, Georgette told me all about it. She had been getting ready to fix supper when the spirits suddenly entered her. Her body became as taut as a bowstring, she was thrown on the ground, and the spirits talked through her mouth in the Hiha language. Some Fofu women gathered around her to listen but they refused to give their messages because all those present were women and it was not worth the trouble to talk to them. Maria felt exhausted for a week after the event and was lucky to have Noela to do the household chores for her.

When I left Nyanya in August 1984 I was confident that a new and successful stage had started in the life of Abiso's family.

When I returned a year later I found Georgette not in the chief's house but in her relative's house closer to the shops. Although she did not tell me, I understood that her affair with the chief had ended. She, herself, explained her move to me in spiritual terms: a relative of hers had put a curse on her in that house.

Georgette's life had not been uneventful during my absence. Indeed, calamity had literally struck her a few months ago and she had nearly died. One evening she had been in bed — she omitted to say she was with a lover — when she was struck by lightning and lost consciousness. She was taken to the mission hospital and subsequently spent much money and time to no avail. Finally she had been taken to a diviner who had traced the cause of her calamity to her father's brother who had caused her trouble as long as Georgette could remember. He was angry with Georgette for fooling around with men and not bringing him bridewealth. That evil man, as Georgette called him, had "killed" Georgette's father years ago and had tried to steal another brother's daughter's bridewealth. After the visit to the shaman, Georgette's brothers had taken the courage to go and compel the uncle to confess that he had practised witchcraft on Georgette. As well as the confession they also collected some of his saliva as a symbol of reconciliation. That was to be mixed with herbal medicine and administered to Georgette by rubbing it on cuts made with a razor blade. Georgette believed that the Zairean medicine had made her feel better.

Georgette was a wonderful source of information of Fofu thinking in the line of witchcraft. She talked about it more than anyone else although I had to make allowances for exaggeration and imagination. I wondered why she was more open about it than others. It seemed to me that she took pleasure in revealing these secrets to a white woman. She also liked to shock people. When I looked at her life, I thought I knew the reason. As she had no children she was an outcast: she was not respected as a real woman. My hypothesis is that she reacted to being marginalised by taking pleasure in rebelling against rules, such as the family rules regarding bridewealth and society's rules concerning moral behaviour. Although she consulted with ancestors according to tradition she disregarded their advice when it suited her.

I was anxious to hear about Abiso's family. Although Georgette said she was weak, she had no trouble in telling me what had happened to the family. It was a gloomy story and my optimistic hopes were shattered.

In February of 1985 Abiso's body had swollen which was of course a sign of witchcraft. He became lethargic and was confined to bed. Everyone could see that he was nearing his death. He called Singoma to him and commanded him to live in peace among his siblings. Then he added that his killer was Noela.

Noela of all people! I was surprised that anyone could accuse a little girl of twelve of witchcraft. However, Georgette, insisted that it was possible and when I asked other Fofu they too assured me that children could kill their parents with witchcraft, especially where parents were divorced and the child preferred one parent to the other. Abiso had told Singoma that Selestina, his second wife, had given Noela the witchcraft when the two had bidden farewell to each other in Bululu. Noela had put the poison in Abiso's food. Abiso knew this must be the case because he noticed becoming ill after eating food cooked by Noela.

Although Singoma told Georgette this, neither of them made it public because they knew that Maria would go wild with anger. I wondered whether even Noela knew about the accusation.

When Abiso died, Deondonne was still away gold digging in a remote place north of Lemura. A message had been broadcast on the radio but there had been no response from him although seven months had now elapsed. Georgette regretted that Abiso had not died in Bululu where he would have had many Logo to bury him. In Komanda he had quarrelled with his relative and gone to live with a Kimbanguist[1] woman. Georgette said that a handful of Kimbanguists buried Abiso. Maria had been at Georgette's during the time of her father's death. When the news about Abiso's death reached Nyanya, Georgette sent Maria to Komanda by bus and she herself walked to save the pennies for the wake feast. Georgette told me virtuously that she had saved money to assist Abiso in building a new house for himself and the children, but she used them for his wake.

After the mourning period Georgette had brought the children who were left in Komanda with her to Nyanya. She had acquired a permanent job for nineteen-year old Singoma at the Protestant mission hospital and lodging for him at her sister's. Her sister lived with her husband and children a few miles from Georgette and was happy to have Singoma as a helper in the family. Georgette had instructed Singoma to be respectful toward the home-givers because without them he would have no place to stay. Singoma had taken her advice to heart and was working well both in his job as a laundry helper and at his new home. Georgette's sister had troubles with her husband and left him several times during the year I was at Nyanya. She told me that she could trust Singoma to take care of the children faithfully while she was away.

Maria with her two daughters and Noela had stayed with Georgette. However, problems had arisen when Georgette had been ill after being struck by lightning.

---

[1] Kimbanguists were followers of Simon Kimbangu who had started an indigenous religious group as an offshoot of an American Baptist mission in the Lower Congo in the 1920s. The religious movement had been banned by the colonial government but after Independence had become one of the three official religions in the country and was still spreading to the east.

Georgette had lent Maria some money to set her up distilling liquor. While Georgette was in the hospital the distilling had failed and Maria disappeared with the money. Georgette knew that she had returned to Komanda, not to Abiso's relatives but to the town. Noela had remained with Georgette but cheated her on school attendance: while pretending to go to school she had walked around the market place. Georgette was furious when she found out and sent Noela away. The two sisters were now living together in Komanda.

I was very saddened with the news of the family. I had hoped that Abiso's move to a different area would be an improvement in his life. It was not to be. According to Western medicine, he was probably suffering from a heart ailment, as Anastasia had in Bululu, and would have died no matter where he lived.

Later the same year, I heard from the Fofu that Maria had sent a letter saying she was planning to return to Bululu with her two daughters and Noela and to work as a prostitute there. She did not like Komanda and missed Bululu.

Nobody heard anything from Deondonne all year. Georgette wondered if he had been killed while digging gold because the pits often collapsed on the diggers. Many husky young men had lost their lives at that dangerous work.

Kato was said to be happy in Beni. I did not see him but was pleased with the news. Sengi stayed with his mother in Bululu and worked at the slaughter's cleaning cow stomachs or herding cows before they were slaughtered.

During the year of fieldwork I often saw Singoma either at the hospital or at Georgette's or her sister's house. Sometimes they used him to carry messages to me. He looked content and was always dressed in clean new clothes. He considered himself lucky to have a home and he served his relatives with humility. I remembered those years when he had worked in the filthy slaughter house in Bululu wearing rags and suffering from jiggers and stomach trouble. I was sincerely happy for him.

As for Georgette, now that Noela had gone, she had acquired a five-year old niece to help her with the household chores. My last image of Georgette was of her firmly giving orders to the little girl. She mentioned that the girl was sick and she, Georgette, would take her to the hospital if God helped her to distil and sell much liquor the following day. Georgette's God, like that of most Fofu, was a friendly God, who always accepted people as they were, regardless of what they did. I smiled to myself when I remembered how I was taught in my childhood not to expect God's blessing over anything illegal. Although I heard missionaries, both Catholic and Protestant, teach the same here, the Fofu ignored such dull dogma. Georgette was a devout Catholic and regularly attended the local Sunday mass.

Some time ago she had taken a lover, a Protestant school teacher, whose wife protested against her husband's new mistress by publicly chopping up their marital bed and moving away with all their furniture. Georgette was pleased with herself for being able to seduce a respectable married man, but refused his offers to pay bridewealth to her uncles. These continued to criticize her and, according to

Georgette, tried their best to kill her with witchcraft. She confided in me that if she tired of this lover later on, she would move to Isiro to be out of the reach of her uncles' witchcraft.

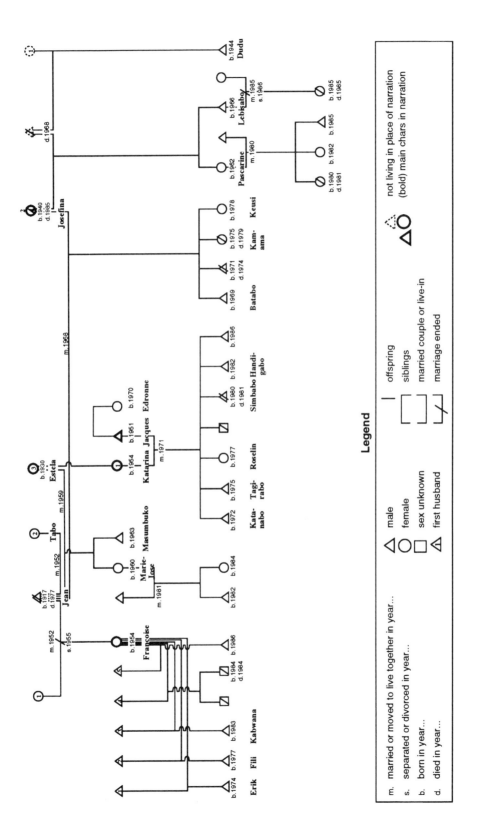

Figure 7.1 Family Diagram for "Survival of the Dependents of a Civil Servant."

7 THE SURVIVAL OF THE DEPENDENTS OF A CIVIL SERVANT

A SUDDEN DEATH

The day I met Jean's first wife, Tabo, could not have been a worse one for her. It was a day of double tragedy. *Mama* Avion whom I had gone to visit was not at home and a neighbour had taken me to find her in another house. There I met with a noisy group of people. The neighbour assumed they were drinking but in fact they were excited about something else.

In the middle of the group was an elderly woman with a black eye, bruises on her face and arm and some open sores. This was Tabo, Jean's first wife. The other Fofu women, *Mama* Avion included, were standing around her, all talking loudly and angrily at the same time. After a little while, I managed to gather bits and pieces of what had happened.

Tabo had been hit by a motorcycle a few hours previously when walking in the main street with a little boy. The motorcyclist, who happened to be drunk, fell and hurt himself. Apparently, he had borrowed the motorcycle, had no money and was a good for nothing, so there was no hope of getting any compensation from him.

A younger woman then joined the group. She had the little boy with her who was about five and was bandaged. She announced that the motorcyclist was still at the zone administration centre and urged Tabo to go back to the dispensary for medical attention. The group dispersed when Tabo did as she was bidden. We thought she would be put right but in fact things soon changed for the worse.

Mama Avion and I were strolling towards my house when we heard a terrible scream. We rushed to the house from whence it came and discovered it was Tabo. She had called at the second wife's house to get something before leaving for the dispensary when a second tragedy hit her. Her husband, Jean, had died two days previously in Buva and had already been buried. Tabo had just heard this news and that was the cause of her screaming.

Mama Avion stood in the road stunned. She was talking about Jean half to herself and half to me. Apparently Jean had gone to Buva to collect some money he had lent to someone. He had been staying with a relative and had obtained the money as planned. Then in *Mama* Avion's words "a stomach disease had captured him," and he had been operated on. He had sent one of his children, who had travelled with him, to fetch his third wife, Josefina, from Bululu, so she could take care of him in the hospital. Josefina was at that moment preparing to go the next day.

Hysterical screaming continued to come from the house. *Mama* Avion seemed to direct her steps towards it. I did not know whether to enter the house or not. In my home country families wanted to be alone in moments of sorrow. I had only just met the widow, was I too much of a stranger to join them? The screams were so piercing that I had goose pimples on my arms. I was scared. Coping with deaths was the hardest part of anthropological fieldwork, at least for me. *Mama* Avion saw my indecision and decided for me,

"Go home and I'll come to see you later."

I walked home wondering how anyone could take two bad shocks in one day. The old woman was already in pain from the motorcycle accident and now she had the added pain of losing her husband. *Mama* Avion came in a few hours. She told me that it would have been appropriate for me to go in the house. Indeed, the widows had been wondering why I had not. Since then I have learned that the Fofu do not consider their mourning to be private. I should have gone and shown my sympathy.

Mama Avion told me the names of the wives and gave me a bit of the family background. The old woman, Tabo, was Jean's first wife. She had no children herself but she had raised the children of Jean's second wife as her own. *Mama* Avion explained that she was like "a mother" to her husband and her co-wives and if she had started quarrelling with her co-wives everyone would have laughed. I interpreted this as meaning that Tabo no longer had sexual relations with her husband and therefore did not compete with her co-wives for him. The wake was to be held in the house of the second wife, Estela, where Tabo had received the sad news. All the wives would mourn their husband together. The mourning period would last four days, which followed the general Fofu tradition. *Mama* Avion went on to explain that if Jean had been a rich man the wake would last a week and the mourners would "eat his wealth in food and liquor." Because he was not rich, the mourners would stay less time. I had never before heard this refinement of the tradition.

Mama Avion asked me to pass the news on to Angelika, my Fofu neighbour. I expressed my surprise that she asked me to go there and did not go herself since she had walked as far as my house. *Mama* Avion dryly explained that she did not want to appear at Angelika's "every day" and she had taken me there to meet Angelika only a few days ago. As soon as *Mama* Avion had left I went to Angelika's and told her the news. She was as stunned as *Mama* Avion had been and told me that she would go to mourn with the widows the same day.

The next morning I walked to the wake. I could see from a few hundred yards away that men were sitting on chairs in the road outside the house since the house had no yard. The road was wide so there was plenty of room. It was also so rough that no cars could pass it. The men were chatting casually among themselves.

Mama Avion had told me that the mourners had bought expensive eucalyptus fire wood to burn through the night. The spirit of Jean would fear the fire and would not come to bother his widows. Otherwise there would have been a great danger of the widows being troubled by their dead husband in dreams.

The women were inside the house, lying on palm mats. Each of the widows was in a different room. In the middle room, into which the front door led, Josefina lay on her side with her face turned down. She was obviously very pregnant. What a time to receive the news of her husband's death!

The first wife, Tabo, was lying prone on a mat in the room to the right and Estela in the room to the left. Each of them sat up when I went to greet them but then returned to the lying position. Tabo mourned aloud. She had received no medication for her cuts and bruises and looked miserable. Life was truly harsh for these widows.

A young woman, Estela's daughter, offered me a chair in the middle room. She took a chair for herself as well. Her name was Katarina and I found it easy to relate to her. She was to become my best friend in Bululu. She had her baby on her lap and she sat with me all the time I was there.

The next morning, I brought some ointment for Tabo's sores. She was lying prone again but sat up when I came and let me apply the ointment. Then she lay down again.

My family had been planning to make a New Year's trip back to Nyanya and Yenyabo. I was away a few days and consequently could not participate in the ending ceremonies of the wake. When I returned all the rituals were over and a young man had arrived from Beni in order to take Tabo back with him. He was the husband of one of Tabo's "daughters." Like Anastasia, Tabo as the first wife, had internalized her role as a "mother" so deeply that she always talked about her co-wives' children as her own.

The man explained that it would be much better for Tabo to live in Beni than in Bululu because she had many relatives in Beni who would look after her. Tabo and the young man were only waiting for Francoise, another "daughter," to return from Buva where she had gone to visit her father's grave and find out more about his death. Tabo was about to go to bid farewell to her tribal sisters in town so I had no chance to talk with her.

I saw Tabo once more before she moved to Beni. She was cutting up cauliflower with another of her "daughters," who had arrived from Beni with a basketful of cauliflowers for the family. It looked as if the family was going to have only cauliflower for their meal because I did not see anything else being prepared. Katarina and some other women kept me company. I asked Katarina what ethnic group her infant daughter belonged to. At that moment Estela was offering the infant, six months old, some beer and the little child took a sip.

"She must be Fofu, she drinks beer as you see!" Katarina answered with a laugh. She stressed that the difference between the Fofu and the Nandi lay in the fact that the former drank liquor all the time while the latter did not.

Estela next offered Tania, then two years old, some beer, too, but she refused after smelling it. Everyone laughed and joked that she was not a Fofu. Fofu children recognized their food, as they called alcoholic beverages, almost from birth.

After a couple of days Tabo left for Beni accompanied by Francoise and the man who had come to fetch her. Tabo never returned to Bululu but we heard that she was doing well in Beni. She fully recovered from her motorcycle accident. Francoise stayed with Tabo in Beni for a while but then returned to Bululu as she preferred to live there.

The wake was the last time the widows were together. After that, they lived their separate lives. Francoise took care of their mutual business at first but later the spirit of co-operation broke down. However, they retained their ties with other Fofu which drew me into the Fofu network which criss-crossed the city.

The following stories describe the life events of Jean's widows and their descendants as they struggled to take care of their families without their husband. Some of their children were already adults or became adults in a few years, and I will sketch their family lives as well. I will start with Francoise, who was Tabo's "daughter." Then I will describe the survival strategies of Estela and her children, of whom Katarina was the oldest. Finally I will recount how Josefina, the youngest of the widows, tried hard to manage but with little success.

First a few words about Jean, whom I never met. He must have been between fifty and sixty years old when he died. He was born at Sezabo in the Fofu country and married a Nyanya girl, Tabo. After their marriage he started working for the colonial government as a driver during which time he lived in Lemura, Beni, Butembo, Buva, and Bululu. Tabo mentioned that Butembo was the place where she aged, meaning that they lived there the longest. It was there that Jean married a couple of other women besides Tabo but only one of them, Estela, stayed with him. She already had two children by another man but Jean welcomed them all into his family. Jean moved to Bululu after Independence was declared in 1960 and continued to work for the government. There he took yet a third wife, Josefina, out of tribal responsibility, as will be recounted in her part of the story.

Nobody spoke spontaneously about Jean after the wake, so I had no knowledge of what kind of man he had been. When I interviewed Katarina about her childhood she gave me a standard answer: her step-father had been strict and had taught her to respect adults. In addition, he had taught her to read and write. Katarina claimed to have loved her step-father very much.

JEAN'S PRESTIGIOUS DAUGHTER

Francoise was the child of Jean and a former wife whom he had taken after Tabo's two children had died as infants. She left her husband for some reason when Francoise was an unweaned baby. Tabo took Francoise as her daughter and, according to Francoise, also breastfed her. Francoise did not remember her real mother and never met her but she knew that the mother was living in Kisangani. Francoise talked highly of Tabo and always referred to her as her mother. After Jean died she contemplated moving to Beni to be near her "mother" but decided against it. However, she made several trips to Beni to visit Tabo.

The very first get-together, which *Mama* Avion had arranged between me and the Fofu women, was held at Francoise's house. At that time she was living in a better house than most of the Fofu because her husband was a customs official. It was generally known that men in his occupation took money and other objects from travellers for their private use. They were considered wealthy and Francoise enjoyed prestige among the Fofu as a wife of a wealthy man.

Francoise was a young woman of 23-years when I met her. She looked pretty and sophisticated. She kept herself neat at all times and wore good clothes. Before she left for town on official business, she carried a bucket of water into her outhouse, took a bath, and dressed up in her best outfit. She spoke in a higher voice than other Fofu women, who tended to have low and harsh voices. The aura of sophistication was also created by her habit of keeping her eyes, which had long lashes, half-closed. Her hair was longer than that of other Fofu women and formed a wider frame for her face. She liked to wear an "antenna" coiffure, in which her hair stuck out as little antennae with balls on the tips.

She had completed eight grades of school education, which was far more than other Fofu women had done, and she was able to speak French. She also understood Kifofu and Kinandi although she did not speak these languages. Because she had French, she was the family representative in official matters. After her father's death, for example, she was sent to Buva to find out more about it. When Jean's widows started receiving compensation from the government (as Jean's employer) it was Francoise who went to the office to receive the monthly payments and distributed it among the widows. She also supervised her "mother's" move to Beni and accompanied her there.

Before she travelled to Buva and Beni on family business, she gave up her rented house and stored her furniture with Fofu relatives. On her return she boarded with Estela, her mother's co-wife until she found another house to live in. She did not like the temporary arrangement because her husband could not sleep with her as long as she was staying at her step-mother's place, due to the in-law avoidance rule.

I was to learn that the ground for much of her prestige was shaky. Although her husband was wealthy, he neglected finding Francoise a place to live. As the months went by Francoise became anxious. During that time I overheard Estela gossiping about Francoise. She said Francoise was upset because her husband had many wives, at least six. (Francoise had told me that he had five wives and that she was the third). Estela went on to reveal that Francoise had seen her husband with other women and had been offended. He played around with women all the time. What made her particularly angry was that he gave these other women extravagant gifts such as tape recorders and radios. This meant that there was less left for her. After hearing this, I was not surprised that he had not found a place for Francoise.

Francoise was contemplating leaving her husband but after six months or so, he established her in two rooms of a very nice house in the slum area, half way between *Mama* Avion and Anastasia. It was a new house, built of concrete blocks and cement, and had a cement floor, a status symbol in the neighbourhood. There were no windows in the rooms for security reasons, but the house featured a ceiling window created by a clear plastic panel in the corrugated iron roof. Three local paintings hung on the walls, and the living room was furnished with a couch and three arm chairs around a coffee table, all locally made. To cap it all, Francoise's husband had provided a transistor radio and a sewing machine. She was able to repair her children's clothes with the machine. She also let her neighbours and friends use it. Sometimes a tailor hired the machine and sewed for other people in her living room. Then Francoise would lie on her couch as if she were a lazy rich woman, chatting with customers and the tailor.

Now there was no more talk about leaving her husband and the Fofu thought that she had it made. They turned to her in their financial difficulties and she gave them money if she had any. Josefina especially kept on going to her for help. I wondered how strong she really was financially. I don't think she was much better off than the other Fofu.

I used to drop by her house often on my Fofu round in the neighbourhood and she grew accustomed to me. She was quite open with me at that time and we both enjoyed chatting with each other. Later on, when her life was no longer going so well she became more secretive and less friendly.

I asked her about her relationship with her husband who was posted about 40 miles north of Bululu at the Rwanda-Zaire border. It was in the mountains at a higher altitude than Bululu and it was always cold there. According to Francoise, the other wives alternated in living with him at his post for a fortnight each but she did not want to go there because of the cold weather. This may or may not have been true. I had overheard Estela say that her husband had taken a new wife at his post. Francoise personally knew two of her co-wives, who were much older than she, had several children each, and lived in Bululu. She sometimes paid them a courtesy visit.

When she was looking for a new house and was frustrated about living at Estela's, I asked why she did not live with the other wives like the rural Fofu did. She shook her head.

"It would only produce quarrels," she prophesied.

"Why don't the rural wives quarrel then?" I tested her.

Francoise thought that the reason was that all the wives were Fofu. In the city, the wives belonged to different tribes and would not get along with each other. The other Fofu viewed the situation in the same way as Francoise and said that it was not wise for the co-wives to live together. Anastasia's unsuccessful attempt was a case in point.

Francoise told me that her husband would come to visit her without warning whenever it suited him, about once in two weeks. She had to be ready to receive him any day. Usually he arrived at night and left early in the morning.

As she was alone most of the time, I asked if she could have lovers while her husband was away. Francoise was shocked. She would not dare to have any! Her husband would be furious if he found another man with her. Even if he did not discover them together he would find out sooner or later. She could not risk it.

The husband was very clever and frequently sent relatives to check on her. They would drop in at any time for a chat and glance around to see that everything was in order. Francoise always appeared submissive and polite to them. Often relatives of her husband stayed overnight in her living room. I saw the inequality of the position of a husband and wife: he had many wives, mistresses and lovers but she had to be faithful. I did not open up a feminist discussion, although her position troubled me.

I asked if her husband gave her money regularly. Apparently he did nothing regularly. Francoise had to make her case for money and he would consider it and give her some if it suited him.

Although I visited Francoise regularly for two years I never met her husband. Her relatively grand accommodation and the Fofu respect for her were the only evidence that he really existed.

Francoise had to earn some money by her own efforts. Like other Fofu women, she distilled liquor and sold it to a bar. As she could not build an open fire on the cement floor of her house she arranged to do her distilling in other Fofu houses which had dirt floors. Sometimes she distilled with Josefina's teenage daughter, Pascarine. At other times *Mama* Avion offered her house and other times she went to her cousin's place, Ida, who was the mother of the Tabo Anastasia had brought up.

Francoise did not seem to miss the company of her husband. She socialized with her neighbours and Fofu people. When I stayed for any length of time at her place, many people dropped in to borrow or return something or simply to chat with her.

Relatives were so important to her that she would take anyone in for a night who claimed to be a relative. One afternoon I met a woman at her place who had arrived from Buva and claimed to be Jean's mother's sister. She was helping Francoise to cook a meal and care for the children. The next day, Francoise was very upset. Her living room was full of local Fofu relatives who were comforting her. Francoise had discovered that the woman had been an imposter. When Francoise had left the house for a while, the woman had collected Francoise's money, salt, soap, and her best clothes in a basket with the intention of stealing them. Francoise caught her in time and chased her away. She repeated the story over and over: how the woman had arrived, how Francoise had believed her, how they had worked together, and how the woman had tried to steal from her. The Fofu shook their heads, amazed that such things could happen. I found it interesting that amid all the lying, stealing and corruption that was going on in Zaire this so shocked them. Relatives are almost sacred to the Fofu.

Francoise had two sons, Erik born in 1974 to her first husband and Fili born in 1977 to her present husband. Erik's father had moved away to his tribal area in western Zaire and Francoise had not wanted to move with him. She kept saying her first husband had paid a lot of bridewealth for her and, according to the custom, he had the right to take Erik. She was expecting him to come at any time and hoped that Erik would get an excellent education with her ex-husband. Francoise also claimed that her present husband had paid much bridewealth for her. Only years later did I realise that she had been lying to me and that she was in fact in a pitiable position. I will elaborate on this later as the story unfolds.

I had a particular interest in childrearing so when Erik had a temper tantrum in my presence I paid close attention. It happened in 1978 when Francoise was living with her step-mother Estela. Tabo, Erik's grandmother, Francoise, and Francoise's teenage step-sister Marie-Jose, were sitting in Estela's living room when Erik burst in, wound the curtain of a cupboard around his wrist and yelled,

"Sugar!"

When nobody paid any attention to him he repeated the demand several times until suddenly Marie-Jose, who was nearest to him, slapped the hand which was holding the curtain. Erik hit her back angrily and burst into tears. Neither Marie-Jose nor the women reacted to him. When Marie-Jose went to another room to get ready for school, Erik took hold of the curtain hanging at the door to that room and again yelled,

"Sugar!"

Still Marie-Jose did not react, so Erik went to his mother.

"Take from the cupboard," she said simply and continued her conversation. The boy did not move but remained there sulking. The matter was forgotten when Francoise and Tabo hurried to get ready to go to town.

When the two women left I went out of the house. Erik was sitting on the ground playing with a teapot lid while Estela and Marie-Jose were pounding manioc. Yet again Erik yelled,

"Sugar!"

When nobody paid any attention to him, the boy threw himself on the ground and cried loudly. This too was in vain.

On my way home I thought back to similar occurrences in the rural areas and concluded that rural parents treated children's temper tantrums exactly the same way as Erik's relatives had: they simply ignored them.

As mentioned earlier, in the year 1979 Francoise was fairly content with her life and the arrangement with the customs man. Erik was then five years old and Fili two. Until then Francoise had been carrying Fili on her back or holding him on her lap when chatting with friends. Now Fili was starting to walk and followed his mother everywhere by holding on to furniture or walls. He was very attached to his mother and cried almost every time she took a few steps away from him. Francoise pampered him, talked to him softly, and gave him his food first. She had weaned him earlier the same year before he was two years old.

Erik roamed the neighbourhood in a peer group and got into many fights. Francoise yelled at him all the time, threatening to beat him. She gave him food only after first feeding the little brother. Erik was not requested to do much work at home because he was a boy but sometimes he carried his little brother when Francoise was busy.

I was surprised to see that gender roles were sometimes reinforced by complete strangers. Once Erik was standing near the charcoal burner roasting a banana for himself when a man who was passing by slapped him hard. Erik ran away speechless while the man bent down to light his cigarette from the burner and then left. A neighbour boy was standing near me and I asked him why the man had hit Erik. The boy explained that the man had jokingly taught Erik that a male's place was not near a charcoal burner! The man's action was inexplicable to me and I had certainly seen no joke in it. A Zairean child on the other hand understood immediately. When the man left, Erik returned to get his banana and then ran off to continue playing.

Like Anastasia's children, Erik and his playmates made cars out of cardboard boxes. His gang invented a way of using manioc paste to stick the pieces of cardboard together. Manioc was a starch and made excellent glue.

Once I happened to call in Francoise's house when it was raining. A neighbour told me that Francoise was not at home but the door was open. She came with me to sit in her living room until the rain stopped. Erik came in for a while but left before the rain was over. When I left I saw him with a handful of playmates splashing about in the stream in the road. The rainwater was gushing down the road in torrents and several groups of children were having fun in it. I noticed some women throwing pails of waste into the stream. On closer inspection I saw that it was the waste from distilling. I had not considered the problem of disposing of the waste from distilling. A fast flowing stream was clearly ideal: the waste would disperse quickly and no investigator could find its source. And, if a stream suddenly appeared in front of your house, so much the better! The children did not mind their water being polluted.

Francoise maintained that she did not want to have any more children for a few years. I asked if she knew about birth control. She had learned about it at school from Catholic nuns. They had taught her that one should abstain from sexual relations for about ten days after menstruation. Francoise had not told her husband about her plan but whenever he visited her during the dangerous time, she would pretend that she was menstruating. When she took this line with her husband he would go to spend the night with another wife. In any event, her husband came so rarely that birth control was not a problem.

After two years, Francoise's husband was transferred to another part of Zaire and he was going to take two wives with him, Francoise being one of them. Again, she dispersed her belongings among her relatives. She left Erik with Dudu, a Fofu relative, because he was fathered by a man other than her present husband but she took Fili with her. Dudu had taken in another relative and did not seem to mind having an extra mouth to feed.

During her absence I saw Erik at Dudu's playing with the children of the family. He seemed to be well adjusted and not bothered by his mother's absence.

After nine months Francoise and Fili came back. She had lost weight and looked miserable. Francoise said her husband had changed and had constantly beaten her. Furthermore, as they were living in a strange area there were no relatives to check his behaviour. She had, therefore, decided to leave the man for good. I don't know where she obtained the money for her return flight but there she was, determined to live near the Fofu again.

Her older co-wives who lived in Bululu were angry at her for abandoning their husband, whom she should have continued to take care of, in their opinion. Estela, her step-mother, and Estela's children would have nothing to do with her after her return. I don't know exactly what caused the total breakdown in their relationships since neither Francoise nor Estela, not even Katarina would discuss the matter with me.

After returning to Bululu, Francoise lived with Viktorina and her husband. Viktorina was a Fofu who lived in a run-down brick building, provided by the government because her husband was a government worker. She features in "A Carpenter's Family."

Francoise was happy to be back and after a while she found herself a place to live. She chose a busy spot near the road between the international airport and the city. She had two small rooms in a dark, wooden building, which was not nearly the same quality her previous house had been.

Because she no longer received money from her husband she started to use her rooms as a bar. She distilled liquor as before and brought in beer. And she did not only serve drinks in her home: she also served the men as a prostitute. When I dropped by, her living room was full of men and smoke. Some of the men were drunk and were flirting with her. One of them took her hands and announced to everyone that Francoise was his wife. Francoise smiled non-committally and did not say a word. Afterwards she told me that the man had been joking.

While this was going on inside, the children were playing outside. There was a small muddy hill in their yard and Fili and his peers were thrilled about sliding down it. I could not believe that such a simple thing could produce so much delight.

Erik was busy building a shack with his friends. He led me to the site along a narrow passage between a brick wall built by a wealthy trader and houses which were crammed together haphazardly. Erik's shack was situated behind two smelly outhouses. The boys showed their creation to me with pride. They had collected scraps of building material from the neighbourhood and made their "house" with them.

I quickly realised that I was not very welcome in Francoise's bar. She was busy earning her living and had no time to chat. She did not have much time to pay attention to the children, either. Moreover, she often complained about headaches. I did not disturb her but if she was at her door when I passed, I would greet her.

When we thought we were leaving Zaire for good, I went to bid Francoise farewell. A neighbour went in to call her while I waited outside. It took a long time before Francoise appeared complaining about a headache. I gathered that I had interrupted her business with a customer in the bedroom. It was noon and I had not thought she would be busy at that time. I apologised for disturbing her but told her that I wanted to see her perhaps for the last time ever. We shook hands and I left her standing at her door with her hand on her forehead.

Three years later, I spent only a day in Bululu but managed to find Francoise with the help of some Fofu. She was living near the place where I had left her three years previously but in a better house. It was made of wide planks painted with black oil which was used motor oil, sold in town. The inside walls were bright green. She had three rooms, and the living room was bigger than ever before. The floors were dirt, not concrete.

Francoise was in the process of plucking a hen. Eating meat, especially chicken was prestigious. That she could afford it told me that she was well off by local standards. A year-old toddler was sitting on the floor near her, staring at me with wide eyes. Fili came in from his play and smiled at me as if he remembered me. Erik was at the lake washing his clothes.

Francoise clicked her tongue out of surprise at seeing me again and asked questions about my personal life, while working on the hen. She appeared content with her life. She ran her household more conventionally again as when she had been married to the customs official. When she told me that she was in fact married to another customs official, I burst into laughter.

"Can't you marry other than these customs officials?" I kidded her.

"Watch out! You would marry another pilot if you divorced your husband," she retaliated. I insisted I would not but she was certain I would.

Her present husband was the captain of a customs boat cruising on Lake Kivu trying to catch coffee smugglers. He came to see Francoise when the boat happened to come to town. He had one other wife in town. When I asked about possible other wives in other cities, she told me that it was none of her business and she did not worry about such matters.

The toddler sitting near Francoise was her new baby, a son called Kabwana. The father was a Rwandese boyfriend, who drove a truck between Kisangani and Bululu. Francoise claimed that she had not had a long term relationship with the man. She was now pregnant by her present husband.

The following year I found Francoise in the same house under the same conditions. She was sitting in her living room with four neighbour women. Kabwana sat on the floor behind Francoise and was so shy of me that he covered his eyes every time I glanced at him. The metal roof heated the house and it was uncomfortably hot inside.

When Francoise walked a little way with me to see me off, I could ask her about personal matters. A few months after my last visit she prematurely bore twins but the infants died the same day. Now she was pregnant again, expecting to have a baby around Christmas time.

I dropped in many times when passing by. She was usually involved with housechores and childcare. The charcoal burner was often outside with a pot of food simmering on it and Francoise inside conversing with her female friends. The youngest son, Kabwana, was generally somewhere near his mother. Eight-year old Fili roamed around with his peer group and sometimes I saw him making cardboard cars, like his older brother had done a few years back.

Erik, now 11, was absent most of the time. I asked about his activities and Francoise told me that he went and played with his friends near warehouses. At home it was his job to fill their water barrel every few days. He attended to this well but she had difficulties with his school attendance. He had dropped out of school last term while in grade three and she did not know if he would agree to continue. Fili had not started school yet but Francoise was going to put him in the first grade in September.

In August I invited Francoise to my house. When she did not come at the agreed time I walked to see what she was up to. I met her near the market in a distraught condition. She was looking for Erik whom she had sent to buy lemons early in the morning. He had not returned and a neighbour had seen him enter a cinema. She was determined to find him and I joined her in the search. We went to the two cinemas in town but they were not showing anything in the morning and there was nobody around. While we were walking to her home Francoise talked angrily about her son. She was sure that he had bought himself manioc cakes with the money for the lemons. He had done it once before and Francoise had become so angry that she had called a soldier to beat him until he apologised. When we arrived at her home she started washing dishes, banging them in her fury.

After a while Erik sauntered in. No sooner had he entered than Francoise attacked him with an accusation of being a thief. She demanded her money back and frisked him to find it. She found a bundle of notes under his shirt but Erik claimed that it was his money, not hers. Telling him to stand against the far wall, she flew out, reappearing shortly with a man who had been passing by. She told him to beat

Erik and went back outside. The man stood at the door wondering what to do. Finally he told Erik to wait for his mother and went away. He may well have proceeded to beat Erik had I not been present. Parents did occasionally obtain others to discipline their children.

After some minutes Francoise came back in, still very agitated. She told Erik that she had sent for a soldier to beat him. Erik threw another bundle of money on the floor and ran out. Francoise bent down and inspected it. It was the one she had given him in the morning. Francoise told me that Erik had only given it up because I was present and because she had threatened him with the soldier.

The next day I asked Francoise what had happened to Erik. She told me that he had not appeared back home until late at night for food. Francoise did not give him anything to eat. Erik cried and apologised but Francoise "closed her spirit" and did not give in with the food. That was a lesson to Erik.

Erik was clearly getting to be too difficult for Francoise to handle. He would not go to school, not even after Francoise called Dudu to talk to him. Fili, however, started school according to her wishes.

Erik's misbehaviour had upset Francoise's planned visit to my home. But another day, when things had calmed down, she called to see me. I invited her to the table with my family since we happened to be eating at the time. She ate with us quietly. When the food had been cleared, the children went out to play and Henry went to fly. Francoise and I were sitting in the armchairs when she suddenly asked for some bread and margarine. I was surprised because we had just finished eating. She explained that she had been "ashamed" of my husband and had not dared to eat enough.

"I am not used to eating with men," she whined, still "ashamed."

I realized that she was serious although it was difficult to believe. It seemed to me that she did far more daring things with men than eat with them. I knew that rural women did not eat with men but I had not noticed that urban Fofu women also, even the more audacious ones, harboured the same sentiment of segregation which was a sign of respect for men. Her remark was an important lesson to me and I brought bread and margarine for her which she now ate in a relaxed way because only I was present.

I went to the rural areas for some months after this and returned about Christmas time when Francoise's baby was due. Her husband had not visited her at all, although he had kept on sending messages that he was coming. The due date passed but there was no husband and no baby. Francoise was getting discouraged. She was huge and uncomfortable and to make things worse her house was extremely hot, even when the door was open.

When I called on her one day there was an elderly man sitting with her in her living room. At first I thought he was her husband but I learned later that he was only a relative of the husband. He was telling Francoise not to worry about her delivery, God was there to watch over her. It seemed to calm her somewhat.

After Christmas I left for the rural areas again and did not visit Bululu again until February. Francoise had still not delivered and she was extremely anxious about it. Soon after my visit, however, she delivered a big baby boy. When I next saw her in May she was in a relaxed mood. The baby was doing fine and her life was back to normal again — or as normal as it could be in the circumstances.

Ever since I had known Francoise she had always tried to give the impression that she was living well and that she was satisfied with her various marital arrangements. Most of the time I had believed her. It was only on my very last day in Zaire that I learned her true feelings.

My final fieldwork project was a survey of bridewealth payments among the urban Fofu. Francoise had put off our interview the entire year. She presented all kinds of excuses why she could not answer my questions: she had to finish sweeping the floor, she had to go to the clinic for her pregnancy check, she had to go to the market etc. She was normally accommodating and had happily answered my questions about childrearing. This made it the harder to understand why she was suddenly so difficult. Finally on my last day I announced that I needed the information about her bridewealth payments now. Only then did the truth come out,

"Please, ask me about children. I like to talk about them. Don't ask me about men and bridewealth. They have not paid anything and never will!"

She looked distressed and ashamed sitting alone in her house. Her life was not what she would have liked it to be. She had only been a mistress to a succession of men, who took responsibility neither for her nor for the children they fathered. She did not even have the self-respect of a woman whose husband had paid proper bridewealth for her. She was really alone fighting for her livelihood and attaching herself to passing men in order to get occasional money to support the children. The stories of bridewealth which she had fed me with all the years were not true.

When I examined her situation, I noticed that modern conditions were more advantageous to men than the pre-colonial times had been. Now it was easier for men to take wives. Previously, they had to pay bridewealth and take responsibility for all their wives, whom they had to take publicly. They could not favour one particular wife because whatever they did was known by all the wives and all the relatives. Modern men took wives and mistresses who did not know about each other and whose families let them go without the bridewealth. There was nobody to check on neglect or favouritism. Francoise's life went up and down according to the whims of her "husbands." When she needed moral support, at the time of her delivery, for example, there was none forthcoming from her husband, who was then staying with one of his many mistresses or wives.

I did not imagine that my matter-of-fact survey could have caused so much anguish. Naturally I did not proceed with it, but her exclamation had revealed the answers to many other questions!

After our last chat Francoise did not sink into self-pity despite her unenviable position. With her youngest child tied on her back, she got up to sweep her house and the yard. Then she was going to distil liquor, go to the market, cook food and eat. She had to be industrious to survive and to take care of her four sons. I left her in a dust cloud as she energetically swept her yard with her baby asleep on her back.

A WELL-BALANCED WIDOW

Estela had become Jean's second wife after his original second wife had left him. She was a Nandi, like most of the people in Butembo where they then lived. Although Estela had two children by another man, who had not paid bridewealth for her, Jean accepted the two daughters with Estela. The daughters were now adults, one of them was living in Beni and the other one, Katarina, was living in Bululu, not far from her mother and was married to a Fofu man. The next story will deal with her family life.

Estela had moved with her husband to live in both Beni and Lemura before settling in Bululu. She bore Jean two children, a daughter, Marie-Jose, and a son, Masumbuko. They were seventeen and fourteen respectively when I became acquainted with the family. Estela herself did not know her age but she must have been over fifty. She had not gone to school at all and did not know how to read or write.

Estela was one of the most balanced persons I knew. She was anxious about nothing. Nothing seemed to affect her. When her husband Jean died she got up after the wake and continued her life very much as before his death. She did not reminisce about her husband nor lament about being a widow as her co-wife Josefina constantly did.

Some time after her husband's death, I asked her if she was planning to remarry.

"What for?" she asked laughing. "I can bear no more children, why should I marry?"

"Don't you marry for any other reasons?" I asked.

"What other reasons are there?" she inquired, genuinely curious.

"Companionship," I suggested. That made her laugh even more.

"We don't marry for companionship, we marry for children," she concluded.

She had already been earning her living by distilling liquor for many years. She had not needed to do it when she was young in Butembo, because Jean's wages supplemented by her fields had been sufficient. Estela had gradually started distilling as Zairean money "lost its force" over the years. Now she was the most regular of the Fofu distillers. Francoise did occasionally, not even once a week, so did Anastasia. But Estela distilled every week without fail and more often than that if she was running out of liquor. She sold her liquor at home to passing men who wanted a drink. They stayed from anything between a few seconds to fifteen minutes. Some of them just gulped the liquor down as if it were water and continued on their way. Estela negotiated the price of the drink before measuring it out. Sometimes men bargained with her and she adjusted the price. Occasionally, if she knew the customer had a regular-paying job she gave credit.

Estela knew all too well that it was hard to make a living.

"Life is tough for us Zaireans, very tough," she sometimes said. And so saying she laughed dryly and busied herself with her work. She did not dwell on the toughness of life, nor did she worry about it, but she organized her life the best she could - and appeared reasonably satisfied.

Estela tolerated me with benevolent humour. She thought I was funny when I asked all kinds of questions that would not enter a Zairean head. Sometimes she brushed me off when she was busy and told me to go to her daughter, Katarina, with whom I had become friends. She came to view me as a special friend of her daughter and even let me go into her back room when she was secretly distilling her liquor. However, she banned me from coming to her house during the time when the "Red Berets" were in town because she was afraid that my presence would attract their attention to her illicit liquor trade. The soldiers stayed in Bululu almost a year and I respected her order to stay away from her house during that time.

Estela had been living in a relative's house long before Jean died and she continued to live in it. She did not need to pay rent for it, which helped her financial situation. The house was a mud hut with a metal roof and was in very good condition. It had three rooms, the middle one being used as the living room and the bar. There was a low wooden table and half a dozen wooden chairs in the room as well as a cupboard in the corner. Estela or Marie-Jose took a glass out of the cupboard when a customer came and used it for the next one without washing it in between. The walls were covered with pictures out of colour magazines, received from Jacques, Katarina's husband. It intrigued me that years after Independence there was still a framed picture of King Baudouin on the wall.

Estela and Marie-Jose kept the house neat. But however neat it was, there were always rats and mice, attracted by the fermenting corn in one of the rooms. The inhabitants of the house were used to the vermin and paid no attention to it.

Both Marie-Jose and Masumbuko were attending a government school. Marie-Jose distilled liquor for her own tuition fees and Estela for Masumbuko's. Sometimes Marie-Jose's distilling failed and she stayed away from school until she had enough money to try again. Katarina told me that teachers of Masumbuko and Marie-Jose occasionally stopped by for free drinks at Estela's and, therefore, the children gained favour in the teachers' eyes.

After her husband's death, Estela told me that the children would not continue at school very much longer because of the difficulty in paying the fees. They continued a few years until Marie-Jose was in grade 11, and Masumbuko in grade 10.

Jean must have had a round face, because both of the children had very round faces and Estela did not. Both of them were fairly large and had obviously been well fed. They were also both very calm and even tempered. Marie-Jose always had a friendly smile on her face when doing housechores. Often she had a neighbour's baby tied on her back. She loved children and they came to her house to hang around her. When she went to visit her step-sister, Katarina, she voluntarily started washing the dishes or caring for the children. She never did any homework for school but she washed herself carefully and put her neat school uniform on before going there. When she was not at school she was either at home or running errands for her mother.

Masumbuko, on the other hand, was seldom at home. Estela shrugged her shoulders when I asked of his whereabouts.

"Who knows about him? Men wander around, women stay at home!"

I heard comments like this a lot in the slums and noted that the double standard for men and women was more marked here than in the rural area, where women also "wandered around." In the villages, women went to work in their fields, to fetch water, to collect firewood, as well as going to the markets far away. There seemed to be much more freedom for women in the villages than in this city.

"Men want to marry women whom they would always find at home," she commented when talking about Marie-Jose's faithfulness in staying at home. When Masumbuko was at home he never did household chores "because he is a man." He usually sat and read magazines, groomed himself, or chatted with his boy friends. Then he would go for a stroll. He always wore nice clothes while his sister, Marie-Jose, wore old working clothes at home and only dressed up to go to town, the pattern followed by most Fofu women. Like his sister, however, he generally had a friendly smile on his face. His movements were very slow and he never appeared to be in a hurry. I wondered if he would ever be capable of work because he seemed to be so pampered by the women folk.

I heard from other Fofu that negotiations concerning Marie-Jose's marriage were taking place. A totally unrelated Fofu man was allowed to sit in at these negotiations which were led by another Fofu man, called Dudu. Dudu was Jean's "brother's son" and several of Jean's descendants looked to him for advice and support over the years. I never knew, however, why Dudu took more responsibility in Marie-Jose's negotiations than in those of Josefina's daughter. Katarina confirmed the rumours. When I was allowed to visit the family again (the Red Berets having left Bululu) I asked Marie-Jose about her marital arrangements. I could not have chosen a more unpleasant subject. The usually friendly Marie-Jose turned to stone,

"Where did you hear such lies?" She spat the words at me and turned away. The topic was closed.

Dear me! I had no idea I would get such a reaction. In the rural area girls willingly talked about their marriage negotiations, as far as they knew about them. I wondered if Marie-Jose had to keep them secret for the same reason that women tried to keep their pregnancies secret: if others knew they might become jealous and try to cause harm.

Estela did not want to talk about the marriage plans either. She claimed that she did not really know about them. However, she was not as hostile as Marie-Jose.

Katarina and other Fofu were more open about them. Marie-Jose's fiance was a young man, a son of a neighbour, who belonged to the Nandi tribe, as did Estela. He was working for Air Zaire and thus had a steady income. As bridewealth he was to pay money, a watch, and some pieces of cloth to Marie-Jose's mother, brother, and other male relatives.

Half of the bridewealth was given to Masumbuko toward his marriage arrangements. It was put in a bank run by Catholic missionaries. Four years later, Estela told me that Masumbuko tried to increase the amount by trading with it. However, as a result of his inexperience (and in my view, laziness) he lost it all. Estela did not seem to mind: she laughed about it. By that time, Masumbuko had already moved away and lived with some other young men in a small apartment somewhere else in the slum area.

"Does he have a girl friend?" I asked.

"I don't know. He would not tell us if he did," Estela replied in a tone which told me that it was proper for the mother not to know.

I could not help contrasting this with the way the marital arrangements were handled in the rural area. There the parents knew about their son's marriage arrangements long before he did. Rural parents would not dream of putting the bridewealth into the hands of a youngster. They handled it themselves because they knew what they were doing. In the city, it seemed to become increasingly more common for sons to have to manage everything themselves.

The traditional rules for arranging daughters' marriages were also breaking down in the city. Anastasia's daughter had borne a child before her father had even started looking for possible husbands. Marie-Jose's step-sister, Pascarine, also became pregnant before any marital negotiations. Some other Fofu daughters ran away with their lovers before their parents knew what was going on. Surprisingly, however, Marie-Jose's marriage was arranged in a "proper" manner.

Some time after I left Africa, Marie-Jose, with the consent of her family, had moved in with her husband although he still owed some money. When I came back, she was living a few doors down the road from her mother. The mother and the daughter could see each others' yards. When I went to visit Estela, I could sometimes see Marie-Jose washing dishes in her yard. She had one daughter, two years old, and she was pregnant for the second time. She appeared content with her life and called at her mother's house several times a day with the little daughter in tow.

Estela told me that Marie-Jose's husband had been laid off by Air Zaire a year earlier and he spent a lot of time in Ruthsuru, a town a couple of hours drive north of Bululu. I felt sorry for Marie-Jose having to stay alone in the city. Estela laughed at my sympathy. She lived with her husband's relatives who took care of her. Marie-Jose was earning money by selling sugar in the market. Estela helped by baby-sitting. She was fine.

"Does her husband have another wife in Rutshuru?" I inquired.

Estela shrugged my question off: "We don't know. None of our business."

I remembered that Marie-Jose had told me several years previously that she did not want to be the second wife but she would not mind being the first of several. I could only wonder what her position was.

A year or so later Marie-Jose was knocked down by a motor cycle and she broke her arm. It was put in plaster but when the plaster was removed they noticed that the bones had not set properly. After that Marie-Jose could not do much with her right arm. She continued to sell sugar in the market, however, and I often saw her there, sitting on a low stool behind a huge bowl of unbleached sugar. She often carried her second baby on her back while the first child stayed at Estela's. Another female relative helped carry the sugar to the market.

DOILIES AND "VIETNAMESE BALLS"

As mentioned earlier, Katarina was Estela's daughter and Estela had her before she had met and married Jean. Although Katarina was a Nandi, she felt at home with the Fofu. After all, she had grown up with a Fofu step-father, Jean, and now she was married to a Fofu, Jacques. She could even understand Kifofu a bit although she did not speak it herself. Finally, during the last year of my fieldwork, her family was planning to move to Lemura, the heart of the Fofu country.

I took an immediate liking to Katarina. She was very frank, so conversation came easily and I knew where I stood with her. When she was distilling liquor, for instance, she told me I should not hang around and draw unnecessary attention to her activity. If she was busy, washing the floors, for example, she told me to go to another Fofu family and come back later. I was glad to just do as she said for it meant that I did not have to worry about whether or not I was intruding. And I knew that when she said I was welcome she meant it.

I felt that she was a real friend, like Cecilia was at Yenyabo. I was not only studying her and her family but I shared myself with her. She was interested in me as a person and often, after my questioning her, she questioned me. I told her a lot about my personal life and difficulties and she listened to me attentively. Sometimes she scolded me if she thought I had treated my husband or a friend badly and told me what I should have done. She did not understand me in everything, of course, and sometimes criticised me from her point of view, which amused and occasionally irritated me. If I said, I was tired, she snapped,

"And what are you tired about? You have so many servants that you don't have to do any work. You cannot be tired!"

She gave me scraps of material to make into clothes for her children. When I frowned at her mounting orders, she stated,

"You have nothing to do anyhow, so you might as well do something useful!"

I did not want to be her seamstress and I thought that I did have something to do. But Katarina did not regard my anthropological investigations as work at all. To show goodwill I repaired her sons' clothes and sewed a few outfits for her daughter, adding some cute details of my own, but I let her know that I was not going to do it continually.

When I first got to know Katarina, she had three children: a five-year old son, Katanabo, a three-year old son, Tagirabo and a six-month old daughter, Roselin. Her husband's seven-year old sister, Edronne, was also living with the family. At that time Katarina had an aura of assurance about her: she was doing what she was supposed to as a woman and a mother and her life was in order. I gradually watched her attitude change, and when I finally left her, she was living with her mother, Estela, in a state of despair.

Katarina and Jacques lived near *Mama* Avion, in a similar terrace as she. A colonial company had built four terraces of ten houses, each house having two rooms. There was a communal yard to each house. With children and relatives a house might accommodate quite a few people, so there could be up to a hundred individuals sharing the use of one yard.

Katarina would invite me into her living room where we could have some peace to talk but while we talked she kept one ear on the noise outside. She would suddenly dash outside, grabbing the stick she kept by the door, and threaten the children. The noise always sounded the same to me but she detected nuances and knew when to intervene. When she hit the children with the stick I asked her if she ever got into trouble with other parents over it. She first told me that she did not but later admitted that sometimes there were disputes between parents which resulted from adults punishing unrelated children.

Figure 7.2 **Boys playing soccer with a home-made ball.**

Fortunately most children attended school, either in the morning or in the afternoon. All schools were so crowded that they had to operate shifts and open on Saturdays as well. Sometimes, therefore, it was quiet enough for us to sit outside. There I could observe how the neighbours interacted. I was amazed how friendly people were to each other and how much they shared. For instance, when Katarina's neighbour cooked porridge, she invited Katarina and her children to eat with her family. She gave a bowl for the children to share, and shared her bowl with Katarina. Similarly, when Katarina made tea, she gave some to the neighbour. Women would frequently borrow sugar, salt, pilipili, and the like from each other. The news and gossip of the city were spread by word of mouth. Passers-by would bring their news to the people when they stopped for a few minutes on their way to the market which was near-by.

Sometimes Katarina said that she had not slept at night because, say, a couple who lived a few doors down had been fighting. Sick children could also keep the neighbourhood awake at night. Instead of complaining, however, everyone was always sympathetic towards the suffering family. If a death occurred, the neighbours would go and sleep in the house of the deceased family and grieve with them.

One morning I was inside Katarina's when a neighbour cried out that her wrap-around cloth had been stolen. A group of women soon gathered to whom she explained loudly how she could not find her skirt. The women exclaimed and wondered who could have stolen it. Then the woman declared that she would go to drink some "medicine" which would reveal the thief to her. She already had an idea who the thief was, a student boarding in their house. The woman went on and on about it and her female audience agreed with her. After the gathering had dispersed, the woman let out another cry: she had found the skirt! The women rushed back to hear the details of how and why she had not been able to find it before.

Spontaneous events like that taught me about many aspects of urban life. They showed relationships between neighbours and relatives, the causes of tension, the extent to which traditional medicine was used, how news was shared, etc. Had I gone armed with a questionnaire, instead of observing what actually happened, I would have got a totally different impression. They would certainly have told me that they never used native medicine to discover thieves. This is the answer students gave when they did one of my questionnaires. So natural observations are a good way of checking information which is gathered more formally.

The men were not around very much. Many of them held jobs but even if they were not working it was customary for men to go out "to walk" while women stayed at home. There was one exception. One of Katarina's neighbours worked at a hotel. When he was on the afternoon shift, he would spend his mornings sitting in front of his house embroidering a table cloth. I was surprised to see a man doing what women normally did in my country! The explanation for the role transfer was that embroidery was a new Western import and men were the first ones to use it. It was the same with handbags. When they were first imported, I saw young men carrying them under their arms. Only later did the women start using them.

Katarina cleaned her house every morning. She swept the floors and washed them. The floors were made of brick and cement, but were so badly worn that there were gaps between the bricks. How she ever got the dirt out of the holes and gaps, was a mystery to me. The children slept on the floor in the living room while Katarina and her husband, together with the youngest child, slept in the other room. The family ate late at night and threw fish bones, banana skins, and the like on the floor. Every morning, there was a lot of garbage to be cleaned out.

Katarina's living room was attractive after she had cleaned it. The walls were lined with pictures of cars cut from magazines which Jacques obtained from work and there were curtains at the window. The room itself was packed with arm chairs and couches interspersed with little coffee tables and a sideboard. And on top of everything, or so it seemed to me, there were little doilies. They were everywhere: on the coffee tables, on the sideboard, on the radio, and on the arms, backs and seats of the chairs and couches. At first I did not know where to sit because I did not want to sit on a doily. Katarina laughed and told me to sit on them. She had bought the doilies from a neighbour who crocheted them. I gathered that doilies were a status symbol in this neighbourhood. Most of the Fofu did not have them.

Katarina did her laundry twice a week. Of all things, her wash tub was the bottom half of an old fuel tank of a car! It was wide and flat and had plenty of room for her to pound the clothes against the bottom. She used very little water because it was precious but made up for it with vigour.

Figure 7.3 Katarina's wash tub was an old fuel tank from a car.

I recall, however, one occasion when Katarina had to do an extra wash — all of the children's sheets. She was angry with me for it was my fault that the children had dirtied them. The children, except the baby, had been at my place the day before doing drawing and modelling tests. Afterwards I had let the children climb in the fruit trees. They loved guava-fruit and consumed them greedily. Since they were the first guavas of the season, their stomachs were not used to them and all the children had bad diarrhea that night and dirtied their bedding. After scolding me furiously, she smiled again, and invited me in.

Katarina's water barrel was in the back room and she filled it with the aid of a five gallon kerosine can. These were known locally as *bido*, from the French *videau*, or 'empty,' an empty kerosine can. Katarina carried her bido about three hundred yards to a tap in somebody's private yard, paid for the water, filled her container, put it on her head and carried it home. She had to make the trip ten times before the barrel was full. So, in three or four days a family of six used about 200 litres of water for all their needs: cooking, drinking, washing themselves, the dishes and clothes, and cleaning the house. She tried to conserve as much water as possible and the children were allowed only a mugful of water to wash with before going to school. Water was not to be wasted! And yet if a neighbour woman came to ask for water, Katarina would give it to her.

Every morning Katarina bathed her baby, Roselin, with about a litre of water. Katarina heated the bath water for her and washed her in a little cooking pot. Then she washed Katanabo, who was five years old, either in the baby's bath water or in cold water.

I was surprised that although Katarina expected her children to perform quite difficult tasks, such as running errands, she did not expect them to be able to wash themselves at school age. She always scrubbed and dressed Katanabo and buttoned his shirt and tied his shoe laces before he went to school. I gather that in Canada children are expected to be able to tie their laces before starting school. Katarina continued to give baths to Katanabo until he was seven. I think that this pampering was partly because Katanabo was male. When Roselin grew older I do not recall Katarina pampering her any more.

Although Katanabo was only five, Katarina and Jacques had told the teacher that he was six, in order to get him into the school. Jacques' identity card, on the other hand, stated that Katanabo was three years old! The discrepancy between this and his actual age was caused by a delay in getting him registered. Jacques had failed to register Katanabo's birth within the time limit and to avoid a penalty he had lied about his age! This was an example of adjusting information to fit personal needs instead of following the "objective facts."

Katanabo was a skinny boy, small for his age and must have been one of the smallest in his class. His parents were very keen for him to start school early. Katarina always reported to me over the years how he was doing at school. When the other children started school, she kept a close watch on how they did as well.

Her attitude contrasted strongly with that of rural Fofu mothers who hardly let their children go to school, let alone care about their progress.

When he was not at school, Katanabo was sent on errands and he obeyed without a word. He was quiet and very obedient and never got into fights with other boys. Tagirabo, on the other hand, was constantly fighting. He was barely three years old but he was already almost as big as Katanabo and in a few years he was bigger than him. He was a happy-go-lucky fellow, roaming around the yard with other toddlers, playing with lids of pots, my bicycle, or anything that he could get his hands on. Katarina was constantly scolding him and he obeyed her good-naturedly, but when Katarina turned her back he did exactly what he was not supposed to do. He loved to eat sugar and would go and open the sugar tin whenever his mother was not looking, even if I was. He had soon learned that I did not tell on him.

As already mentioned, Jacques' sister, Edronne, who was seven-years old, lived with the family. Katarina would boss over her, commanding her to help with the cleaning, washing and baby care. Edronne was quite slow compared with Katarina, but she did a high proportion of the housechores, receiving much scolding and little thanks for it from Katarina. The older she became the more she was expected to do. She attended school as well, Jacques paying for her tuition fees and school uniform. Edronne looked on her brother Jacques and Katarina as her parents. When I asked her to draw a picture of a family, she drew Jacques, Katarina, and their children and called them her parents and siblings.

Between all her housework and schooling she occasionally found time to play. I once watched her playing hop-scotch with the neighbourhood girls. Roselin was bouncing up and down on her back as she hopped. In a way she was working even then! Edronne often entertained Roselin with singing and hand-clapping. She seemed to enjoy being part of the family.

Katarina ruled the house strictly, and, it seemed to me, somewhat harshly. However, the suckling baby was pampered. Roselin's cries were always attended to and she was held in bodily contact with her mother or Edronne a large proportion of the time. Katarina was glad to be a mother, as God had created her to be, and she knew she was a good mother because when God created her, he gave her the ability to be one. This is how she explained it to me. Unlike Western mothers, she had no doubts about the quality of her motherhood. She was confident in her role as Fofu women always were.

I did not see very much of Jacques because he usually came home from work after dark when I was not there. He was generally at home at the weekends, however. He did not help with the housework except for the ironing, which he did with a heavy charcoal iron. The reason for this exception is that irons were a status symbol because they were classified as being part of Western technology. They were therefore a male prerogative. Jacques would stand at a table in the yard and iron the clothes listening to his bright-red radio covered with — what else, but a red doily.

Figure 7.4 Edronne babysitting, peeling fruit and playing with neighborhood children.

When Roselin learned to walk she also learned to dance. When her father ironed and listened to the rhythmic Zairean music on the radio, Roselin would dance. Her little hips made her dress flap in a funny way, and the neighbours would clap their hands and laugh.

Jacques spent most of his leisure time just sitting in his living room or in the yard and chatting with his male friends. Occasionally, he would hold Roselin in his lap, if Katarina was busy. Once, when he was watching his sons play marbles with their friends, he suddenly got up and joined in. I was amazed to see a Fofu man playing with his children and went closer to observe the remarkable event. Then I noticed that he was not actually playing with them — he was playing marbles by himself while the boys watched. When he had enough of marbles, he got up and left the boys, who resumed their game. So Jacques had after all acted as an ordinary Fofu father, who refrained from becoming intimate with his children and could interrupt their play as he wished.

Jacques was 26 years old when I got to know him, a muscular man of medium height, with a pleasant round face. His clothes always looked nice and he kept his pants well pressed. I thought that he must be very attractive to other women and asked Katarina if he had affairs. Katarina replied in her frank way,

"Surely he does not lack girl friends but he won't tell me about them!"

She did not worry about her husband's fidelity at all. She, on the other hand, was obliged to be faithful, because she lived in his house and bore his children. Katarina did not see anything wrong with society's rules being different for men and women. Later on, however, Katarina actually let rip at her husband about his infidelity, but it was only on account of Roselin. The infant had become very sick with diarrhea, despite the protection of "medicine" hanging in a little bag from a string around her hips. When the diarrhea persisted Katarina took the child to a native healer. He diagnosed Jacques' infidelity as the cause of the trouble. Katarina then told Jacques in no uncertain terms that he was to quit fooling around with other women. Jacques was frightened and obeyed immediately. Katarina was pleased when Roselin became better very soon afterwards.

One morning, when I went to greet Katarina, Marie-Jose was sitting on the door step looking into the house, which was packed with people. When I reached the door I could see Jacques lying on the floor, propped up with cushions. There were many familiar Fofu faces.

In his calm, kind way Jacques explained to me that he had received a message from Lemura the day before that his younger sister, about 20-years old, had died. He had started the wake as soon as he heard the news. Word had been sent to all the local Fofu, who had come to sleep in the house, as had Jacques' immediate neighbours, whether they were Fofu or not. The conversation was not sad, although the occasion was a wake. I heard, for instance, Georgette telling the others how she had prevented some "Red Berets" from stealing money from her. Everybody laughed as she imitated the stupid soldiers and her stubborn resistance.

Jacques stayed on the floor for three days, as was customary. Then he got up, had his hair cut by a Fofu man, and washed his sorrow away. His wife, children, and Edronne went to the barber as well. Jacques told me that he had his hair only cut because his late sister was young. If she had been an adult he would have had to have had all of his hair shaved off. The wake ended with a big communal meal, prepared by *Mama* Avion and Estela. I noticed that as Estela mixed the porridge, she kept the manioc pot in place with her bare feet and her toes touched the porridge. I smiled to myself as I thought of Western hygiene! Men ate from a big bowl, women from another one, and children from yet another.

Soon after the wake Katarina miscarried and had to spend a few days in hospital. Estela came to do all Katarina's housework. She stayed with the children during the day but returned to her own home at night because it was not proper for a woman to spend a night at her son-in-law's place. Katarina was back to normal in a few days and took over the daily routine in her household again.

Jacques worked as a sales clerk in an auto part shop. He told me openly how much he earned, which covered the rent but only part of the cost of food for his

Figure 7.5 Hair cut is part of the ritual in the wake.

family. Then he added, equally openly, that he made much more than this on the side by adding a bit to the price of the parts and pocketing the difference.

"But don't you give a receipt to the customer and a copy of it to your boss?" I asked.

"If a customer demands a receipt I tell him that the part should really be put in by our men. Then he'll forget about the receipt."

I did not follow the logic and Jacques had to explain to me what was obvious to most other people, namely that the shop workers would steal other parts out of the car while putting in the new part. It was better for the customer to have the part put in under his own supervision or, better still, do it himself. A customer would no longer insist on a receipt if it meant the shop mechanics working on his car. Jacques would then write a receipt for his boss for the proper price and everyone was happy.

Katarina was satisfied with the way Jacques provided for his family. She told me that he bought the clothing for the children and she did not need to bother about it. She added to the family income by distilling liquor, but she did not need to do it often.

Jacques claimed to be on excellent terms with his boss and proudly showed me a clock that he had received from his boss as a gift. When I passed the auto shop downtown I saw that there was hardly anything on the shelves. Shop keepers were finding it difficult to get stock to sell and Jacques was laid off. But his boss liked him so much that he asked Jacques to start a new business with him and Jacques agreed. The two men commenced smuggling gold from Zaire across the border to Rwanda.

This new occupation meant Jacques was often away from home buying and selling gold. It was a risky life but he and his boss had ways of avoiding the law. They probably bribed custom officers to cooperate with them. Katarina did not worry about him so long as there was enough money to live on.

To cover his illegal activities, Jacques arranged for Katarina to carry on a legal trade, so that people would not start wondering how the family had money when the father was out of work. He gave Katarina the capital to buy used clothing wholesale which she then sold retail in their yard.

With Jacques' money Katarina bought a huge round bundle (two yards in diameter) of "Vietnamese" clothes from a warehouse and carried it home on top of her head. She sorted the clothes, divided them into piles and sold them on the roadside. I wondered why the clothes were called Vietnamese when I saw Sears tags in them. Katarina told me that all the people had died in Vietnam and their clothes had been sent to Africa! So much for a native explanation of the country of origin.

A buyer of a "Vietnamese ball" had no control over the content, as she was not allowed to undo it before purchasing. Sometimes Katarina was disappointed with the content, sometimes pleased. Neighbour women came to inspect her stock on the road side. They were especially partial to slips and soon most of the local female population was wearing Sears slips: pink, peach, powder blue, and white — with and without lace! They liked to wear them at home as work clothes over a wrap around skirt. Such outfits were coveted and became popular throughout the city, all due to the Vietnamese balls!

Katarina would spread her clothes on sacking on the roadside in the morning and keep one eye on the clothes while doing her housework. Edronne helped her with both activities. Katarina could do much of the food preparation near the clothes. Often I saw her peeling manioc or sweet potatoes, or shredding cabbage while both selling and looking after her youngest baby Simbabo (born in 1980), who would be crawling around nearby.

Katarina offered to buy my family's unwanted clothing. I collected clothes which my children had grown out of and my old clothes together and brought them to her. I let her set the price and was curious to see if she would pay the agreed sum. Fofu often left their debts to me unpaid. To my surprise, she paid to the last penny, little by little.

Katarina continued to distil liquor as well. If I saw smoke coming through the cracks of the house I knew what she was doing and did not call on her.

About the time Jacques was laid off, housing became an acute problem for Katarina. Right from the beginning she had told me that their house was falling apart and that they should get out before it collapsed. They were lucky to pay very little rent because they had gained the landlady's favour by the mere fact that her son was Jacques' namesake and was about his age, too. (The reasoning was delightful!)

The matter became more urgent for Katarina when she realized that the amicable neighbour, the one who shared her porridge with her family, was too interested in Jacques. Her own husband was too old for her, was Katarina's explanation for it. Although Jacques swore that he was not interested in the woman, Katarina was determined to move. She spent hours criss-crossing vast areas of Bululu looking for suitable accommodation for the family. She returned home exhausted and depressed.

Then Katarina had a stroke of luck. A woman across the road, some 100 yards away, offered her house to Katarina. The woman had lost her child in an accident in the house and her husband was blaming her for the accident. She could not bear to stay in the place that reminded her of the unhappy event. The accommodation was in a building which had served as a dispensary during colonial times but had since then been divided into two living units. Katarina and Jacques were glad to buy one of them.

The new house had one big room, which Jacques divided in two with coarsely woven mats. The new place was no bigger than the other one but it was in a better condition. Katarina had been right about the state of their old place: in the middle of the night, soon after they had moved out, the back wall collapsed. The occupants were unharmed because it collapsed outwards rather than inwards.

When Simbabo was born, Roselin was no longer pampered. The new baby inherited the position of favourite in the family and Roselin was relegated. She and Tagirabo became good friends and often played together. Edronne was assigned to take care of Simbabo much of the time. Around that period I sometimes took Tania, then five years old, to play with Roselin. The girls enjoyed each other's company and I could leave Tania under Katarina's or Edronne's supervision while visiting other Fofu.

While Katarina traded Vietnamese balls and distilled liquor, Jacques continued to smuggle gold. At first his trips did not last long and he was at home several days a week. On those days he often chose to sit across the yard in a deserted house whose walls had long since collapsed but whose roof, supported by the corner posts, still gave shelter from the sun. Katarina's family had appropriated this tumbledown house for various household activities and Jacques would sit there smoking, listening to his radio, and observing life around him. That was perhaps the happiest time for the family.

Jacques used to make himself comfortable in his den and often sent Edronne to bring him some liquor. If Katarina was out of liquor, Edronne had to run to one of the neighbour's to buy a bottle. Once she came from a neighbour with a bottle in her hand and tripped and broke the bottle. Edronne cried as she saw the precious liquid soak into the ground. She stood as if paralysed.

"There you see!" Katarina exclaimed as if she had predicted the calamity.

Jacques was smiling in anticipation of his pleasant drink. When he saw what had happened the smile froze.

"I will beat you hard!," he threatened his sister, pointing at her with his forefinger.

Edronne mechanically picked up the broken glass, walked to the garbage heap and threw the pieces onto it. Then she went to sit on a stool, limp from the trauma.

"What now?" Katarina yelled, "Isn't there any work?"

Edronne slowly rose and prepared to wash the dishes. She behaved as if all her strength was gone and the job was too much for her.

I knew from interviews with children that breaking something was one of the worst things they could do. Such a crime meant a beating.

Jacques growled and frowned at his sister and complained about "her stubbornness . . ."

Next day I casually asked Jacques if he had beaten Edronne. He had not, he had only scolded her severely and forgotten the matter. He went on to tell me what kind of punishments he used on his children. He explained that sometimes he made Edronne stand on her hands with her feet up against the wall. When I did not understand, Katanabo was eager to show me. Later I heard many parents, both rural and urban, describing the same punishment. Teachers were said to use it at school, too. I even observed a criminal being punished that way by the authorities at the zone headquarters! I don't know how often the parents actually used that punishment. Probably only rarely, but the threat of it — and that of beating — usually kept the children in line.

Some time after the birth of baby Simbabo, Jacques started spending more time in Lemura, sometimes several weeks at a time. Katarina became restless and worried. I thought Jacques had a lover in Lemura but Katarina was not bothered about that aspect. The economic worries were the greatest for her since she had been troubled with no such worries before. Roselin had to bear the brunt of her anxiety. Once I heard screaming and yelling from far off. When I arrived Katarina was beating the four-year old Roselin on her head and back. Roselin was screaming and jumping and she continued to sob long after the tears had dried on her cheeks.

The reason for the beating was that Roselin had dirtied the outhouse, the outhouse, which was about one yard square, had a wooden floor with a hole in the middle. Katarina washed the floor every day and kept the house locked, so strangers would not dirty it. Roselin had missed the hole when defecating and had to bear the harsh consequences. What a contrast to Katarina's attitude only two years previously! Then she had allowed her to urinate and defecate in the house. Once, realizing that Roselin's faeces were on her sandals, Katarina calmly wiped them without a word. Now Roselin was no longer the youngest and higher standards were expected. It must have been hard for her.

Another morning I found Katarina sitting on a low stool in the yard. She was holding the chubby Simbabo on her lap, while Roselin played at her feet. Suddenly Katarina pushed Roselin roughly and the little girl started crying. I did not see what had happened but guessed that Roselin had bumped into her mother while playing. Katarina yelled at her,

"Be quiet!" Roselin moved two yards further away and cried even louder. Then Katarina picked up a small stone and threw it at Roselin. It hit her in the stomach and as the little girl lost control of herself, urine trickled down her legs. Katarina, disgusted at her daughter's lack of control said,

"A great shame!"

Roselin ran round the corner of the house howling desperately. Passers-by paid no attention. I was very upset for the little girl but realized that Katarina's bad temper was caused by the severe stress she was under. After a little while Roselin returned to her mother, picked up Simbabo and started playing with him on the ground as if nothing had happened.

When the children were peacefully playing Katarina opened her troubled heart to me. She had spent all the money her husband had left for her. She had also spent the proceeds from her Vietnamese clothes. She had put her last pennies into liquor distilling but it had failed. There was no word from her husband and her head was full of "thoughts." Things could not have been worse for her and there was an enormous heaviness about her, which I had not seen before. Tears welled in her eyes.

While we were sitting in her yard several neighbour women came by. They were very sympathetic and asked to taste her liquor. Katarina got up with a heavy sigh and brought a glass of the failed liquor.

"It is only water," Katarina apologised weakly.

The glass went around the circle as the women tasted it, trying to think what had gone wrong with the distilling. Each of them had experienced a similar failure at least once during her "professional" career. A woman then suggested distilling the failed liquor again. Katarina would get very little liquor from it but at least she would recover her expenses. Katarina's face lit up, the concern and advice of their neighbours had clearly raised her spirits, and I left her to work alone.

The next day she told me that her friend's suggestion had been a good one, at least she had recovered her expenses, even if there was no profit.

Now that money was getting short, Estela, Katarina's mother, advised her to stop feeding her family several times a day. She scolded Katarina especially for serving tea with generous helpings of sugar between meals. She pointed out that most people in the neighbourhood had abandoned these habits long ago. Katarina had lived much better than most people around her. It was time for her to wake up to reality. Katarina had used in ten days what most families would stretch to last a month.

When I left Africa in 1981 Katarina was very insecure: she had little money and did not know where her husband was. When I returned to Africa in 1984 I spent only one day in Bululu. I managed, however, to visit Katarina. In fact, I found her at her mother's. At first I thought that she was visiting her, as she had often done previously but she told me that she had moved in to live with her mother.

Jacques was then living in Lemura and was the manager of a bar. He had a house through his work but he was in the process of finding a house of his own. Katarina was prepared to move to Lemura when the house was ready.

"Does he have another wife?" I asked Katarina.

"Would he lack one?" snapped Katarina and then added, "Travellers from Lemura tell me that he has one but I don't know whether they have any children."

I studied her face, trying to decide what her feelings were but I could not tell much. Then I asked her how she felt about it.

"We can kill each other!" she said in her blunt way.

She was not overly upset but the assurance and contentment with her lot was no longer there.

"It is no good for the children here. I would like to send at least Katanabo to Lemura," she muttered.

A small boy was holding onto Katarina's knees as we talked. I looked at him and thought that Simbabo should have been bigger. I recognized the other children: Edronne, Jacques' sister, was fourteen and looked like a young woman; Katanabo, Tagirabo, and Roselin looked familiar, although they had grown, of course.

"Simbabo died of measles," Katarina said quietly and explained that Handigabo was born in 1982 the year after I left. Another Fofu family whom I knew very well had lost two of their children in one week, also of measles.

"There is suffering here in Zaire. Suffering. We are being tortured," Estela stated. She had always acknowledged that life was hard but seemed to feel it more now that her daughter was suffering.

Katarina told me that she and her mother took turns in distilling liquor. A few days before, Katarina had been fined by soldiers for her illicit activity which was an unwelcome expense in their tight budget. The fine did not stop the women from continuing their work, however.

It amazed me that no matter how much liquor was produced, there were always buyers. No matter how poor people were, they always had money for "one more drink." The slum area was like a sponge that soaked up all the liquor poured into it.

Marie-Jose had heard I was visiting and came to show me her son, about Handigabo's age. Everybody smiled at the little one. Katarina told me that she and Marie-Jose had weaned their sons at the same time, when Katanabo and Tagirabo had been baptized.

I gathered that Jacques had finally brought his baptism papers from Lemura, so his marriage with Katarina could be validated in the church and the boys baptized.

Years back Katarina had mentioned that although the bridewealth had been paid, Jean's certificate of baptism was still in Lemura. This had prevented a formal church wedding and the baptism of their children. It seemed that Roselin would be baptized later after attending preparatory classes.

When I returned to Bululu a year later, I found Estela at home taking care of Katarina's children. Katarina had gone to visit Jacques in Lemura and had taken the youngest child, Handigabo with her. Estela scolded the children as she talked to me, and the children stole outside not to bother us. They were curious, though, and peeked through the door to hear what we were talking about and see if I had brought them anything. Estela was concerned about Jacques. Something was wrong. Travellers had told her that his boss had accused him of stealing money and he had been thrown into jail. She did not know how Katarina was doing in Lemura.

It was too much for Estela to take care of the children. Next time when I called she was in the dark back room in bed. She had been taken to hospital with high blood pressure and she was still exhausted. She begged me to persuade Katarina to come back to Bululu as she could not make enough money for the school fees.

Luckily Edronne was mature enough to do all the housechores and distil liquor. She was busy in the yard peeling manioc for a meal. Marie-Jose was pounding flour nearby. She stopped when she saw me and told me empathically,

"Mom will not have enough money for the children's tuition fees. Katarina must come and help us!" I promised to pass on the message to Katarina. Estela was going to dictate a letter for Edronne to write and I was to take it to Katarina in Lemura.

When I went to the Fofu country in September I found the bar where Jacques was working, with the aid of directions given to me by Estela. I arrived at 11 o'clock in the morning, when the bar was being mopped out. The owner called Jacques who came with uncertain steps and glazed eyes. Drunk at this time of the day! Jacques' drinking had not been a problem in Bululu. I wondered if he had started drinking excessively during his travels, through the loneliness of being away from his family. He had gained weight and had a few grey hairs at the temples. He claimed to be fine, having two wives. The rumours about him being in jail were incorrect. I could not ask him more about the matter because his boss was probably within earshot wondering what a white woman had to do with his employee. Jacques confirmed that Katarina was in town and found a youngster to show me the way to her.

Katarina was standing in front of a neat mud hut, which was plastered with sand and blended in with the sandy surroundings. She was happy to see me, a friend from her beloved Bululu, and to have someone to listen to her troubles. At heart, however, she was desperately unhappy.

She had a co-wife — she pointed across the road to a woman with an infant on her back who was standing in a yard peering in our direction. Katarina did not get along with her at all. Her life in Lemura had been miserable. No sooner had she arrived than she had fallen ill with malaria and lost much weight. She had regained some of it but not all. She did not like Lemura at all. Furthermore, Jacques was drinking too much and was not taking care of her. Handigabo was her only company, Katarina claimed, and picked the little boy up to sit on her lap. I noticed that she was pregnant, and calculated that it was at least her seventh pregnancy (at 33 years of age). I could not be sure as she may have had miscarriages which I did not know about. She said she was preparing to travel to Bululu to fetch the rest of the children, to relieve her mother. Katarina did not read her letter while I was there but listened to me attentively when I told her about her mother's health.

The next time I saw Katarina at Estela's place in Bululu in December when I went home for Christmas. When I asked her what the journey had been like, I heard a horror story, so typical of the country. Katarina related it in a matter-of-fact way while I reacted with exclamations of shock. On a mountainous section of the journey, the bus in which Katarina and Handigabo had been travelling, had gone off the road and down a steep bank. I was horrified but Katarina calmed me down by saying that the bus had been so packed full that there was no room for the passengers to be tossed around. Consequently nobody was hurt, except for bruises. Fortunately the bus had landed the right way up. Another vehicle had pulled it out and the bus was able to continue the trip all the way to Bululu. Because it was night time when they arrived in the city, everybody had stayed in the bus sleeping until dawn. Nobody dared to walk in town in the depths of the night.

The journey no longer concerned Katarina but she had other worries. Her time of delivery was approaching and Jacques had sent no money for the family. Katarina was distilling liquor and tried to make ends meet but it was tough. She was angry with her children, telling them to go outside and not show their dirt to a white woman.

During December her anger and bitterness grew. She said that, in contrast with her original plan, she was not going to return to Lemura until the end of the school year. It was no use going there anyway because her husband had divided his love and loyalty between her and the other wife.

Before I returned to the Fofu country myself, Katarina wrote a letter to her husband, or rather she dictated it to Katanabo, for me to deliver. She let me read it. It was a very bitter letter telling him in no uncertain terms that he was neglecting his family and wife who was taking care of five children alone, one of them his own sister. And a sixth one was about to be born. She told me to scold her husband in the presence of his boss so his neglect would be publicly known. He had to send her some money. My heart ached for Katarina when I saw the despair in her tearful eyes.

I took the letter to her husband at his work place in Lemura as requested. Surprisingly Jacques was not drunk but looked quite sober. He promised to send Katarina some money. Before I flew to Bululu for a few days in February, I went to ask him if the money was ready. It was not but Jacques wrote a letter wherein he solemnly promised to do his utmost to send Katarina some money.

The letter comforted Katarina a little. I tried to encourage her by telling her that Jacques had been sober when I saw him. This made little impression on Estela who was standing by, listening to my news. In her opinion, a person who liked to drink could not stop drinking. She thought that Jacques would drink himself to destruction. Her mother's gloomy forecast did nothing to help Katarina's state of mind. Her baby was to be born soon, in fact, she confessed to me, she was already in labour, although very mildly. When I remembered how Suzana in Nyanya had hidden her severe labour pains from me I was gratified that Katarina trusted me enough to tell me that she was in labour. She had no money for the maternity ward, let alone for her children's clothing. I gave her some money which she used for the maternity payment the next day. She bore another son, and was relieved to get the delivery over with.

I was doing fieldwork at a Catholic mission station on the outskirts of Lemura and saw Jacques when I went to town. I pressed him to remember Katarina and finally he brought me an envelope fat with money. I sent it to Katarina with Henry when he next had a flight to Lemura.

I saw Katarina next in May. She had kinder thoughts of her husband after receiving the money from him and she praised Henry as a trustworthy man for bringing it to her without delay.

On this visit, I was surprised to see Katarina feed her three-month old baby some porridge with a spoon. Roselin had only had her mother's milk for well over a year, as was usual among the Fofu. Edronne was making tea and Estela was distilling liquor in the back room. Marie-Jose came in with her two children, the younger one less than a year old. She was all smiles and talked softly to the children. Tagirabo, Roselin, Handigabo, Katarina, and Estela were all drinking and dipping their bread in tea. When I looked at the group of relatives enjoying their tea, I realized that a woman found greater security with her consanguineal (blood) relatives than with her husband. The blood relatives would always be loyal to her while her husband's loyalties could be divided at any time. Marie-Jose seemed to be content to live near her mother, whom she could look to for support.

One Sunday that May I had many Fofu children, including Katarina's, in my house to complete a questionnaire for me. Roselin, although nine years old, was not able to write her answers herself, so I did it with her orally while the other children filled in their forms. She was sitting beside me on the porch and little by little, she edged closer to me until she was leaning on me so heavily that I had difficulty in writing. In Zairean fashion, she looked for physical human contact for comfort.

I don't know if Katarina ever returned to Lemura to live with her husband. I saw neither her nor her husband after that May because I was working in Fofu villages. If she did go to Lemura, her life would have been tough with an alcoholic husband who had two wives to make demands on his money. In my opinion, she would have been better off in Bululu, where she at least had the support of her family. Whatever she decided to do, I know that her life will not have been easy.

A BIT OF A NUT CASE

Before becoming Jean's wife, Josefina had been married to another Fofu man who had died. Jean had obeyed his sense of responsibility for a Fofu "brother" and married his widow in order to keep the children with the Fofu. Anthropologically, the marriage could be viewed as "applied levirate." Other Fofu spoke respectfully of Jean's third marriage as an act of tribal responsibility.

Josefina was a Havu, a tribe that dwell on the island on Lake Kivu and had kept many old traditions and linguistic features because of its isolation from the mainland. Josefina, for example, spoke Swahili in a funny way inserting aitches between syllables. Her first husband had gone to the island during colonial times as a nurse at a dispensary. Later the couple had moved to Bululu. When Josefina's first husband died, Jean feared that Josefina might return to the island and the Fofu would lose the children. By marrying Josefina, he secured the children and that, for the Fofu, was the most important thing.

Josefina's two oldest children, 15-year old Pascarine and 11-year old Lebisabo, were fathered by her first husband. Jean was the father of the next four: an 8-year old son, called Batabo, another son who died as an infant, a two-year old daughter Kamama, and a baby girl, Keusi, who was born immediately after her father's wake in the new year. Josefina was, therefore, a widow with five children to care for. She did not know her age, but she must have been younger than her co-wives, about 40-years of age in my estimation.

Josefina was a bit of a nut case. I don't know if she had always been one or if she changed when she became a widow for the second time. It seemed to me that she had given up the struggle for survival and decided not to worry: she just joked and drank. She was disorganized, irregular, and casual in her child and home care. She was active most of the time but not organized.

Josefina accepted me as belonging to the people of her husband. She would greet me in Kifofu, which she had learned through her marriages to Fofu men. When we walked together on the road she would announce to her neighbours,

"This madam is one of the Ituri people, she comes from Kisangani!"

I don't think she understood my anthropological task at all. She was unable to concentrate on interviews and could only cope with a few questions at a time. I don't think she even tried to be truthful. She would happily say anything she thought I might like to hear. I had a dreadful time trying to verify her answers. She could not have cared less.

Josefina had not gone to school at all and was completely illiterate. Pascarine and Lebisabo had both completed three grades before dropping out. Batabo was in grade three when his father died and from then on Josefina was bombarded with demands for school fees and the like. I once saw her on her way to beg money from Francoise because the teacher had told each student to bring two zaires to school to build new outhouses. Francoise had no money to give and Josefina's appeals to the teacher to be merciful to a widow's son fell on deaf ears, so finally Batabo dropped out of school.

At the beginning of her second widowhood, Josefina blamed it for everything and used her widowhood as a general excuse. Once she was at Anastasia's sharing the food with the family when she announced that she was going to visit me. Anastasia uttered dryly,

"Be sure to wash yourself before going on your visit, and remember to wash your neck, too, it is very dirty!"

Josefina was ramming beans into her mouth but she managed to answer,

"I am a poor widow, I can't keep myself clean!"

This cut no ice with Anastasia who promptly countered,

"If I were to become a widow, I wouldn't stop washing myself." Then she turned to me and said, "She has always liked to be dirty, not only now." Josefina seemed oblivious to the criticism and continued enjoying her food. I was intrigued that Anastasia was so critical of Josefina's cleanliness, when she let her own son Kato go dirty! Children belonged to a different category from that of adults and different rules applied.

"I am a poor widow," was often on Josefina's smiling lips but nobody seemed to be impressed.

Josefina lived in six different places during the four years I observed her. She was kicked out of each through non-payment of rent. Francoise gave her a portion of Jean's pension and it would have covered the rent but by the time she received it each month, she was already deep in debt to neighbours and relatives and had to pay first those who cried for their money the loudest.

The house where she was living at the time I became acquainted with her, was in a deplorable condition. I saw it for the first time after a rainy night and was appalled. It was a mud hut with only a few leaves for the roof which consequently let water like a sieve. The floor was comprised of ankle-deep mud and puddles and was littered with bowls of half eaten food, dirty pots and pans, potato peelings and banana skins. Josefina owned only one bed, which she slept in with the two youngest daughters, the rest of the children lay on the floor on sacking. It must have been impossible to sleep on a wet night. Although the state of her home shocked me, Josefina remained unperturbed. She jabbered happily with her children and walked around in the mud of her home. The other houses she lived in were in a better condition than the first one, but they were never the best in the neighbourhood.

During the first year of our acquaintance, Josefina worked quite regularly. She got up before dawn and walked to the place where liquor boats arrived from her home island. Because it was illegal, the boats were unloaded before dawn. Josefina was one of the women hired to carry the loads to their mainland destinations. She would return home in the early afternoon. If she came earlier, it meant that it was too dangerous for the boats to land. I suspect that she spent several hours drinking before coming home.

After a while, she did less work and more begging and drinking. When I walked through the slums she could pop up anywhere where there was liquor for sale. I don't know if she ever paid for her drinks or if she begged free ones with the excuse of being a poor widow.

Pascarine helped to provide for the siblings. She would take a tray of roasted peanuts down town to sell. Occasionally, she distilled liquor with her mother or her step-sister Francoise. Once I overheard her and Josefina trying to decide if it was safe to distil. Josefina told her to leave it at least for a week because the soldiers had been roaming around lately trying to catch people at the illegal activity.

Pascarine was a moody young woman. She could look like thunder when she was shouting at her siblings. Other times she was happy and smiled, showing a beautiful row of even white teeth. She did whatever chore Josefina asked her to do, but she in turn made sure her younger siblings ran around after her. She was a nurturant caretaker for her two youngest siblings, and she often took the youngest one on her back when she went to sell peanuts — in fact she carried her more often than Josefina did.

After his father's death, Lebisabo moved to live with his step-brother, Dudu, who was Josefina's first husband's son by a co-wife. Dudu was a middle-aged man, about Josefina's age. He worked as a clerk in a Catholic school office and had a family of five children. He lived in one of those terraced houses where *Mama* Avion and Jacques lived, which had only two rooms. When I asked Dudu's wife if it was not difficult for her to accept an additional child into her family she looked at me as if I had come from outer space.

"But Lebisabo is my husband's brother. He is one of the family!"

I was sure that financially, Dudu had trouble feeding one more mouth but nobody complained. Lebisabo was part of the family.

Lebisabo worked hard at Dudu's. He pounded flour, ran errands, swept floors, baby-sat, and was told to bring me a chair when I visited. Lebisabo obeyed and looked contented. However, after a few months he moved back to his mother's. Nobody offered me an explanation but I could see that he was needed at home more than he was at Dudu's. After all, Dudu had other children to do the jobs Lebisabo did.

Lebisabo was the chief baby-sitter at home. His brother Batabo, was more often free to roam in the market place while Lebisabo stayed at home pounding flour and keeping an eye on his young sisters.

Although Josefina did not seem to take life seriously, she was firm on one thing, namely Lebisabo's babysitting. Once in 1978 I was standing in her yard with a crowd of people who were watching two government officers inspecting outhouses with tanks of chlorine on their backs. There was a cholera epidemic, and the government was desperately trying to improve hygiene conditions in the city. Twelve-year old Lebisabo was so fascinated by these officers that he stood watching, ignoring the fact that his baby sister, who was crawling on some sacking, was eating her faeces and crying.

The door burst open and Josefina charged out and swiped Lebisabo around the face.

"Neglecting the baby!" she shrieked. Lebisabo ran behind the house howling with all the might of his lungs. None of the crowd paid the least attention to them. Josefina picked up Keusi, wiped the faeces off her, turned the sacking over, sat on it and nursed her. She complained of having a headache and said the baby's cry had interrupted her sleep.

Keusi was almost as big as Kamama although she was about two and a half years younger. She was certainly stronger and often beat her sister. I once saw Josefina slap her for this. Something was wrong with Kamama. She walked and talked but she was a bit simple and had no control over her bowels. Many a time did Lembabo remove her dirty pants and carry her faeces to the garbage on a hoe.When her brothers and sisters were not around she would wander about, talking nonsense and singing an eerie tune to herself. She was always happy, laughing at everything. Even Josefina left her at home alone. In one respect she was sharper than normal: she could spot Josefina coming home long before anyone else.

While I was away on a vacation one year, the two girls had measles. Keusi survived the disease but Kamama died. When I came back, Josefina mentioned her death casually, and life continued as if she had never existed.

I used to enjoy watching the children at their play. One day I saw Lebisabo and Batabo playing "Red Berets." They made miniature red berets and epaulettes and attached them to their heads and shoulders with sticky grass, which was as good as, if not better than, velcro. They dashed around their yard catching people, taking them to "prison," and beating them.

Another time I was surprised at the amount of fun the children got out of a simple thing. A big crowd of boys had gathered around Batabo who had a plastic bird which he had got from the market. If you filled the bird with water and blew into it, the bird "sang." The sound fascinated them. I stayed in the yard for an hour and the boys' interest in the bird had not waned the least.

Sometimes the play was more practical. Batabo often came home from the market with scraps of meat, vegetables and pieces of charcoal which he had picked up from the ground. He would cook the food on the charcoal in old tins. Children from the neighbourhood gathered around to help him cook and eat the food. This was of no significance nutritionally but it helped their hunger and gave them an interesting activity.

As I focused on childcare, I paid close attention of Josefina's way of mothering. I noted that Josefina did not carry Keusi on her back as much as other nursing mothers did. In fact, Pascarine carried the baby three times more than the mother did. Keusi was a strong-willed infant. Although she could only say a few words clearly at 17 months, she talked nonsense assertively.

As soon as Josefina came home Keusi would run to her and seek her breasts and Josefina would oblige. Josefina did not wean Keusi until she was 30 months old, which was a long nursing period for an urban baby, whose average weaning age was around 20 months. Josefina explained that as she would not get pregnant again she would not bother to wean her. It was generally the case that the last child was breast fed longer than the other children. This was because the other children would only be breastfed until their mothers became pregnant again, a pregnant woman's milk being considered poisonous.

I happened to drop by the very day Keusi was being weaned and observed the process which I had heard much about. Keusi seemed agitated, walking behind her mother, who in turn was angry with her. Josefina pointed at some broken plants on the ground and told me that in the morning she had smeared her breasts with their sap. Keusi only tried to nurse once and the juice turned her off for good. To prove this, Josefina turned to Keusi and offered her breast. Keusi knew better than to try it and stamped her feet in anger.

Then a neighbour woman arrived with a glass of liquor and let Keusi drink it. She drank as if it was milk! All the women laughed approvingly. Until then I had no idea that infants were weaned with liquor. However, during the years of fieldwork in the slums there had been numerous occasions when children were given alcoholic beverages, so weaning with liquor should not have surprised me.

I offered Keusi some candy thinking that sugar would not be as dangerous as alcohol, but the little girl refused.

"She thinks it is bitter medicine and refuses it!" Josefina giggled.

No matter how I tried to explain that it was not medicine but sweet candy she still would not take it. She went for the liquor instead, and was in a better mood afterwards.

I don't know where Keusi got her stamina from, but she was a strong baby, and developed into a strong child. I had a soft spot for her because I had followed her progress right from the unhappy birth.

Pascarine turned eighteen and continued to care for the family. I did not notice anything unusual about her until Josefina once remarked to me laughing,

"Have you noticed that Pascarine is pregnant?"

Pascarine glanced at her furiously. I knew that Josefina was breaking the rules by speaking about a pregnancy. When we were alone, I asked her more. Josefina told me that the father was her landlord's son who already had one wife and two children. No bridewealth had been paid yet but it was the job of her step-son, Dudu, to negotiate with the groom's family in order to obtain bridewealth. I was to see the problem of Pascarine's bridewealth haunt Josefina to her death.

When Pascarine's baby was born and she was in a better mood, I could ask Pascarine herself how she felt about it. She told me then that she had been very afraid, not of her mother, but of her half brother, Dudu, whose responsibility it was to get her married. Marriage negotiations were inappropriate during the pregnancy but now that the child was safely born, her step-brother could proceed with them.

Although the negotiations were delayed, Pascarine moved in with her boy friend, who rented a room for them in the neighbourhood. Josefina was invited to live in the big house of the parents of the boy friend, rent free. This union was really a stroke of luck for Josefina and the rest of her children. It meant she could beg money from Pascarine who would get it from her boy friend or from her own work. The boy friend also paid Pascarine's brothers for helping him with his butchering business.

Pascarine had intended to deliver the baby at home but she was in labour for such a long time, that in the end, with the aid of her mother, husband and some friends she walked to a dispensary one night and delivered the baby there.

When I called at Pascarine's new home, I often found Josefina taking care of the baby while Pascarine was out on business. She walked across the border to Rwanda, bought a case of beer, smuggled it into Bululu and sold it at home. It was not typical for Fofu mothers to leave their new born babies at home six to eight hours at a stretch. The baby cried a lot and Josefina would rock her and give her water all day.

Something was wrong with the baby. The complaint was called Kasai's sickness. The soft spot on the baby's head was concave which was considered serious. In addition, the baby had a cleft palate. Once I saw Pascarine bending over the baby while a woman, Katarina's neighbour, administered native medicine to the roof of the baby's mouth, her scalp and rectum. The woman had some black powder which she smeared on her fingers. She showed Pascarine how important it was to administer different spots with certain fingers. Pascarine was very concerned about her baby and the Fofu shook their heads saying that she was dangerously ill. When I described the symptom's to an American nurse she thought that Kasai's sickness might be dehydration which would, indeed, be dangerous for the child.

The baby seemed to recover from Kasai's sickness. I remember looking at her carefully when Pascarine and a neighbour were playing with her. She was beautiful. Pascarine had painted eyebrows as half circles around her eyes. I was a bit surprised that the baby did not cry when a neighbour turned her upside down but she looked at us with calm eyes.

Two days later she died in her sleep. I arrived when the Fofu, to my horror, were hammering her coffin lid down in the midst of the terrible screaming and crying of the women, especially Pascarine and Josefina. Pascarine screamed and moaned heartbreakingly at the grave side and turned back for home before the grave had been filled in.

"I am leaving my child alone in the grave," she lamented, supported by two women who had also prevented her from jumping in the grave.

I went to the funeral with the Fofu and went back to the house for the wake. Josefina was there crying and lamenting about whom she would carry in the future now that the little one she had been carrying had died. She was so distressed that she did not go to the grave at all.

Pascarine had been nursing her baby, of course, and her breasts were bulging with milk, no longer needed by the dead baby. Part of the ritual of the wake was to tap Pascarine's breasts lightly with a bundle of thorny twigs. The woman performing the ritual told me that it would help dry up the mother's milk. Pascarine stood straight during the ordeal and did not react although it must have hurt her.

After the wake, Pascarine stayed at home for a few months. She was sure that the death of her baby was caused by her co-wife. She told me that her bitterness would not disappear until she had another baby and she did indeed look very down at heart for a long time after her baby's death. So much for my theory that Zaireans got rid of their sorrow by mourning intensively for a few days!

About a month after the death, Pascarine resumed her beer trade and I again saw her around with a case of beer on her head, followed by her brother Lebisabo carrying a bundle of her belongings.

When I returned to Bululu three years later, I found Josefina sitting on a mat at a friend's place. A group of Fofu women gathered to chat with us. Josefina was extremely thin except for a huge belly, which was as big as a pregnant woman's. Her skin was yellowish. Something was seriously wrong with her, although I could not diagnose it. I wondered whether she was suffering from a liver disease, caused by heavy drinking. We all helped her to husk beans.

Figure 7.6   True to type, Josefina talked in a carefree manner as if there were no troubles in this world.

True to type, she talked in a carefree manner as if there were no troubles in this world. Her voice was loud and cheerful. She said that she was not in the least surprised to see me because she had dreamed about me a week before. She knew I was coming.

Keusi, who was playing with neighbour children nearby, had grown a little but not as much as I would have expected. Her hair had turned red and Josefina thought that she had intestinal parasites. Lebisabo and Batabo had gone to the lake to wash their clothes. Pascarine was no longer trading beer but she was rushing off somewhere or other and her husband was leaving for his butchering job. They hardly had time to greet me. Josefina proudly pointed out to me a little two-year old girl playing with Keusi. She was Pascarine's daughter, Mami.

Although Josefina spoke in a carefree way, I gathered that one matter bothered her greatly. It was Pascarine's bridewealth. Her husband had not paid any of it yet. Josefina blamed Dudu, her step-son, for not fulfilling his duty, as the oldest brother of Pascarine, of extracting the bridewealth from her husband.

In the old, familiar way, Josefina begged me for some money to buy Fanta, a soft orange drink. I gave her some and she quickly hid it inside her skirt. We all knew that she would buy something other than Fanta and that it would do her liver no good.

I took pictures of her and other Fofu, promising them a copy the following year.

"I will have died of my disease by the time you bring the pictures back," she said as a joke. I felt cold shivers go through me when she said it but she was smiling broadly.

She was true to her word. When I took the pictures the following year I heard from the other Fofu that she had died. The old people were convinced that someone had bewitched her, because her belly had swelled, but they had not been able to find out who had caused it. Concerned Fofu had dragged her to the hospital where a doctor had removed gallons of fluid from her abdomen several times. She had suffered a great deal. Her last words had been,

"I have not drunk one sip of Pascarine's bridewealth."

THE TAXIS WERE IN HIDING

I would not have known where Pascarine had moved to, had I not happened to spot Keusi when I was at a market with Tania. Keusi was now seven-years old. She had been sent by Pascarine to buy something and she was about to return home. She was barefoot and was wearing a torn dress covered with a wrap-around cloth. She was carrying some salt, wrapped in brown paper. We went home with her which was about half a mile away. She paid careful attention to the traffic, checking left and right all the time, and when she saw a car coming, she stepped aside to wait for it to pass. Her hair colour had returned to normal and she seemed to be a well adjusted, balanced child. She did not talk to us, as children were not expected to, but she confidently showed us the way home.

Pascarine was waiting for her, grabbed the salt from her and turned to her cooking. Keusi took the wrap-around cloth off and gave it to Pascarine who wound it around her hips. I inferred that she had given the cloth to Keusi to dress up when going to the market. Then she went to wash dishes, but first stopped to look at us more carefully because Tania was with me. She smiled and asked about our news and details of our living conditions. A strange woman entered and wanted to read Tania's palm, but Pascarine strongly forbade it and told the woman to leave.

It was typical of her. Sometimes she ignored me, sometimes she was very friendly. Whatever her disposition, she never agreed to be formally interviewed. If she did not want me around she flashed an angry glance at me, a glance that could have frozen the sunshine. Once during my last year in Bululu, I greeted her when passing by her home, wondering if I was welcome to stay a while. She did not answer. Lebisabo who was standing at the door remarked to her,

"Do you see madam?"

"I saw her yesterday," Pascarine snapped and continued her chores without lifting her head. It was more than clear to me then that I was not wanted so I did not hang around.

After Josefina's death, Keusi lived with Pascarine and acted as both a baby-sitter and playmate for Mami. Lebisabo had taken a wife without paying any bridewealth and was living with her and his brother Batabo. They had two rented rooms in a dilapidated mud hut near Pascarine.

An old Fofu woman, Chika, expressed grave concern about the unpaid bride-wealth of this family. It was very bad that Pascarine's husband had not paid any-thing and it was bad that they, the Fofu, had not gone to talk to him about it. The fault lay mainly in Pascarine's half-brother, Dudu, who did not dare or care to take the formal step of demanding bridewealth. Lebisabo's unpaid bridewealth was a source of worry for his wife's father, who was known to be angry at Lebisabo for "stealing" his daughter but did not want to disturb the peace while his daughter was pregnant. Pascarine was pregnant again, too, but after the delivery, the Fofu should , in Chika's view, smarten up and go to talk to the husband about the bride-wealth. Things would go wrong if the matter was not straightened out. Chika was living alone and had time to worry about the private matters of Fofu families.

During my last year in Bululu, Lebisabo and Batabo were still occasionally helping Pascarine's husband with butchering. Each of them sold meat in different markets. There was a lot of competition in the market and both of them occasionally got into fights with other butchers. Once when I was at Estela's I saw a crowd of young men go by. The arms of one of the men were tied behind his back and a soldier was walking with him. Lebisabo explained to Estela that the fellow had stolen 1,000 zaires from the others. This did not deter Lebisabo, however, and later the same day, I saw him continuing his sales in the market.

As a result of one of these disputes at the market Lebisabo was once badly beaten on his face. He stopped work for a while and spent his time playing cards or board games with local youngsters. He was free for discussions with me then and came to my house several times for interviews. He did not mind my dropping in on him, either.

He was dressed like other young fashionable men in the slums. He bought used clothing and I don't know exactly what features made him look so fashionable. Perhaps the tightness of his shirts, or the vest he wore, or the fact that a certain number of shirt buttons were undone.

He did not take such a serious view on bridewealth as the old Fofu people did. He said that it was acceptable nowadays to take a wife and pay liquor later when a few children were born. He casually mentioned that his "wife," Marie-Jarinne, had still been living at home when she became pregnant. Her father had beaten her to find out her lover's name and when she did not reveal it, he denied her food as a punishment. Marie-Jarinne then ran away from home to Pascarine, who fed and sheltered her. Later she moved in with Lebisabo.

If it was acceptable to take a wife this way, was it a good way, I asked. Lebisabo admitted that it was not good but when the guy did not have money, what else could he do? I wanted to know how much he would have to pay for his bride if he did have money. He gave the following figures: two cases of beer, two gallons of a liquor called kasiksi, and a gallon of another kind of liquor. I don't think he knew exactly what he was supposed to pay because no negotiations had been held. On the other hand, the father-in-law would have been happy to drink even a small amount of liquor as bridewealth for his daughter.

The bridewealth in the form of liquor was very different from the rural bridewealth of cows and goats. Liquor brought only a momentary pleasure to the parents, cows and goats grew and bred and brought prolonged benefit for the family. It was also important that the livestock could be returned if the marriage did not work out but liquor could not since it had already been consumed.

Lebisabo reminded me that he was in such a position because Pascarine's husband had not paid anything for her. Had he paid, he could have used her bridewealth to pay for his bride. (In this matter Lebisabo continued to hold onto the rural ideology despite the fact that the liquor would have been drunk before he could have got married!) He also confirmed the story that Josefina had lamented not having had a sip of Pascarine's bridewealth on her deathbed. This seemed to be regarded almost like a curse hanging over the family. However, Lebisabo was not the one to press for the bridewealth because he was dependant on his brother-in-law for a job. Urban relationships were much more complicated than rural ones. In the villages, it was much easier for the girl's relatives to go after her bridewealth than here in the city.

Lebisabo was worried because his brother, Batabo, was interested in his wife and took advantage of her while he was out. Perhaps Lebisabo's lack of interest in work was caused by the fear of his brother hanging around his wife. He told me that he beat his brother whenever he discovered he had been fooling around with his wife and Batabo always swore to leave her alone — but only did so until the next time. Batabo was getting into trouble in the market place, too. Both Lebisabo and other Fofu told me that he was a pickpocket. The angry victims came to Lebisabo to complain and he would pay damages for his brother. When Batabo was thrown into jail, Lebisabo paid to get him out. Lebisabo thought that Batabo had changed drastically after their mother's death. Until then, things had gone fairly smoothly. I wondered if this was true because I vaguely remembered Batabo getting into trouble before then. When his mother was still alive neighbours were saying that he stole food at the market.

I noted how the siblings, although they had differences, were still supporting each other, both morally and economically. They all looked up to Pascarine, who as the oldest, took the most responsibility for them.

Although Lebisabo was not facing one responsibility, namely paying his bridewealth, he was putting another area of his life in order. He was attending baptism classes in the Roman Catholic cathedral twice a week with his sister Pascarine. He seemed to be looking forward to becoming a full member of the church.

I tried to get to know Lebisabo's wife, Marie-Jarinne, who was a member of the Nandi tribe. I passed by their place on my way to see Pascarine and greeted Marie-Jarinne. At first she stared at me wide-eyed, not being able to understand my role among the Fofu. Soon she treated me naturally and I guessed the other Fofu must have explained to her about my "Fofu grandfather." She became friendly and I often called on her for a chat. Keusi spent time at her place, too, and ran errands for her as well as for Pascarine. I sometimes saw her playing "cooking" in front of Marie-Jarinne's house with her friends. The little girls used old tin cans as pots, and dirt, sand, grass, and pebbles as food.

All the neighbourhood seemed to use Keusi as their messenger. One day I was sitting at Pascarine's with a few other women when Keusi pulled the door curtain aside and walked briskly up to one of the women,

"They need you at home. They are starting the *bugali* water," she informed the woman, clearly and confidently.

The woman was holding someone's baby. She gave it to another woman, got up immediately, and left the room. I looked at Keusi and marvelled at her strong character and confidence. I wondered how it was possible for her to become secure and happy after all the hardships she had suffered. I decided that her stubbornness was part of it. Lebisabo had criticized her for being bullheaded and sometimes refusing to run errands. Pascarine had chastised her many a time for this fault. Although stubbornness was not appreciated when it was demonstrated against the authority of the family, it was undoubtedly an asset when it came to surviving in the slums.

Pascarine duly had her third baby in hospital. She had to walk home from the hospital with the help of the old woman, Chika. Pascarine's husband had given Chika some money for a taxi but they were all in hiding that day because word had gone round that the taxi permits were being inspected. Most taxis did not have permits and so they went underground for a few days, until the inspection was over.

Her neighbours arranged a feast for her when she came out and I went to it, too. All the women of the neighbourhood gathered to sing and dance for Pascarine, who smiled broadly as she sat on the edge of her bed, holding her baby boy in her arms. The women danced so vigorously that the earth of Pascarine's little mud hut quaked. She welcomed me that day, especially when I gave her a gift of baby clothes.

Then there was an incident which illustrates how the Fofu introduce mock hostility on certain occasions, for example, births and weddings. Some young men came to the door. They looked in to the living room and ridiculed Pascarine good humoredly:

"Pascarine bore a robber!"

The women clapped their hands and shooed them away: "As you are robbers! Robbers bear robbers!"

The young men disappeared. After all, the occasion was only for women. Still more women were arriving. They filed past Pascarine and said,

"Thank you, Pascarine, for bearing a boy!"

I asked the women if it was especially good to bear a boy rather than a girl. They claimed that both were good, a human was a human, but a boy was good after a girl and Pascarine already had a girl.

In fact, Mami, Pascarine's daughter was upset by the turmoil of the feast. She hung on to her mother and cried. The women had no sympathy for her, however, although she was only three.

"What's the matter, Mami?" they yelled and pushed her around. I felt so sorry for her that I went to buy some candy to console her. She immediately shared it with Keusi and other children.

When I left the feast with some other women, the girls were playing outside. Keusi told us Mami was drunk. I looked at her and noticed that she had glazed eyes but I did not see any other symptoms. I gathered that the dancing women had comforted her by giving her liquor and I remembered Keusi being weaned with liquor a few years back.

Pascarine was happy that day. I gathered from the gossip that she and her husband had gone through a bad patch. Pascarine had a ruptured appendix about a year ago which was removed in hospital. While she was in there the doctor told her that she had syphilis. The Fofu women were quick to blame Pascarine's husband. They claimed that she would have become pregnant much earlier if he had not given her syphilis. The main source of annoyance lay in the fact that the husband had stopped his wife bearing children regularly. The delay in her becoming pregnant again was unforgivable. Chika told me that Pascarine's biggest worry was that the doctor had operated on her womb instead of her appendix without her knowing. When a new baby was born after all these worries one could understand the family joy.

A few months later I saw Pascarine nursing a neighbour's baby. I heard a recent Fofu immigrant to the city criticising Pascarine for helping a stranger in this way.

"You should do it right! You should nurse only your bigger sister's baby, not a stranger's baby!" she protested irritably.

The other Fofu women sitting with Pascarine tried to placate her.

"We are now living in Bululu and we follow the white people's customs."

Pascarine told me that the mother of the baby had a breast infection and could not nurse it herself. Many neighbours were also helping her. The strange baby sucked greedily. Pascarine nursed it on one breast only and then took her own baby and put him on the other one.

Pascarine's husband seemed elusive at first and I wondered if he would be willing to talk to me at all but he turned out to be a very congenial young man. He did not talk about emotional matters as women did but he was quite open about his trade of butchering. He did it in quite a small way. Each operation started with a group of friends lending him money to buy a cow. When he had butchered and sold the meat, with the help of Pascarine's brothers, Anastasia's son, Sengi, and some other little boys, he would return the loan to his friends without interest. When I passed through the market place I often saw him selling his meat. The work was irregular because the supply of cows to the city was spasmodic and prices fluctuated. Nevertheless, the family survived with his activities and, as importantly, with Pascarine's distilling enterprise.

I was told by Fofu women that his first wife had become so angry at his favouring Pascarine that she had gone to Butembo. There one of her two children had died. She was embarrassed about the death and did not dare to return to her husband. The husband would not go to fetch her either, because she had gone on her own accord, he had not sent her away. This kind of gossip gave me a glimpse of the intrigues of husband-wife relationships.

While Pascarine managed her family life despite various obstacles, her brother Lebisabo failed in his attempt to establish a family. Marie-Jarinne was expecting her baby in a couple of months. However, it was born prematurely and died after a few days. Lebisabo later told me that his parents-in-law had come to the wake but did not face him nor talk to him because of the in-law avoidance rule. Although they had to sit in the same room because the house was so small, they kept their backs turned to Lebisabo. Nothing had been said about the bridewealth. Lebisabo knew that the parents had tried to persuade Marie-Jarinne to go home but she had not wanted to.

Sadly, the relationship between Lebisabo and Marie-Jarinne deteriorated after the loss of their baby. The Fofu reported violent fights between them. One morning, old

Chika, who lived in the neighbourhood, told me that she had heard Lebisabo beating his wife at night. It had kept her and her neighbours awake.

"Didn't you intervene?" I asked.

"No, we did not because we knew that no bridewealth had been paid."

I saw that Chika was bothered by the fight among the young people. She was not related to them but felt responsibility as a Fofu. I knew that rural parents habitually intervened when their married children quarrelled and it seemed that it was only the matter of the unpaid bridewealth that prevented it in this case.

In the event, however, some non-Fofu neighbours, who were not fettered by the same bridewealth rules, did intervene and separate the spouses. I went to Lebisabo's home soon after the fight. Lebisabo was not there but Marie-Jarinne was lying on the bed in the back room. Keusi ran to get her for me. She came slowly, holding her hand to her cheek. She looked wretched and must have been in terrible pain. Her cheek was very swollen and one eye was black. She told me she had lost a tooth and her ear had bled. I saw blood on her blouse and on the curtain between the living room and the bedroom. As she told me this, a rat ran down the wall. I jumped when I saw it which made Marie-Jarinne turn to look at it, too. She laughed derisively, as if to say that the rat was the least of her worries.

I tried to discover what Pascarine thought about the situation but she was in a terrible mood and looked at me murderously. Perhaps she was too upset to talk about it. I left the city for good in a few days but heard from the other Fofu that Marie-Jarinne had finally gathered her belongings together and gone home to her parents.

Lebisabo and Pascarine continued to attend their baptism classes in the Catholic cathedral twice a week and were duly baptized. I have not heard whether Pascarine's bridewealth ever arrived. I have my doubts about it. Neither do I know whether Lebisabo has taken a new wife, but I dare say he has. Batabo may have taken a wife as well, so he does not need to borrow his brother's — on the other hand, he may have been thrown into prison for good. By now, Keusi should be in her teens and flourishing. However, one cannot be sure, because life in the slums is so unpredictable.

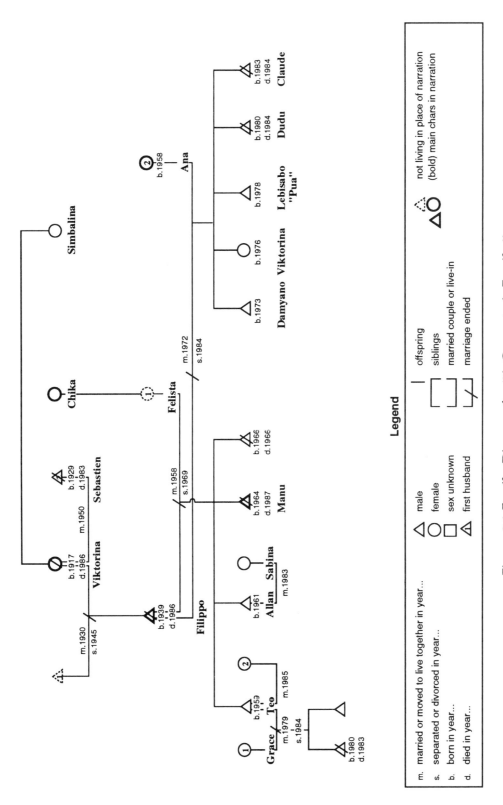

Figure 8.1 Family Diagram for "A Carpenter's Family."

8 A CARPENTER'S FAMILY

"WE FOFU SHOULD HELP EACH OTHER"

I became acquainted with Filippo while visiting Anastasia. He lived a few hundred yards from her and used to stop to chat with Anastasia and Abiso when passing by. After seeing him several times at Anastasia's, I asked to visit his family.

He was proud of his skill as a carpenter and he had built a shelter with a work bench in front of his house. His life revolved around carpentry and Filippo working in his shelter while chatting to somebody and his little children playing in the yard was a typical sight.

I never felt completely at ease with him because he tried to get material goods out of me and his technique for extracting them was to try to make me feel guilty. In the beginning, for instance, I thought I would order some furniture from him to support his business. However, when we started serious negotiations he did not set any firm prices. He told me that he would like me to help him to repair his house. To start with, I should give him two sacks of cement, a return air ticket to Lemura (to visit his relatives), and some pills. I realized that there would be no end to his demands and I would never know when I had paid for the furniture. The uncertainty would spoil our relationship and might even affect my relations with the rest of the Fofu in town. Furthermore, I did not know what his work was like. What if the drawers did not fit properly? Could I complain to him, a Fofu, about it? I decided to order the furniture from a shop in town instead. That offended Filippo although he did not say anything at first. Only later when he was drunk did he rebuke me. In his opinion, I should have sponsored his business because he was a Fofu.

"We Fofu should help each other," he said.

I did not argue with him and once he had vented his anger, he got over his disappointment.

Then Filippo started bragging to me about how much he knew about Fofu history and customs. He claimed that I would not have enough note paper to record all his knowledge. I had only to pay him and he would open the gates of his vast knowledge. I saw this offer as being similar to the one of his carpentry and told him that I had to find the information somewhere else.

Thereafter, he kept asking me what I was going to give him and his "poor" family. I gave him gifts in the same way as I gave the other Fofu gifts. I know he liked them but he always belittled them saying that I never gave him anything. During the final year of my fieldwork, I finally hit upon the Fofu way of handling him. I started talking back to him the way he talked to me, although it went against my Finnish upbringing according to which the giver plays down the value of the gift. I reminded him of all my gifts and told him he was rude not to acknowledge them.

"I have wasted so much on you and you only complain!" I finished coldly.

He shut up and became friendly. I wished I had been brave enough to have done it earlier. I had observed how the Fofu remembered the gifts they gave and received. For Filippo not to acknowledge my gifts was contrary to Fofu custom. He only wanted to manipulate me with his complaints. He had learned, perhaps from his white teachers at school, that white people easily feel guilty.

Although he complained a lot during the early years of our acquaintance, he was flattered by my visits to his home. I was doing the timed observations when I visited each Fofu family for a specified time during each day. One morning, I was at his house at six. I overheard him bragging to some neighbour women,

"Madam left her good house just to visit me"!

Another time he boasted to his neighbours, "Madam likes me, look how often she comes to see me here, she wants to marry me." The women burst out laughing.

I think that beneath all the manoeuvring, Filippo accepted me and even understood my anthropological task better than most other Fofu, because he had been educated by white people.

His wife, Ana, seemed curious the first time I walked into their yard. While chatting with Filippo near his shelter I could just see her creeping closer to listen to us, with an outstretched neck. I am sure she consulted *Mama* Avion and other Fofu to ascertain whether I was a malignant person. Thereafter she accepted me as part of the picture and was generally friendly to me, but I did not come to know her very well. When the authorities gave them a hard time and Filippo was in captivity for two months, she turned cold towards me and I thought it better not to visit her during that period.

Had Filippo and Ana not liked me, they only needed to report me to the "Red Beret" soldiers who were roaming around the neighbourhood at that time. Although I had permission for my research, they would have arrested me first and asked questions later. Ana once mentioned that the soldiers had asked her about me and she had simply stated that I was one of the Fofu and harmless. I was thankful to her for that. I knew I was taking a risk by continuing my field work during the occupation by the "Red Berets."

Filippo's house desperately needed repairs. It was a mud hut with two rooms and was subsiding badly. The back wall was almost symbolic: there were holes big enough for children to crawl through, the rats did it all the time. The roof was made of flattened oil drums, now rusty.

Despite the desperate state of repair, Filippo never did anything to the house and when I left Bululu almost a decade later, the house had subsided even further. The front room served as a living room and a storage room for Filippo's tools and materials and Ana's distilling barrels. I was surprised Filippo's tools stayed intact, as anyone could have broken in and stolen them. There was also a table, a side board, and a couple of chairs in this room. The second room was used as a bedroom and had two beds: one for the parents and the youngest child, and another one for the rest of the children.

The outhouse was made of woven mats and was situated a few yards from the house. There was a garbage pit near it, which Ana guarded jealously. I once heard her shout at a neighbour who had thrown a pot of water onto it.

Filippo's shelter comprised four poles with a few flattened oil drums on top as the roof. A work bench was attached to two of the poles. Whenever I arrived, one of Filippo's children would carry a chair to the shelter for me so that I could sit in the shade. Often the children were playing in or near the shelter.

The ground of Filippo's yard was lava rock and did not, therefore, become muddy during the rains. It was not shared with other families but people had the customary right to pass over it. The rocky yard was quite a nice place for the children to play in and Ana grew squash in part of the yard. Filippo's lot was on top of a small hill and when standing in his yard I would often gaze at the ocean of roof tops. Most of the roofs were made of flattened oil drums, like Filippo's. Poorer people used leaves. There were only a couple of corrugated iron roofs in sight. There was no planning in the area: the houses were jammed in haphazardly.

Filippo was born in Lemura 39 years previously. He received his primary school education of five years in a Catholic boarding school there and spent a further two years learning carpentry at the Catholic mission. During this time his father had moved from one mining area to another.

Filippo's mother had left his father when he was a few years old and married another man with whom she moved to several cities before settling in Bululu before Independence. After his schooling Filippo decided to visit his mother in Bululu and never again returned to the Fofu country. He attended a technical school in Bululu for a year and then started working as a carpenter. In 1958 he was sent to work at a furniture factory in Buva but he moved back to Bululu after a year.

Filippo had worked for many furniture companies in Bululu. He said that work opportunities had diminished after Independence when a large number of white people had left the country. He now worked for an Italian whom he had served for fifteen years but did not pay well. He quarrelled with the employer several times and stopped working for a while. When he was arrested by the military police, he lost his job for good. After being released, he worked at a Zairean carpentry shop. He also did private jobs in his shelter after normal working hours. After a while, he only worked as a freelance carpenter from home.

Filippo should have been better off than he was. After all, he had a steady income, although he did not reveal the exact amount of it to me. If I asked about his profits, he played them down and begged me to loan him money for materials. I never did. I knew from another Fofu carpenter that it was customary to demand half of the price of a piece of furniture as a down payment for raw materials, and the rest on delivery. He did not need my money for materials.

Filippo once lost some of his income to the soldiers. He was returning from a customer to whom he had delivered a table. Unfortunately he did not make it back home before the dark. The soldiers stopped him on the road, found the money for the table hidden in his shoe and took it. This kind of thing happened to everybody at one time or another and Filippo did not bemoan his loss for very long.

Ana's childhood had been far less stable than her husband's and when I interviewed her about it, I was touched by the severity of it. She was only two years old when the country gained its independence in 1960. Her mother was living in Kisangani, in central Congo, at the time but her father was away on military service. They never knew where he was. After Independence, the country was plunged into a civil war and Kisangani was a centre of turmoil for many years. Ana's father was serving in the national army while Kisangani was occupied and terrorised by the Simbas (the Lions), a rebel army who supported Patrice Lumumba. Ana remembered that she had to run with her mother into the bush many times when the Simbas were coming. She saw mothers abandoning their infants lest they reveal their hiding places. The whole society was in chaos. It must have been a devastating experience for a little girl. After Mobutu took power in 1965, things gradually calmed down and Ana's family was reunited, although her father still served in the national army until the 1980s.

Ana did not stay idle by her husband's side. As other Fofu women, she earned money by distilling liquor at least once a week. She had a standing agreement with a bar which bought all she distilled. I often saw her engaged in some distilling activity or the other, either in preparation for it or on the way to the bar with a heavy basket of bottles. Ana may not have been regular in cooking the meals for the family but she was regular in her distilling.

Ana used to say that she did not need to fear soldiers finding out about her distilling because she had friends among them. Her father had lived in the Bululu barracks for many years when he had been posted there as a soldier. The "Red Berets," however, did not know her father. One night one of Ana's customers informed on her and led the soldiers to her door. Filippo opened it, thinking that they were customers for a late-night drink but the soldiers invaded the house, shouting and causing havoc by overturning the fermenting barrels. Filippo offered them money to appease them and finally they left. Ana lost that batch of liquor and her savings for the next one. She had to wait until Filippo earned some more money before she could start up again. She did not give up distilling, however. To her, getting caught was an occupational hazard which had to be endured.

At first I thought that Filippo's household was a nuclear family but I was soon to learn that the family ties spread to other parts of the city. Filippo had first married a Fofu girl, Felista, while in Buva in 1958. Felista had born him four sons, of whom one died as an infant. They had subsequently lived together in Bululu until the late

1960s when she left her husband and sons and moved to Bujumbura where she remarried.

Filippo's sons from his first marriage did not live with him but with his mother, Viktorina, who lived about half a mile away. Filippo said that his present house was too small for two sets of children: his mother was glad to have them with her.

Filippo never mentioned why his first wife had left him. During my fieldwork, Felista moved back to Bululu with her old mother, Chika, and settled in Filippo's neighbourhood. I often saw the two women when they walked by Filippo's and chatted with Ana and I know that the older boys used to visit their mother, Felista. When I asked Felista why she had left Filippo, she answered briefly that she was tired of being constantly beaten by her husband. I heard such answers from many women and never knew how to take them. Men were said to beat their wives all the time, in fact, if they did not, they were not thought of as loving their wives. At what point was their beating rejected by women? I suspected that there must have been more to this alleged beating of Felista. Her mother's story was that Filippo had taken a second wife when Felista's youngest son was born. Felista had become very jealous of her and left Filippo because of her. As nobody else mentioned Filippo's second wife I did not know whether to believe Chika, either.

After Felista had left Filippo and her sons had gone to live with his mother, Filippo found another young Fofu girl, Ana, and married her. According to the dates they gave me, Ana would have been only 14-years old when she married Filippo. She bore Filippo a son, Damyano, when she was only 15. A daughter was born three years later and they named her Viktorina, after her grandmother. During the years I knew the family, Ana bore three more sons, of whom two died. The deaths caused her to leave her husband in the end, but I will return to that topic later. I will first describe family life at Filippo's and then the kind of life his older sons had, living with their grandmothers.

BOWS OVER THE DOOR

Filippo and his first wife, Felista, had spoken Kifofu at home but Ana did not speak it. Although she was a Fofu, her parents had been living away from the Fofu country for many years and used Lingala, which was the language of the president of the country and the language of the military. Filippo and Ana spoke Swahili at home, although I heard Ana using Lingala in conversations with some of her neighbours. The children spoke Swahili. Filippo would sometimes, but not consistently, speak Kifofu with some of the older Fofu.

When I first got to know the family Ana was pregnant with her third child (although she did not reveal it to me) and spent much of her time sitting in front of her house feeling nauseated. Little Viktorina was two years old and had been recently weaned because of her mother's new pregnancy. She was a cranky child, cried a lot and suffered from diarrhea. She would let the diarrhea run down her legs any time any place. Ana never scolded her but wiped her legs with a dirty rag and threw some dirt over the ground to cover the mess up. If her older half-brother Manu happened to be visiting, he took care to clean the spots that Viktorina had dirtied.

During this period Ana directed her children and neighbour's children from a reclining chair in which she sat with a piece of cloth around her shoulders, like a shawl.

"Tie the child on your back better!" she once commanded a strange girl who was walking across her yard. The girl did as she was told.

One morning when I arrived at their house, Ana was heating left-over beans from the previous night on a charcoal burner. She put the pot of beans on the dirt floor in the living room and told 5-year old Damyano, Viktorina, and two neighbour children to eat them. The children sat down on the ground and started eating straight from the pot with their fingers, as was usual. Viktorina tried to pull the pot onto her lap but Ana did not permit it.

"I'll hit you if you take the pot!" Ana warned her.

Viktorina's bottom lip quivered. She got up, ran outside, threw herself on the ground and screamed.

"If you don't stop crying, I'll hit you!" Ana threatened.

Viktorina got up to run further away and threw herself on the ground again, still crying loudly. Nobody paid attention to her. Soon she got up and returned to the living room where the other children, having eaten enough, had abandoned the pot. Viktorina sat down on the ground, put the pot on her lap, and finished the beans. Damyano started picking up the beans that had fallen on the floor.

"Sweep them up!" Ana commanded. Damyano took a handleless broom and tried to sweep the floor, while Ana instructed him with curt commands.

By this time Viktorina had finished her meal and she bent down trying to help Damyano to clean the floor. Suddenly she burst into tears.

"You are a short-tempered child!" Ana scolded her.

Viktorina took offence at this, ran outside, threw herself on the ground yet again, and howled. Ana ignored her and continued her chores. Filippo was planing some wood in his shelter. He called softly to Viktorina, who went slowly to her father. Interrupting his work, Filippo sat down on his bench, took Viktorina on his lap, and talked to her gently. The little girl calmed down immediately, and when Filippo continued his work, she walked to her mother who picked her up. The two then sat together on the chair outside the door of their house. Meanwhile Damyano had finished his sweeping and was struggling to put sneakers on. Ana noticed that he was putting them on the wrong feet.

"I'll hit you if you don't change the shoes to the right feet," she told him sharply.

Damyano stared at his feet and slowly switched the shoes. Then he ran to play with his neighbours.

Little Viktorina had fits of crying many times during the early months of our acquaintance. I attributed her behaviour to the trauma of weaning and to her sickness. If she was suffering from amebic dysentery, as her mother claimed, it is no wonder that she felt miserable. I had it a few times in Africa and it made me feel like screaming, too. Ana's reaction to little Viktorina's temper tantrums was first to scold her, then to ignore her and only finally to comfort her. Nobody thought of taking her to get medicine. Later on, Viktorina seemed to be better and happier. Also Ana became more energetic as her pregnancy progressed and spent less time sitting in the yard.

In the July of that year, Ana bore a son. I visited the family two days afterwards and Filippo and Ana told me how it happened. Ana had apparently delivered the baby all by herself on the bedroom floor, which she had covered with a piece of plastic normally used for distilling. Filippo stayed outside listening to Ana's groans through the door. He suggested going for a *mademoiselle* (midwife) to help but Ana belittled her difficulties. Neighbour women came to cut the umbilical cord once the baby was born.

I noticed that in the city the mother was left alone to deliver, while in the rural areas the husband would assist his wife, if related women were not available. A solitary delivery was very rare in the Fofu villages.

When I was told the story of the birth Ana was sitting in the yard with the tiny baby on her lap. She was moaning and told me that her uterus was hurting. However, she got up and went in and out of the house while we chatted. Again, there was no talk of getting medical help. Suffering was a normal part of life for the Fofu.

Filippo said he was going to arrange a special outcoming ceremony to name his son and to mark his entry into the community. I knew that the rural Fofu had such a ceremony four days after the birth of a son. Filippo, however, saved money for the festivity for almost a month before he called the Fofu of the city together for the naming ceremony. I was glad to be invited.

The ceremony took place on a Sunday morning. When I arrived at Filippo's at 9 o'clock, Ana was fetching water and Filippo was taking a bath in the outhouse. Filippo's mother, old Viktorina, *Mama* Avion, Ida, and some other older Fofu women were preparing a meal. When Ana returned with the water, she changed her own and the children's clothes. Filippo also donned clean clothes and the feast could begin.

Dudu, who officiated at most of the Fofu funerals, appeared at the door carrying the baby in his arms. He laid the baby on its back on a piece of cloth on the ground and put a bow and arrow under its arm. I was amused to see that the traditional male symbol of hunting was preserved, although the Fofu never hunted in the city and only rarely did it nowadays in the rural areas. A baby girl would have received a wooden ladle to represent her role as a cook in the family.

After giving the child the bow and arrow, Dudu picked the baby up and carried him to the shelter where the men (and I) were standing. There he announced the baby's name, Lebisabo, which old Viktorina had suggested. Filippo stepped forward and kissed the baby's forehead and chest which had black marks on them. Dudu told me later that he had made the marks out of palm oil and salt and that he had made similar marks on the baby's mother and grandmother as well. They like the marks made on a bride represented the energetic force the ancestors were giving the new born as well as their blessing. With the ritual, he was received into the family and into the lineage, which extended beyond the living.

Next the women brought out bowls of food to the shelter for the men, and a little bit later for the women sitting on the ground near the house. I was asked to go inside where I found a bowl of potatoes and meat, European food. While I ate alone, the others ate in groups sharing a bowl with the others of the same sex. Everyone ate swiftly; nobody used the time for conversation but dedicated it solely to eating.

After the meal, the women brought out bottles of beer, home distilled liquor, and *mandaragua*, native mild beer. The atmosphere became light and people were laughing and joking. Dudu, Filippo, and some old Fofu women served the drinks while Ana sat in the house holding the baby and occasionally letting Filippo's mother hold it. I left close to noon, when the Fofu were ready to dance happily together in celebration of the arrival of a new Fofu.

During the following days, the memory of the naming ceremony brought happy smiles to the faces of the Fofu. Many of them told me that they tried to arrange

Figure 8.2 Filippo (left) enjoying his child's naming ceremony.

**Figure 8.3 Viktorina (right) participating in her grandson's
naming ceremony with other Fofu women.**

such a feast for at least one of their children. They showed me half rotten bows, which still hung over their front doors, where the father had installed them after the ceremony. Nobody ever mentioned holding a naming ceremony for a girl although in theory, they should have been held, too.

The baby was not called Lebisabo in every day parlance, although this name was entered in the parents' identity cards and would be used in official documents. *Mama* Avion called him Pua, which means 'a nose' in Swahili because, in her opinion, his nose was big. Thereafter the baby became known as Pua among the Fofu and their friends.

When I called at Filippo's during the following year, it was typical to see Ana going about her distilling or household chores with the baby on her back. As Pua grew bigger Ana would sometimes leave him on a half-finished bed near Filippo's shelter or on a piece of sacking on the floor of his shelter. But Ana was never far away. When Ana was distilling, for example, she would go into the house to tend to her work, then come out to kiss Pua and sing to him or play with him before going back in to the distilling. Pua was a happy, chubby baby, very responsive to other people.

Ana never left the baby to be baby-sat by Damyano or little Viktorina but these older children would often go to the baby, coo and talk softly to him. Filippo was never in sole charge of Pua but if he was working in his shelter, he would stop his work if the baby needed attention. Once Ana left the baby with the grandmother,

Viktorina, while she went to deliver a batch of liquor. But this was exceptional, generally Ana took care of Pua herself.

When Damyano was six-years old, he spent much of his time playing with neighbour boys, and sometimes, but less frequently, with neighbour girls. Little Viktorina, then three, hardly ever joined in but she often followed the bigger children at a distance and watched them admiringly. She seldom left the secure boundaries of her own yard, while Damyano was often out of sight roaming the neighbourhood. Like Josefina's and Anastasia's sons, Damyano was crazy about the "Red Berets." He spent hours playing at them, copying their marching exercises, their singing, their gymnastic exercises, and finally their work of capturing and imprisoning people. Damyano continued to imitate the "Red Berets" in his play for a year after they left Bululu. Once he also pretended to be the president of the country, flying with his jet and coming to Bululu for a visit. Occasionally he played "house" with boys and a few girls. The children marked out a house on the ground with flour, brought by a neighbour girl in her mother's pot. In the middle of their game, the mother came and angrily retrieved her flour pot.

Most of the time Damyano was allowed to play undisturbed. His play was seldom interrupted to run errands. Once his mother told him to kindle the fire in the charcoal burner, but Damyano answered that he was tired and suggested his sister do it. It was typical of a male not to want to do female jobs. His mother answered him with a question, as the Fofu often did,

"Is she a human being?."

Her question revealed to me that Viktorina was not yet regarded as a human being and was consequently not required to take responsibility. Damyano, on the other hand, was considered to be a human being and, in the absence of female humans, had to perform female tasks. The mother repeated the order so many times that Damyano had no option but to go and kindle the fire.

This was not the only time I observed Damyano trying to get out of an unpleasant female duty. One morning in 1979 I found Ana nursing Pua in front of the house and Damyano sitting on a rock nearby with his head drooping. He did not join his playmates who were kicking a ball in the road.

"You are refusing to do what I say. Don't sit!" Ana told him quietly but firmly.

Damyano moved two yards further away and continued sitting and staring at the ground. Little Viktorina arrived back from a neighbour's and sat next to her brother. Ana, who was in the process of scrubbing black pots with sand brought from Rwanda, threw a glance at her son.

"Go further away to sit. Don't you sit here!" she ordered.

Damyano got up, walked about 10 yards and sat down again. Ana continued her work while Viktorina protected a water pot from Pua's hands. I asked Ana what the matter was with Damyano.

"I asked him to do something and he refuses to do it," she explained briefly.

Damyano kept aloof sulking and did not answer neighbour girls who tried to catch his attention when passing by.

"See, what did I say? Now you are feeling the hunger." Ana snapped at him while scrubbing a lid energetically. I gathered that she would not give him breakfast unless he did the job. A man who was passing by, bent down and washed his hands in Ana's dishwater. The man's companion picked up Pua and made him walk by supporting him under the arms. Then the men continued on their way. Ana smiled at them and exchanged greetings.

Damyano got up and walked very slowly toward his mother, stopping a few yards from her.

"I'll beat you severely!" she threatened him.

Damyano walked very slowly into the house and made some dishes clutter. Apparently the noises sounded right and Ana directed him about the utensils he was going to need.

"Take the whole bag," she advised him.

As if in a slow-motion movie, Damyano rolled a mortar outside then went back to get the pestle, then equally slowly, returned to get a manioc bag.

"E-e!" he exclaimed faintly when he saw Pua smearing himself with his faeces. Ana got up and lifted the baby up, telling Damyano to hold him while she went in to get some rags to clean the child with. Damyano did not oppose holding his brother.

After this diversion, Damyano had nothing else to do but to obey his mother and pound the manioc. He did it lazily and took every opportunity to interrupt his work. He would, for example, stop Pua from crawling too close to him or sit down on the ground and taste the flour. Nevertheless, he stuck to the task the whole hour I was there, while Viktorina chatted with Pua and Ana scrubbed the dishes.

If it was hard for Damyano to do female jobs, he gladly ran male errands for his father. One day I heard his father calling him in from his play with neighbour boys. Damyano went in immediately. Filippo gave him orders and money to buy cigarettes. When the boy was on his way, the father called after him,

"For fifty makuta (pennies)!"

"Ee," Damyano answered, the Swahili "yes," while walking briskly.

Filippo sat down on his work bench to wait and sent little Viktorina to the house to get matches. He was ready for a smoke.

In about eight minutes, Damyano returned without the cigarettes.

"Where are the cigarettes? Was the place closed?" Filippo inquired with a frown.

"I did not know how to say it," Damyano explained.

"Sporti, fifty makuta worth. Repeat it now!" Filippo taught his son.

Damyano repeated it haltingly and Filippo corrected him until he was satisfied. "Go and walk fast!"

Damyano set off again, walking as fast as he could. In less than five minutes he was back holding five cigarettes in his hand.

"*Voila!*" Filippo exclaimed in French, took the cigarettes and immediately lit one. Damyano returned to his play with his friends. Later on he had no difficulties in performing this task for his father and he did it gladly.

Little Viktorina was a sweet girl, very trustful of people. She would follow her mother and sit near her when she was nursing Pua. Visitors often asked her to sit on their laps and she went happily to them. Once a man came to talk to Filippo for a few minutes. He stretched his arm toward Viktorina, who immediately walked to him and leaned against his thigh letting the man hold her hands. She would come to me, too, if I asked her to. She helped her mother by fetching her soap, palm-oil, salt, and the like from the house. She also shared any food she had with the baby once he was big enough to eat solid foods.

When visiting the family I had the opportunity to observe the husband-wife relationship. Filippo, for example, shared his news with Ana when he came home from his trips to town. Ana would listen attentively and comment on the news and the people Filippo told her about. Not all Fofu men chatted with their wives like Filippo did, but kept their world apart from that of their wives. I saw mutual appreciation in their relationship. Ana viewed it differently, however, she thought her parents loved each other more than she and Filippo did,

"Because there was more to eat in their home than in ours."

This was typical of the Fofu: they thought that material conditions were a barometer for human relations. If economic conditions were good then human relations would automatically be good and vice versa. It was as simple as that. Later, when Ana left Filippo, other Fofu viewed her departure in economic terms as well.

Ana enjoyed singing and attended a Catholic choir practice twice a week in a nearby chapel. She had a notebook filled with hand-written songs which she read during the week. I never noticed it myself but other Fofu criticized her for spending hours drumming and singing in an intoxicated condition when she should have been cooking food for her family.

Pua was weaned when he was 19-months old and I gathered that Ana was pregnant again. As before Ana delivered alone in the bedroom. This time it was in the middle of the night, while the other children were asleep. When Filippo noticed that his wife "wanted to deliver," as he put it, he excused himself and went to the outhouse. A neighbour woman called a *mademoiselle* to cut the umbilical cord. Everything was soon over and Ana said she felt fine. In a month the baby was named in a naming ceremony, just as Pua had been over two years previously. The new baby was called Dudu after his grandfather in Lemura.

After the birth of another baby Pua turned into an unhappy and aggressive toddler. He cried much of the time, as Viktorina had done at two, had temper tantrums, and constantly hit other children. His mother threatened to hit him, ignored him, and at times comforted him. It was unfortunate that I tried to do Bayley tests on Pua during this unhappy period. He hated me for it and refused to do much at all. About six months later, he changed back into a happy child and joined Viktorina in her play. Then he liked me again: as soon as he spotted me on the road coming toward his home, he would run to shake my hand, grinning broadly.

Then Filippo was thrown into jail for allegedly stealing a soldier's rifle while he was drinking Ana's liquor. Occasionally I saw Ana in the vicinity of the *gendarmerie* downtown when she was taking her husband food. However, she did not want to talk to me. Her extra responsibilities gave her a worried look. I am sure she was suffering financially without Filippo's income. The Fofu did not want to tell me about the affair of the rifle and so I did not pester them with questions. I felt the pressure of the unresolved case hanging over the family and affecting the Fofu generally. After two months detention Filippo was back at his work bench, several pounds lighter than before. He had lost his regular job in a carpenter's shop. After a while, he found another job in a Zairean shop but was not very happy with it. Filippo rebuked me for not visiting him in prison.

When little Viktorina was five years old, she was ailing again. Her skin turned grey and dry and her hair became straight. She was apathetic and had lost her happy smile. Her mother took her to a dispensary where she was diagnosed as having an intestinal parasite, Ascaris, a worm that looked like a pale earth worm. During the treatment Ana claimed to have counted 148 worms in the stools she did on the ground. She could not of course count any of the stools she did in the pit in the outhouse!

It was not uncommon for children to get parasites. I treated my own children for them about twice a year and I, myself, suffered from Ascaris once. At the time of Viktorina's illness, I gave a cure to Pua as well. One day I saw two worms crawling out of his rectum while he was sitting on the ground. The same thing often happened to my son Tom: after a bath there might be several living worms in the bathtub! The cure we used did not kill the worms but prevented them from clinging to the intestines.

I tried to help Viktorina by bringing her meat, since I decided she was suffering from lack of protein. Once I brought her two hamburger patties in a plastic container. The neighbour women gathered around Viktorina and stared at the meat.

"White man's meat," they murmured with curiosity and broke off pieces to have a taste. In the end there was only half of a hamburger left for Viktorina. I told them to leave the food entirely for the little girl but they said that they had to have a taste of the peculiar food. I noticed that my good intention had not produced good results.

By the following year Viktorina was getting her natural skin colour back and her hair was curly again. She was giggling and playing with Pua in the yard while Filippo banged nails in his shelter. Life was not too bad for the family then.

BETTER ONE CHILD THAN NUN?

There was something secretive and shameful about the move of Filippo's mother to Bululu. Over the years, Viktorina, herself, and Manu, the youngest of Filippo's first set of children, referred mysteriously to her deed but only at the end of my last year in Africa, did I understand why there was so much stigma attached to her departure.

"They would kill her if she went back to Lemura," Manu revealed once.

"Why on earth would they do that?" I exclaimed.

"She left her legal husband who had paid the bridewealth," he explained to me.

There had to be more to it than that, for Fofu women were always leaving their husbands. I had to think hard to understand why Viktorina's departure had been worse than that of other Fofu women. The reason was that she had failed her lineage and that of her husband by leaving the marriage that her family had arranged for her and for which her husband's family had paid the bridewealth. The wealth had been used for her brother's marriage and could not, therefore, be returned to her husband's family. Part of the bridewealth should have been returned because Viktorina had only produced one child for him. Had she produced three children, no bridewealth need have been returned and her leaving her husband would not have been condemned so harshly. As it was, it was looked upon as a breach of contract.

Viktorina considered herself a failure. In my first interview with her, she sighed deeply and told me that when she was young she was expected to become a Catholic nun but she left the convent because she wanted to bear children. With hindsight, it was hardly worth leaving the convent, as she had borne only one child and she had done that with great difficulty. She felt she had not accomplished much in life.

Filippo did not think as pessimistically about her. He put it in a more positive way,

"I am now delivering the children who were in the stomach of my mother."

He ignored the fact that Viktorina was not increasing her husband's lineage as she should have, according to the Fofu patrilineal rule.

Viktorina was sixty-years old when I got to know her. She was a bitter old woman with a stern face and a thin voice. She passed rude remarks to people with her quiet voice but nobody dared to oppose her because she was old. One of the young Fofu women told me that Viktorina's facial expression showed that she was able to kill people by witchcraft. In this way, she held some power over people by keeping them in fear of her. Another negative comment came from a Fofu man, who had moved to Bululu with his family and borrowed some money from Viktorina to get started with a new life. He told me that it was the last time he would borrow from her, because Viktorina was always at his home nagging him to return the money. A third Fofu complained that Viktorina did not know how to converse with friends. Her way of talking took away his desire to visit her and he stopped going to her house. Then Viktorina kept on complaining that Fofu ignored her and did not go to see her sick husband.

With her stern face and her bitterness, Viktorina was somewhat like Anastasia. But whereas Anastasia acted like a magnet and was the central figure for the Fofu, Viktorina drove people away from her. Notwithstanding this, Viktorina faithfully attended the Fofu funerals and other feasts and her interaction with the Fofu was considerable. She allowed for example the wife of the aforementioned family, who moved to Bululu, to use her kitchen hut for distilling and taught her how to distil in the local way. She also had contact with Francoise who helped her to get her husband's salary from the government office. Finally, when Francoise returned to Bululu after leaving her husband, Viktorina let her and her children stay in her house until the young woman found herself a suitable place.

Viktorina was suspicious of me and although she never talked about it directly she made sure that other Fofu knew about her suspicions and passed them on to me.

"Viktorina fears that the authorities will start wondering why a white woman is always at her door. She thinks they might take you for a spy," a Fofu man told me. I sent word back to Viktorina that I had permission to study the Fofu customs and the authorities knew that.

Then another message came through:

"It is not good that madam keeps asking about our past."

"All right, I will not ask about her past," I sent in reply.

"You are allowed to visit her but you are not allowed to ask her any questions," was the answer she sent me.

I followed her instructions and only called on polite Fofu visiting terms, with no interviewing. I was glad that I had already interviewed her before she turned against the idea. Then she let me know through a third party that she no longer wished me to visit her. I respected her wish and for over a year Viktorina did not even greet me. If we happened to meet on a road she pretended not to see me. Then suddenly, at the funeral of Pascarine's baby girl, she stepped in front of me and greeted me forcing a smile on her face. After that I visited her again but was extremely careful not to offend her in any way.

When I went back to Bululu for my last field trip I sensed that Viktorina was lonely and that she looked forward to my visits. She even started telling me about herself voluntarily. Right at the end I invited her and Filippo to a meal at my house. Filippo could not come because he was very sick. Viktorina came alone and she talked to me openly as if she were giving me her last words. Perhaps she thought that she did not have much longer to live. If so, she was right, for she died not long after my departure.

Her present husband Sebastien, whom she had married after leaving her Fofu husband, was twelve years her junior but was in a worse physical condition than Viktorina, because he constantly suffered from asthma. He worked for the government in a regional office but he was off work sick most of the time. In the early days when I went to see Viktorina, Sebastien answered my *hodi* calls at the door from his sick bed in the dark back room. He was always friendly and during the first year he would get up to chat with me and allowed me to interview him. Later on he would call out that Viktorina was not at home. I did not see him at all during the last two years. I, myself, had never noticed any symptoms of asthma; he seemed normal to me, even when he claimed he was ill and was in bed.

Sebastien was a Nyanga, but he was born somewhere near Kisangani where his father had been working for the colonial government. He attended school in Buva and Beni, living with his uncles. After finishing school, Sebastien was a secretary in the colonial government and was posted to many different places. When he was working in Butembo, he met Viktorina who had left her first husband and was visiting relatives. He and Viktorina got married and moved to Bululu in 1954. When Independence came in 1960 he continued to work for the Zairean government.

Sebastien had the use of half of a duplex which the colonial government had built. There were at least ten similar houses in the row and they were now interspersed with mud huts which had been jammed in afterwards. It was an old house built of brick with a concrete floor and a tiled roof. The glass in the bedroom windows had long since broken and Sebastien had replaced them with cardboard. Some window panes were also missing in the living room and these were patched the same way. The brick walls were black with dirt and cracking in places. Grass and occasionally other plants grew on the roof. Although the houses were deteriorating they provided sturdy shelter, better than many other people had.

Long ago Sebastien had sent Filippo, his stepson, a ticket to enable him to come to Bululu as a young man and had then helped him with the fees of the technical school. He had also acquired Filippo's first wife, Felista, for him in 1958. That marriage had produced three children: Teo born in 1959, Allan in 1961, and Manu in 1964. Felista had left her husband in 1969 and since then, these three eldest sons of Filippo had lived with Sebastien and Viktorina, who had no children of their own. When Filippo remarried in 1972, the boys did not go to live with their father "because his house was too small and he had a new wife," as Manu explained it. Actually, his house was as big as Viktorina's, so the latter reason must have been the main one for the boys not moving in. Furthermore, both Sebastien and Viktorina took pride in providing for the boys because it made them look like proper parents which earned them both prestige and the respect of their friends.

The boys had slept in Sebastien's house until they were "big." Now that they had grown (Teo was 18, Allan 16, and Manu 13), Viktorina had rented the boys a room in a long mud hut a few hundred yards from her house. She also rented them a kitchen, which was situated across the yard from the boys' room. Viktorina could distil her liquor in the boys' kitchen because it had a dirt floor and an open fire would not damage it. I was never clear to what extent Filippo contributed towards the expenses of his older sons and how much Viktorina and her husband paid.

Viktorina blamed Filippo for not paying his share, while Filippo insisted that he paid part of his boys' school fees. Manu told me that Viktorina did not provide him with any money, so he made some money himself by selling his toy cars. Viktorina, on the other hand, complained that the boys did not give her any of their earnings. I think they did and that she was just in the habit of complaining.

Whatever the financial arrangements, Viktorina regularly cooked the boys' meals and went to the lodging several times a day to check on them. In return they often dropped in on her and helped with her chores, especially Manu as the youngest. Also, when Sebastien went to work, he would walk via the boys' house both ways and see how they were doing.

When I became acquainted with the family, neither Manu nor Allan were attending school. They had completed the sixth and seventh grades respectively. Teo, however, was attending grade nine in a government school, which, according to him, had lower tuition fees than other schools. Teo was a tall, handsome youngster but he was withdrawn and never showed his emotions. He never looked at people when he talked to them and he tried to keep himself aloof. I never got to know him very well, although he always answered my questions. Suddenly Teo dropped out of school for a month, stating that the fees were too high for him to pay. However, this was not the real reason. The other Fofu told me that the government was recruiting young men for army service and schools were the first place they went to. Young men were generally scared of dying of starvation in the army and avoided schools until the danger had passed. After a month he returned to school.

Years later I discovered the astonishing truth behind Teo's school fees. I was visiting Teo's maternal grandmother, Chika, when in came a huge and noisy woman. She flung herself in a chair and complained about Teo to Chika.

"Not even one likuta from Teo for Roger's circumcision, not even one likuta!"

Chika hastily gave her a drink of her liquor. It was obvious that Chika was trying to calm her down. I wondered what claim the woman had on Teo and soon found out. She had been Teo's lover and had paid all his school fees.

"Why would you do that," I asked, amazed that a woman in this society would go out of her way to spend money on a youngster.

"*Amour* (love)," she said simply.

Her use of French instead of Swahili was revealing. Such relationships were foreign to the Fofu and only a foreign word could express it. The woman explained that she had been so much in love with Teo that she had provided him with the money for school. She was double the size of Teo and about ten years his senior. Teo took advantage of her love, he let her provide for him, fathered her son, and then left her for another girl. The woman was now begging him to give some money for their son's expenses but he refused to help. When she left, Chika stated that Teo had not taken her into his house as a wife, so he did not need to bother about her. After meeting her at Chika's, I saw her many times near Katarina's, where she lived in one of the small terraced houses.

When I first got to know Filippo's family, Allan was living with his mother in Bujumbura. Then he returned to Bululu and moved in with his brothers. There was one bed between the three of them. He was a difficult person for me to handle, similar to his father. He would always try to cadge something from me when we met, so I did not want to talk to him much. Toward the end of my research I noticed that he behaved very differently when he was in my house. So I started inviting him to my house for interviews and there we talked peacefully without his begging. I then found him open and friendly.

One summer, Filippo let Teo visit his mother in Bujumbura during the school holidays. Allan was not part of the plan but he went anyway. In the fall the boys returned to school. Teo attended grade 10 and Allan a kind of nursing school of the Red Cross, to enable him to work in a dispensary.

Manu was the youngest of the brothers and the most friendly and open of them. He obeyed Viktorina humbly, running errands for her and helping her to pound flour for distilling liquor. He was growing fast and looked unsteady and clumsy

Figure 8.4 Manu and his friend pounding flour for distilling liquor.

with his long limbs. I kept in contact with him over the years and had motherly feelings toward him. When he grew up, I was pleased and amazed that he told me openly about his love affairs, something I did not think a man would do. He became an easy-going cheerful young man.

I visited the boys' house regularly over a period of time to see how often they did certain things. One day I found a young woman in the kitchen. The neighbours told me laughingly that Teo was married and had brought his wife in. In fact Teo had made his classmate pregnant and the girl had moved in. The girl, Grace, had dropped out of school but Teo was still going there.

Grace was a happy young woman. She ran the house for the boys and was always busy doing something. Viktorina no longer needed to cook for them but she still called in every day to check they were all right.

When Teo brought Grace into the house, Manu slept on the kitchen floor and Allan moved back to Viktorina's house, so the young couple had the whole of the boys' room to themselves. Teo did not show any feelings, no happiness nor sorrow, not even embarrassment, when the neighbours kidded him about having a wife. As usual, he only looked apathetic. I was never able to understand why he behaved this way.

Grace's father was not happy about losing his daughter without any bridewealth but he kept quiet for the time being because peace was necessary for a safe pregnancy and delivery. Grace was the opposite of Teo: her face was very expressive and she smiled and laughed a lot, sang while doing her chores, and chatted happily with the neighbours. I liked her immediately and kept in touch with her as long as she stayed in Bululu, whether she was living with Teo or not.

Manu was an errand boy, not only for Grace and his brothers, but also for the neighbours, who often sent him to buy cigarettes. He interrupted whatever he was doing to obey. He often took care of the neighbours' little children. But he also had time to play and was an avid builder of cars out of wire. He made them much more skilfully than Anastasia's or Francoise's sons, but then he was older, now 15. He was especially fond of his latest model, which was a "Mercedes," three-foot long and 18 inches high with very soft suspension. He looked content when he played with it.

One day Filippo appeared in the boys' yard. He was puffing after walking briskly from his home. He called Manu who was crouching down, checking something in his Mercedes. The father was on his way to town and ordered Manu to run back to his home to get a tool which he had forgotten. Manu's face turned sour. His lips quivered as he wrinkled his nose, an expression out of character to him. One could see that he was not happy about the order but he uttered not a word of protest. Instead he walked his precious car into the kitchen and strolled towards his father's house. Filippo sat in an armchair which a neighbour pulled up for him and was soon engaged in deep conversation with the neighbours. It took Manu at least half an hour to return with the tool. He handed it to his father who only said, "Ee," got up and hurried off to town. Manu returned to play with his car.

I don't know how much Viktorina paid towards Teo's expenses but I noticed that he made an effort to earn some money. He barbecued little pieces of meat on charcoal and sold them in the street at night. His school attendance was not very regular and I sometimes saw him preparing the meat during school hours. He was very slow and clumsy and I wondered how well his business was doing. Manu was selling his cars at the same time and bought clothes for himself with the money. I don't know who paid Allan's fees at the nursing school but I never saw him earning any money.

When Grace had the baby, a son, her father made her leave Teo and go to live with relatives out of town. This was his way of making Teo pay the bridewealth. From the expression on his face (or lack of it) it seemed to make very little difference to Teo, whether Grace was there or not.

After about six months Grace returned to Bululu but lived with her father and not Teo. She was as happy and smiling as before. The child looked very much like Teo and was a well-fed, chubby baby.

Teo tried to earn money for the bridewealth and left school officially. He was hired by Air Zaire to load cargo onto the planes but was soon laid off. However, having been kept apart for about a year, the young couple was allowed to live together again, on the understanding that Teo would pay the bridewealth at some time in the future. They rented a room not far from Grace's parents. I often called in to observe the mother-infant interaction. I also filmed Grace with her baby. During the same year Teo attempted to build his own house on Filippo's lot. He got as far as erecting the poles but then his natural apathy got the better of him and he gave up. The poles eventually fell down and rotted on the ground.

About the same time, Viktorina stopped paying the rent for Allan and Manu's room. The youngsters moved out and slept in Viktorina's living room. When Teo's attempts at building had failed, Allan decided to try his skill and started building in the same place as Teo's poles were rotting. He was working at a Red Cross dispensary by then and seemed to be doing well. When I left Zaire for three years, his building was further advanced than Teo's had been, but not yet finished.

One day I was approaching Viktorina's home when I saw a huge crowd of people in her yard singing Catholic hymns. It was a funeral. My heart was in my mouth: could it be Sebastien? With trembling legs I walked closer and saw that everyone was looking towards the neighbour's and not Viktorina's. So it was not Sebastien, I sighed with relief!

I joined the crowd and Viktorina and some other people told me what had happened. It was quite terrible and typical of the atrocities of Zaire. A young man boarding at the neighbour's had been stopped by soldiers in the street at night. The soldiers had taken his money and identity card. When he politely asked for his card back the soldiers simply shot him dead. The army had admitted guilt and sent a truck to transport the body to the graveyard. It had also arrested the soldiers, but the people had no faith in justice and did not believe they would be punished.

"Zairean soldiers, you know them. They will soon be released."

Viktorina had an encounter with the soldiers as well. They raided her "distillery" and arrested her, only letting her go after she paid a fine. The experience acted as a deterrent and, unlike many other Fofu women, who occasionally paid fines but continued distilling, she quit. Instead, she started selling charcoal at the market. In 1981 before I left Zaire, I often spotted her sitting in the market among the row of charcoal sellers. It tied her up for the entire day, but she had no little children at home who needed care. She had the time to spend her days away from home. She did not look happy but then, she never did.

UNHEEDED HYMNS

When I spent one day in Bululu in 1984, I caught up with the news of Filippo's family from a variety of sources: Dudu, the official mouthpiece of the Fofu (who for example, directed Filippo's baby's naming ceremony), friends and relatives, and Filippo and Ana themselves. I sat a long time with Ana and Josefina, who was then living in the neighbourhood. As usual Filippo was at his work bench, making a bed for sale. He complained that it was very difficult to make a living, more difficult than before. The government had imposed a tax on his work shelter and he did not know where he would get the money to pay it. The family could not eat every day. The furniture he made did not sell well and there was no money for Ana to distil liquor. I did not know whether he was telling the truth or whether he was up to his old trick of presenting a gloomy picture in the hope that I would give him money. The other Fofu were managing better, although everyone complained about hard times. There had in fact been enormously high inflation during the three years of my absence.

The Fofu shook their heads when talking about Filippo's family. They had noticed that Ana was going dirty, a sign of serious neglect. Things were not well there. Some said Filippo drank all his earnings.

Ana had a year-old baby son, Claude, whom she was holding while helping Josefina husk the beans. Little Dudu had been taken to Beni by Ana's parents. She explained that her parents had passed through Bululu when her father was transferred to Beni from Kindu. Her mother saw that Dudu was suffering from malnutrition and promised to take good care of him in Beni. The other children were hanging around smiling at me, they all remembered me, including Pua. I did not think they had grown much in three years, which was surprising. I realised that the picture Filippo was painting was real: the family did not have enough to eat.

By that time Damyano was in grade three and was continuing his schooling. Little Viktorina had finished the first grade but her father could not afford to let her continue.

Allan had finished building his new house on Filippo's lot and was now living in it. It was the tiniest I had seen, having only one room. He had been unemployed for a year and still had no work. Despite this he looked well dressed and by no means suffering. He had a wife, a Nandi girl called Sabina, who had moved to Bululu after my departure. She was pregnant. She sat with us and helped to husk the beans but did not speak much. But she listened carefully and her reactions and facial expressions showed her to be a warm-hearted girl. I suppose she felt uncomfortable with me, and also, as a daughter-in-law, she should not be very talkative in the presence of her mother-in-law, anyway. It was Josefina who did most of the talking.

Teo's son had died of measles, as had many other children. He had another son but he had quarrelled with his wife and Ana thought that she had left him for a while. Teo was living near his parents in the general direction of Anastasia's old house.

Viktorina's husband, Sebastien, had finally died of asthma during the previous year. She had subsequently been evicted from the government house and was living in a rented house near the market. Her younger sister from Lemura was staying with her on a visit. Manu lived with the two old women. I did not see him that day because he was on a trip to Kisangani. He was a trader between Rwanda and the interior of Zaire.

I had no time on that brief visit to talk to each person individually and to hear their inner feelings. But when I returned in a year I spent a lot of time with the Fofu, including Filippo's family. There had been a turn for the worse. I met Filippo emerging from his house with some food in his mouth. Damyano, Viktorina and Pua left the pot they had been gathered around and came to greet me with a smile. There was no Ana in sight.

A week before my arrival, Filippo had dreamt that I had come with my bicycle to greet the family, just like I used to. He shook his head in wonder at his forecast. I did not have a bike, but I did come to greet his family, as before, so his dream had partly come true.

Filippo complained about the misery of life more than ever. Two of his children had died, one in Beni and the youngest one here in Bululu. He had heard the news of Dudu's death in Beni one Saturday morning, and the very next morning, Claude, the youngest one, had died in his hands. Filippo was very sick at that time with a swollen foot and could not even go to bury his son. Before that, Josefina had died and when her coffin was carried across his yard, Filippo was lying on the ground with his sore foot and was not even able to get up to show respect to Josefina's corpse. This had seriously upset Filippo. He had been sick about half a year during which time he had earned nothing.

That Christmas Ana had left for Beni to see Dudu's grave. Over seven months had passed and she had still not returned. Filippo had recently received a radio message from her father stating that she was about to come back.

As Filippo told me this, little Viktorina saw her friends going to get water. She ran inside to get a water container and joined them. Allan's wife, Sabina, was sitting by her door. She had miscarried her baby. Allan was still unemployed but made some money by helping Sabina distil liquor. Later that year, Filippo would wink if they were distilling so I would know not to ask about their whereabouts. I learned from Allan that the price of liquor was going down because of overproduction.

Once when I called I found the young couple sorting a big wooden box of papers. They told me that during the previous night, rats had run around noisily in the box, disturbing the sleep of the house and destroying most of the papers.

Teo's wife had not returned. The neighbours were angry at her for having left without saying good-bye to them. Teo was angry that she had left without a word to him, either, and he was not going after her. And finally, Filippo was angry at Teo for letting his wife go with his child.

Meanwhile, he had taken another wife, also without paying any bridewealth for her. She was from Gisenyi, across the border, and her father owned a carpenter's shop. The young wife was doing the bride's service at old Viktorina's and Teo was doing the groom's service by working for his father-in-law for nothing. This was a new arrangement that had arisen out of urban conditions. It was a kind of compensation for not paying the bridewealth: traditionally, a man did not have to serve the bride's father. Teo also tried to please his father-in-law by embracing Islam, as the in-laws were all Muslims.

I saw the new wife at Viktorina's when I went to greet her. She was a teenager, a small, thin girl. She was very frightened of me on my first visit and hid inside. On subsequent visits she was braver and obeyed Viktorina when she told her to bring me a chair. She did not stay at Viktorina's very long but moved to Gisenyi to live with Teo who continued to work for her father.

I did not see Teo during my year in Bululu but Viktorina kept me informed about his life. The family arrangements were not satisfactory to Teo because he was not paid for his work. Apparently, he could not demand a salary because he had not paid the bridewealth for his wife. Yet, there was no agreement as to how much unpaid work would compensate for the unpaid wealth. Eventually he stopped working for his father-in-law and moved to live and work independently of him.

Viktorina's younger sister, Simbalina, was still living with her but she was preparing to go back to Lemura any day. A Fofu who worked for a transportation company had promised her a free pass in a truck to Lemura. She had to be ready to leave at a moment's notice.

Simbalina was a lively and talkative woman, very different from her stern sister. Many years ago she had gone to a Catholic school. One day when I was visiting the sisters, she started giggling and then got up to demonstrate what was amusing her.

"The sisters taught us that we must greet our husbands with a kiss when he comes home from work!" she giggled. Then she stretched her arms in the air, as if around a man's neck and gave exaggerated kisses on the imaginary man's cheeks. The nuns also told the Zairean girls that they should eat with their husbands and she solemnly mimed in slow motion the Western method of eating with a fork and knife. She was doubled up laughing, trying to tell me how funny the white customs were. I was well acquainted with the Fofu view of our habits and smiled as I said,

"Fofu don't do that, do they?"

"No! No way!" she emphatically assured me.

After mocking white customs, Simbalina started imitating the way the Rwandese talked Swahili. She did not like it and claimed that this terrible accent made her dislike Bululu. She exaggerated their speech by putting aitches between every single syllable and was such an excellent actress that I could not help laughing. Viktorina did not laugh, however. She was sitting upright on her stool, weaving a basket and glanced at her sister with a stony face.

Viktorina was still selling charcoal in the market, but not very regularly. She had started to weave baskets for sale and so did her sister, while in Bululu. The skill of basket weaving had spread from Rwanda to Bululu and many women had learned to weave during the four years I had been away. I ordered two baskets from Viktorina, one for myself to carry my fieldwork equipment and a smaller one for Tania. I asked Viktorina to make extra long handles, so I could carry the basket over my shoulder. As she made non-standard baskets for me, I gave her extra money for them. This brought a faint smile to Viktorina's face which was a lot for her. Just then a man came to ask Viktorina to repay the debt she owed him and Viktorina proudly gave him some of the money she had just received.

While I was there one day, Manu came to greet Viktorina. He no longer lived with his grandmother but with two male friends in a rented room, a few hundred yards away. He invited me to see his place and we walked over there together. Manu had grown tall since I had last seen him and had very long legs which he had learned to use more gracefully than when he was in his teens. Although he strolled easily I had to walk briskly to keep up. He had a friendly smile on his face all the time. The boys had divided the room with a deep blue curtain, having their bedroom with one large bed behind it. All three boys shared the same bed. The boys had a few pieces of furniture in the other section of the room and the walls were covered with colour pictures of rock singers, clipped from Western journals.

The mother of one of the boys lived in the same compound and cooked for them. When I asked about the economics of their arrangement, Manu told me that each of them paid her a little, whenever they happened to have money. If they did not have any for a while, nobody got upset.

Manu earned his living by smuggling goods in and out of Gisenyi. I wondered if he was ever caught by soldiers or border guards. I occasionally saw soldiers stopping people in the slums and examining their loads and I frequently saw people running away from soldiers, as if for their lives. Manu casually told me that he sometimes had to pay fines, but that if God helped him really well, he was not caught.

I chuckled when he referred to God. It was typical of the Fofu to regard God as being on their side, no matter what they did. To me, who had been brought up to respect the law and the authorities, it was funny to hear the Fofu claim that God protected them in their illicit activities. When I thought the matter over some more, I realized that the people did not consider the soldiers' authority to be legitimate. The soldiers were there as representatives of a government which followed the form of the old colonial government and had nothing to do with indigenous concept of justice. To the Fofu, it was perfectly legitimate to make one's living in any way one wished.

"The soldiers are taking people for their hunger," Manu explained. The wages of the soldiers, as those of most professions, was below the subsistence level and they needed bribes and the like to survive.

He was very relaxed and his dangerous work did not seem to create any stress. He did not work every day. He wore good clothes and told me that he had some money put away in the Catholic fathers' bank. Later on that year, I was to find out what he was saving for.

Although his son was managing to escape the soldiers, Filippo had a confrontation with them that August which made his life more miserable than ever. One evening as he went out after dark to buy some cigarettes, soldiers captured him in his own yard and accused him of spying. They took him to the airport to be beaten and released him the next morning. Filippo was so sore that he slept badly for a long time. However, he tried to continue his carpentry although he was bent double with pain.

In those days the soldiers were like angry bees. Filippo said he heard shots almost every night. He considered himself lucky not to be beaten as badly as Dudu, who had been taken from his yard and beaten until he was covered with his own blood, urine and faeces. Filippo's beating was moderate by comparison.

Filippo did not seem to bear grudge against the soldiers but accepted the beating as a fact of life. I was horrified and could not accept such injustice. Filippo's friend, a retired soldier was leaning on Filippo's work bench while we talked. I turned to him and asked,

"What do you think of the beating, you, an old soldier?"

"It's their job," he stated simply. There was nothing to add to it.

Some Fofu women were less accepting of the atrocities of the soldiers. Older women, such as *Mama* Avion and Chika, even voiced their opposition. Around the time of Filippo's capture, many of the Fofu attended the funeral of the soldier husband of a Fofu woman. After a fair amount of liquor had been drunk, Chika opened her mouth to scold the soldiers who were attending the funeral. Chika told me about it later and said that the soldiers did not mind her rebuking them and even agreed with her. One of the soldiers had taken some money from *Mama* Avion a few days previously and when he saw her at the funeral he lowered his eyes in shame. *Mama* Avion warned him,

"God will remember the money, he will keep it in mind!"

The soldier tried to pacify her, saying that she was not the only Zairean to lose money and she should not take it so seriously. *Mama* Avion's warning was like a curse, and being an old woman, it might work. Even the soldier feared it, although he did not return the money.

If the authorities and the general population had different ideas about what was legitimate power, there was also a discrepancy between the Christian teaching, which the indigenous population claimed to follow, and their actual behaviour. Chika was a clear example of this, but it applied to all of the Bululu Fofu.

I came to know Chika, the mother of Filippo's divorced wife Felista much better now than during the earlier years. The two women took great interest in the general affairs of the Fofu and Chika was one of the ritual leaders at funerals. During my last year in Bululu, Chika treated me like a granddaughter and invited me in every time I passed by her house.

Chika attended the Catholic chapel regularly every Sunday, almost every morning, and twice a week for choir practice. Her faithfulness surprised me because no other Fofu went so frequently. I asked her why she went so often.

"Because I'll get to heaven when I die," she responded quickly.

"Don't other people get to heaven?" I inquired her.

"I don't know, not my business to know," she stated.

I asked if she had already got any benefit from her regular attendance. Indeed, she had. If she became sick, the members of the church would come and visit her and assist her with food and money. She herself joined the group once a week for a sick visit and gave her zaires for those in trouble. Later that year, Chika was laid up in bed for several weeks with a bad back. Then she reaped the benefits of being a member of the Christian community and felt cared for.

One day I asked Chika if I could go to a choir practice with her to see what it was like. She was surprised but agreed. The participants were even more surprised to see a white woman accompanying the old Chika but they soon forgot about me. There were 22 women and six men present. Two of the men led the singing and corrected any mistakes, two more accompanied the singing with drums and the others sang with the women. The younger women were holding babies on their laps while singing. Everybody was enthusiastic.

The two leading men taught a new song which the women learned line by line. The song was written on a black board and one of the men read one line at a time for those women who were illiterate. The choir repeated each line after them. The drumming gave rhythmical support and lifted the spirits of the women, who sang as loudly as they could.

The words intrigued me and I was curious to see how the women would react to them. The verses gave instructions as to how to lead a good Christian life, one thought in each verse. The import of the chorus was that those who did not follow the instructions would perish and the ones who did would be saved.

The first verse was a reminder that God gave good feet to people and they should not spoil them by walking indiscriminately. In the same vein, God gave people hands to do work and they should not spoil them by stealing. Thirdly, God gave lips and they should not be spoilt by telling lies. Finally, God gave us a pure voice. We should not spoil it by drinking liquor all the time. The exact words of the last verse in Swahili and in translation are as follows:

Sauti safi — ee. Mungu alikupa kuimbia — ee.
Unaiharibu kwa ku kunywa pombe — ee, pahali pote.

Sweet voice - yes. God gave you to sing, yes.
You are spoiling it by drinking liquor, yes, everywhere.

There was no reaction to the song until the last verse, then the women smiled a little.

Laughter was welling inside me throughout, however, and I had a hard time concealing my amusement. The discrepancy between the teaching and the reality was enormous, as I had seen over many years. I wondered how many of the choir distilled liquor: I was sure that they all drank it in huge quantities. Fofu always claimed that the main difference between Catholics and Protestants was that the former were allowed to drink while the latter were not. The reality was that the Protestants drank secretly while the Catholics drank more publicly. So there was not really a difference and everybody drank like fishes.

After the choir practice Chika and I strolled back to her house. Chika could not walk fast, especially after her back trouble. On the way, we stopped at a house where Chika picked up a gallon of liquor.

"I can't lie to you, it is liquor," she told me. "I buy it here and sell it in my house."

"Don't you remember the song you sang in the chapel?" I asked innocently.

"We have to live," she stated dryly.

We had hardly got back when an elderly man put his head round the door. He was startled at seeing me in the living room and quickly went out.

"Don't worry, come in," Chika reassured him. "Madam is our sister, she will not tell on us."

"I was looking for my tea," he whined.

Chika went into her bedroom, brought the gallon container out and measured a drink for the man. He gave her the money hastily, gulped the drink down and continued on his way.

No Christian teaching has made the Fofu believe that either alcohol or illicit distilling is bad. They classified alcoholic beverages as food, because they took away the sensation of hunger. They made a person feel better and happy. The downside was usually not discussed. The excessive drinking of only one person, Ida, was severely criticized by the Fofu. She drank "too much" and neglected her children, whom the other Fofu had to care for. She behaved stupidly at funerals and brought shame on the Fofu. The drinking pattern of the other Fofu was not seen as a problem.

Distilling was not only acceptable but women took pride in their skill and cursed be the one who dared to criticise their liquor! One day when I was approaching

Felista's home I could see she was in a terrible rage. I could not understand her words exactly but she was swearing as loud as she could. She spat over her shoulders in disgust, swung her arms around like a windmill and looked absolutely furious. An audience of passers-by had gathered around her who gazed at her with quiet amusement.

Apparently Felista had served her liquor to some customer who had not liked it and had told her that it "tasted like piss." This was the worst insult she could imagine.

That one could, however, exist in the slums without distilling was proven by a family living next door to *Mama* Avion. They belonged to the indigenous Kimbanguist church and the wife did not distil liquor because her church forbade it. To earn money she cooked waffles on charcoal and sold them to passers by. But I noticed that she had to work harder at it than those women who distilled alcohol.

The liquor trade had another advantage, too: it was compatible with childcare, because the mother did not need to be away from home for as long a time as those women who traded in the market. The Fofu saw the liquor trade as a good way of earning money and whatever the Christian teaching, they believed that God loved, understood and forgave them, regardless.

Illicit distilling amid terrible poverty was not so distant in my own culture. At school I had read many Finnish novels about rural poverty, which the peasants tried to overcome or blot out by illicit distilling or heavy drinking at the beginning of the 20th century. The phenomenon was very similar to what I was observing in Zaire.

AT LAST VIKTORINA TALKS

Manu had always been the most open of Filippo's sons and during the last year we became good friends. When I was on my Fofu rounds I would call at his place to greet him. I often saw him in other houses, too, especially that of his real mother and his maternal grandmother. He often begged the latter to give him a drink on the promise to pay in the afternoon.

"You liar! You are a bandit!" Chika remonstrated contemptuously as she measured a drink for him. One could see that despite her protestations, she loved her grandson dearly.

Manu would stretch his long legs and sip the clear liquor in a relaxed manner while Chika gossiped and wove a mat.

Manu claimed to greet his father once or twice a week but his father complained about his rare visits. I never happened to meet him at Filippo's.

I asked Manu if he was planning to get married and he told me that, in fact, he had a girl in mind. He had met her at a dance in a night club in town and fallen in love with her. Her name was Salome and she was from Kasai. She lived with her parents in the slums, not very far from Manu.

Manu went to see her every evening between seven and eight o'clock. He would send a male friend to her father's house to ask her to come out. The girl would sneak out and they would stand in the road for a few minutes chatting. The girl enjoyed the visits and insisted that Manu come every day.

Manu also got his male friends to spy on the girl. She was attending school (grade ten) and Manu's friends watched to see if she talked to other men in the street or at school. Manu told me that it was not worth asking her directly if she had other boy friends because a girl would never reveal the truth: sending trusted spies was the only way of finding out.

Manu claimed to be saving money for bridewealth. He thought that a man who paid his dues was respected more than the man who did not. I asked if he had negotiated with the girl's father but he had not. He felt it would be better to have an amount ready before he went to face the father with his brothers, Allan, Teo, and some friends. To date, the father had no knowledge of either his existence or intentions.

In a round-about way Manu had found out how much Salome's father wanted for his daughter. One night Manu had followed Salome's father to a bar and sat within earshot. As the father was getting drunk he started bragging about his beautiful daughter and telling his companions what her bridewealth would be. Possibly Manu's friends prompted the father to talk about the topic. The bridewealth would be 5,000 zaires. I doubted whether such a sum would be within Manu's reach but he was optimistic. He had already about half of it saved in the Catholic fathers' bank and he would keep putting money aside from his tool sales.

In addition to his own savings, Manu's relatives in Lemura had written to his grandmother that they were willing to donate one cow towards his marriage arrangements. I questioned what use a cow in Lemura was. Manu said that he intended to fly to Lemura, sell the cow there, and bring the money back. I calculated that the air fare would be nearly as much as the proceeds from the cow but Manu did not let it discourage him. He still wanted to go to Lemura. He thought that in six months he would have the bridewealth ready and the necessary gifts of beer and liquor. Then he would go to the father, offer the wealth and take the girl into his house.

"What if the father will not agree with the amount you offer?" I asked pessimistically.

"Then I take the girl without his agreement. He cannot do anything about it," he stated calmly.

Girls eloped all the time and Salome was ready to do it, if her father did not cooperate. Manu regarded himself as a nice guy who at least tried to follow the respectable rules but he was not going to bend over backwards. Salome's father would understand this and be realistic. Manu appeared confident about his plans.

I asked to go with him on one of his secret assignations with Salome and he agreed. Afterwards, however, I thought it was tactless and cancelled the plan. I now regret that decision. It would have been a wonderful opportunity to observe urban Zairean courtship.

When I questioned Manu about his sex life he claimed that he had no sexual relations with his girl friend. If this was true it showed he was following the traditional Fofu rules in the matter. He did, however, visit prostitutes about twice a month. I asked if he was not worried about venereal diseases and he claimed he was not. If he was infected he would take medicine as necessary. He obviously did not know about AIDS and did not believe me when I told him about it, although people in Kinshasa, the capital, some thousand miles away, were hysterically afraid of it. Most people in eastern Zaire, like Manu, had not even heard about the disease. I feared for these people and the following years proved that my fear was justified: many people in the area have died of AIDS.

I wanted to know what the father's role was in the urban marital arrangements and asked Filippo whether Manu was getting married, without letting on what Manu had told me. Filippo answered me with counter questions, such as: Where would he bring a wife? Has he got a house? Where does he get the money for the bridewealth?

I suggested he might get the bridewealth from his trade but Filippo played it down,

"His trade is slow. Nobody buys the tools he tries to sell."

How different from rural marital arrangements! A rural father directed his son's marital arrangements with authority while this urban father did not even know about his son's marriage plans. It seemed to me that the different attitudes were caused by the poverty of the urban fathers. The rural fathers controlled marriages because they provided the bridewealth from their own stock and from their fields. Urban fathers could barely feed their families let alone save for their son's bridewealth.

Filippo seemed to confirm my view when I asked him about the departure of Teo's first wife in 1984. Many Fofu had told me that Filippo was angry at Teo for letting his wife take their son with her. However, as Teo had not paid bridewealth for his wife he had no right to his son, so little could be done about it. Filippo, who was unable to help with the payments, concluded,

"We fathers shut up because we do not give the wealth to our sons."

My discussion with Manu had taken place around Christmas. When I next saw him in May, I asked how his marriage plans were coming on. Manu casually informed me that Salome had other male friends, a fact which his spies had relayed to him, and he had dropped his plan to marry her. He talked about the matter as if it did not upset him at all, it was one of those things that could happen to anybody in this life. He was looking for another girl friend. He did not appear anxious or heart-broken but carried on with his life as if nothing had happened.

His reaction was similar to that of rural young men and women whose marital plans failed. I had often been surprised how little the breakdown seemed to affect them emotionally. I had to conclude that the persons filling the roles did not matter, the important thing was to get married: Manu had not dropped his plans to marry and girls could always be found. The problem lay in finding the money.

The last year was remarkable not only in gaining Manu as a friend but also Viktorina, who until then had been hostile to me. I called on her regularly and she seemed to be looking forward to my visits.

Her house was fairly new and looked much sturdier than a mud hut because it was made of rocks which were cemented together. One day, however, something happened which made her move out. She was in the living room pounding manioc and had to go to the back room for something. While there, she felt a tremor as in an earthquake and when she returned to the living room, she saw that one of its walls had tumbled down and the room was full of rubble.

"God is!" her sister Simbalina said, raising her arms theatrically. She meant that God had protected her and Viktorina. She was still waiting for her ride to Lemura and continued her economic activities of distilling and weaving baskets to support herself while in town.

Viktorina found some other rooms to rent, in the house of one of Filippo's neighbours. It bordered on Filippo's yard but had an entrance on the opposite side. Being so near made it easier for the two households to help each other and I often saw Pua and little Viktorina help Viktorina with her housechores. Damyano, on the other hand, was near the slaughter house most of the time playing football or scouting for scraps of meat.

By May Simbalina had finally left and Manu moved in with Viktorina. By then she was blind in one eye and losing her sight in the other. I could see that her strength was waning but she kept on weaving when her back allowed it.

Filippo had come to visit me in my house several times during the previous year but Viktorina had not yet come. As the end of my stay in Zaire drew near I arranged for Viktorina and Filippo to come to dinner at my house. On the agreed date I went to fetch them in my car. Viktorina was dressed up in her best clothes and eager to come. Filippo, however, was not ready. He had been suffering from diarrhea for several weeks and he was losing weight. As he continued to work at his carpentry, I thought that he was not too bad. But now I saw him coming from the outhouse bent over and with his belt undone: he was obviously suffering from stomach cramps.

Looking very sick and weak, he shook his head, he was not coming. Allan invited himself with us but I refused to take him. Now Viktorina was at last coming to visit me, I wanted to talk to her in peace. Allan would only dominate the conversation.

Viktorina and I had a meal together and we talked a long time. She opened her heart to me about her life and expressed her aspirations and disappointments. Things had gone wrong for her all her life.

I already knew about her disappointment of only having one child, Filippo. In this culture bearing children made a woman "good" and not bearing them made her "bad." Although Viktorina had suffered from this method of valuing a person she was ready to judge Allan's wife, Sabina, in the same way.

"She is very bad, she does not bear children," she uttered with contempt.

It did not count that Sabina was a very pleasant person and put up with Allan's unemployment and moody personality without complaint. She also humbly served her father-in-law and Viktorina. Furthermore, during the past year Sabina had started a new enterprise to earn money for the family. She went to a big market south of Bululu by truck and bought large quantities of charcoal and firewood which she transported back to town and sold in her yard. On one trip she had fallen from a crowded truck and hurt her arm so badly that she could hardly use it at all. Despite her endeavours, Sabina was still "bad."

Another matter which troubled Viktorina was her husband's death. His side of the family came to her home after his death, accused her of killing him, and confiscated all the large items of furniture. Viktorina was left with a few stools.

"That's the way it is with us, the widow is always held responsible for the death of her husband," she sighed sourly.

The third worry was Ana's departure from Filippo. As mentioned earlier, Ana's mother had arrived from Beni and persuaded her to go to Beni to see the grave of her deceased child. Viktorina was sure that the mother already had it in mind to take Ana away from her husband for good. Although Filippo was sick with a swollen foot, off Ana went to Beni.

Suddenly I remembered that Filippo had once mentioned that he thought Ana's father had something against him. It occurred to me that Filippo might not have finished all his bridewealth payments, although he claimed that everything was taken care of. He had reacted to my questions in the same way as Francoise had, trying to brush unpleasant questions aside. Perhaps he, like Francoise, was trying to fend off my painful questions, knowing that things were not in order. Ana's parents were probably angry with Filippo for the poor conditions she lived in, many Fofu had remarked that Ana was going dirty. Finally, the parents might have held Filippo responsible for the death of two of their children.

As I was turning this over in my mind Viktorina disclosed that Ana had born a baby in Beni and wondered whether it was Filippo's.

"Do you think she is living alone?" she asked me.

Viktorina thought she must have moved in with another man and forsaken Filippo forever. Viktorina told me that she had urged Filippo to take another wife, for it would be shameful for the family if Ana returned and found Filippo still single.

I, too, had asked Filippo if he was going to take another wife and he had answered with a counter question,

"Well, who is taking care of my children?," which I took to mean that he would take a wife to take care of his children.

I wondered why Ana's father kept on sending the messages on the radio that Ana was returning, if she had already remarried. Also, despite her pessimistic view, Viktorina seemed to half expect Ana to return. There were so many illogicalities and contradictions that I could not understand it at all. I suppose Viktorina was trying to prepare herself psychologically for all eventualities.

Viktorina was so eager to talk that she did not eat much. Or perhaps she did not eat much now anyway. Perhaps she did not make enough money to eat every day. It was Filippo's duty to help her but she kept on blaming him for neglecting her. Manu, on the other hand, told me that his father took good care of her.

I looked at old Viktorina, half-blind, wrinkled, and bitter. She talked in short sentences and gasped for air. I did not know if her shortness of breath had a physical cause or whether it was because talking about personal matters agitated her. Many a time she had refused to talk to me at all but now she wanted to tell me intimate details as her last words to me.

I put the left-overs of our meal — meatballs, rice, and spinach — in bowls and asked her to take them for herself, Filippo, and her grandchildren. She stacked the bowls on top of each other, tied them together with her scarf, and carried the bundle by the knot of the scarf. When I dropped her off in the slums a neighbour woman looked at her bundle with jealous eyes.

"Why didn't you bring anything for me?," she whined.

Viktorina did not answer nor change her stern expression. She disappeared into the ocean of decaying mud huts. That was the last I ever saw of her.

I did not expect her to live long but I expected Filippo to recover from his sickness, after all he had survived many before. I was confident that Manu would get married soon.

During the following year I received two letters from Dudu, the spokesman for the Bululu Fofu. The letters contained news of the Fofu in brief statements with little detail. The news concerning Filippo's family overwhelmed me. I had not expected things to go so bad. This is what Dudu wrote:

"Today, with a very bitter heart, I pass you this news that our brother Filippo died November seventeen 1986. That is the bad news which departs from the family of the Fofu in Bululu."

A year later, I received another letter which stated that Manu had died. Manu, the strong and young one! It was not possible. I left him healthy and happy!

Finally, soon after Manu's death, Viktorina died. I was sorry that she had to have the pain of seeing her only son die. I am sure it must have taken away much of her will to live. I was also sorry that Manu died before her, because he was Viktorina's moral support in her old days.

I was crushed by the news. The decade that I had lived in Zaire had not taught me to accept the cruelty of life there. I was again very angry that lives were wasted.

Those people should have lived! I could have accepted Viktorina's death, since she was 70-years old. But I could not accept that a father of three died at the age of 47, and especially, that a young man died at the age of 23.

Dudu has not written to me for six years now and I don't know how many of the Fofu are alive. Perhaps Dudu has died. I do not know how much AIDS is affecting Bululu now. My European friends have told me that many people, whom they knew, have died of AIDS in the neighbouring country Rwanda. Perhaps Manu was a victim, too. I have no way of knowing.

9 AN ANTHROPOLOGIST'S CONCLUSION: STRENGTH IN THE FIELDS INDEED

Throughout the narration there is an underlying assumption that the rural area is a better place to live than the city. This is reflected in the titles of the two parts "Our Strength Is In Our Fields" and "Who Can Survive In This City?." The urban Fofu themselves carried on their daily activities without complaining, even under the most severe conditions, and made the best of their situation. But every once in a while there was a little remark that showed that they too were aware of the special difficulties of the city. For example, Suzana (in "The Dissolution of a Marriage"), who is living in Lemura, the city in the Fofu area and in many ways a more comfortable place to live in than Bululu, stated that it was tough to live in the city with no fields for one's livelihood and with low wages which did not go far. Although the women of Bululu carried on their distilling in a business-like manner, they were conscious that it was something that circumstances had forced upon them. Katarina, for example (in "The Survival Of The Dependents Of A Civil Servant") once commented that during colonial times, the salaries of their husbands had been so good that the wives did not need to lower themselves to such dangerous and illegal activities. In this final chapter, I want to compare and contrast the rural and urban ways of life. May it also serve as an example of how an anthropologist would go about analyzing the data she has recorded in her notes.

Although the first part of the book covers communities which I call rural and the second part depicts life in the city of Bululu, this is really too simplistic as some of the "rural" communities are more rural than others. In fact, all of the communities could be placed in a rural-urban continuum in the following order: Gangu, Yenyabo, Nyanya and Bululu.

Gangu, where Sofia's second marriage took her, is the most traditional community of all. The four original lineages of the village were so organized that the more closely related the men were to each other the closer they lived to each other. There were few outsiders to the village and those lived apart from the original villagers. The outsiders were mostly people involved with the school, the church, or the only shop in the village. The villagers emphasized the difference between themselves and the outsiders all the time, as if to protect the village from outside contamination, and did not accept them as fully-fledged members of the community.

Yenyabo had been very similar to Gangu until recently when the Bible school arrived, bringing with it a large number of outsiders in the form of staff and students. Unlike Gangu, Yenyabo welcomed outsiders although it experienced some difficulties in adjusting to the newcomers. Although, for example, the shortage of land, water and firewood was already becoming a problem, it still allowed Hiha pastoralists to share the village lands, as told in "Persevering Cecilia." Also in contrast to Gangu, Yenyabo had no shops.

The third community, Nyanya, was less traditional than the first two, owing to its location next to the mission station and hospital. Although its basis was a traditional village with its original lineages, these were overrun by the influx of newcomers, whom the chief welcomed because they paid him for land, their houses and for fields. Nyanya inhabitants complained that the fields which were rightly theirs rent free were being sold off by the chief who was "eating" the money. They were consequently confined to small fields, which they had to cultivate over and over again thereby impoverishing the soil. Nyanya also had a large number of shops, bars, hotels and brothels. Furthermore, transient people from a wide area stayed there while their relatives stayed in the mission hospital.

The final community, Bululu, was the least traditional in its composition, being a colonial city. It was a mixture of tribes with no traditional structure. No complete lineages resided there but families were fragmented into nuclear families or single parent households. The Fofu were a tiny minority of about one hundred, in a population of 100,000. Western influences were to be seen everywhere: shops, government offices, medical services, schools, churches, and even an international airport.

Various aspects of Fofu life can be related to the rural-urban scale. The more rural the community, for example, the greater the importance of the fields to the inhabitants' livelihood. Thus the people of Gangu and Yenyabo obtained their livelihood almost exclusively by cultivating their land. Sofia and Remi (in "Two Wives Who Left"), for example, got up early in the morning to hoe in their fields and their children helped them with it. They proudly showed me their fields. Maladi, who was training to give villagers Western medical aid, got up even earlier in the morning to be able to hoe his gardens before the patients arrived. Teresa, who was a teacher, also hoed her fields as did all the other teachers in these villages. Cecilia (in "Persevering Cecilia") worked hard in her fields and also used hired help to expand them. Although her husband Herabo was a preacher and a business man, his main concern was his fields and he took great pride in them. When his son had finished at elementary school and wanted to continue his education in Nyanya, Herabo told him, "There is much work at home, work at home." He meant hoeing the fields. He calculated that his son could make more money by cultivating huge fields and selling the produce in the market, than as a professional teacher with a monthly salary. In these two villages, the most rural, the fields were paramount. There was an outcry if someone's goats destroyed crops. On one such occasion, Sofia (in "Two Wives Who Left"), for example, attacked a man and knocked him to ground in her fury. And her mother-in-law, whose movements were slowed down by arthritis, was nevertheless impelled to run when a thief got into her precious sugar cane.

The attitude of Nyanya inhabitants to their fields was becoming less traditional. Women still cultivated and held their fields in high regard but many men were concentrating on other enterprises. Suzana, for instance, was often in her fields when I went to see her but Jacques gave them no attention. He was a tailor and tried many other business ventures, both legal and illegal. These non-agricultural interests took him away from Nyanya and in the end caused him to forget his family and his duty to arrange good marriages for his daughters. He was said to have married a white woman in another city, which illustrates the ambition of many urban Zaireans to be like white men, with wealth and prestige at the cost of traditional values.

Bululu was truly urban and people had hardly any access to fields there. Abiso tried to grow beans at some distance from the city and it helped feed the family for a while. Ana had a small patch of squash growing in her yard, but it did not go far in satisfying the nutritional needs of the family. The other Fofu grew hardly anything. Instead, Fofu men were either employed or self-employed or from time to time unemployed. Abiso (in "Anastasia, The Focus Of The Fofu") had been a driver but was unemployed all the time I knew him. Jean (in "The Survival Of The Dependents Of A Civil Servant") was a civil servant and left a small pension for his widows. Jacques, Katarina's husband, had several occupations. Initially he worked in a shop, selling spare parts for cars. When the owner laid him off, he went into smuggling gold. Finally he moved to Lemura to be a bar tender. Francoise's two "husbands" were custom officials, who received hefty bribes on the side. Pascarine's husband worked as a free-lance butcher, selling the meat in a market place. Her brothers worked for him for wages. Manu (in "A Carpenter's Family") smuggled tools across the border and had to beware customs officials and the military police. Filippo was a self-employed and sometimes an employed carpenter.

City wives did not know exactly how much their husbands earned but it was never enough for the family needs. They consequently tried to earn money themselves. All of them either distilled liquor or had done so in the past. It was illegal and they had to be careful. Ana, Viktorina (in "A Carpenter's Family"), and Katarina (in "The Survival of The Dependents Of A Civil Servant"), for example, were fined by the military police and it made Viktorina quit the business although Ana and Katarina continued. Josefina (in "The Survival of The Dependents of A Civil Servant") carried liquor ashore from the smugglers' boats and could only work when the military police were not around. Her daughter, Pascarine, smuggled beer across the border from Rwanda for some time. Although the women did not complain and they were very supportive of each other, it was very stressful to earn their livelihood by such uncertain and dangerous means. Some women tried other, more legal ways of making money as well. Katarina sold "Vietnamese balls," Viktorina sold charcoal and wove baskets, Pascarine sold roasted peanuts in the streets, and Anastasia fried manioc cakes and sold them on the road side. The women were industrious and steadily earned money while their husbands often roamed around, neglecting their families.

Housing is another thing that varied according to the community's position on the rural/urban scale. Living quarters were not as good, clean or spacious in the city as in the rural area, where people obtained raw materials from the bush and forest. In Nyanya, some items had to be bought but earth for mudding houses was free. In Bululu, everything had to be bought and consequently repairs were delayed, often until it was too late. The stone wall of Viktorina's house, for example, came crashing down one day. Katarina wisely moved from her apartment just before it collapsed in the middle of one night. Francoise's living quarters varied according to her husbands' whims: sometimes she lived in a cement plastered house, at others she was sponging on relatives. Filippo's house leant badly to one side and had large holes in the walls, which he never repaired. Josefina had the worst housing because she was not able to pay her rent. Another difference is that rural houses always had some space around them but city houses were crowded together and had very small yards. Nights were especially noisy as quarrels and sick children crying could be heard by the whole neighborhood. It was common knowledge, for example, that Josefina's son Lebisabo beat his live-in girl-friend and finally the neighbors intervened. Some houses, such as Katarina's, were terraced which exacerbated the problem. She had many sleepless nights on account of the noise.

Soldiers were a threat to the civilians in the whole country, even in the villages, but they appeared there only rarely. My discussions with soldiers at Herabo's dinner table in a village and at Filippo's in the city revealed that the duty of soldiers was considered to be that of arresting and beating people and they performed it diligently. Cecilia's son Richard and his cousin Mateso narrowly escaped the draft when they spotted soldiers at Gangu market place. Similarly, Teo in Bululu avoided school at the time of the draft. But many of the urban Fofu men fell prey to the roaming soldiers: Filippo and Dudu were captured by soldiers in their own yards, taken to a military tent at the airport and beaten so that they were sore for months. Earlier, Filippo lost the money he had received for a piece of furniture to a soldier who found it in his shoe when searching him. On yet another occasion he spent a few months in prison, accused of stealing a soldier's gun while the latter was drinking his wife's liquor. The Fofu attitude to the military varied on lines other than ruralness. The men did not complain even after harsh treatments by them, they were just glad to be alive. But their wives talked about avenging the violence with witchcraft. Children looked on the soldiers, especially the fierce "Red Berets," with admiration and awe, and imitated them in their play.

The relationship between children and their parents was similar both in urban and rural areas. It was the children's responsibility to run errands, help with household chores, and act as babysitters. The narrative contains numerous observations of what children did in each family. For example, in the village, Herabo sent Kato to buy coffee beans from a neighbor even though it was raining hard and in Bululu, Filippo sent his son, Damyano, to buy "Sporti" cigarettes. Both boys were glad to oblige. Cecilia's daughters and occasionally sons took care of the twins when they were small and I saw Tajeki carry Kato tied on her back although he was of school age. When Cecilia's oldest son Jean-Pierre got married and had a baby, it was thought natural that Rozalin should be the nanny and she skipped school for this duty. Being absent from school was also considered normal when her mother needed help in harvesting the crops. After all, school did not count as work, the real work was at home.

Children made their own toys both in the rural area and the city. In the latter they had a wider choice of materials; old shoe boxes, wire stolen from the fence of the airport, beercaps and thongs, while in the rural area the boys used organic material from the gardens and the bush. Anastasia's and Francoise's children often made cars and Manu still made and sold them when in his late teens. In the city the children had the luxury of pretending to drive in real cars that had been abandoned, while the rural children used more imagination by pretending that a mortar and some pot lids were a car. Rural children played at medical clinics and sung church hymns as they had seen done at real mission clinics but the urban children played "Red Berets," who beat people up and imprisoned them. This difference of play reflected the fundamental difference between the environment of the village and the city. The village was a relatively safe place while dangers lurked everywhere in the city, where you had better watch out!

The city was not only dangerous but also a smelly and dirty place to live in. The stench of the outhouses was sometimes very strong in the slums, rats and mice ran around all the time and got into pots and pans even during the day. At night they bothered those who slept on the floor, who were invariably children. Many of the Fofu boys were involved with butchering and that was an extremely filthy and unhygienic business. Children clearly suffered from intestinal parasites in the city more than in the villages. Most important of all, rural children got their stomachs full from the food their parents grew, but the urban children could not be sure when the next meal would appear and what it would offer. Yenyabo people noticed this difference when they sent their children to attend the mission school at Nyanya where they boarded with local families. Although they had to send sacks of food from their fields in payment for boarding, their children never ate as well away as in their home village. As mentioned earlier, the chief had reduced the size of the fields in Nyanya and so the people there had to reduce their appetites. Bululu, of course, was much worse off for food. I saw Anastasia's family eat only rarely although her single relative Kristina, who rented rooms from Anastasia, was continuously cooking meals for herself. Katarina used to serve tea and bread or porridge to her children several times a day in addition to a daily big meal but later she had to reduce her cooking to the minimum. Her mother rightly reminded her that most families lived on a shoestring budget and Katarina had just been lucky until then.

Not that villages were perfect places without problems. There was much sickness and death in them, as we saw in the story of Cecilia, when Kato fell in the boiling water pot and the healthy twin became ill and died in the hospital at Nyanya. Other examples are Sofia having lost three of her infants by her first husband and Teresa's cheerful daughter Mami dying in the hospital. There were many child deaths in the city, too. Josefina, Anastasia, Katarina, Teo's wife, Grace, and two of Josefina's children all lost one infant and Ana's two youngest ones died just a few days apart. The biggest difference seems to be, however, in the number of adult deaths in the city. Jean, the civil servant, died the day I became acquainted with his family, Anastasia after a long illness, and Viktorina's husband suffered for years before he passed away. Anastasia's well-fed renter Kristina died mysteriously. Abiso, who had dreamt about starting a new life after Anastasia's death in the rural area, departed the city as a sick man and wasted away before he had built a house for himself. Josefina died troubled by and bemoaning the lack of bridewealth. Finally, Filippo's family was drastically reduced when his mother Viktorina, his adult son Manu, and he himself all died within a few months.

I do not know how much of the urban death toll was due to alcohol. I suspect that some of it may be attributable to the heavy drinking in the city, although distilling was becoming more common in the rural area, too. Herabo told me that in the old days alcoholic beverages were served only on ceremonial occasions. After the introduction of a monetary currency, villagers could distil liquor and sell it to others when they needed cash. The alternative was to butcher a pig or a goat. When gold digging was made legal, villagers noticed that it was very profitable to sell alcoholic drinks to the young diggers after their day's work. As the school principal at Gangu once said, distilling was a good source of income. Both Sofia and Teresa were happy to exploit it even though their Protestant husbands protested it because it was in breach of church rules. Yenyabo people, however, did not care to dig gold and distilling did not take off there, although some individuals, such as Sofia's first husband, were known to drink to excess. Nyanya inhabitants had a bigger market as they could sell alcoholic beverages to transient people. Suzana also gave liquor parties to her neighbors (which I innocently disturbed). However, nowhere was Fofu alcohol abuse as rampant as in Bululu, where even babies were weaned with liquor, such as Josefina's daughter, Keusi. Adults habitually drank first thing in the morning and as they walked about in the slums. The amount of drinking came as a surprise to the Fofu who moved into the city from a rural area and other ethnic groups remarked upon it and even joked about it.

It can be seen, therefore, that there are many differences in the Fofu lifestyle in the rural and the urban areas, although there are, of course, also many similarities. The importance of land should not be underestimated as it directly affects housing conditions and the way the Fofu obtain their livelihood. In the form of fields, it also has implications for the gender roles.

As already mentioned, the children's relationship to their parents was similar in the villages and in the city: they were obliged to help their parents wherever they lived. The gender differentiation was made quite early, more pressure being applied on girls to do household chores than boys. Sofia, for example, excused Felisi from carrying a baby because he had already done it for several hours, although girls would be expected to have more endurance. Similarly, his neglect of the beans was excused but a girl's similar behavior would not have been. Furthermore, he only had to do girls' jobs at all because there were no daughters. Also, in the city, Filippo's son Damyano was compelled by his mother to pound flour even though he disliked this female task and tried to get out of it. His sister was deemed too young to help and more jobs, therefore, fell to him. Anastasia had both sons and daughters, and although the boys had to babysit and help with the cooking the heaviest responsibility fell on the girls. I observed a stronger tendency in the city to differentiate the jobs according to gender and even strangers would sometimes enforce the rules. Francoise's son, for instance, was slapped on his hand by a passer-by when roasting a banana for himself, a job that should have been performed by a woman. I noticed similar behavior on other occasions. Once, for example, a young Fofu man in his early twenties was ridiculed and mocked at by a passing woman for helping his mother pound corn. The man quit and disappeared into his house until the woman had left and then he returned to continue his "feminine" work.

Boys could be very pampered in the city. Although Katarina's oldest son Katanabo ran errands for her at the age of seven, he did not dress himself to go to school. Katarina did everything for him, even buttoned his shirt and tied his shoe laces. Her mother, Estela, still had two teenage children living with her when she was widowed. The daughter distilled liquor to pay her tuition fees but Estela did the distilling for her son's school fees. The daughter was always busy doing chores at home and taking care of neighborhood children, while the son just dressed in his best clothes, groomed himself, conversed with his male friends and went for walks. When I once asked where he might be, Estela shrugged her shoulders, "Who knows about him? Men wander around, women stay at home!"

The situation was different in the rural area. Both boys and girls were taught the importance of fields and many had their own sections to hoe. When they came home from school, they went to hoe for a while. They also helped the mother harvest. I observed teenage boys taking a walk to admire their fields on Sunday afternoons, when they did not work there. Everybody took pride in their fields from early childhood on. Women also worked in the fields and as they could be several miles away, it was normal for the home to be empty. Accompanied by their daughters, they also went to the markets to sell their produce and could be away all day, sometimes overnight. The fields, therefore, had an equalising effect on the gender roles: women and girls were by no means expected to stay at home in the rural area.

The fields also affected the extent to which parents were involved with the marriages of their children. In the rural area, it was the parents' duty to find a spouse for their children and make all the arrangements for the marriage. At Yenyabo, for instance, Herabo cycled several times to prospective brides' homes to check on the suitability of the families. His son, Jean-Pierre, the groom-to-be, meanwhile played at home with other children, totally oblivious of these arrangements. Later, Cecilia and Herabo considered the request of an elderly cattle owner to make their daughter, Rozalin, one of his ten wives. They refused because none of his wives was familiar to them and they could not be sure Rozalin would be well looked after. Women were active in trying to find suitable young girls to be the wives of their brothers' children, or even of their own children. Cecilia, for example, spotted a suitable girl for Richard at the wedding of some other village boy. Herabo then rounded up the cows and goats that were needed for his son's bridewealth. In other families I noticed that mothers also worked for the bridewealth, by selling their garden produce and saving the money to buy animals. In one family, the prospective groom helped by carrying the sacks of sweet potatoes to the market on his bicycle for his mother to sell. Market traders were expected to be female.

Children did not always follow the tribal rules concerning marriage even in the rural areas, but the lapses were never condoned. Herabo's daughter, Tajeki, eloped. Herabo was furious and cursed her, which caused tension in the family. Tajeki and her baby were eventually taken back into the family home without damages being paid by the fellow and married off properly a couple of years later. At Nyanya, one of Jacques' daughters also eloped. Unlike Herabo, who reacted strongly in accordance with the tribal rules, Jacques had neglected his parental duties by leaving his family for another city. His sister kept on worrying about the fulfilment of bridewealth obligations, and his brother went to negotiate with the groom, as was only proper in the Fofu culture. Jacques' neglect was severely condemned by his lineage at Gangu and in the Nyanya neighborhood in general.

In the rural area, the father sometimes even took responsibility for his married son. When Herabo's son, Richard, fathered a child outside his marriage, for instance, Herabo paid damages of a cow to the girl's family, although he was, of course, angry with Richard for this extra cost. This shows that the way young people behaved after marriage was also of concern to the parents.

The position was very different in the city of Bululu. The young people there were left to choose their partners and to make the arrangements themselves. The ideal even in the city was for the parents to perform these tasks but there were difficulties, the chief one being the inability of the groom and his family to pay bridewealth. There are many instances of this in "Who Can Survive In This City." All four of Francoise's husbands, for example, had paid nothing for her. Abiso did not get any damages from his daughter's lover who already had several wives. Teo got his classmate pregnant and brought her to live with him in his rooms without any payment made. Her father tried to get some bridewealth and Teo promised to pay it, but he never did so. Pascarine's case is a good example of the conflict between the ideal and the actual. She eloped with her landlord's son, who already had another wife. Because her father had died, the Fofu looked to Dudu, her older stepbrother, to approach the groom's family to initiate the bridewealth negotiations. He never did. Pascarine bore a child, no bridewealth paid. She bore another child, again no bridewealth paid. And then a third child, still no bridewealth. Old Fofu women often gossiped to me about it and predicted a catastrophe on account of the non-payment of bridewealth. When Pascarine's mother was dying, her last words were: "I have not drunk a sip of Pascarine's bridewealth."

The city men feared marriage negotiations. This was probably partly because of their poverty and partly because of feelings of inferiority. Their children often took spouses from other ethnic groups who had different bridewealth measures and who also ridiculed their customs. Some demanded a length of cloth for the mother of the bride, and a watch, a radio, money etc. In the rural areas people very rarely married into other ethnic groups, so there was nothing unfamiliar or intimidating about the bridewealth payment. They always consisted of cows and goats. And as cultivating one's own fields was far more stable than being a waged worker in the city, the rural Fofu were more able to pay bridewealth. The city Fofu used liquor as the unit of currency for bridewealth. Manu, for example, had set the amount of liquor that he was willing to pay to the father of his girlfriend. The father did not know about this, but Manu had made up his mind independently and assured me that if the father did not accept it, he would take the girl anyhow. This was a bold statement for a groom. When I asked Manu why he bothered to pay anything for her, if the father's wishes did not matter, Manu answered that it gave him status to be a man with a properly arranged wife. Many urban men and women lived without this status, however. Francoise, for example, was embarrassed about the lack of it.

As it turned out, Manu's plan fell through because the girl was flirting with some other guys. It was typical of the urban situation that Manu's father, Filippo, did not know anything about the marriage plans. The role of parents was very different compared with the rural areas, where parents were the masters of all arrangements.

In the rural areas the bridewealth payments established a reciprocal relationship between the wife-givers and the wife-receivers. It involved the lineage group of each party, who lived in different villages. The men married in their childhood villages which comprised their clan members, while the women left their clan homes and went as strangers to their husband's village. There they had to be submissive, for example, a young *ngoli* humbly knelt down when handing something to her husband's relatives as related in "The Dissolution of a Marriage." The *ngoli* had many duties, such as drawing water for her parents-in-law. On the surface the men had the better deal but women had a lot of power, too. A woman's home village watched to see how she was being treated and if it was not satisfactorily, her home village protested. It might also take action if other things did not go according to their wishes. For example, a man from a village which had sent two women as wives to Yenyabo told me they were no longer letting their girls marry Yenyabo men because one of their girls could not conceive and the other one's infant had died.

The wife's home village acted as a refuge. If the husband or his family mistreated her, she could always "run back" to her home village. That's why women liked to marry in a village within walking distance of home. When she returned, she was guaranteed a field to cultivate and moral support in her dispute with her husband.

Suzana, for instance, lived long periods in her home village when her marriage with Jacques was shaky and when she had a dispute with her second husband in Lemura. Cecilia went home many times during her marriage and Sofia spent three months at her home village between husbands.

It was humiliating for a husband to have an absent wife. Her absence pronounced her dissatisfaction much more forcefully than her presence could have done. Often the threat of running home was enough to keep a husband in line. If he wanted his wife back (which he usually did), he had to approach his wife's village humbly with gifts to soften his in-laws' hearts. Sometimes he had to endure rebukes or rebuffs. Cecilia remembered with glee the humiliation of Herabo, when he came to beg her back several times and had to sleep on the ground in the yard for a couple of nights to prove his sincerity. If a wife wanted to, she could refuse to return and pick another husband, as Sofia did.

In the city, the bridewealth was often not paid in which case the contractual relationship never arose. On the contrary, the two groups had to avoid each other. This became very clear to me in the case of the dispute between Josefina's son, Lebisabo, and his live-in girlfriend. The whole neighborhood heard him beat her. The Fofu relatives could not intervene because no bridewealth had been paid. Unrelated neighbors then went to her help on humanitarian grounds. Even where the bridewealth was paid, the situation was still different in the city. The urban Fofu lived in nuclear families so there were no large kin groups for a woman to fall back on if her marriage failed. Fictive kin terms were used of non-relatives, but the numbers of even these were not great. When Katarina was neglected by her husband, she went to live with her mother there being no other relatives around. The two women tried to take care of her children, but it was tough without any fields.

Another difference is that in the city, men could escape their responsibilities more easily than in the village. Not that rural men did not try to escape them too, but life was too public for them to succeed. Herabo, for example, tried secretly to take a mistress in the village of Yenyabo, but his plan failed when she caused a scandal by beating Cecilia. The village community unanimously condemned him, Cecilia's home village was enraged, and Herabo's reputation smeared. At Nyanya a similar event took place when Suzana's husband Jacques took another wife without asking Suzana. This angered her and her village but Jacques did not care. He broke the tribal rules by abandoning his family and his status fell. It would have been very hard to recover his position if he had ever dared to return.

In the city, however, men got entirely away from their responsibilities. Francoise's husbands are a good example. They all neglected her for much of the time. Her latest husband neglected her when she was pregnant and ready to deliver. Instead of coming to support her, he persistently stayed away. Katarina's husband, although very congenial for years, abandoned her and their children when she was pregnant and left her with no money. Maria, Anastasia's daughter, was a single mother and her lover had no intention of helping her raise their child. When her brother, Deondonne, fathered a child he left the mother and went gold digging. Teo took advantage of a woman for his school fees but did not support the child he fathered. These are just a few of the many examples.

In the city, women did not bother to look for new husbands because no men would take the burden of them and their children. Katarina expressly stated this when I suggested that she remarry. In the rural area, the children stayed with their fathers, who wanted them to enlarge their kin group, and the divorced women were free to remarry. Sofia, for example, left her first husband after bearing six children and started a new family with Remi. Teresa's sister had done the same. Suzana left her husband after having five children and married a man in Lemura. Rural women were wanted both as producers of offspring and producers of crops. They were proud of both abilities. And they knew that if their husbands were unsatisfactory, they could always go home and cultivate fields there. Whether in their home village or their husband's, they would live off of the fruits of the land. Their strength, as that of the entire rural culture, was truly in their fields.

REFERENCES AND RECOMMENDED READINGS

African Women or Families:

Aronson, D. R. 1978. *The City is Our Farm: Seven Migrant Ijebu Yoruba Families.* Cambridge, Mass.: Schenkman Publishing Company.

Bappa, S., J. Ibrahim, A.M. Imam, F.J.A. Kamara, H. Mahdi, M.A. Modibbo, A.S. Mohammed, H. Mohammed, A.R. Mustapha, N. Perchonock, R.I. Pittin (eds.). 1985. *Women in Nigeria Today.* London: Zed Books.

Blendsoe, C.H. 1980. *Women and Marriage in Kpelle Society.* Stanford: Stanford University Press.

Bukh, J. 1979. *The Village Woman in Ghana.* Uppsala: Scandinavian Institute of African Studies.

Glazer Schuster, I. M. 1979. *New Women of Lusaka.* Palo Alto, California: Mayfield Publishing Company.

Kilbride, P. L. and J. C. Kilbride. 1990. *Changing Family Life in East Africa: Women and Children at Risk.* University Park and London: The Pennsylvania State University Press.

Little, K. 1973. *African Women in Towns: An Aspect of Africa's Social Revolution.* Cambridge: Cambridge University Press.

Moran, M. H. 1990. *Civilized Women: Gender and Prestige in Southeastern Liberia.* Ithaca and London: Cornell University Press.

Obbo, C. 1980. *African Women: Their Struggle for Economic Independence.* London: Zed Press.

Robertson, C. C. 1984. *Sharing the Same Bowl: A Socioeconomic History of Women and Class in Accra, Ghana.* Bloomington: Indiana University Press.

Life Histories of Africans:

Mirza, S. and M. Strobel. 1989. *Three Swahili Women: Life Histories from Mombasa, Kenya.* Bloomington & Indianapolis: Indiana University Press.

Paulme, D. (ed.). 1971. *Women of Tropical Africa.* Berkeley: University of California Press.

Romero, P. W. 1987. *Life Histories of African Women.* London and Atlantic Highlands, N.J.: The Ashfield Press.

Shostak, M. 1981. *Nisa: The Life and words of a !Kung Woman.* Cambridge: Harvard University Press.

Smith, M.F. 1954. *Baba of Karo: A Woman of the Muslim Hausa.* Reprint, New Haven: Yale University Press, 1981.

Winter, E. H. 1959. *Beyond the Mountains of the Moon: The Lives of Four Africans.* Urbana, University of Illinois Press.

The Fieldworker in Action:

Bowen, E. Smith. 1954. *Return to Laughter.* New York: Harper & Brothers.

Marshall, E. Thomas. 1965, 1981 (reprint) *Warrior Herdsmen.* New York: W.W. Norton & Company.

Turnbull, C. 1961 *The Forest People: The Study of the Pygmies in the Congo.* New York: Simon and Schuster.

Articles and Books Discussing Dialogical Anthropology:

Clifford, J. 1983. "On Ethnographic Authority." *Representations* 1(2): 118-146.

Clifford, J. and G.E. Manus (eds.). 1986. "On Ethnographic Allegory." In *Writing Culture: The Poetics and Politics of Ethnography.* Berkeley: University of California Press. Pp. 98-121.

Geertz, C. 1973. "Thick Description: Toward an Interpretive Theory of Cultures." In *The Interpretation of Cultures.* New York: Basic Books. Pp. 3-30.

Handler, R. 1985. "On Dialogue and Destructive Analysis: Problems in Narrating Nationalism and Ethnicity." *Journal of Anthropological Research* 41(2): 171-182.

Sapir, E. 1921. *Language.* New York: Harcourt Brace.

Tedlock, D. 1979. "The Analogical Tradition and the Emergence of a Dialogical Anthropology." *Journal of Anthropological Research* 35(4): 387-399.

Tyler, S. A. 1986. "Post-Modern Ethnography: From Document of the Occult to Occult Document." In *Writing Culture: The Poetics and Politics of Ethnography.* J. Clifford and G.E. Manus (eds.). Berkeley: University of California Press. Pp. 122-140.

Other References:

Foster, G.M. 1965. Peasant society and the image of limited good. *American Anthropologist* 67: 293-315.

Weber, Max. 1947. *The Protestant Ethic and the Spirit of Capitalism.* New York: Scribners.

QUESTIONS AND TOPICS FOR DISCUSSION

You will notice that, on the one hand, the ethnography is a narrative of fieldwork by an anthropologist and, on the other hand, an account of the everyday lives of six families which the anthropologist became acquainted with. One may read the narrative purely for pleasure but for the purpose of this course, you should read it as an anthropologist seeking to understand the underlying structures and rules behind the reported behavior and speech. Your task is to act as an anthropologist by extracting information on one of the topics below and analyzing it. You could also read the relevant passages in your introductory text book and consider how your ethnographic discoveries fit with the theories described therein. When reading, you could write down examples of events which illustrate the point you want to make. You can use the names of characters in your essay.

1. ENCULTURATION AMONG THE FOFU.

Analyze how children are raised among the Fofu, the values they are taught, the responsibilities they are given and at what age. Are there differences in the upbringing of boys and girls? When does childhood end? When do the children get married and who chooses their spouses? How is the ideal personality of the Fofu inculcated in children and what purpose does it serve in the society? Is rural enculturation different from urban?

2. FAMILY COMPOSITION AND RELATIONSHIPS AMONG THE FOFU.

Are families nuclear or extended, monogamous or polygamous? What residence rules are followed and how do the rules influence the male and female experience? Discuss the duties and rights of family members and affinals. Who are in authority and who must obey? What ideology is behind the authority structure? Explain the organization of work in the family. Consider the place of the family in the wider society. Compare villages with the city.

3. CULTURAL CHANGE AMONG THE FOFU.

Although the narrative covers the present, there are indications throughout the text about the past. Attempt to reconstruct the traditional society of the Fofu (for example, the social, economic, political, and religious aspects) and suggest ways in which the colonial and mission rule and urbanization have changed the society. How have the Fofu reacted to the changes imposed on them? To what extent do they accept or reject the new way of life and the new rules? How well have the Fofu adjusted?

4. MALE - FEMALE RELATIONSHIPS.

Economics. How do Fofu men and women differ in the way they make their living in the villages and in the city? How secure are they financially? To what extent are their jobs legal? How much time do males and females spend away from home because of their work? Do adults share their earnings with their spouses? Do they know how much their spouses earn? Do the wives expect to be supported by their husbands? How does polygyny affect the finances of the family?

Marriage & affairs. How do men and women choose their spouses or lovers? Does one gender have an advantage over the other? How much control do women have over their husband's choice of mistresses and other wives? How much time do the spouses spend together? Do men and women take equal responsibilities in maintaining their unions? Are there any special conditions in rural or urban life which give one gender advantage over the other?

Home life. Who has the main responsibility of childrearing in the family? What tasks do men and women do for children and housekeeping? Which gender spends more time at home and how is absence from home viewed along the gender line? What recreation do men and women participate in?

The role of the relatives. What part do the families of rural and urban young women and men play in their marriage arrangements and bridewealth payments? Why are urban people becoming increasingly frustrated about the way marriage arrangements are conducted? How much moral and/or economic support can married men and women expect from their parents and other relatives if their marriages go wrong? Which is the stronger bond: the conjugal or kin bond? Are there special constraints that the urban living puts on relations between the kin as compared to the rural living?